GROWING UP IN ANCIENT ISRAEL

ARCHAEOLOGY AND BIBLICAL STUDIES

Brian B. Schmidt, General Editor

Number 23

GROWING UP IN ANCIENT ISRAEL

Children in Material Culture and Biblical Texts

Kristine Henriksen Garroway

SBL PRESS

S B L PRESS

Atlanta

Copyright © 2018 by Kristine Henriksen Garroway

Library of Congress Cataloging-in-Publication Data

Names: Garroway, Kristine Henriksen, author.
Title: Growing up in ancient Israel : children in material culture and biblical texts / by Kristine Henriksen Garroway.
Description: Atlanta : SBL Press, [2018] | Series: Archaeology and biblical studies ; Number 23 | Includes bibliographical references and index.
Identifiers: LCCN 2018014650 (print) | LCCN 2018015668 (ebook) | ISBN 9780884142966 (ebk.) | ISBN 9781628372113 (pbk. : alk. paper) | ISBN 9780884142959 (hbk. : alk. paper)
Subjects: LCSH: Children—Palestine—History—To 1500. | Children—Palestine—Social conditions. | Households—Palestine—History—To 1500. | Sociology, Biblical. | Social archaeology—Palestine. | Household archaeology—Palestine. | Palestine—History—To 70 A.D. | Palestine—Antiquities. | Bible. Old Testament—Antiquities.
Classification: LCC DS112 (ebook) | LCC DS112 .G297 2018 (print) | DDC 305.230933—dc23
LC record available at https://lccn.loc.gov/2018014650

Printed on acid-free paper.

For my parents and my grandparents

Contents

9.2. The Vulnerable Child
9.3. The Gendered Child
9.4. The Playing Child
9.5. The Next Years

Preface

This book resumes my research into the world of children in the ancient Near East, a world that I find endlessly fascinating. My first book, *Children in the Ancient Near Eastern Household* (Eisenbrauns, 2014), expanded my dissertation research and was one of the early forays into the field focusing on children in the biblical world. At that time, much of the previous scholarship had either addressed children through discussions of the family or listed children as another statistic in the burial assemblage. Exploring both texts and archaeology, *Children in the Ancient Near Eastern Household* concentrated specifically on the legal and social status of children in the ancient Near East. The textual database for that study included Mesopotamian legal codes, private legal documents, and the Hebrew Bible. Archaeological data was gleaned from the ancient Near Eastern burial record, with an emphasis on interments in the Southern Levant. The book concluded, first, that a child's status was not binary and, second, that a child's membership within the household was tied to the child's social age.

In researching *Children in the Ancient Near Eastern Household*, I noticed that not much had been written on the lives of children in ancient Israel. Even as Bible and ancient Near Eastern scholars began showing an increased interest in child-centered studies, a noticeable gap remained: no one had written a social history addressing what it was like to grow up during the Iron Age in ancient Israel. Unlike *Children in the Ancient Near Eastern Household*, the present book has a smaller regional focus, addresses a narrower time period, and investigates the process of growing up rather than social and legal status. The study analyzes material culture, the Hebrew Bible, epigraphic data from the ancient Near East, and ethnographic accounts. In doing so, *Growing Up in Ancient Israel* offers the first of hopefully many discussions of what life was like for children in ancient Israel.

While writing this book, I found an academic home with a growing group of scholars who also shares an interest in this subject. To my colleagues and friends of the Society of Biblical Literature's Children in the Biblical World sessions, Julie Parker, Laurel Koepf-Taylor, John Martens, and Sharon Betsworth, you have been there championing our field and in this way supporting me. Deepest thanks go to Shawn Flynn for being a real mensch of a colleague through this whole process.

Many people, institutions, and libraries have been instrumental in helping the book come together. Thanks go to my home institutions, the Hebrew Union College-Jewish Institute of Religion and University of Southern California, and to Sally Nakanishi who provided invaluable help locating sources; to Fuller Theological Seminary, where doors opened by Chris Hays allowed me access to the library, and a scholarly community in Pasadena; and to Sadie Goldstein-Shapiro who edited the manuscript.

Unless otherwise noted, biblical translations are my own; however, the illustrations in the book are from several sources. Jim Eisenbraun and David Ilan kindly gave permission to reprint figures and illustrations from publications by Eisenbrauns and The Nelson Gleuck School of Archaeology in Jerusalem respectively. The Metropolitan Museum of Art's Open Access policy made images in the online collection available through Creative Commons Zero designation. Paul Butler of Rutgers University also made his collection of ancient and classical art available; and the Ashmolean, via the help of Alice Howard, provided me with photos from their collections. The remainder of the images I drew myself. Thanks, Dad, for spending many hours taking me out to sketch when I was little.

Most importantly, I offer my thanks to my friends and family. To my YMCA family, you kept me sane and balanced and are a continual source of positive energy. To my three boys: Cyrus, Leo, and Abner, you continue to make my research come alive. And, of course, to my *eṭlu*, Josh, for your unending love and tireless support.

List of Tables and Figures

Tables

Figures

All drawings, unless otherwise attributed, are by Kristine Garroway, modeled after the sources listed.

Abbreviations

AA	*American Anthropologist*
ÄAT	Ägyptologische Abhandlungen
AB	Anchor Bible
ABD	Freedman, David Noel. *Anchor Bible Dictionary.* 6 vols. New York: Doubleday, 1992.
Abst.	Porphyrius, *De abstinentia*
AASOR	Annual of the American Schools of Oriental Research
AEM	Archives épistolaires de Mari
AfO	*Archiv für Orientforschung*
A.J.	Josephus, *Antiquitates judaicae*
ANET	Pritchard, James B., ed. *Ancient Near Eastern Texts Relating to the Old Testament.* 3rd ed. Princeton: Princeton University Press, 1969.
Ant.	Josephus, *Antiquities*
AoF	*Altorientalische Forschungen*
ARC	*Archaeological Review from Cambridge*
ARM	Archives royales de Mari
ASOR	American Schools of Oriental Research
ASV	American Standard Version
AUAM	(aka HMA): tablets in the collections of the Andrews University Archaeological Museum
b.	Babylonian Talmud
B. Bat.	Bava Batra
BA	*Biblical Archaeologist*
BAM	Köcher, Franz. *Die babylonishc-assyrische Medizin in Texten und Untersuchungen.* Berlin: de Gruyter, 1963–.
BAR	*Biblical Archaeology Review*
BARIS	Biblical Archaeology Review International Series
BASOR	*Bulletin of the American Schools of Oriental Research*

BDB	Brown, Francis, S. R. Driver, and Charles A. Briggs. *A Hebrew and English Lexicon of the Old Testament*. Oxford: Clarendon, 1907.
Beit Mikra	*Beit Mikra: Journal for the Study of the Bible and Its World*
Ber.	Berakhot
Bib. hist.	Diodorus Siculus, *Bibliotheca historica*
BJS	Brown Judaic Studies
BM	Museum siglum of the British Museum, London
BTB	*Biblical Theology Bulletin*
CAD	Gelb, Ignace J., et al. *The Assyrian Dictionary of the Oriental Institute of the University of Chicago*. 21 vols. Chicago: The Oriental Institute of the University of Chicago, 1956–2010.
CHANE	Culture and History of the Ancient Near East
CT	Cuneiform Texts from Babylonian Tablets in the British Museum
DDD	Van der Toorn, Karel, Bob Becking, and Pieter Willem van der Horst, eds. *Dictionary of Deities and Demons*. Grand Rapids: Eerdmans, 1999.
EA	El-Amarna tablets. According to the edition of Knudtzon, Jørgen A. *Die el-Amarna-Tafeln*. Leipzig: Heinrichs, 1908–1915. Repr., Aalen: Zeller, 1964. Continued in Rainey, Anson F. *El-Amarna Tablets, 359–379*. 2nd rev. ed. Kevelaer: Butzon & Bercker, 1978.
Emar VI	Arnaud, Daniel. *Recherches au pays d'Aštata, Emar VI*. 4 vols. Paris: Editions Recherche sur les Civilisations, 1985–1987.
ERV	Easy-to-Read Version
ESV	English Standard Version
FAT	Forschungen zum Alten Testament
FGrHist	Jacoby, Felix, ed. *Fragmente der griechischen Historiker*. Leiden: Brill, 1954–1964.
Gen. Rab.	Genesis Rabbah
HAR	*Hebrew Annual Review*
HBM	Hebrew Bible Monographs
Hit Gilg	Hittite Gilgamesh Tablet
HUCA	*Hebrew Union College Annual*
IAA	Israel Antiquities Authority
IEJ	*Israel Exploration Journal*
ISV	International Standard Version
JAMA	*Journal of the American Medical Association*

JANES	*Journal of the Ancient Near Eastern Society*
JBL	*Journal of Biblical Literature*
JFSR	*Journal of Feminist Studies in Religion*
JNES	*Journal of Near Eastern Studies*
JPF	Judean Pillar Figurine
JPS	Jewish Publication Society
JSOT	*Journal of Old Testament Studies*
Jub.	Jubilees
KBo	Otten, Heinrich. *Keilschrifttexte aus Boghazköi.* Leipzig: Hinrichs, 1916–1923; Berlin: Gebr. Mann, 1954–.
KJV	King James Version
KTU	Dietrich, Manfried, Oswald Loretz, and Joaquín Sanmartín, eds. *Die keilalphabetischen Texte aus Ugarit.* Münster: Ugarit-Verlag, 2013. 3rd enlarged ed. of *KTU: The Cuneiform Alphabetic Texts from Ugarit, Ras Ibn Hani, and Other Places.* Edited by Manfried Dietrich, Oswald Loretz, and Joaquín Sanmartín. Münster: Ugarit-Verlag, 1995.
LNTS	Library of New Testament Studies
LXX	Septuagint
Lyc.	Plutarch, *Lycurgus*
m.	Mishnah
MAH	Museum siglum of the Musée d'Art et d'Histoire, Geneva
Maqlû	Knut L. Tallqvist, *Die assyrische Beschwörungsserie Maqlu.* Helsingfors: Societas Scientiarum Fennicae, 1894.
Menah.	Menahot
MLC	Morgan Library Collection, siglum of the Yale Babylonian Collection, New Haven
Msk	Tablet siglum of texts from Meskene
MT	Masoretic Text
NASB	New American Standard Bible
NCBC	New Cambridge Bible Commentary
NEA	*Near Eastern Archaeology*
Nid.	Niddah
NIV	New International Version
NJPS	New Jewish Publication Society
NLT	New Living Translation
NRSV	New Revised Standard Version
O.	Museum siglum: Antiquités (orientales), Musée du Cinquantenaire

OEAE	Redford, Donald B., ed. *The Oxford Encyclopedia of Ancient Egypt.* 3 vols. Oxford: Oxford University Press, 2001.
Or	*Orientalia*
OTL	Old Testament Library
P.Oxy.	Grenfell, Bernard P., et al., eds. *The Oxyrhynchus Papyri.* London: Egypt Exploration Fund, 1898–.
P.Berlin	Erman, Adolf. *Zaubersprüche für Mutter und Kind aus dem Papyrus 3027 des Berliner Museums.* Berlin: Königlichen Akademie der Wissenschaften, 1901.
P.Petr.	Mahaffy, J. P., ed. *The Flinders Petrie Papyri.* Dublin: Royal Irish Academy, 1981–1905.
PBS	University of Pennsylvania, Publications of the Babylonian Section
PEQ	*Palestine Exploration Quarterly*
pl.	plate
PN	personal name
R.	Rawlinson, Henry, et al. *The Cuneiform Inscriptions of Western Asia.* 4 vols. London: Bowler, 1861–1909. 1R = vol. 1 (1861); 3R = vol. 3 (1870).
RA	*Revue d'Assyriologie et d'archaélogie orientale*
Resp.	Plato, *Republic*
Rosh Hash.	Rosh Hashanah
Sanh.	Sanhedrin
SEL	*Studi epigrafici e linguistici*
Shabb.	Shabbat
SJOT	*Scandinavian Journal of the Old Testament*
StBibLit	Studies in Biblical Literature
Strata	*Bulletin of the Angelo-Israel Archaeology Society*
STT	Gurney, Oliver R., Jacob J. Finkelstein, and Peter Hulin. *The Sultantepe Tablets.* 2 vols. London: British Institute of Archaeology at Ankara, 1957–1964.
t.	Tosefta
TA	Tell el-Amarna tomb
TA	*Tel Aviv*
Ta'an.	Ta'anit
TIM 1	Al-Zeebari, A. *Old Babylonian Letters.* Texts in the Iraq Museum 1. Baghdad: Dar Al-Jumbari Press, 1964.
Tusc.	Cicero, *Tusculanae Disputationes*
TynBul	*Tyndale Bulletin*

UET	Ur Excavations: Texts
UM	Tablet siglum of the University Museum, Philadelphia
VS	Vorderasiatische Schriftdenkmäler der (Königlichen) Museen zu Berlin
VT	*Vetus Testamentum*
VTSup	Supplements to Vetus Testamentum
WA	*World Archaeology*
ZA	*Zeitschrift für Assyriologie und vorderasiatische Archäeologie*
ZÄS	*Zeitschrift für ägyptische Sprache und Altertumskunde*
ZAW	*Zeitschrift für die alttestamentliche Wissenschaft*
ZDPV	*Zeitschrift für des Palästina-Verins*

Introduction

There is a set season for everything, a time for every experience under heaven: A time for being born and a time for dying.

—Eccl 3:1–2a

"Where are the children?" This question has been asked now for over twenty-five years by archaeologists who have recognized that where there are men and women, there should also be children. But this question has only recently entered the arena of biblical and ancient Near Eastern scholarship. Previously, children were included as part of discussions about families, households, and women. This picture is slowly changing with published studies increasingly focused on children. Such works challenge the long-held assumption that exploring the lives of children is fruitless because there are very few texts about them and even less material culture indicating the presence of children.[1] As the new wave of child-centered biblical scholarship has proven, children are present in texts and material culture. By readjusting analyses of sources from adult-centric to child-centric approaches, this book engages in a childist methodology to find the children and answer the practical question of what it was like to grow up in ancient Israel.

---

1. On the historic struggles of the archaeology of children and ways to move forward, see Kathryn Kamp, "Dominant Discourses; Lived Experiences: Studying the Archaeology of Children and Childhood," in *Children in Action: Perspectives on the Archaeology of Childhood*, ed. Eva Baxter, Archaeological Papers of the American Anthropological Association 15 (Arlington: American Anthropological Association, 2006), 115–22.

Childist Interpretation: A New Method

Scholarship focusing on children in biblical and ancient Near Eastern texts and cultures is so new that those engaged in it have not agreed on a single nomenclature. Some call it childist theory, while others refer to it as child-centered interpretation.[2] The field is quickly expanding as scholars have become more aware of the importance of children within ancient Near Eastern households.[3] This new wave of study owes much to Philippe

---

2. When Julie Parker first suggested the term *childist* as a name for the field, she did so with a specific methodology attached to it. In recent years others have expounded on the methods used to address children. For a discussion on the term childist, see Kathleen G. Elkins and Julie Parker, "Children in the Biblical Narrative and Childist Interpretation," in *The Oxford Handbook to Biblical Narrative*, ed. Danna Fewell (New York: Oxford University Press, 2014), 422–34. The following are a list of those most recent monographs on children: Laurel Koepf-Taylor, *Give Me Children or I Shall Die* (Minneapolis: Fortress, 2013); Julie Faith Parker, *Valuable and Vulnerable: Children in the Hebrew Bible, Especially the Elisha Cycle*, BJS 355 (Providence, RI: Brown University, 2013); Kristine Garroway, *Children in the Ancient Near Eastern Household* (Winona Lake, IN: Eisenbrauns, 2014); Shawn Flynn, *Children in Ancient Israel: The Hebrew Bible and Mesopotamia in Comparative Perspective* (Oxford: Oxford University Press, 2018). Naomi Steinberg, Stephen Wilson, and Daniel Justel do not define their scholarship with either theoretical term but offer a similar approach to children. Naomi Steinberg, *The World of the Child in the Hebrew Bible*, HBM 51 (Sheffield: Sheffield Phoenix, 2013); Stephen Wilson, *Making Men: The Male Coming of Age Theme in the Hebrew Bible* (New York: Oxford University Press, 2015); Daniel Justel, *Infancia y legalidad en el Próximo Oriente antiguo durante el Bronce Reciente (ca. 1500–1100 a. C.)* (Atlanta: SBL Press, 2018). Older works, which functioned as a sort of springboard for the new wave of childist scholarship include: Danna Noel Fewell, *The Children of Israel: Reading the Bible for the Sake of Our Children* (Nashville: Abingdon, 2003); Andreas Kunz-Lübke "*Schaffe mir Kinder ...*" *Beiträge zur Kindheit im alten Israel und in seinen Nachbarkulturen*, ABG 21 (Leipzig: Evangelische Verlagsanstalt, 2006); Marsha Bunge, ed., *The Child in the Bible* (Grand Rapids: Eerdmans, 2008). An extensive bibliography can be found in Parker, *Valuable and Vulnerable*, and Flynn, *Children in Ancient Israel*.

3. New Testament and early Christian scholars have also begun focusing specifically on children: Cornelia Horn and John Martens, *Let the Little Ones Come to Me: Children and Childhood in Early Christianity* (Baltimore: John Hopkins, 2007); K. O. Sandnes, O. Skarsaune, and R. Aasgaard, eds. *Når jeg så skal ut i verden: Barn og tro i tidlig kristendom* (Trondheim: Tapir, 2009); Reidar Aasgaard, *El Evangelio de la Infancia de Tomás* (Salamanca, Spain: Ediciones Sigueme, 2009); A. James Murphy, *Kids and Kingdom: The Precarious Presence of Children in the Synoptic Gospels* (Eugene, OR: Pickwick Publications, 2013); Sharon Betsworth, *Children in Early Christian*

Ariès's investigation of childhood, and Victor Turner's study of liminality for bringing children into the scholarly discourse.[4] Based on Ariès's theory of childhood as a particular period in a child's life, initial works in the field started to investigate if childhood as we know it today existed in the ancient world.[5] These studies presented children from a historical-critical approach and were concerned with whether children were treated as Ariès thought, as miniature adults, or as children, in the modern sense of the term.[6] Recent scholarship has begun to challenge the assumptions of these early works and to examine what the ancient writers of the Hebrew Bible thought about children and childhood.[7]

At its core, childist theory addresses issues raised by its elder hermeneutic: feminist theory. Like feminist theory, it seeks to assign a voice to the silent other. To a contemporary Western reader, the notion of children as silent might seem foreign. One way of thinking about children with a voice that is not heard is to understand them as a muted group.[8] Children

---

Narratives, LNTS 521 (London: Bloomsbury, 2015); Ville Voulanto, Children and Asceticism in Late Antiquity. Continuity, Family Dynamics and the Rise of Christianity (Farnham: Ashgate, 2015); Katarina Mustakallio, Christian Laes, and Ville Voulanto, Children and Family in Late Antiquity: Life, Death and Interaction (Leuven: Peeters, 2015). Reidar Aasgaard's working project, "Tiny Voices from the Past: New Perspectives on Childhood in Early Europe," focuses on bringing together early Christian texts, material culture, and theological, philosophical and political thought (ca. fifth century BCE–eighth century CE) regarding children. For an extensive bibliography of 2200 plus entries concerning children in the ancient world through the early Middle Ages, see the project curated by Voulanto et al., "Children in the Ancient World and the Early Middle Ages: A Bibliography," https://tinyurl.com/SBL1729o.

4. Philippe Ariès, Centuries of Childhood: A Social History of Family Life, trans. Robert Baldick (New York: Vintage, 1962); Victor Turner, The Ritual Process: Structure and Anti-structure (Chicago: Aldine, 1969). Ariès understood children as miniature adults who went through various life cycle events in the process of growing up. Turner expanded Ariès's work, investigating the transformative stages of the rites of passage.

5. For a review of scholarship concerning how Ariès's theories have been received, modified, and challenged, see Parker, Valuable and Vulnerable, 11–15, 31–39.

6. Joseph Blenkinsopp, "The Family in First Temple Israel," in Families in Ancient Israel, ed. Leo Perdue et al. (Louisville: Westminster John Knox, 1997), 48–103; Philip King and Lawrence Stager, Life in Biblical Israel (Louisville: Westminster John Knox, 2001); Bunge, Child in the Bible.

7. Parker, Valuable and Vulnerable, 12; Flynn, Children in Ancient Israel, 5–9.

8. This term is borrowed from Edith Specht, "Girls' Education in Ancient Greece," in Children, Identity and the Past, ed. Liv Helga Dommasnes and Melanie Wrigglesworth (New Castle: Cambridge Scholars, 2008), 125.

are muted in the sense that they have something to say that will add to our understanding of ancient Israelites if they are only given the freedom to do so. Child-centered interpretation liberates children to tell their stories. Again, like feminist scholars, childist scholars also point out a bias in the text; for childist scholars it is the adult-centric, rather than the androcentric bias. Using various methodologies, childist scholars also seek to "fill in the gaps," but with respect to children, not women. For some, like the current work, this means interpreting the sources to highlight children, and for others, it means reading the extant source material differently.[9] In these ways, child-centered interpretations of children in the biblical world also have a strong affinity with the field of childhood archaeology.[10] Many of the questions and issues childist biblical scholars are addressing are the same concerns that childhood archaeologists have: What is the relationship between the child, their world, and adults? What did it mean to be a child in the past? When do children become gendered? What role did children have in the household economic system? Can we talk of childhood in past societies? Both fields recognize the presence and importance of children and are calling for more scholars to include children in their studies and reconstructions of past societies.[11]

---

9. Parker, *Valuable and Vulnerable*; Koepf-Taylor, *Give Me Children*; Wilson, *Making Men*; Garroway, *Children in the Ancient Near Eastern Household*; David Bosworth, *Infant Weeping in Akkadian, Hebrew, and Greek Literature* (Winona Lake, IN: Eisenbrauns, 2016).

10. Liv Helga Dommasnes, "Introduction: The Past-Worlds of Children and for Children?," in Dommasnes and Wrigglesworth, *Children, Identity and the Past*, xv. With respect to childhood archaeology in ancient Israel, see the groundbreaking work of Rona Avissar-Lewis, "Childhood and Children in Material Culture of the Land of Israel from the Middle Bronze Age to the Iron Age" [Hebrew] (PhD diss., Bar-Ilan University, 2010); Avissar-Lewis, ילדי קדם מבט ארכיאולוגי וילדות בארץ ישראל בתקופת המקרא [Children of Antiquity: A View of Archaeology and Childhood in the Land of Israel during the Biblical Period] (Haifa: Haifa University, forthcoming).

11. An early foray into children came in Moore and Scott's seminal book addressing women and gender. Jennie Moore and Eleanor Scott, eds., *Invisible People and Processes: Writing Gender and Childhood into European Archaeology* (London: Leicester University Press, 1997). More recent scholarly collections concentrate on children and showcase various multidisciplinary approaches for discovering them in the archaeological record. Joanna Sofaer Derevenski, ed., *Children and Material Culture* (London: Routledge, 2000); Julie Wileman, *Hide And Seek: The Archaeology of Childhood* (Stroud: Tempus, 2005); Eva Baxter ed., *Children in Action: Perspectives on the Archaeology of Childhood*, Archaeological Papers of the American Anthropological Associa-

In line with childist scholarship and those studying childhood archaeology, the present work investigates the life of the child, the child's world, and the relationship between the child, their world, and the adults in it. To do so the study favors an interdisciplinary approach. Whereas some previous childist works examine the intersection of gender, linguistics, and literary theory to glean new insights about children from the Hebrew Bible, the approach taken here veers slightly; it incorporates a wider historical perspective, looking to the textual as well as archaeological sources of the larger world from which the Hebrew Bible arose.[12] In doing so, the book aligns itself with the goals and methods used in childhood archaeology.[13] My intention in adopting a similar approach is to look beyond the Hebrew Bible to the life of the child in ancient Israelite society.[14] My approach owes

---

tion 15 (Arlington: American Anthropological Association, 2006); Dommasnes and Wrigglesworth, *Children, Identity and the Past*; Güner Coşkunsu, ed., *The Archaeology of Childhood: Interdisciplinary Perspectives on an Archaeological Enigma* (Albany: State University of New York, 2015). In addition to representations of children in art and iconography, the material culture presented in these collections reveals other means of finding children. For example, fingerprints and footprints left on ceramics can be used to identify the age and size of a child and to determine if an object is a toy. Spatial analysis can also help determine where children were allowed and whether items left in the area could belong to children. Evidence of children in the work force can be seen in skeletal and muscular stresses and small tools. The most heavily studied realia are those of child burials.

12. Flynn's recent work, *Children in Ancient Israel*, uses a similar methodology by looking to Mesopotamian societies to inform our understanding of the biblical text. Whereas this book starts with the biblical evidence and moves outwards to surrounding lands, his book begins with the Mesopotamian corpus and moves towards the Hebrew Bible. Read in tandem, these two books provide methodologies that can deepen one's understanding of children in the biblical world. Nadia Pezzulla's thesis focuses primarily on children in Mesopotamia, but she, too, references the material culture and burials found in Israel, as well as the texts in the Hebrew Bible. Nadia Pezzulla, "Neonati, Infanti e Bambini nel Vicino Oriente Antico" (Master's Thesis, Università ca' Foscari Venezia, 2012).

13. Brigitte Röder, "Archaeological Childhood Research as Interdisciplinary Analysis," in Dommasnes and Wrigglesworth, *Children, Identity and the Past*, 68–82.

14. Ian Hodder, "Agency and Individuals in Long Term Processes," in *Agency in Archaeology*, ed. Marcia-Anne Dobres and John Robb (London: Routledge, 2000), 21–33; M. Johnson, "Concepts of Agency in Archaeological Interpretation," in *Interpretation of Archaeology: A Reader*, ed. Julian Thomas (London: Leicester University Press, 2000), 211–27; Jennifer Dornan, "Agency and Archaeology: Past, Present, and Future Directions," *Journal of Archaeology and Theory* 9 (2002): 303–29.

much to the pioneering work of Carol Meyers, who uses archaeological realia, sociological data, and ethnographic and extrabiblical materials to inform her interpretation of the biblical text and bring to life the silent other.[15] What biblical scholars have done for women in ancient Israel, I hope scholars will begin to do for children in ancient Israel. I offer this book as a starting point.

Who Are Children?

Finding children requires knowing who qualifies as a child. For the human, the biological life cycle includes ten stages.[16] Stage one begins at conception, called the prenatal period. Stage two is birth, generally thirty-eight to forty weeks after conception. The period right after birth is called the neonatal period, lasting from birth to twenty-eight days postbirth. Infancy starts at end of the second month but ends when the infant is weaned, or by thirty-six months. During this time, the mother provides the infant with milk/nourishment, and the infant cuts its first teeth and begins to develop motor skills (e.g., rolling over, crawling, smiling, and waving) and cognitive abilities (e.g., simple problem solving).[17] Stage four, childhood, is unique to humans. It begins at age 3 years and ends at age 6.9 years. Unlike other mammals that continue to grow rapidly from infancy to the juvenile stage, humans slow down their growth, creating a longer period of dependency upon adults. Childhood is marked by the loss of some milk teeth, the ability to digest more complex foods, and the completion of brain development. Between six to eight years of age humans undergo a mini-growth spurt and gain some body fat.[18] The juvenile period, stage five, is often associated with an "older" child. For females, it is ages seven to ten years, and for males, ages seven to twelve years. At this point a child can survive without a mother's support, as he has the physical and cognitive

---

15. Meyers has written extensively on the subject, a bibliography of which can be found in her recent book. Carol Meyers, *Rediscovering Eve: Ancient Israelite Women in Context* (Oxford: Oxford University Press, 2013).

16. Barry Bogin and Holly Smith, "Evolution of the Human Life Cycle," in *Human Biology: An Evolutionary and Biocultural Perspective*, ed. Sara Stinson, Barry Bogin, and Dennis O'Rourke (Hoboken: Wiley & Sons, 2012), 521.

17. Bogin and Smith, "Evolution of the Human Life Cycle," 533.

18. Bogin and Smith, "Evolution of the Human Life Cycle," 537–41.

ability to feed and protect himself.[19] Puberty, lasting days or a few weeks, leads to adolescence, which lasts five to ten years. The adolescent starts the journey toward social and sexual maturation and experiences a second, greater growth spurt.[20] Adulthood marks the completion of skeletal, cognitive, and sexual maturity. Females reach adulthood around age eighteen to twenty, while male adulthood is reached between ages twenty-one to twenty-five. The final stage of life is old age, starting at either forty-five or fifty-five years old for females and males respectively.[21]

From a biological perspective, the following chapters cover the prenatal through juvenile stages.

However, we should not assume that all past societies adhered to these seemingly natural biological categories.[22] Indeed, ancient Near Eastern societies were more reliant upon social ages and stages, rather than chronological ones. Both textual and archaeological sources favor social ages as opposed to chronological ages. Julie Faith Parker's recent analysis of over twenty-eight words used to describe infants and children in the Hebrew Bible highlights this.[23] Social ages can be fluid, meaning person A may reach the age sooner than person B. By the same token, person B might experience the social age for a shorter period of time than person A. The complexities do not stop there. Some terms can even cover multiple social stages. Shawn Flynn has demonstrated the metal gymnastics a reader must perform when trying to determine to what social age a term refers.[24] For example, he notes that much like the Akkadian term ṣeḥrum, biblical Hebrew ילד (yeled) can span a wide range of social ages. Adding to these difficulties, the biological categories themselves can span a range of both chronological and social ages. Here infancy is a good example of how even biological ages are related to social stages.[25] The end of infancy is defined

---

19. Bogin and Smith, "Evolution of the Human Life Cycle," 541.

20. Bogin and Smith, "Evolution of the Human Life Cycle," 541–44.

21. Bogin and Smith, "Evolution of the Human Life Cycle," 544–48.

22. In some cases, human categories do not even work! Dommasnes points to the permeable boundary between the human, animal, and spiritual world in ancient Egypt, "where pharaohs, although human, were also gods and could take animal forms" (Dommasnes, "Introduction," xiv).

23. Parker, *Valuable and Vulnerable*, 41–74.

24. Flynn, *Children in Ancient Israel*, 9–13.

25. In examining past societies, and especially children in past societies, the separation of biological and social ages has been called into question. Current research calls for something of a rapprochement between the two areas. Siân Halcrow and Nancy

as the moment the mother stops nursing the baby, that is, when the baby is weaned. Yet, weaning does not happen at the same time for every baby. In societies like ancient Israel where infants were fed on demand, the infant could nurse for up to three years. Reasons for weaning might include a loss of interest by the infant, or the mother's desire to stop nursing so that she could start ovulating again and become pregnant.

Because of the complex relationship between biology and culture, it is necessary to define the terminology used in the following chapters.[26] If possible, the biological and chronological ages will be referred to. If social ages are referred to in textual, archaeological, or ethnographic literature, then these terms will be used. However, often, the simple terms infant/baby and child will be employed. An *infant* is one who is still nursing. A *child* is one who, if left on his own, could not survive; while weaned, a child is still dependent upon an adult. The terms *younger* and *older* child are used to refer to an individual at either end of the child spectrum. Finally, the generic term *child*(*ren*) will be used as an umbrella term for both infants and children.

The experience of being a child, and the topic of childhood itself is one that "straddles the traditional dualism of nature and nurture."[27] The study conducted here in the pages of this book recognizes that childhood is both biologically determined and culturally constructed. Each of the eight chapters acknowledges this relationship by exploring a different part of a child's life that is biologically or culturally determined: conception, birth, infancy, dangers in childhood, the growing child, play, dress, and death.

The World of the Child

Grete Lillehammer, an early pioneer in the world of childhood archaeology, noted that finding the child in an ancient society can be done only if one first knows the adult world; a child's engagement with their world is an

---

Tayles, "The Bioarchaeological Investigation of Childhood and Social Ages: Problems and Perspectives," *Journal of Archaeological Theory and Method* 15 (2008): 190–215.

26. It should be kept in mind that age delineation in any fashion is ultimately a construct. The terms used here attempt to address the child in texts and realia with terms that stay true to the ancient materials and to which the modern reader can relate.

27. Baxter, *Children in Action*, 5.

engagement with the world created by the adults for the children.[28] Children acculturate to the adult world in the process of becoming socialized and enculturated into their society as they physically mature. Considering this, the fact that previous studies of ancient Israel have focused first on men and more recently on women should be seen as a net positive, for these previous adult-centric studies have paved the way for this exploration of children in ancient Israel.

Children in the World of the Bible and Archaeology

As the title of the book suggests, the work here explores the lives of children in ancient Israel. This designation might seem somewhat ambiguous, but it is meant to cast a broad net as will be discussed below. Since the book uses the Hebrew Bible as its starting point, the term *biblical Israel* might be a better fit. However, the term biblical Israel does not always link neatly to the material culture that is also explored in the book. As used here, the term *ancient Israel* refers to the lands of the Southern Levant, the lands where the Israelites, as reported by the Hebrew Bible and other epigraphic references (*inter alia* the Merneptah Stela, Mesha Stela, and Neo-Assyrian inscriptions) are said to have lived.

From an archaeological perspective, the term ancient Israel might be broken down further into early Israel (Iron Age I ca. 1200–1000 BCE) and Israel (Iron Age II ca. 1000 BCE–586 BCE). The identity of the Israelites in the Iron Age I is in some respects a fraught subject.[29] On the early end, one could identify early Israel with the group called "Israel"

---

28. Grete Lillehammer, "A Child Is Born: The Child's World in an Archaeological Perspective," *Norwegian Archaeological Review* 22 (1989): 90, 99.

29. Various models and terms for the development of early Israel have been offered (and rejected) throughout the years: conquest, peaceful infiltration, tribal amphictyony, peasant revolt, gradual emergence. For the debates surrounding these and bibliographies, see inter alia Albrecht Alt, *Die Die Landnahme der Israeliten in Palästina: Territorialgeschichtliche Studien* (Leipzig: Druckerei der Werkgemeinschaft, 1925); William F. Albright, *The Archaeology of Palestine* (Harmondsworth: Penguin, 1949); Martin Noth, *The History of Israel*, 2nd ed. (New York: Harper & Row, 1958); George Mendenhall, "The Hebrew Conquest of Palestine," *BA* (1962): 65–87; Ernest Wright, *Biblical Archaeology*, new and rev. ed. (Philadelphia: Westminster, 1962); Israel Finkelstein, *The Archaeology of the Israelite Settlement* (Jerusalem: Israel Exploration Society, 1988); Norman Gottwald, *The Tribes of Yahweh: A Sociology of the Religion of Liberated Israel, 1250–1050 BCE* (Sheffield: Sheffield Academic, 1999); William G.

in the Merneptah Stela (1207 BCE).[30] While the exact location of where Merneptah's Israelites resided is unknown, archeology has demonstrated that a group of people, which can be called early Israel, came into being in the Central Hill Country during the twelfth–eleventh centuries BCE. To quote Israel Finkelstein, "The rise of early Israel was the latest phase in *long-term, cyclic processes* of settlement oscillation and rise and fall of territorial entities in the highlands."[31] This cyclic process accounts for the continuity between much of the material culture of the preceding Late Bronze Age with that of the Iron Age. On the later end of the timeline, ancient Israel might also be broken down into the northern kingdom of Israel (ca. 930 BCE–722/721 BCE) and southern kingdom of Judah (ca. 930–587/586 BCE).[32] While there were undoubtedly microcultures within the southern Levant throughout the Iron Ages, it is impossible to address all those cultural nuances here.[33] Rather, the book addresses meta-issues and stages of a child's life. Such an approach might be criticized for possibly missing microcultural differences. However, the current method allows the conversation regarding children to begin and sets a baseline from which later studies can proceed in order to find those microcultural differences. When possible, the term ancient Israel will be qualified to specify which time period and which subgroup of Israelites is being discussed.

The book examines the Iron Age broadly for three reasons. The first has to do with an essential practicality: the available data. The Iron Age

---

Dever, *Who Were the Early Israelites, and Where Did They Come From?* (Grand Rapids: Eerdmans, 2006).

30. Merneptah identifies a people group called "Israel"; however, it is difficult to assign a *specific* territory to the group. Israel Finkelstein, "Ethnographic Origins of Iron I Settlers in the Highlands of Canaan: Can the Real Israel Stand Up?," *BA* 59 (1996): 200.

31. Finkelstein, "Ethnographic Origins," 209, emphasis original.

32. When applicable, the terms *Israelite* and *Judean* will be used to distinguish the children of the Northern and Southern Kingdoms, respectively.

33. The peoples living in the land of ancient Israel were not a homogenous ethnic group. For example, Yifat Thareani has demonstrated how trade routes affected the demography of cities of the Negev and its frontier. Yifat Thareani, "Ancient Caravanserais: An Archaeological View from 'Aroer," *Levant* 39 (2007): 123–41; Thareani, "The Judean Desert Frontier in the Seventh Century BCE: A View from 'Aroer," in *Unearthing the Wilderness: Studies on the History and Archaeology of the Negev and Edom in the Iron Age*, ed. Juan Tebes (Leuven: Peeters, 2014), 227–66.

provides a wide variety of textual, iconographic, and archaeological sources. Archaeology in Israel has long focused on the biblical period. The excavations of the nineteenth and early twentieth centuries sought to find a connection between the text and the land of the Bible. During this time archaeologists dug with the Bible in one hand and the spade in the other. With the establishment of the State of Israel in 1948, Israeli archaeology also looked for that biblical connection, often for the purpose of nation building. Recent excavations continue to add to the considerable wealth of Iron Age data.

The second reason concerns the household structure of ancient Israel, the בת־אב (*bēt-ʾāb*). Literally meaning "house of the father," this term is used in the Hebrew Bible to refer to the extended family or a family compound.[34] Archaeologically, the בת־אב can be thought of as the conglomerate of people, activities, and physical structures that make up a household.[35] Archaeologists estimate that upwards of 90 percent of Israelites lived in agricultural settlements, meaning the בת־אב remained the core social structure from the Israelite settlement until the fall of the monarchy.[36]

---

34. For a discussion of the בת־אב as a kinship term, and a comparison of the בת־אב and the בת־אם, see Cynthia Chapman, *The House of the Mother: The Social Role of Maternal Kin in Biblical Hebrew Narrative and Poetry* (New Haven, CT: Yale University Press, 2016), 20–74.

35. Richard Wilk and William Rathje, "Household Archaeology," *American Behavioral Scientist* 25 (1982): 618; Catherine P. Foster and Bradley J. Parker, "Introduction: Household Archaeology in the Near East and Beyond," in *New Perspectives on Household Archaeology*, ed. Bradley J. Parker and Catherine P. Foster (Winona Lake, IN: Eisenbrauns, 2012), 4.

36. Shunya Bender, *The Social Structure of Ancient Israel: The Institution of the Family (*beit ʾab*) from the Settlement to the End of the Monarchy* (Jerusalem: Simor, 1996); Douglas Knight, *Law, Power and Justice in Ancient Israel*, Library of Ancient Israel (Louisville, KY: Westminster John Knox, 2011), 70; Carol Meyers, "Household Religion," in *Religious Diversity in Ancient Israel and Judah*, ed. Francesca Stavrakopolou and John Barton (T&T Clark, 2010), 119–20; Meyers, *Rediscovering Eve*, 112; Garroway, *Children in the Ancient Near Eastern Household*, 159. Note that while the Hebrew Bible refers to Israelites living in cities, this does not mean they lived in small houses with immediate family members. The English word *cities* is a bit of a misnomer: "the Hebrew term (עיר > *ʿîr*) usually designates walled towns that lacked truly urban functions and features" (Carol Meyers, "Household Religion," 119).

On population and population distribution estimates, see Finkelstein, *Israelite Settlement*, 330–56; Finkelstein, "Environmental Archaeology and Social History: Demographic and Economic Aspects of the Monarchic Period," in *Biblical Archaeology*

Thus, the three basic elements of a household (humans, physical structure, and activities) with which children interacted remained relatively stable throughout the Iron Age.

The third, and related reason, concerns the relationship between the ancient Israel found by archaeologists and the ancient Israel created by the authors of the biblical text. The Israel of the biblical text was produced by many hands that composed, complied, and shaped the narrative over many years (ca. late eighth to fifth century BCE). As the principle source coming out of the region and time period under investigation, it has been analyzed and interpreted for thousands of years, for many different purposes.[37] The goal here is to highlight the muted children preserved therein and place them in their world. Such a task is not often easy, for the Hebrew Bible is layered with theological ideology and nationalist propaganda.

Since *Growing Up in Ancient Israel* examines many issues that are related to females, as well as children, it is important to note the bias of the biblical text towards men.[38] This is not a revelatory statement; feminist

---

Today, 1990: Proceedings of the Second International Congress on Biblical Archaeology, ed. Avraham Biran and Joseph Aviram (Jerusalem: Israel Exploration Society; Israel Academy of Sciences and Humanities, 1993); Gunnar Lehmann, "The United Monarchy in the Countryside: Jerusalem, Judah and the Shephelah during the Tenth Century B.C.E.," in *Jerusalem in Bible and Archaeology: The First Temple Period,* ed. Andrew G. Vaughn and Ann E. Killebrew (Atlanta: Society of Biblical Literature, 2003), 130–36. See also Dever's discussion of various sized settlements and their population estimates. William G. Dever, *The Lives of Ordinary People in Ancient Israel: Where Archaeology and the Bible Intersect* (Grand Rapids: Eerdmans, 2012), esp. 47–105, and fig. IV.1.

37. The Hebrew Bible has become a foundational document for our understandings of children. Sayings such as "spare the rod and spoil the child!" and demands like "honor your father and mother!" have shaped the way Western culture has historically thought about children. *Growing Up in Ancient Israel* reexamines the Hebrew Bible and these understandings so that one might apply the biblical text in a more informed manner. For example, §6.2.2 discusses the "coat of many colors." After reading what this was and why it was given to Joseph and Tamar, one might reevaluate Sunday School projects that teach favoritism. The book does not make these connections explicit but leaves it up to the reader to reconsider the biblical narratives.

38. Rather than bemoaning the androcentric nature of the text, a more fruitful way forward is to think about men writing narratives about children and to acknowledge when they did and why they did. For example, the metaphor for the relationship between YHWH and Israel is often one of a parent and child. When Jeremiah states that Rachel weeps for her children (Jer 31:15), he uses a metaphor of the mother and child bond to talk about national calamity. The use of child-centered imagery is

biblical scholars have been pointing out the androcentric nature of the text for many years. However, this bent also affects the study of children. Considering that men were not allowed in the birthing room, descriptions of birth are likely second-hand, if not idealized.[39] In fact, much of the biblical text is idealized, written by elite men. We might suspect their interest in children, as well as their description of children and the events of childhood, to describe those on the higher end of the socioeconomic ladder. Indeed, the children with the most "page time" are boys who grow up to be great leaders (Moses, Joseph, David, Samson). This does not mean one should discount the biblical text as nonrepresentative of children. Rather, one should keep in mind that the information provided in the Bible comes from a certain bias. A rather obvious example is that of the child as lion-tamer/lion-killer. Samson kills a lion with his bare hands (Judg 14:5–9), and similarly, David keeps lions from his father's flock (1 Sam 17:34–37). Encounters with savage animals are not something that most children survive. However, such rhetoric is common amid kingly feats of bravery, such as those the Assyrian king Ashurbanipal had carved on his palace walls at Nineveh. The inclusion of this motif in the Bible might therefore serve to instill confidence in up-and-coming national leaders.

Despite these difficulties, trying to shed light on ancient Israelite children demands using all resources available, and fortunately, the Hebrew Bible is not without its references to everyday children and daily activities. As Meyers writes, "incidental or background information in the Hebrew Bible is useful, no matter what the date of the text in which it appears, because the economic basis of Israelite society remained relatively constant over the many centuries of Israelite existence."[40] The key then to using biblical texts for understanding a child's world is context. Killing or taming lions will not be listed under David's "playtime activities." Instead, the book will try to identify those background or incidental details common to everyday children. In this way, the fact that David watched his father's flocks becomes useful as it sheds light on the daily activities of a child.

---

powerful because it is relatable; it was relatable to Jeremiah's audience and it remains relatable today.

39. Tarja Philip, *Menstruation and Childbirth in the Bible: Fertility and Infertility*, StBibLit 88 (New York: Lang, 2006). For a counterargument, see John Makujina, "Male Obstetric Competence in Ancient Israel: A Response to Two Proposals," *VT* 66 (2016): 78–94.

40. Meyers, *Rediscovering Eve*, 25.

Furthermore, the text will focus on those areas that reflect general, rather than religious or theologically informed, statements regarding children.[41]

A Comparative Approach to the Child's World

A comparative approach is needed for a variety of reasons.[42] Kathryn Kamp notes that "patterns in the experience of children differ both spatially and temporally, and of course, show considerable variation within a single society."[43] Since this is no doubt true for ancient Israel, it is vital that multiple sources are investigated to add to the picture of ancient Israelite children. Kamp's statement acknowledges the experience of the child. However, the experience of the reader is also important to consider. Each person brings cultural assumptions and reading strategies to a text. For those not so familiar with the ancient world, the comparative approach used in the book provides some cultural literacy needed to understand what is being said about children.[44]

Multiple sources and interdisciplinary methods are also necessary because there are gaps in the biblical record.[45] This is true not just for children, but for other groups as well. Concerning mothers, Beth Alpert

---

41. See also Flynn, *Children in Ancient Israel*, 18.

42. For a history of scholarship on the comparative method, see Christopher B. Hays, *Hidden Riches: A Sourcebook for the Comparative Study of the Hebrew Bible and Ancient Near East* (Louisville: Westminster John Knox, 2014), 15–38. On reactions against biblical archaeology and the comparative method, see the discussion in James Hardin, *Lahav II: Households and the Use of Domestic Space at Iron II Tell Halif: An Archaeology of Destruction*, Reports of the Lahav Research Project (Winona Lake, IN: Eisenbrauns, 2010), 186–94.

43. Kamp, "Dominant Discourses," 115. Multiple sources and angles must be employed. Limitations in data occur even when we think that the record is relatively complete for a certain group of society. "Even in situations where documentation of family histories was prized, such as the Egyptians, there are barriers. For most of history the Egyptian protocol was to only include daughters on monumental art. Such practices limit our knowledge and understanding of the Egyptian birth record for the royal families." Aidan Dodson, *Amarna Sunset: Nefertiti, Tutankhamun, Ay, Horemheb, and the Egyptian Counter-Reformation* (Cairo: The American University in Cairo Press, 2009), 14–16.

44. On the lack of cultural literacy and the issues faced by most contemporary (nonacademic) readers, see Hays, *Hidden Riches*, 3.

45. For a similar methodology, see Flynn's examination of the child-deity relationship (Flynn, *Children in Ancient Israel*, 16–18).

Nakhai writes: "Written evidence from ancient times that bears on motherhood or describes individual mothers is scant.... The corpus of relevant texts is not large.... It is, therefore, all the more important to look at alternate ways to reconstruct the role of the mother in the societies of the ancient Levant."[46] Thus, one way to fill in the gaps is by using comparative sources. Such sources are important because the people writing the Hebrew Bible did not live in a vacuum; they were influenced by their own cultural environments and those of surrounding civilizations.[47] Additionally, due to the paucity of information regarding the lives of children, a comparative approach is quite helpful.[48]

The first half of the book addresses the prebirth, birth, and immediate postbirth stages of the ancient Israelite infant. As one might expect of the male biblical writers who are attempting to provide the history of a people, in-depth descriptions of these stages in an infant's life are not a top concern. Indeed, as Joseph Blenkinsopp has noted, "On the birth and nurture of children, our information [in the Hebrew Bible] is not abundant."[49] Here, too, the archaeological record of Iron Age Israel is also rather silent. Fortunately, the few biblical references to elements of an infant's life, such as transporting the baby, that are present can be filled out using comparative sources. At times, however, inferences must be made for processes and stages that are not mentioned in the Hebrew Bible but that must have taken place. For example, the umbilical cord must have been cut by some

---

46. For Nakhai this means turning to the archaeological record. Beth Alpert Nakhai, "Mother-and-Child Figurines in the Levant from the Late Bronze Age through the Persian Period," in *Material Culture Matters: Essays on the Archaeology of the Southern Levant in Honor of Seymour Gitin*, ed. John R. Spencer, Robert A. Mullins, and Aaron Jed Brody (Winona Lake: Eisenbrauns, 2014), 169.

47. Acknowledging this relationship between the Hebrew Bible and surrounding areas, Hays calls the biblical texts "exceedingly 'respiratory': they breathe in the culture of their times, and breathe it back out in a different form" (Hays, *Hidden Riches*, 4).

48. Karel van der Toorn, "Parallels in Biblical Research: Purpose of Comparison," in *Proceedings of the Eleventh World Congress of Jewish Studies, Division A: The Bible and its World* (Jerusalem: World Union of Jewish Studies, 1993), 1–8; Van der Toorn, "Israelite Figurines: A View from the Text," in *Sacred Time, Sacred Place: Archaeology and the Religion of Israel, ed. B. Gittlen* (Winona Lake, IN: Eisenbrauns, 2000), 45–46. Comparison is "a requirement for anyone who aims at explanation" (Stan Stowers, "Theorizing Ancient Household Religion," in Household and Family Religion in Antiquity, ed. J. Bodel and S. Olyan [Malden, MA: Wiley-Blackwell, 2008], 7).

49. Blenkinsopp, "Family in First Temple Israel," 68.

means, and while the archaeological data from ancient Israel and the Hebrew Bible do not go into detail, other ancient Near Eastern sources do. Thus, by necessity, the first half of the book engages more heavily with the ancient Near Eastern world to offer suggestions for what might have been happening in ancient Israel.

The second half of this book covers the growing and dying child in ancient Israel. Once the child is born, the biblical text begins to pay more attention to the figure of the child. Even so, there are subjects in the biblical text that can be further elucidated. In these cases, examining the material culture from Iron Age Israel sheds light on the life of a child. One obvious source is the skeletal remains of children. Burials, and the presence or absence of children in the burial record, have led to insights regarding population sizes and the perception of children within a society.[50] The skeletal remains of the children also provide information on disease and other stressors that may have led to the child's death. Other avenues to explore include the realia created by children or used by children. To this end, the field of childhood archaeology has developed various techniques for locating children in the archaeological record.[51] Exciting work has been done using fingerprint and footprint analysis to determine ceramics made by children.[52] Work like this is relatively new for ancient Israel, but an exemplary study of a slightly earlier period site, Middle Bronze Tel Nagila, has provided a model for understanding not only what ceramics were used

---

50. Patricia Smith, "An Approach to the Paleodemographic Analysis of Human Skeletal Remains from Archaeological Sites," in Biran and Aviram, *Biblical Archaeology Today, 1990*, 2–13; Andrew Chamberlain, "Minor Perspectives on Children in Past Societies," in Derevenski, *Children and Material Culture*, 206–12; Yossi Nagar and Vered Eshed, "Where Are the Children? Age-Dependent Burial Practices in Peqi'in," *IEJ* 51 (2001): 27–35; Röder, "Archaeological Childhood Research," 68–82.

51. A child's place in the labor force has been explored through skeletal and muscular stresses found on bodies, and the presence of small tools in a site (Nyree Finlay, "Kid Knapping: The Missing Children in Lithic Analysis," in Moore and Scott, *Invisible People and Processes*, 203–12; Linda Grimm, "Apprentice Flintknapping: Relating Material Culture and Social Practice in the Upper Palaeolithic," in Derevenski, *Children and Material Culture*, 53–71).

52. Blythe Roveland, "Footprints in the Clay: Upper Palaeolithic Children in Ritual and Secular Context," in Derevenski, *Children and Material Culture*, 26–38; Miroslav Králik, Petra Urbanová, and Marin Hložek, "Finger, Hand and Foot Imprints: The Evidence of Children on Archaeological Artifacts," in Derevenski, *Children, Identity and the Past*, 1–15.

and created by children, but also how ceramics can be used to determine in which areas of a house children were permitted and which areas were off-limits.[53] Finally, depictions of children on monumental reliefs can also provide a glimpse of what children might have looked like.[54] Thus, as both textual and archaeological materials from Israel itself become more readily available, the discussion of the data in the second half of the book focuses more on the Hebrew Bible and the material culture of ancient Israel and less on the comparative ancient Near Eastern materials.

Ethnography in a Comparative Approach

Anthropological and ethnographic reports also add another layer to the lives of children and can help us think about those "considerable variations within a single society" that Kamp calls us to recognize.[55] A final means of supplementing the biblical record is, therefore, through the social sciences.[56] Noting the difficulties of using the Hebrew Bible as a source for

---

53. Joel Uziel and Rona Avissar Lewis, "The Tel Nagila Middle Bronze Age Homes—Studying Household Activities and Identifying Children in the Archaeological Record," *PEQ* 145 (2013): 284–92.

54. Iconography depicting children also offers a picture of children in past societies providing information on a child's adornment, stature, relationship to adults, and activities (inter alia, Lesley Beaumont, "The Social Status and Artistic Presentation of 'Adolescence' in Fifth Century Athens," in Derevenski, *Children and Material Culture*, 39–50; Specht, "Girls' Education in Ancient Greece," 125–36; Irène Schwyn, "Kinderbetreuung im 9.–7. Jahrhundert: Eine Untersuchung anhand der Darstellungen auf neuassyrischen Reliefs," *Lectio Dificilor 1* [2000]: 1–14).

55. Archaeologists and anthropologists today employ the theories of both historic analogy and comparative analogy. For a description of these theories and a history of their development, see R. Lee Lyman and Michael J. O'Brien, "The Direct Historical Approach, Analogical Reasoning, and Theory in Americanist Archaeology," *Journal of Archaeological Method and Theory* 8 (2001): 303–42.

56. Carol Meyers has used this approach in much of her work. See, for example, her various interpretations of terracottas. Carol Meyers, "Terracottas without a Text: Judean Pillar Figurines in Anthropological Perspective," in *To Break Every Yoke, Essays in Honor of Marvin L. Chaney*, ed. Robert Coote and Norman Gottwald (Sheffield: Sheffield Phoenix, 2007), 115–30. "Central to the recent research on pre-historic terracottas, as to Ucko's approach, has been the emphasis on the explanatory value of arguing parallel cases in the literature of anthropology and ethnography." P. R. S. Moorey, *Idols of the People: Miniature Images of Clay in the Ancient Near East*, The Schweich Lectures of the British Academy 2001 (Oxford: British Academy, 2003), 6.

understanding ancient Israel, Meyers explains how the "social science approaches make the social actors—the women, men, and children of ancient Israel—more discernible as figures in the ancient landscape."[57] For the purposes of this book, ethnographic studies can provide clearer examples of things experienced by children that might appear obscure in the ancient record, or frankly, seem impossible for the contemporary Western reader to understand. Cross-cultural, or indirect data, can provide useful information. "Comparisons of this sort can draw attention to aspects of culture that are unique to one group, highlighting the need for explanations of the observed differences."[58] Cross-cultural data are thus beneficial for showing wide-scale patterns or divergences from patterns.

The best ethnographic studies, however, are those that provide direct data.[59] Direct data come from similar societies that are geographically and temporally close to the area under investigation. James Hardin notes four benefits of using direct data.[60] First, the sites are subject to the same ecological restraints. Second, the sites are demographically similar. Third, the resources available to the ethnographic parallel are similar to those available to the ancient counterpart. Fourth, the previous three points all contribute to a similar social organization. Here it is notable that the social structure in the ethnographic reports discussed below finds numerous similarities with the biblical text and ancient Near Eastern written sources.[61] In addition to illuminating aspects of the social structure, the ethnographic data will be applied to the ancient material record through relational analogies as a means of testing possible interpretations of objects and attitudes. As a whole, ethnography offers another lens through which

---

57. Meyers, *Rediscovering Eve*, 13.

58. Hardin, *Lahav II*, 165.

59. Ian Hodder, *Symbols in Action: Ethnoarchaeological Studies of Material Culture*, New Studies in Archaeology (Cambridge: Cambridge University Press, 1982). Much work in the field of household archaeology has engaged with ethnography and ethnoarchaeology, see Assaf Yasur-Landau, Jennie Ebeling, and Laura Mazow, *Household Archaeology in Ancient Israel and Beyond* (Leiden: Brill, 2011); Bradley Parker and Catherine Foster, *New Perspectives on Household Archaeology* (Winona Lake, IN: Eisenbrauns, 2012).

60. Hardin, *Lahav II*, 165.

61. Hardin notes of villages in Palestine and western Iran: "their social structure along with that of many other contemporary societies in the Near East is in many respects virtually identical to the social structure described in biblical texts and attributed to Iron Age Israel" (Hardin, *Lahav II*, 166).

to view customs and objects because one can see why x, y, and z occur. Even when this lens appears blurry, when the people themselves do not know exactly why they do something or what it means, one can adopt Hilma Granqvist's optimistic outlook: "Sometimes they may only answer: 'It is the custom.' But one can in this way learn general rules, get an insight into the thought and attitude of the individual–into folk psychology."[62]

In the category of direct data, the studies of children in early twentieth century Palestine by Granqvist are invaluable.[63] Not only does Granqvist study children, but she does so for reasons similar to those informing the present work: she wants to help people understand the cultural background behind the Bible. She found the study of children in particular to be of utmost importance: "The child in the Bible has not been studied enough.… Customs among the present day Arabs also show many parallels with biblical habits and customs, and illustrate the life described in the Bible."[64] Her reports are particularly useful in that she pays careful attention to noting when customs are similar to, but not necessarily the same as, those found in the Bible. Studies a little farther afield covering mid-twentieth century western Iran, by Erika Friedl and Patty Jo Watson respectively, offer similar pictures.

Issues in Comparisons

It should be noted that many of the textual examples from surrounding cultures present a picture of the upper class. Annals, letters, poetry, prophecies, rituals, incantations, all of these were, not unlike the biblical text, written by the elite males of society and therefore present a specific view. However, this does not mean the ancient Near Eastern data should be ignored or deemed useless for purposes of comparison. Since work in the field of children is relatively new, these comparisons will serve as a starting point for future research to use, modify, or even with which to disagree.

---

62. Hilma Granqvist, *Birth and Childhood among the Arabs: Studies in a Muhammadan Village in Palestine* (Helingsfors: Söderström, 1947), 26.

63. Hima Granqvist, *Marriage Conditions in a Palestinian Village* (Helsingfors: Societas Scientiarum Fennica, 1931); Granqvist, *Birth and Childhood among the Arabs: Studies in a Muhammadan Village in Palestine* (Helingsfors: Söderström, 1947); Granqvist, *Child Problems among the Arabs: Studies in a Muhammadan Village in Palestine* (Helingsfors: Söderström, 1950).

64. Granqvist, *Birth and Childhood among the Arabs*, 17–18.

Additionally, in many cases class difference does not matter. For example, a royal infant and slave infant alike were breastfed. *Who* breastfed the baby presents an opportunity to comment on the possibility of social class affecting the child's life.

As noted above, the focus of the book is on ancient Israel and the Iron Age; however, at times comparisons are made with earlier periods. Such comparisons are done for a few reasons. First, J. D. Schloen's cross-cultural work on the בת־אב has shown the extended family to be the governing social structure not only within ancient Israel but across the Levant from the second through the first millennia BCE.[65] Because the structure remained generally static, in cases where there is no stellar information from the Iron Age, examples are drawn from earlier periods. When discussing creation and the birthing process, for example, the biblical text is abstract, while the Babylonian myths describe the process in more humanly relatable terms. Pictorial evidence of birthing chairs and bricks are not found in Iron Age Israel, but there are examples from Middle Kingdom Egypt and Bronze Age Mesopotamia. At other times comparisons demonstrate continuity with the previous periods, such as the use of figurines, rattles, bottles, and protective amulets.

Drawing on earlier periods is not without its difficulty, for there is always the possibility of cultural change. Comparisons with earlier periods can also show a shift in practice. Consider the use of Late Bronze Age Egyptian amulets at Tel es-Sa'idiyeh. In the Late Bronze Age, adults wore them as status symbols, but in the Iron Age children wore them for protection.[66] This conclusion calls attention to the fact that while items might have enjoyed continual use, the motivation for their use might change with time (or region).[67] As this example demonstrates, caution needs to be used when engaging in comparisons with any time period. To this end, ethnography can be useful. When the practices represented in earlier periods are also found in more contemporary ethnographic societies from the Middle East (see above), the likelihood for some measure of continuity in practice

---

65. J. David Schloen, *The House of the Father as Fact and Symbol: Patrimonialism in Ugarit and the Ancient Near East*, Studies in the Archaeology and History of the Levant 2 (Winona Lake, IN: Eisenbrauns, 2001).

66. See §6.4.1.

67. Differences such as these show the benefits of being able to work with a single site. However, not many sites have such well-preserved burials, much less well-preserved burials spanning a long period of time.

(i.e., that they also existed in the Iron Age) is, in my opinion, high. When it is possible, the change or development in items or practices will be noted.

The outcome of a comparative approach results in a work that provides an overview of a child's world. The discussion is expansive, and perhaps even encyclopedic in the manner of Martin Stol's investigation of birth in the biblical world.[68] In its explorative nature, the book starts with the Hebrew Bible and fills in the gaps where necessary with ancient Near Eastern comparanda, primarily from Mesopotamia, Egypt, and the Hittite world. Since it is impossible to relate every piece of data, the evidence presented should be taken as representative of a larger corpus. As this field is yet young and this is the first work of its kind, more information will inevitably come to light or be reassessed regarding its relationship with children. With respect to the ancient Near Eastern comparanda discussed, it should be noted that sometimes the discussion will focus on a particular geographical region over another. For example, while all cultures have a creation narrative, the Atrahasis Epic is particularly helpful in considering the human birthing process as experienced in the ancient world. Consider too, the discussion of transporting a baby by wearing him. In this case the available iconographic data from Egypt provides insightful information. Due to the availability of data, no one single social age category discussed has a certain formula of what type of data is used, rather the discussion provides a broad picture of the issue at hand.[69] In addition to the broad overview of data provided, at times multiple cultures or sets of data are available allowing the discussion to delve more in-depth into a specific topic. In these instances, the text focuses on using a case study approach. As with any work striving to bring together a disparate and expansive corpus of materials, the texts and examples within are meant to serve as examples of key areas.

The Process of Growing Up

The first chapter begins by exploring who is involved in creating children, noting that the physical act of sexual intercourse was understood as only

---

68. Martin Stol, *Birth in Babylonia and the Bible: Its Mediterranean Setting* (Groningen: Styx, 2000).

69. As a caveat, at times the available data cause a discussion to be Mesopotamian heavy in the comparanda, while another section may lean on the Egyptian or Hittite data.

one part in the creation of children. The other part, the divine will, was needed in order for the human component to work. Children were understood, not unlike today, as a "gift from God." In light of this, barrenness was considered both a physiological and spiritual problem, which elicited various ancient responses. After discussing these responses, the chapter shifts to the texts describing situations in which a pregnancy is prevented. It explores methods of birth control (abstinence, coitus interruptus, anal intercourse, and breastfeeding), as well as the laws, medical texts, and attitudes concerning spontaneous, intentional (abortion and sorcery), and accidental miscarriages. In closing, the chapter addresses what happens during a successful pregnancy, how the news is announced, and the ancient methods for determining the sex of the child.

Chapter 2 covers the mechanics of birthing a baby, from the prebirth preparations through labor, and on to the immediate postpartum actions. It opens by comparing the creation account in Genesis with the Atrahasis Epic. Preparations for birth meant calling the midwives, preparing the atmosphere of the room, and getting into a birthing position. Ritualized behavior brought order to the chaos of the birthing chamber and the use of ritual objects, such as birthing stones or wands, had both a practical and magicoreligious purpose. Notably, most information regarding the labor in the Hebrew Bible comes from prophetic texts, which draw a parallel between the experiences of birth and war. Once a baby was finally born, certain ritual actions were taken: (1) the umbilical cord was cut, (2) the infant was cleaned, and (3) the infant was swaddled. Each of these steps finds parallels in the lands surrounding Israel, and a look at the visual representations of these rituals helps contextualize some of the birthing rituals for a modern reader. The chapter then addresses the legal repercussions of not providing these rituals for the infant. It closes with a discussion multiple births. The discussion looks first at how multiples are handled today in comparison to the Hebrew Bible and ancient Near East and concludes that ancient attitudes towards twins depended upon foreknowledge of twin births and the type of twins (identical or fraternal) born.

Once the child was born a new set of issues needed to be addressed. Chapter 3 begins by explaining the naming process and what names meant for the ancient Israelite. Oftentimes mothers named the babies, an act that began the out-of-womb gendering process for the child. The process of gendering can also be viewed in light of the period of separation between the mother-infant unit and the rest of society. While boy and girl infants were secluded for different periods of time, the seclusion itself can be understood not only as gendering, but as a practical measure to allow the baby to bond with the mother and keep him or her safe from illness. The bonding process was continued through the process of feeding via nursing, a wet-nurse, or feeding cup. Baby-wearing, a popular part of attachment parenting in modern times, finds its origins in the ancient world. Keeping the baby close with a wrap or sling could help calm cranky infants, as did lullabies and rattles. Parents had a vested interest in comforting their infants so as to keep themselves sane, the baby happy, and the household gods from exiting the premises and leaving the house and the newborn unprotected.

The ancient Near East was full of dangerous spirits. Chapter 4 explores various means of confronting this fact. Women sought to protect their children with items that are both easily identified as having a magicoreligious function and with items that might also have a practical function. An example of the first category would be the use of sympathetic magical rituals, as well as the hanging of amulets or images of the demon to repel it. Actions like these were done to ward off Lamaštu, Pazuzu, and the *kūbu*, as well as the evil eye. Women might also use protective measures, such as clay guard dogs, spells, wands, and lullabies to secure the infant. These latter measures combined the power of the written word, the spoken word, and the visual image. Objects with both a magicoreligious and practical function are perhaps the most intriguing because they emphasize the fact that material culture is a complex set of symbols. This category includes items that are both easily identifiable as having a protective use, as well as items that might easily be overlooked as protective. Here the seemingly mundane objects, like lamps and rattles, whose primary use was of a quotidian nature, serve as a prime example. Lamps provided light and rattles were noisemakers. But these too shielded the newborn from harm; lamps embodied divine protection and rattles kept the protective ancestors at peace. Objects, used either alone or in conjunction with other protective items, provided the mother with a multitude of ways to harness her protective instincts. While the exact ritual or use of each object might seem a bit unclear to the contemporary reader, what should be evident is that the much-desired baby was not left to fend for itself.

Chapter 5 focuses on how gender affects the way an ancient Israelite child grew up. Since children are quite literally the way a society reproduces itself, it would be logical that teaching children how to grow up to be proper male and female adults within society is important. In the ancient world each child was not privy to a formal education; however, each child did attend "the school of life" in which they began to learn gender by witnessing adults performing gendered acts. This chapter explores ways in which adults gendered boys into men and girls into women. For example, girls learned household obligations, while boys learned how to shepherd, farm, or carry on the family business. The chapter also investigates ways in which the ancient Israelites enculturated their children so that they would be able to carry on Israelite traditions. For boys, this meant undergoing circumcision, as well as learning the manly traits associated with war. With respect to girls, the chapter focuses on learning the religious activities associated with household religion.

Clothing is unique to humans and the clothes one wears can tell volumes about who the person is. Chapter 6 begins by noting the relationship of clothing to a coming-of-age motif seen in the Bible and Mesopotamian literature. Both Adam and Enkidu are naked before they experience a sexual awareness. They don clothing to symbolize their transition to men. The stories of young Joseph, Samuel, and David also include references to clothing that signify a special social status within their family and communities. Reliefs from Assyrian palaces and Egyptian temples continue to present the relationship between clothing and social status; both artistic traditions depict Israelite infants without clothes and wearing a sidelock. The Lachish reliefs provide a case study demonstrating that the depiction of clothing seen on Judean children seems directly correlated to a child's age. Young children are dressed simply, while older children wear more elaborate clothing. The bodies of the children themselves are also instructive. Burials might not show clothing, but they do show evidence of adornment, such as earrings, bracelets, anklets, and necklaces. The subject of dress can be rounded out by ethnographic accounts of what children wear and how they are adorned in rural, modern Middle Eastern villages.

The life of a child was not all work; there was also time for play. Chapter 7 examines the importance of play and what play might have looked like for the ancient Israelite child. After examining the ambiguous instance of Isaac and Ishmael playing, the chapter navigates the gap between play in the ancient and modern world by focusing on cross-cultural categories of play. The Hebrew Bible refers to non-object-centered play such as joking, playing tricks, and dancing. This picture is complemented by the archaeological record, which presents evidence of object-centered play such as board games, dice, figurines, and other toys. Some of the objects and games even have modern counterparts. Children today tell stories, play tricks on one another, and dodge their parents to avoid work. They too play jump rope, have running contests, dance, and play with board games and toys. In seeing the objects and reading the ancient accounts, the modern reader can get a sense of how an Israelite child might have spent his or her free time.

Chapter 8 addresses the reality that infants and children died. With a mortality rate upwards of 40–50 percent, it is fair to say that childhood death touched every family, if not directly, then certainly indirectly. Reactions to death can reveal a lot about how a society understood their children and what value they placed on them. The chapter explores two categories of deaths: those that were intentionally inflicted by human hands (cannibalism, sacrifice, and infanticide), and a more generic category of other deaths (disease, accidents, etc.). Both kinds of deaths find their way into the Hebrew Bible. However, these deaths are usually part of a larger narrative. For example, child sacrifice and infanticide are often discussed in the context of improper worship. Even the death of King David's first baby with Bathsheba is about something else; this baby's death is linked to the extended narrative of his father's acts of adultery and murder. After discussing examples of various deaths, the chapter asks: did ancient Israelites care when their children died? The answer to this question involves interacting with examples from ethnographic studies, ancient Near Eastern sources, and the burial record of ancient Israel.

The book concludes by exploring a few different meta-themes that can be seen spanning the course of the book. First, in each of the chapters, the duality of value and vulnerability can be seen. As the youngest members of society, children were dependent upon others to provide for them and keep them safe. While this is not always explicitly said, it nonetheless remains an implicit fact. Second, from the moment a child is born, they enter the process of gendering and socialization so that they may grow into an Israelite man or woman. Finally, because a child lives within a world and by necessity interacts with that world, he or she leaves his or her imprint on it. At times, this imprint is quite visible, while at other times, it is harder to see. By refocusing the way in which one thinks about texts and the archaeological record, the hidden, muted children can become more visible.

1

What to Expect When You're (Not) Expecting

The Israelites understood that sex was a key component in creating children. While there was not a specific word for sex, there were plenty of euphemisms for it: Adam "knew" his wife Eve (Gen 4:1), Abram "went in" to Hagar (Gen 16:4), Isaac "took" Rebekah (Gen 24:6), and David "lay with/ slept" with Bathsheba (2 Sam 11:4–5). Yet the physical action was not understood as the sole reason a woman became pregnant. For the Israelites, one of God's facets was fertility.[1] Similar to the Mesopotamian belief in the goddesses Inanna or Ishtar, or the Ugaritic and Canaanite belief in El and Asherah, the Israelites believed that God was ultimately in control of the womb.[2] Isaiah 54:1–3 praises God for his capacity to provide a plethora of descendants to the once childless woman. It was up to the divine whether to open a woman's womb and allow her to become pregnant.[3] Stories of God opening a woman's womb are found throughout biblical narratives. In Genesis, God not only opens Sarah's womb when she is well into menopause (Gen 21:1–7), but also opens the womb of Leah, a young

---

1. Tivka Frymer-Kensky, *In the Wake of the Goddesses* (New York, NY: Free Press, 1992).

2. For references to El or YHWH as child-giver in the Bible, see Gen 16:2, 17:15–16, 21:1–2, 30:2; Judg 13:5; Ruth 4:12–14; 1 Sam 1:11; Job 1:21.

3. Reports from villages in Palestine preserve the continuance of this belief. They reason that only the divine allows conception to occur, otherwise a woman would become pregnant every time a couple copulated (Granqvist, *Birth and Childhood among the Arabs*, 34–35). When God opened the womb, it was a fragile time for the woman. Because jinn and Satan are always around, one must say God's name during intercourse to get them to leave. If one forgot to do this, evil would enter the women, and the child would become a child of the devil. Such was rationale behind children who had fits—their parents did not bless the sexual union. If the parents said the name of God, then the child would be a merciful child (30). Similarly, if a woman was impure at the time God opened the womb, then the child would have a bad smell (33).

woman (Gen 29:31). While the former example again uses a euphemism to describe the process of opening a womb, "YHWH took note and did for Sarah as He had spoken," the latter text specifically uses the verb פתח (*pātaḥ*; "to open."). As the opener and closer of the womb, God was the one who initiated pregnancy. This is a fitting role since God is described as the first creator and the one who created humankind in the divine image (Gen 1:26–27).

1.1. Barrenness and Infertility

In a world where children were valued in multiple ways (as the ones to carry on the family name, as the perpetuators of the cult of the ancestors, or as part of the family workforce), producing children was of utmost importance.[4] As in today's society, infertility was also a reality in ancient Israel. Most of the biblical texts suggest that infertility had more to do with females than males. For example, a man could take a second wife or a concubine to produce children when his primary wife was past childbearing age or was incapable of having children. The biblical narratives address infertility through a common literary pattern: "the barren woman/matriarch" motif.[5] Sarah (Gen 18:9–15), Rebekah (Gen 25:19–25), Rachel (Gen 30:1), Hannah (1 Sam 1), and the wife of Manoah (Judg 13) are all barren women who miraculously give birth to a son.[6]

Barrenness was an undesirable state, akin to having a disability or a curse.[7] Women without children were stigmatized; no children meant no

---

4. Charles Fontinoy, "La naissance de l'enfant chez les Israélites de l'Ancien Testament," in *L'enfant dans les Civilisations Orientales*, ed. Aristide Théodoridès, Paul Naster, and Julien Ries (Leuven: Peeters, 1980), 103–4; Meyers, *Rediscovering Eve*, 110, 136–69.

5. Robert Alter, "How Convention Helps Us Read: The Case of the Bible's Annunciation Type-Scene," *Prooftexts* 3 (1983): 115–30.

6. Sarah is called עקרה (*ʿăqārāh*; "barren") in Gen 11:30, Rebekah in Gen 25:21, Rachel in Gen 29:31, and the Wife of Manoah in Judg 13:2–3. Hannah's song, perhaps an abstract reference to her own plight, gives praise to God for giving multiple sons to the barren (1 Sam 2:5). The poetry in Isa 54:1 places the barren woman in parallel with the woman who has no child, suggesting that the two were understood as one and the same.

7. Joel Baden, "The Nature of Barrenness in the Hebrew Bible," in *Disability Studies and Biblical Literature*, ed. Candida Moss and Jeremy Schipper (New York, NY: Palgrave Macmillan, 2011), 13–27.

future financial security. Rachel is so beside herself that she wishes to die rather than to remain alive and childless (Gen 30:1).[8] She understands herself to be socially disabled. In Gen 20, King Abimelech mistakenly takes Abraham's wife, Sarah, into his household. As a result, God closes the womb of all the women in Abimelech's household (Gen 20:1–17). Here, barrenness is used as curse for a misdeed. The stigma surrounding a disability or a curse is due in part to a departure from social norms. A woman's place is in the home with a house full of children. An exemplary tale of caution can be found in the Mesopotamian myth about the rogue goddess Inanna. She, like Rachel, has no children; however, instead of wishing for death, she uses her position to her advantage. Unattached to the home, she roams about doing whatever she wishes. Her husband, Dumuzi, has no control over her. Inanna becomes a proof text for how dangerous women can be if they are not tied down to the domestic sphere, thus reinforcing the social standards that women needed to be mothers.[9]

While most biblical texts fault a woman for a childless marriage, in the case of the Shunamite woman the reason for her childless state is attributed to her husband's old age (2 Kgs 4:8–17).[10] Where the Hebrew Bible is relatively silent on the issue of male infertility, ancient Near Eastern texts can provide some insights. The nonvirile state is undesirable and many texts reference it metaphorically, through battlefield and treaty language. In battle, a man's fertility is linked to his battlefield prowess.[11] For example, a "weak showing" militarily was akin to emasculating a man today by stating he wears "small shoes." The following Assyrian incantation uses battlefield accoutrements as metaphors for the male anatomy: "May the [qu]iver not become e[mp]ty! May the bow not become slack! Let the batt[le] of my

---

8. For an overview of the scholarship, as well as cases studies concerning barren women, fertility, and infertility in the Hebrew Bible, see Koepf-Taylor, *Give Me Children*, 33–63.

9. Some accounts of the goddess mention that she has two children; despite this, she remains a young and beautiful femme fatale in the literature. Tikvah Frymer-Kensky, *Studies in Bible and Feminist Criticism*, JPS Scholars of Distinction Series (Philadelphia: Jewish Publication Society, 2006), 190–92.

10. Another possible case of male impotency may be found in the two husbands of Ruth and Orpah, whose names Mahlon and Chilion mean "sickly" and "annihilation" respectively. These men died before producing any offspring, meaning that they were potentially "less than ideal reproductive specimens" (Koepf-Taylor, *Give Me Children*, 39).

11. Koepf-Taylor, *Give Me Children*, 39–42.

love-making be waged! Let us lie down by night."[12] A quiver full of arrows is also referred to in Ps 127:4–5a: "The children born when one is young are like arrows in the hand of a warrior. How blessed is the man who has filled his quiver with them!"

Metaphors of war torn land also can relate to impotence. In curse sections of ancient Near Eastern treaties, any vassal who breaks that treaty is said to have salt sown upon him; that is, the man will become impotent.[13] Rather than drawing on salt's preservative qualities, the metaphor draws upon salt's dehydrating properties. Just as the salted land is dehydrated, so the man's life-giving forces (sperm) are depleted. Hittite military oaths also include a salt related curse upon the one who breaks a vow: "And as salt has no seed, so may [it happen to] such a man that his name, his descendants, his house, his cattle, and his sheep shall perish."[14] The reference to salt in the curse is a way of poetically cursing someone or something with impotence. The biblical text also curses those who break the covenant with, among other things, soil devastated by sulfur and salt (Deut 29:22 [23]). Likewise, those nations who trouble Israel will be cursed with barren, salty, land (Zeph 2:9). In light of the ancient Near Eastern texts, one might see in these biblical texts a link between male impotence and salt, rather than barren women and salt.

1.1.1. Means of Curing Infertility

Without the services of modern day fertility doctors, people in ancient Israel looked for other ways to secure children. Within the Bible, prayer is the most common means of reversing infertility. In the case of Abimelech, a prayerful petition by Abraham, a nonrelated third party, results in God healing all the women of the household, along with Abimelech. At times, husbands prayed for their wives. Isaac prays on behalf of his barren wife, and God answers by causing Rebekah to conceive (Gen 25:21). Hannah prays for herself, petitioning God in such agony that her lips move, but no sounds come out (1 Sam 1:13). Sometimes, however, the reversal of

---

12. Robert Biggs, ŠÀ.ZI.GA Ancient Mesopotamian Potency Incantations, Texts from Cuneiform Sources 2 (Locust Valley, NY: Augustin, 1967), 37, text 18.3–5.

13. F. Charles Fensham, "Salt as a Curse in the Old Testament and the Ancient Near East," BA 25 (1962): 49.

14. Fensham, "Salt," 48–50; Johannes Friedrich, "Der Hethitische Soldateneid," ZA 35 (1924):161.

barrenness is introduced into the narrative without a formal petition. In the case of Abraham and Manoah's wives, מלאך־יהוה (mal'āk Adonai; "a divine messenger") appeared and announced the impending pregnancy (Gen 18; Judg 13).

The biblical text also relates some magicoreligious practices. When Rachel cries out "Give me children, or else I die!" Jacob offers no prayer on her behalf, nor is there a response from a divine messenger. Rachel instead turns to the aphrodisiacal plant, the mandrake, or "love apple." The fruit of the plant is fleshy and juicy. It grows close to the ground and gives off a pleasant fragrance. The lovers in Song 7:14 count mandrakes among the list of plants and flowers associated with fertility. In antiquity, the mandrake may have been associated with fertility because the root of the plant resembles a person. We are not told what Rachel does with them: if she prepares them in a special manner to ingest, or simply places them near the bed to enjoy the fragrance. Sforno, the sixteenth-century Spanish biblical commentator, notes that the mandrake had a good smell and seeds that induced fertility. Modern chemical analyses of the plant reveal trace amounts of human hormones.[15] Due to its hallucinogenic properties, it might also be that ingesting the mandrake helped a woman destress and therefore increase her chances of becoming pregnant.[16]

While the Bible mentions only one such method of curing infertility, the Mesopotamian literature attests to a rich array of magicomedical practices meant to help a woman conceive.[17] The Mesopotamian corpus provides treatments for women past menopause who, like Sarah, are too old to conceive. It also provides treatments for younger women who are

---

15. Sarah Oren, "A Small Plant Gives Birth to Great Drama—The Mandrake," Neot Kedumim Park website, https://tinyurl.com/SBL1729h.

16. A. D. Doman, P. C. Zuttermeister, and R. Friedman, "The Psychological Impact of Infertility: A Comparison with Patients with Other Medical Conditions," *Journal of Psychosomatic Obstetrics and Gynecology* 14 (1993): 45–52; L. O. Hanus, T. Rezanka J. Spízek, V. M. Dembitsky, "Substances Isolated from Mandragora Species," *Phytochemistry*, 66 (2005): 2415–16; John Riddle, *Goddesses, Elixirs, and Witches* (New York: Palgrave MacMillan, 2010), 75.

17. Erica Reiner, "Babylonian Birth Prognoses," *ZA* 72 (1982): 124–38. The Mesopotamian corpus also includes a list of physical characteristics to look for on a woman's breast and stomach to determine whether or not she is infertile (Stol, *Birth in Babylonia and the Bible*, 34).

having difficulties conceiving, and women who are considered barren.[18] Such remedies prescribe inserting a suppository or pessary consisting of a piece of wool soaked in medicines into the vagina. The pessary is checked after a period of time to see whether it has changed color. Other pessaries are simply left in the vagina. For example, one prescribes: "To make a no[n?] childbearing woman pregnant: You flay an edible mouse, open it up, and fill it with myrrh; you dry it in the shade, crush and grind it up, and mix it with fat; you place it in her vagina, and she will become pregnant."[19]

Another technique from the Mesopotamian corpus is the fumigation of the vagina. This remedy assesses whether some physical blockage was preventing pregnancy. If the woman could indeed conceive but was "blocked up," then she took a potion to help her open up and become pregnant. Identifiable plants involved in these potions and pessaries include alum, juniper, various resins, and a "white plant." Many of the recipes also have follow-up instructions that the woman and her husband should have sex.[20] Such pessaries may seem to the modern mind counter-productive, functioning as a means of preventing, rather than encouraging, conception.[21] Yet, the number of detailed texts describing how to prepare a pessary and what to do with them shows pessaries were understood to be effective. In addition to herbal remedies, a woman might also keep a special stone meant to induce pregnancy. Such stones were hollow with a pebble inside.[22] It seems logical that some sort of

---

18. For a woman in menopause see BAM 241 and BAM 243 *ša alāda parsa*. See also BAM 244.8 for references to a barren woman as SAL NU PEŠ4 (Reiner, "Babylonian Birth Prognoses," 128–29).

19. An unpublished text cited by Martin Stol and attributed to I. L. Finkel (Stol, *Birth in Babylonia and the Bible*, 53).

20. UET 7 123 and STT 98 as found in Reiner, "Babylonian Birth Prognoses," 134–38.

21. The Egyptians, on the other hand, seemed to understand pessaries as birth control. Like the Mesopotamian recipes, the Egyptian pessaries also include animal and vegetal ingredients: crocodile droppings and mucilage and natron mixed with honey. P.Petr. 21 and 22. While the papyrus is incomplete, Fontinoy reports the missing parts are most often filled in according to this interpretation (Fontinoy, "La naissance de l'enfant," 106 n. 19).

22. Jo Ann Scurlock, "Baby Snatching Demons, Restless Souls and the Dangers of Childbirth: Medico-Magical Means of Dealing with Some of the Perils of Motherhood in Ancient Mesopotamia," *Incognita* 2 (1991): 159 n. 5.

sympathetic magic might have been operative here, with the object representing the desired outcome.

One set of Mesopotamian incantations called ŠÀ.ZI.GA even addresses what to do for a male who is at fault. It suggests that male impotency and erectile dysfunction were real issues faced by men, referring to the problem as "the rising of the heart."[23] Rather than prescribing herbal remedies, this collection of texts details ways to cause the "heart to rise." Incantations include those for the man once full of vigor (like a stag, lion, or mountain goat), who has gone limp and whose heart is "blocked up." In addition to the incantation, a medical remedy is given which includes a combination of *puru*-oil, magnetic iron ore, and pulverized iron rubbed on the penis, chest, and waist, or the penis and vagina. I hypothesize that perhaps, like the magnetite used to stop miscarriages discussed below, the combination of the precious oil with something magnetic was meant to draw up the penis and attract it to the woman.

Barrenness, by way of the woman who has stopped bearing, has a prominent place within the ethnographic literature as well. Granqvist notes many methods used by Palestinian Arabs to help a woman conceive.[24] For example, a woman who "stops having" children is thought to have been wronged.[25] To cure this, the wronged woman must collect the urine of the offending party. The wronged woman then pours it over her head, washes, and rinses herself. Another method of curing infertility is to collect some dust left under an afterbirth, mix it with water, and then bathe in the mixture. The power of the afterbirth somehow opens the womb. Finally, a woman might resort to walking over the grave of a murdered person. She collects stones from the grave, puts these in water, and then washes herself with this water. Each of these remedies involves cleansing the woman, perhaps with the idea of (re)birth in mind.

---

23. Vern Bullogh, "Deviant Sex in Mesopotamia," *The Journal of Sex Research* 7 (1971): 191; Biggs, *ŠÀ.ZI.GA*, 13, 17, 18.

24. Hilma Granqvist, *Child Problems among the Arabs*, 78.

25. There is no mention of miscarriage or barrenness in the literature at this point. The phrase "stops having children" seems to be an observation made about a woman whom the villagers think should be capable of having more children, but who, for whatever reason, has ceased bearing.

1.2. Unsuccessful Pregnancy:
Contraception, Birth Control, and Miscarriage

In their desire to convey the importance of children, some biblical texts unwittingly describe means known to prevent pregnancy. Contraception prevents the egg from fertilizing or implanting. The most obvious form of contraception is abstinence. Actively withholding from sexual relations seems contra to the commandment given to humans: "be fruitful and multiply" (Gen 1:28, 9:1). However, the early Israelites may well have engaged in this practice. Meyers suggests that Gen 3, rather than being a set of curses, is a text encouraging the pioneers forging a living in the Central Hill Country. Trying to farm on rocky soil is not exactly an easy task, and both men and women needed to work constantly to make ends meet. Meyers states that in subsistence farming situations such as the early Israelites faced, there was neither a lot of time for baby making, nor a desire to procreate. In her reading, Gen 3:16 encapsulates "cultural values encouraging childbirth to maintain or even increase population."[26] The garden of Eden narrative becomes one meant to reassure women that they should want to desire their husbands, and moreover, that their husbands would take care of them. The men would do the heavy labor of tilling the ground, leaving the women to work closer to home and tend to the children.[27]

The Bible also references *coitus interruptus*, which can be understood as another form of contraception. Genesis 38 tells the tale of Tamar. Her first husband, Er, displeases God, so God strikes him dead. Tamar's father-in-law then sends Er's brother, Onan, to marry Tamar in order to fulfill his "duty by her as a brother-in-law, and provide offspring for his brother" (Gen 38:8).[28] Onan was none too pleased with this arrangement, knowing that the child Tamar would bear would not be counted as his own heir but as his brother's heir. Onan's solution was to withdraw every time they had intercourse so as not to inseminate Tamar. In spilling his seed, Onan seals his fate; his act was displeasing to God, and Onan too is struck dead. Whether Onan died because he broke the law and did not fulfill his levirate duty or because he wasted the seed of potential life is hard to say. What is clear is that he actively avoided impregnating Tamar.

26. Meyers, *Rediscovering Eve*, 101.

27. Meyers, *Rediscovering Eve*, 81–102.

28. The institution of levirate marriage was known throughout the ancient Near East; Middle Assyrian Law A 33 and Hittite Law 193 legislate the practice.

Anal intercourse could be another means of preventing pregnancy. Genesis 24:16 states that Rebekah was a בתולה (*bətûlāh*), whom no man had known. The midrash in Gen. Rab. 60:5 tries to explain what this could mean. Until recently, בתולה was understood to mean virgin. So how, asks the midrash, could Rebekah be a virgin *and* not have known a man? The midrash reasons that since the Bible is never redundant, we must try to understand why both terms are included. It concludes: she was both a virgin (vaginally intact), as well as a virgin "whom no man had known" *anywhere* else (i.e., anally or orally). This sets her apart from the daughters of the gentiles who did engage in such practices as a means of protecting their virginity. While Genesis Rabbah was written centuries after the Israelite period, it demonstrates that later Jews knew about alternative orifices for sex and viewed it distastefully, likely because it too, "wasted seed."[29]

Breastfeeding acted as another means of reducing the chances of pregnancy. Active breastfeeding, such as feeding on demand, done in many agricultural societies, lowers the chances that a woman's menses will restart. The hormone prolactin, responsible for encouraging lactation, suppresses gonadotropin, the hormone responsible for setting off menstruation. Thus, breastfeeding causes lactational amenorrhea, a halting of menstruation due to lactation.[30] Ethnographic studies show that in countries similar to ancient Israel where mothers nurse constantly, carrying their babies around throughout the day and sleeping with them at night, menses can be stopped for eighteen months.[31] The !Kung are a contemporary people group who live in Namibia and southern Angola. They breastfeed exclusively and use no intentional form of contraception, which results in an average of 4.7 children spaced 4.1 years apart. This long span between births is attributed to breastfeeding. Demographic estimates for ancient Israelites hypoth-

---

29. Some Mesopotamian priestesses, such as the *entu*-priestesses, were allowed (and encouraged) to have sex for religious rites. However, these women were not allowed to have children. The *nadītu* and *kulmašītu* were also priestesses who could marry but were not allowed to have children. See Rivkah Harris, *Ancient Sippar* (Belgium: Nederlands Instituut voor het Nabije Oosten, 1975), 303. Regarding these priestesses one text reads "A nun will permit anal intercourse in order that she not become pregnant" (Stol, *Birth in Babylonia and the Bible*, 37 and n. 79; CT 31.44. obv.i.10 [*CAD* 4:325]).

30. R. V. Short, "Breast Feeding," *Scientific American* 250.4 (1984): 36–38. Granqvist notes that some Arab women choose to nurse for a long time so as to avoid becoming pregnant (Granqvist, *Child Problems among the Arabs*, 78).

31. Short "Breast Feeding," 36.

esize a family size of two adults and three to four children.[32] If a woman married in her teens and lived into her forties, she would have upwards of six pregnancies to gain two to three living children.[33] Accounting for miscarriages and breastfeeding, the span between children may have been upwards of four or more years. Some biblical passages hint that the connection between breastfeeding and lactational amenorrhea was known. Hosea 1:8 states that Gomer weaned her first child, a female, in order that she could give birth to another child. The cultic laws in Lev 12 may also support this belief. After birthing a girl, a woman is impure for twice the amount of time as she is after birthing a boy. If boys were desired more than girls, then a woman would want to stop breastfeeding as soon as possible to become pregnant with a boy. The writers of Lev 12:1–5 can be understood as legislating against this practice by mandating that a woman continue breastfeeding the girl child in order to establish a bond with her.[34]

The previous discussion addresses ways in which pregnancy was prevented, yet there are times when a pregnancy begins but does not come to full term. Miscarriage is defined as the expulsion of a fetus from the womb before it can survive independently. Spontaneous miscarriages occur early on in a pregnancy, often without the woman's knowledge. As such, they can be understood as another natural means of birth control. Biblical texts describe a miscarriage as a נפל (nēpel) one who is[has] fallen (out). Some more poetic texts describe a miscarriage as one who never sees daylight (Ps 58:9 [8]; Job 3:16). In Num 12:12, Aaron prays concerning Miriam's skin ailment. He likens it to one who is dead, whose skin is half consumed when it comes out of his mother's womb. The miscarriage there is described in graphic terms, like the phrasing found in a list of Mesopotamian omens where a miscarriage is described as giving birth to individual body parts (i.e., not a whole child), or a membrane, or a membrane filled with blood.[35] In these cases, the miscarriage happened naturally.

---

32. Meyers, *Rediscovering Eve*, 110; Dever, *Lives of Ordinary People in Ancient Israel*, 71–72, 151–58, 201.

33. Meyers, *Rediscovering Eve*, 98–100.

34. Mayer Gruber, "Breast-Feeding Practices in the Bible and Old Babylonian Mesopotamia," *JANES* 19 (1989): 68. For references to childbirth laws in ancient Near Eastern and other cross-cultural societies, see Jacob Milgrom, *Leviticus 1–16*, AB 3 (New York: Doubleday, 1991), 763–65. See also §3.2.

35. See omens 28–40 in tablet 1 of the *Šumma izbu* series: Erle Leichty, *The Omen Series Šumma Izbu* (Locust Valley, NY: Augustin, 1972), 34–35.

In addressing miscarriages, the issue of intentionality comes to the forefront. Some miscarriages were accidental.[36] Exodus 21:22–25 describes a case where a pregnant woman is in the wrong place at the wrong time.[37] The protasis, or causal part of the law is clear: she gets caught up in a fight and is pushed by a man. The apodosis, or resulting action states, "and should her child/ 'birthing' [ילדיה; yəlādêhā] come out," then the one responsible shall indeed be fined according to what the woman's husband places on him, the payment based on reckoning. If damages occur, the penalty shall be life for life, eye for eye, and so on. The issue here is to what the term ילדיה refers.[38] Most modern commentators understand this passage to mean that her baby has fallen out; that is, she has had a miscarriage. The possibility of a miscarriage happening per this scenario during the first trimester is low but goes up as the woman reaches the second and third trimester. While the correlation between abuse and miscarriage is still debated, many people still believe punching or hitting a pregnant woman will cause her to lose the baby; this argument is seen in numerous modern day criminal cases.[39] If the biblical text describes a miscarriage, it is clear that the fetus is not considered a human being, because its life is recompensed with money, not with *lex talionis*.[40] Any time a human life is

---

36. Fontinoy, "La naissance de l'enfant," 107.

37. The law is not about miscarriage alone but about the larger issue of third party injuries. William Propp, *Exodus 19–40*, AB 2A (New York; Doubleday, 2006), 221–22.

38. Steinberg, *World of the Child in the Hebrew Bible*, 112 and n. 16. The Samaritan and Septuagint read *wəlādāh* "her child," while the MT reads *yəlādêhā*, "her children." "This must be taken as referring to either the potential for multiple pregnancies— '(all) her babies, (however many)'—or else to all the stuff of childbirth: water, blood, child(ren), afterbirth" (Propp, *Exodus 19–40*, 222).

39. Sara Torres et al., "Abuse during and before Pregnancy: Prevalence and Cultural Correlates," *Violence and Victims* 15 (2000): 303–21. For case examples, see Andy Rathbun, "Prescott, Wis.: Man Accused of Punching Pregnant Woman in Stomach," *Saint Paul Pioneer Press*, 10 July 2013; "Ex-Pc Jailed for Attempt to Cause Miscarriage by Beating Woman," *The Yorkshire Post*, 8 September 2012; Theresa McClellan, "Man Charged with Trying to Hurt Fetus; He Is Accused of Attacking His Pregnant Girlfriend with the Intention of Causing a Miscarriage," 3 Edition, *The Grand Rapids Press*, 11 September 2003: A.18.

40. Because v. 22 implies a miscarriage, the "harm" (*'āsôn*) in v. 23 is understood by most interpreters, myself included, to refer to harm done to the woman, not harm done to the fetus. Martin Noth, *Exodus*, OTL (Philadelphia: Westminster, 1962), 181–82; Brevard Childs, *Exodus*, OTL (Philadelphia: Westminster, 1974), 471–72; Propp, *Exodus 19–40*, 222. In the case when the woman incurs an injury or death (*'āsôn*),

taken, the Bible demands the death penalty (Exod 21:12; Lev 24:17). Like Exodus, various ancient Near Eastern law codes require payment for the loss of a fetus.[41] In addition, they also reference the case of a woman intentionally sabotaging her pregnancy.[42] For example, the Assyrian law code describes abortion as a heinous crime. Middle Assyrian Law A 53 states that if a woman is found trying to abort the fetus, she shall be impaled, and her body left unburied.

Other miscarriages were intentional and therefore abortive in nature. The ritual of the Sotah, found in Num 5:11–31, prescribes what to do when a husband suspects his wife of adultery. She is taken to the priest, administered an oath and made to undergo a potion drinking ritual.[43] The biblical ritual consists of drinking a mixture of tabernacle dirt and holy water. The priest calls this mixture the "the waters of bitterness that induce the spell/curse" (מי המרים המאררים; Num 5:24). The outcome is this: If the woman is innocent, she shall remain fertile and able to become pregnant. If she is guilty, then the spell water will make her "belly distend and her thigh sag" (Num 5:27). This curse has been interpreted to mean a few different things.

---

then *lex talionis* would come into play. Carol Meyers, *Exodus*, NCBC (Cambridge: Cambridge University Press, 2005), 192–93. For an alternative view, see Propp, *Exodus 19–40*, 222–23. Despite the preborn state of the ילדיה, Flynn argues the issue is the "child's potential value to the economic, cultural, social and religious benefit for the domicile" (Flynn, *Children in Ancient Israel*, 131).

41. Stol, *Birth in Babylonia and the Bible*, 38–39; Fontinoy, "La naissance de l'enfant," 107; Propp, *Exodus 19–40*, 226–27; Code of Hammurabi 209–214; Middle Assyrian Law A 21, A 50–53; Hittite Law 17–18.

42. While one could argue the issue of intentional abortion was absent from the biblical law code and Egyptian texts because it was simply not done; this argument is one from silence. Another answer is that the child was considered the property of the father, but in these cultures an embryo was not comparable to human life (i.e., the embryo was property, but not a human life). Thus, for the biblical text at least, abortion was not proscribed, but probably had a severe punishment (Fontinoy, "La naissance de l'enfant," 108–9).

43. Similar laws for the suspected adulteress are found in Code of Hammurabi 131 (a ritual oath) and 132 (a water ritual). Unlike the Sotah ritual, the "trial" in Code of Hammurabi 132 is not exactly fair and appears to deem the woman guilty until proven innocent. The woman must jump into the river where the river god (ID) will decide if she is innocent or not. Keeping in mind that many Mesopotamians did not have swimming lessons, this seems like a sure death sentence. In a slightly humorous depiction that gets to the point of people not knowing how to swim, the Northwest Palace at Nimrud shows Neo-Assyrian soldiers using "floaties" to swim across the river.

One possibility is sterility caused by a distended uterus. It could also refer to a miscarriage.[44] Modern day miscarriage inducing drugs include Misopristol and Cytotec. The former acts much like the "waters of bitterness." It has a bitter taste and causes "bleeding, cramping, swelling and finally the evacuation of the womb."[45] Logically, the proof that she was an adulteress would be pregnancy. Thus, the miscarriage of the *mamzer*, the fetus produced by the illegitimate union, would not only prove the affair (provided her husband was not lying and that she had not slept with him in recent months), but also would terminate the illegitimate child.

There is one other cause of miscarriage: sorcery. While the Hebrew Bible does not overtly link miscarriage and sorcery, it does note the relationship between sorcerers attempting to mitigate who lives and who dies (Ezek 13:18–19). In Babylonia, a miscarriage caused by a sorcerer's curse could be avoided by performing a ritual to Assur.[46] Some texts describe the use of remedies such as magnetite.[47] The ore's magnetic properties were thought to keep the fetus inside the womb, like a magnet. Remedies also included tying knots, again binding the fetus inside in a magical way. When the woman reached her due date, the knots were untied, thus opening the womb and allowing the baby to pass through.[48] Such texts also

---

44. For further discussion and bibliography on the matter see: Jacob Milgrom, *The JPS Torah Commentary: Numbers* (Philadelphia: Jewish Publication Society, 1990), 303 n. 64; Jaeyoung Jeon, "Two Laws in the Sotah Passage (Num V 11–31)," *VT* 57 (2007): 181–207.

45. Teresa J. Hornsby, *Sex Texts from the Bible* (Woodstock, VT: Skylight Paths, 2007), 132. When a pregnancy was lost it needs to expel itself. There is no record of the modern practice, dilation and curettage, which surgically removes the dead tissue from the woman. An Old Babylonian letter records the plea of a woman to her lord in which she states that the baby has been lost and "dead in my belly since one month and nobody takes care of me" (Stol, *Birth in Babylonia and the Bible*, 28; TIM 1.15; A. L. Oppenheim, *Letters from Mesopotamia* [Chicago: University of Chicago Press, 1967], 85). Failure of the tissue to naturally expel itself can result in infection or heavy bleeding, which in turn could endanger the woman's life. Stillborn babies, identified with the *kūbu* in Mesopotamia, are known in ancient Israel from an archaeological context and are discussed further in ch. 4.

46. Stol, *Birth in Babylonia and the Bible*, 143.

47. Scurlock, "Baby Snatching Demons," 138; Walter Farber, *Schlaf, Kindchen, Schlaf! Mesopotamische Baby-Beschwörungen und-Rituale* (Winona Lake, IN: Eisenbrauns, 1989), 110 §39:7–14.

48. Scurlock, "Baby Snatching Demons," 139; F. Thureau-Dangin, "Rituel et Amulettes Contre Labartu," *RA* 18 (1921): 161–98.

prescribed burying a potsherd under the threshold of the house as a form of sympathetic magic meant to stop the exit of the fetus from the mother.[49] Attesting to the deep desire for a successful birth, the Babylonian corpus also offers a solution for stopping a miscarriage, no matter what the cause, from occurring: "If a woman is about to lose a fetus in either the first, or the second, or the third month, you dry a hulû mouse, crush and grind it up, (add) water three times, and mix it with oil; add alluharu (a mineral). You give it to her to drink, and she will not lose the foetus."[50]

1.3. Successful Pregnancy

Once conception took place, the pregnancy went through different stages.[51] By the time of the Mishnah (200 CE) and Talmud (ca. 500 CE), certain Jewish understandings about these stages had been widely established (b. Ber. 60a; b. Menah. 99b; m. Nid. 3:3). However, within ancient Israel, the exact progression of pregnancy's stages were not so clear. References to the trimesters and the development of the fetus were not of much concern to the biblical writers. Without describing different stages, the prophet Jeremiah does note that God formed him in his mother's womb (Jer 1:5). Psalm 138:13–16, Job 1:5, and Isa 44:2, 24 also present this belief. A few biblical texts reference a woman while she is pregnant in a generic sense. For example, Hagar puts on airs when she becomes pregnant, causing strife between her and her mistress, Sarah. Hagar did not know if the child was a girl or a boy, but in her mind, the mere fact that she was pregnant elevated her status within the household (Gen 16). Rebekah, too, experiences a range of emotions while pregnant. Once barren and pleading for a child, she suffers greatly from the pregnancy as the "children struggled in her womb" (Gen 25:22). So great is her pain and misery that she wonders why she should keep living. The Lord answers Rebekah's cry and tells her she has two nations in her womb. These texts represent the exceptions

---

49. Scurlock, "Baby Snatching Demons," 138.

50. Stol, *Birth in Babylonia and the Bible*, 28 and n. 13. Based on an unpublished inscription from I. L. Finkel.

51. Flynn investigates some of the wide variety of Mesopotamian literature addressing the child in his or her prebirth (preconception and postconception) stage. He concludes that the attention paid to the preborn child expresses from the earliest possible moment of a child's life the value Mesopotamian society placed on him (Flynn, *Children in Ancient Israel*, 24–30).

when it comes to discussing pregnant women. More often, after the reader learns the woman has conceived the next important information given concerns the birth. Consider the following: "She/the woman conceived and bore a son" (Gen 30:23; Exod 2:2). "The two daughters of Lot came to be with child by their father. The older one bore a son … and the younger one bore a son" (Gen 19:36–38). Whether this hints at superstition around the period of pregnancy is hard to tell. It might be that the biblical author is simply not interested in the length of the pregnancy, but only in the life of the child once she or he is born. If so, this could represent a radically different approach to pregnancy and the issue of when life begins from that of the rabbis.

Where the Bible is silent about the length of pregnancy, the Mesopotamian texts are more helpful.[52] These texts tell us that pregnancy lasted nine to ten months.[53] We know now that the average pregnancy lasts forty weeks, or nine months. Just as today, a woman in the ancient world could deliver past her due date. Any pregnancy that lasted longer than exactly nine months was considered a ten-month pregnancy.[54]

Thus, the stages of a pregnancy are conception (via the divine hand), birth, and the postpartum period of impurity. Again, a more detailed version of pregnancy is found in the Mesopotamian texts, which address pregnancy according to the kinds of dangers a pregnant woman might face. In early pregnancy (the first trimester) a fetus is susceptible to sorcery

---

52. Egyptian texts were also vague concerning the length of pregnancy. Instead of numbering months, the Egyptians understood pregnancy to occur "when she has completed the months of childbearing" (Rosalind M. Janssen and Jac J. Janssen, *Growing Up in Ancient Egypt* [London: Rubicon, 1990], 4). The Talmud breaks down pregnancy as follows: "Within the first three days a man should pray that the seed should not putrefy; from the third to fortieth day he should pray that the child should be a male; from the fortieth day to three months he should pray that it should not be a *sandal* [a miscarriage looking like a flat fish]; from three months to six months he should pray that it should not be stillborn; from six months to nine months he should pray for a safe delivery" (b. Ber. 60a; Stol, *Birth in Babylonia and the Bible*, 18).

53. Martin Stol, "Private Life in Ancient Mesopotamia," in vol. 1 of *Civilizations of the Ancient Near East*, ed. Jack Sasson (New York: Scribner, 1995), 491.

54. Hittite miscarriage laws reference the tenth month of pregnancy, as well as the fifth month (Hittite Law 17, 18). The fine for causing miscarriage in a woman in the tenth month is twice that of a miscarriage caused in the fifth month. Presumably these time frames refer to a woman whose pregnancy is full term versus preterm.

and disease.[55] In the later trimesters and also at birth, a fetus/baby is prone to attacks from the demoness Lamaštu.[56] This demon could attack either the mother or the fetus and Mesopotamian women took precautions to ward themselves from danger.

Considering these superstitions regarding demons, one might think that pregnancy would be kept secret. Yet pregnancy within the biblical text, especially for the barren, was a state to be celebrated. In the barren women narratives discussed in §1.4, the annunciation of pregnancy was heralded as a happy occasion. Manoah and his wife cannot believe their ears and must have the announcement repeated (Judg 13). Abraham and Sarah both laugh in disbelief (Gen 17:17, 18:12). When Hannah hears she will conceive, her countenance becomes joyful (was no longer downcast) (1 Sam 1:18). However, these texts are the exception, as mentioned pregnancy is most often relayed to the reader by the narrator in a generic, emotionless fashion: "[the woman] conceived."

1.4. Announcing the News

The impending birth of a child is important and exciting news. While we have no record of parents sending out birth announcements, the narratives of the barren women do include what is called an "annunciation scene" which is formulaic in nature. First, a divine being, or a man of God gives an oracle to the husband and/or wife.[57] God speaks to Abraham stating that Sarah will bear a son (Gen 17:16), and later, three messengers visit Abraham and Sarah at their tent to announce that Sarah will give birth in the coming year (Gen 18:9–15).[58] In the case of Rebekah, she herself receives a direct communication from God regarding the children

---

55. Note the conception of fetal development in Mesopotamia: upon conception the fetus is half a grain long; at ten days it is five grains long; at one month, three fingers; and at ten months, the fetus (or baby if born) is one cubit. JoAnn Scurlock and Burton R. Andersen, *Diagnoses in Assyrian and Babylonian Medicine: Ancient Sources, Translations, and Modern Medical Analyses* (Chicago: University of Illinois Press, 2005), 264.

56. See the discussion in §4.4.1.

57. Such a person can be called an angel/divine messenger (מלאכים; *maleʾākîm*) or, in the case of Elisha, a man of God (איש האלהים; *ʾîš hāʾĕlōhîm*).

58. The visitors in Gen 18 are described as men (אנשים; *ʾănāšîm*), but the context suggests that at least two of them are divine emissaries. Two of the men continue to Sodom where they are called angles (מלאכים; *maleʾākîm*) in Gen 19:1.

she will bear (Gen 25:22–23). The entire chapter of Judg 13 is taken up with the repeated appearances of the angel (מלאך) who tells first the wife of Manoah and then Manoah himself that they will have a son. Similarly, Elisha announces to his Shunamite hostess that she will have a child in the next year (2 Kgs 4:16). In these stories, the parents-to-be react with disbelief. Such a thing is too good to be true! However, the promises given to these couples do come true. Because the barren women narratives announce the birth of a son *before* he is conceived, the annunciation scenes serve more as an announcement of conception, rather than pregnancy.[59] The pregnancy itself is never publicly proclaimed. Perhaps in this way, the biblical texts hint at some unspoken idea surrounding pregnancy similar to the idea that "if we do not talk about it, then nothing bad will happen."[60]

In today's world, many couples eagerly await the twenty-week mark and the ultrasound that can reveal the sex of the child. Texts outside of the biblical corpus suggest that couples in the ancient world were also eager to find out if they were having a boy or a girl.[61] Egyptian medical papyri prescribe urine tests. A pregnant woman was to urinate on wheat and barley seedlings. If both sprouted, she would bear a child. If the wheat alone sprouted, she would have a boy, but if the barley sprouted, she would deliver a girl.[62] If neither sprouted, she would not have a child.[63] Mesopotamian texts discuss throwing oil on water and reading the webs that form: "If I have thrown

---

59. For a broader treatment of the birth narratives, see Timothy D. Findlay, *The Birth Report Genre in the Hebrew Bible*, FAT 12 (Tübingen; Mohr Siebeck, 2005).

60. This notion is most assuredly present among Arab Palestinians, who go through great lengths to avoid drawing attention to a pregnancy or newborn child for fear of Karine and the evil eye (Granqvist, *Child Problems among the Arabs*, 101–14. See also §4.4). One might also think of the power of the "performative speech act"; see Stanly J. Tambiah, "The Magical Power of Words," *Man* 2/3.2 (1968): 175–208.

61. Instead of looking for observable signs, Rebekah turns to a more traditional means of finding out information about her baby; she seeks answers from God. While not stating outright that she has twin boys, the language used and the reference to two nations implies that the children are both male: "Two nations are in your womb, two separate people shall issue from your body; one people shall be mightier than the other, and the older shall serve the younger" (Gen 25:23). In this way, we can infer that Rebekah learns the sex of her children through a prophecy.

62. John F. Nunn, *Ancient Egyptian Medicine* (Norman: University of Oklahoma Press, 1996), 190–91.

63. Janssen and Janssen, *Growing Up in Ancient Egypt*, 2–3.

oil on water and two films go out from the middle of the oil, the one large, and other small: the wife of a man will give birth to a male [*zikaru*]; as to a sick person: he will recover."[64] The Mesopotamian corpus also includes a few omen series, which Mesopotamians understood to function as a sort of medical almanac. These texts are arranged in a cause and effect format: if (*šumma*) X, then Y. Like the Egyptian texts referenced above, the Mesopotamian texts rely on observable behavior or signs. In the omen series *Šumma izbu*, the first four tablets concern pregnant women. The subsequent tablets address malformed births and will be discussed in the next chapter. This series makes predictions about the future of the child, of its family, and at times, of the entire country. For example, if a woman gives birth to a child without a vulva or testicles, pregnant women (everywhere) will miscarry.[65] Another series, called *Šumma ālu*, includes predictions for the sex of a child based on observation of nature: "If a skink walks to and fro on a pregnant woman, that woman will give birth to a male."[66] It also includes predictions that allow the parents to be more proactive in choosing their child's sex: "If the foundations of a house are laid in month V, that house will have sons."[67] A more mystical omen series comes from the Assyrian Dream Book, which, just as it sounds, interprets a person's dreams. A few of the texts are concerned with dreams in which the dreamer (a man) urinates. For example, "If he urinates against the wall, and on [...] he will have sons."[68] Notably, the Mesopotamian omen series focuses its attention on male offspring, again highlighting the wish to have sons rather than daughters.

Even though male children were more desirable, due to the laws and beliefs about abortion, texts do not suggest terminating the pregnancy if it was a girl.[69]

---

64. Stol, *Birth in Babylonia and the Bible*, 206; CT 5.4.4. Oil on water is also a permissible form of divination in the Bible (Milgrom, *Numbers*, 471–73). Indeed, we see Joseph possessing a cup of divination (Gen 44:5). The Hebrew word for divination is נחש, which comes from the same root as snake. The idea is that the oil "snakes" about on the top of the water. While conjecture, it could be that the Israelites too utilized this form of divination to discern a child's sex.

65. Leichty, *Šumma Izbu*, 61, tablet 3.70–71.

66. Stol, *Birth in Babylonia and the Bible*, 104.

67. Stol, *Birth in Babylonia and the Bible*, 104. The Babylonian Talmud also mentions ways to ensure the birth of a son, including making sure the woman "emits" first (b. Nid. 31a).

68. Stol, *Birth in Babylonia and the Bible*, 105.

69. Female infanticide, however, is another matter and is covered in ch. 8.

The desire for a boy and the celebration of a boy's birth comes through clearly in the ethnographic literature from Palestine. Boys build up the house, but girls ruin it as they leave the house through marriage and build up another man's house.[70] The anticipation for the birth of a boy rises when a woman looks like she is carrying a boy. Such a woman is said to look like a "beehive." Women who carry their pregnancy at their hips are said to be carrying a girl.[71]

1.5. Summary

The belief expressed in the adage "children are a gift from God" holds true in ancient Israel as well. As the discussion above demonstrates, God was responsible for opening and closing the womb. Barrenness or infertility was most often attributed to issues with a woman's womb. Male infertility was known but seems to be so embarrassing or emasculating that texts only hint at it. Yet, while it was more socially acceptable to discuss a woman's infertile state, this too had a stigma attached to it. Not being able to produce children meant no heirs, no elder care, and no one to tend to the cult of the ancestors when the parents passed on. The socioeconomic pressures to have children were so intense that an early death seemed preferable to being childless and growing old (Gen 30:1). Throughout the Bible, couples employed prayer and supplication to get God to open the woman's womb. Both the Bible and extrabiblical texts attest to a compendium of remedies known to cure infertility. Herbal remedies could be drunk or eaten. A woman's insides could also be corrected by combining various floral and faunal elements into a pessary that was inserted into the vagina, or by simply fumigating the vulva. In addition to spiritual and medical means, magicomedical remedies were also employed. For example, certain stones were thought to have special powers that could make the woman pregnant.

The information on how to get pregnant and stay pregnant focuses on either divine or human action, and at times, a combination of both. The Bible discusses nurses or midwives being present at birth, and we know from Egyptian and Mesopotamian texts that women from these cultures were also helped during pregnancy. As the traditional keepers of

---

70. Granqvist, *Birth and Childhood among the Arabs*, 79.
71. Granqvist, *Birth and Childhood among the Arabs*, 70.

remedies, midwives played an important role in passing along the chain of knowledge. However, the documents left behind are not the diaries or lists of remedies from midwives, but rather those belonging to members of the professional class such as doctors and exorcists (a sort of magico-medical specialist).

As for pregnancy itself, one could have a successful or unsuccessful pregnancy. Women who were actively trying to avoid pregnancy could do so through abstinence, *coitus interruptus*, breastfeeding, or by engaging in anal sex. Once pregnant, a woman had to contend with the possibility of a miscarriage. Again, miscarriages were understood to come about as either a divine act, or through human actions. Intentional miscarriages were not condoned, and both biblical and ancient Near Eastern laws were enacted against humans trying to carry out such a deed. Mesopotamian texts of a more medical nature also give suggestions for herbs and pessaries that can be applied to stop a miscarriage.[72]

Successful pregnancies lasted nine to ten months and resulted in a healthy child. Like today, ancient Israelites and their neighbors wished to know the baby's sex while it was still in utero. People tried various methods, such as urinating on different grains, as well as looking to prophecies, omens, and dreams to reveal this precious knowledge. The accuracy of such tests are unknown, but regardless of whether the results indicated a boy or a girl, the family took precautions to protect the fetus from divine and human harm until it came to term.

Each of the sections above stresses the importance placed on children and the value they had within the family. Actively wasting the opportunity to have a child was frowned upon (Gen 38) and violates one of the first commandments given to Adam and Eve to "be fruitful and multiply" (Gen 1:22). The biblical text is rather silent about what went on during pregnancy, which makes sense since the male writers were not concerned with detailing domestic life. Yet, when the male writers do address pregnancy, it is the lack of pregnancy that they stress via the multiple barren woman narratives. Through these barren-women narratives the biblical writers celebrate the opening of a mother's womb and impending birth of a child. The ancient Near Eastern texts addressing ways to get and stay pregnant were also written by men and also demonstrate the value of

---

72. The Babylonian lexical series ḪAR-RA lists botanicals helpful for getting and staying pregnant (Flynn, *Children in Ancient Israel*, 28).

children in these cultures. Here we can understand that men, as well as women, desired children.

Boys were preferred for their usefulness in agricultural and other heavy labor and passing on inheritance and the family name, yet we can infer that girls were also seen as valuable. This can be deduced by the attitude surrounding voluntary ending of a pregnancy. If pregnancy "tests" revealed it was a girl, the family still kept the pregnancy. The Middle Assyrian Laws took a strong stance on aborting a pregnancy, punishing the woman with a humiliating death and an unburied body.[73] Even the reactions to unintentional miscarriages carried a fine. While this says something about the legal status of a fetus (nonperson), it does show that a pregnancy had value. Placed in this milieu, the Sotah laws are the one case where it appears something akin to an abortion is condoned. The issues behind the Sotah law are adultery and determining the paternity of the child. However, these issues go back to who owns the potential child and whose heir the child will be, which again demonstrates the value parents place on having a child whom they can call their own.

Every pregnancy came with the potential of a valued child. In a world where infant mortality rates were extremely high, carrying a pregnancy to full term was only the beginning of the journey. Chapter 2 will explore what occurred during the next stage, birth.

---

73. Such a burial, or nonburial as it were, separates a person from the family tomb and the cult of the ancestors.

2

How to Birth a Baby

A baby's entrance into the world was met with great joy. It was also a time of great danger, and a successful birth depended upon many factors. As will be seen, it was necessary not only to create the correct environment for the birthing room but to have the proper people in attendance and equipment on hand. As the previous chapter discussed, not much is known about the actual birth process in ancient Israel. Therefore, this chapter will rely upon the surrounding regions and ethnographic data to offer insights into what occurred just prior to, during, and right after the birth.

2.1. Preparing for Birth

The creation myths of Genesis and the Atrahasis Epic record the birthing process in a mythological context, with YHWH and the mother goddess Mami acting as divine creators and midwives. In Gen 1:26–27 God said, "let us create man in our image, after our likeness.... And God created man in His image, in the image of God He created him; male and female He created them." In a slightly different fashion, Gen 2:7 has God creating man "from the dust of the earth. He blew into his nostrils the breath of life, and man became a living being." Woman comes along a few verses later: "While he [the man] slept, He took one of his ribs and closed up the flesh at that spot. And the Lord God fashioned the rib that He had taken from the man into a woman" (Gen 2:21–22). While God is the divine midwife who births the first humans, the process by which humans themselves are birthed is unlike any birth known to humankind.[1] The description is

---

1. On the relationship between human midwives and divine creation, see Flynn, *Children in Ancient Israel*, 34.

completely abstract. Unlike Genesis, the Atrahasis Epic offers more relatable details and can serve as a starting point for investigating the birthing process as it took place in the ancient world.

> The birth goddesses were assembled,
> And Nintu [sat] counting the months.
> [At the] destined [moment] the tenth month was summoned.
> The tenth month arrived
> And the elapse of the period opened the womb.
> With a beaming, joyful face
> She performed the midwifery.
> She girded her loins as she pronounced the blessing
> She drew a pattern in meal and placed the brick,
> "I have created, my hands have made it."
> Let the midwife rejoice in the house of the wet-nurse.[2]
> Where the pregnant woman gives birth
> And the mother of the baby severs herself,
> Let the brick be in place for nine days,
> That Nintu, the birth-goddess, may be honoured.[3]

Unlike modern American culture, where many women write up a birth plan, ancient women did not have the opportunity to choose things such as who would attend the birth, whether the birth would be natural, what music should be playing, and so on.[4] Instead, as the myth suggests, the birth process was ritualized. It is worth noting that adhering to a ritual not only gives the event religious significance, but also provides the participants with a routinized, process-oriented set of instructions. Order can be calming during the chaos of birth.

––––––––––––

2. This line follows the translation of Alasdair Livingstone, "The Pitter Patter of Tiny Feet in Clay," in *Children, Childhood and Society*, ed. Sally Crawford and Gillian Shepherd, BARIS 1696, IAA Interdisciplinary Series 1 (Birmingham: University of Birmingham, 2007), 17.

3. Wilfred Lambert and Allan Millard, *Atra-hasīs: The Babylonian Story of the Flood* (Oxford: Oxford University Press, 1969), 63–65.

4. Granqvist records popular stories among the Palestinian Arabs of Arab and Bedouin women giving birth out in the open. After giving birth the women would wrap the baby and the afterbirth up in the long folds of their sleeves and head back on their way (Granqvist, *Birth and Childhood among the Arabs*, 52–56).

2.1.1. Creating a Safe Space

Men were not a part of the birthing ritual and were not even allowed in the birth chamber.[5] Instead, a midwife or a helper attended the mother in the birthing room. The Mesopotamian texts refer to these women as *šabsūtu* and/or *qadištu* (a priestess or holy woman). These women provided the laboring woman with medical expertise, as well as a happy countenance. Women were encouraged to stay upbeat and positive during the sometimes long and perilous birth process. Exodus 1:15–17 records the narrative of the Hebrew midwives, Shiphrah and Puah. These women defied the orders of Pharaoh and continued to deliver male babies. Not only were these midwives wise in the ways of women, but they were also strong women themselves. One can imagine the calming, reassuring words spoken to the frightened mother-to-be who was wondering not only whether the delivery would go smoothly, but also if her baby would be killed immediately per Pharaoh's orders.

Midwives remain an important fixture in the birthing room of Palestinian Arabs. Midwives must be old women who are past menopause, which is important for they are not in danger of becoming impure through menses. They, like the midwives of old, learned their trade empirically. When the midwife enters the room, she orders quiet among the various female friends, relatives, and visitors present. Part of setting the mood in the room and instilling a peaceful and calming mood is to remind the women that during labor the gates of heaven are open.[6]

Reassuring words would help create a safe space, which as more contemporary studies point out, is an essential part of the birthing experience. We know that mind-body connection is significant. For example, one modern account states: "No conversation of a depressing character would for one moment be allowed.... The only words that should be then spoken are the few words of comfort from the doctor."[7] That calm and positive words were understood to have a soothing effect can be seen in

---

5. Scurlock, "Baby-Snatching Demons," 140; Fontinoy, "La naissance de l'enfant," 117.

6. Granqvist, *Birth and Childhood among the Arabs*, 60–62; Alois Musil, *Arabia Petraea*, Ethnologischer Reisebericht 3 (Wien: Kaiserliche Akademie der Wissenschafter, 1908), 214.

7. Judith W. Leavitt, *Brought to Bed: Childbearing in America 1750–1950* (New York: Oxford University Press, 1986), 103.

the ancient literature as well. Consider the midwife's reassuring words to Rachel during her difficult labor with her second child: "Do not be afraid, you have another son" (Gen 35:16–19). Presumably the announcement of a son was meant to have a soothing effect that would bolster Rachel's spirits.

Part of creating a safe environment came about through words, while another part came via ritual objects. Perhaps the best-known objects from the ancient world are the birthing bricks, found in both Mesopotamian and Egyptian sources, and perhaps even the Hebrew Bible.[8] In the Bible, the reference to birthing bricks, or more likely birthing equipment, is found in Moses's birth narrative. The aforementioned midwives delivered babies on אבנים (ʾobnāyîm). This word has been translated as birth/delivery stool or chair. Some translations, noting the dual form of the noun, suggest it is related to the word אבן (ʾeben; "stone") and translate it as two stones.[9] However, this translation has now fallen out of favor.[10] All of these translations rely on the notion that Egyptian women squatted during birth.[11] Egyptians were not the only ones to use this position; anthropologists and ethnographers alike note that many historical and non-Western societies do not lay down to give birth, but rather squat using stools or bricks. Squatting allows gravity to aid in the birth process.[12] In studying Persian women, a nineteenth century ethnographer puts it rather bluntly:

---

8. The Atrahasis Epic states bricks are placed in the house where a woman will give birth. A few other references to birthing bricks occur in association with some of the mother goddesses, such as Dingirmah and Gula (Marten Stol, *Birth in Babylonia and the Bible*, 118–20. The Egyptian bricks are discussed at length in §4.2.1.

9. BDB, s.v. "אבן."

10. Philologists note that the plural of אבן should be vocalized as "*abnayim*, not *'obnayim*." Kevin McGeough, "Birth Bricks, Potter's Wheels and Exodus 1:16," *Biblica* 87 (2006): 307–9.

11. For more on the squatting position and crouching, see Makujina, "Male Obstetric Competence in Ancient Israel," 86. The article as a whole addresses how much knowledge males in ancient Israel had of the birthing process. See also, Philip, *Menstruation and Childbirth in the Bible*; Eran Viezel, "The Influence of Realia on Biblical Depictions of Childbirth," *VT* 61 (2011): 685–89.

12. Romans, sixteenth-century Puritans, nineteenth-century Persians, Fellahin of Modern Egypt, and Arabs in twentieth-century Palestine (McGeough, "Birth Bricks, Potter's Wheels," 305; Stol, *Birth in Babylonia and the Bible*, 119–20). Bedouin women in Palestine were also observed getting into a staggered crouch as birthing position, like a sprinter starting a race (Granqvist, *Birth and Childhood among the Arabs*, 52–56).

the woman squats like she is defecating.[13] An overview of pre-Westernized practices in Iraq finds that lying down is an imported (Western) custom. Traditionally: "The Jewish woman supports her heels on bricks, and clings to the *jidda* (midwife), or to a stool, when the *jidda* goes behind her to deliver the child. Moslem and Christian women crouch and cling to a woman, and marsh-dwellers and Mandean women hold on by the reed bundle which supports the roof, while the *jidda* takes the child from behind."[14] Since labor is a painful process that can take a long time, the bricks or chairs support the woman in labor. When the time comes to push the baby out, the woman leans forward onto a stack of bricks or squats on the chair. The ground beneath the chair or the bricks is dug out, allowing the midwife to have room to catch the baby; after she has done so, the hole can act as a receptacle for the afterbirth.[15] Hittite birth rituals from the end of the second millennium BCE describe a platform made of boards, on top of which, a bowl is held in place by pegs on either side.[16] The woman squats over the bowl during labor so that after birthing the baby, the afterbirth could pass into the bowl.

In addition to bricks and bowls, Mesopotamian texts reference the use of stools. Stools again require the woman to be in a squatting position, and the birth stool referenced in Mesopotamian texts also utilizes gravity. While no stools have been recovered, there are some terracotta plaques that show a woman squatting on a chair. One such example can be seen in figure 2.2. The piece comes from the "house ruins" at the site of Tell Uhamir (Kish).[17] It shows a woman in a position similar to the way birthing positions are commonly described. The woman sits on a stool while grabbing her ankles and opening her legs.[18] If this were a birthing stool, the seat of the chair

---

13. "*Ita ut in defecatione.*" Jakob E. Polak, *Persien: Das Land und seine Bewohene*, Ethnographische Schilderungen 1 (Leipzig: Brockhaus, 1865), 219.

14. Ethel S. Drower, "Women and Taboo in Iraq," *Iraq* 5 (1938): 109–10, especially n. 1.

15. This is true also for women in Palestinian villages (Granqvist, *Birth and Childhood among the Arabs*, 62 n. 13).

16. Gary Beckman, "Hittite Birth Rituals" (PhD diss., Yale University, 1977), 107–18, text A; Beckman, *Hittite Birth Rituals: An Introduction* (Malibu, CA: Undena, 1978), 8.

17. The piece is housed in the Ashmolean, AN1924.259.

18. Some scenes with women in this position are understood as childbirth, but scholars are not all in one accord. Other scenes include male genitalia, leading scholars to understand them as fertility plaques or as a depicting a dominant woman

Fig. 2.1. Woman in labor, Persia, circa 1860.

would have an opening for the baby to fall through during the birth process. Chairs continue to be used in early twentieth century Palestine among the Arabs. The so-called birth chair, favored by traditional women in larger cities, is an actual chair with a hole in the center. The village women create a chair of stones for the woman to sit on. The ground under the makeshift chair is scooped out into a special pit (*jôra*), which allows sufficient space into which the infant and afterbirth might descend.[19]

2.2. Labor

The closest thing the Bible contains to a birth-room scene comes from a short story in 1 Sam 4:19–22. The narrative starts with an unnamed woman, identified as the high priest Eli's daughter-in-law and the wife of Pinchas, about to give birth. She hears the distressing news that the ark of the covenant has been captured by the Philistines and her husband is

in sexual position. See P. R. S. Moorey, "Bronze Age Catalogue—Akkadian to Old Babylonian Periods in Babylon," *Catalogue of Terracotta Figurines in the Ashmolean*, 102–3, fig. 113, http://www.ashmolean.museum/ash/amocats/anet/pdf-files/ANET-23 Bronze1MesII-Catalogue-1.pdf.

19. Granqvist, *Birth and Childhood among the Arabs*, 62 n. 13.

Fig. 2.2. Woman on a stool, Tell Uhaimir (Kish), Isin-Larsa/Old Babylonian.

dead. The narrative encourages the reader to understand that the news is so distressing it causes her immediately to give birth. She "crouched [squatted] and she gave birth for her labor pains [travail] turned upon her" (1 Sam 4:19). The following verse says that her attending women (lit., the ones standing [with her]) encouraged her, from which we can infer that multiple women assisted in the birth. Her entourage likely included one midwife (such as in Gen 35:17) and one or more female helpers. After the birth, the mother provides the child with a symbolic name (Ichabod, the glory has departed from Israel) and the narrative abruptly moves on to follow the wandering ark. Not much information is given regarding the birth room, the women attending her, or any specific birth rituals.

Whereas biblical narrative contains few references to birth, the poetic literature often employs birthing imagery, especially when discussing war. Micah 4:9, Jer 6:24, 49:24, and 50:43 all describe a person becoming weak before the enemy as being like a woman seized by labor pangs and writhing in childbirth. The word חזק (ḥāzaq; "seized") plays nicely with the war imagery and implies not only that the writhing is out of the woman's control, but also that she experiences a sense of terror. So, too, Ps 48:6 uses the metaphor of childbirth to compare the reaction of enemy nations to the glory of God at Zion; they shall be like ones seized with trembling like a woman in the throes of labor.[20] Isaiah 13:8 describes the Babylonians as ones who will "writhe like a woman in travail," when the enemy armies come to defeat them. When connected to childbirth, the word for writhing, חיל (ḥîl) denotes the severe discomfort childbirth brings on. The pain is so much that a woman cannot lie still. Isaiah 66:7 uses the metaphor of childbirth to describe a reversal of fates: Jerusalem will bear a child without pain. Here the text implies that the usual process of childbirth is filled with pain.

The text of Gen 3:16 has been intentionally removed from the above discussion because of its fraught interpretation. Various translations render the first half of this verse to mean Eve's action caused childbirth to be painful. "I will make most severe your pangs in childbearing," (NJPS); "I will greatly increase your pangs in childbearing" (NRSV); "I will greatly increase your pains in childbearing" (NIV). Meyers persuasively argues that this text neither depicts the fallen state of women, nor the afflictions by which God cursed woman. Rather, a close reading of the text describes the stark reality facing women in Iron Age Israel (ca. 1200–1000 BCE). Meyers translates, "I will make great your toil [ʿiṣṣabon] and many your pregnancies [heron]; with hardship [ʿeṣeb] shall you have children," so that post-Eden women "will work hard and also have many pregnancies."[21] Meyers points out that the noun עצב (ʿeṣeb) can mean both physical and mental anguish and uses the word "hardship" to try to capture both meanings. As she points out, parenting is both physically and mentally taxing. Thus, while women experience pain in labor and delivery, the pain did not increase due to Eve's actions.

Mesopotamian texts are also full of rich metaphors depicting the woman in labor that help us to better understand how the ancient world perceived the birthing process. One such metaphor is reminiscent of the warrior imagery in biblical Hebrew poetry: "Like a warrior in the fray, she is cast down in her blood. Her eyes are dimmed; she cannot see. Her lips are covered; she cannot open (them)."[22] Another common metaphor is that of a boat loaded with precious cargo that needs to be steered through

---

20. In the Hebrew, the verse is Ps 48:7.
21. Meyers, *Rediscovering Eve*, 91.
22. Scurlock, "Baby-Snatching Demons," 144.

waters, or one that is detained at a quay.[23] This second image parallels the pregnant belly waiting to be unburdened with a ship looking to dock and unload its cargo. Like with a long war, this image conveys the sense of an arduous task.

The travails of labor carried with them the risk of complications. Here again the detailed Mesopotamian corpus can fill in what those practical measures taken to help the laboring Israelite woman might have looked like. When the birth was not going well, the Mesopotamian texts called for incantations, salves, and prayers uttered by midwives.[24] Sometimes, even in the hands of an experienced midwife, complications could occur during delivery. Mesopotamian texts tell us that when this happened, a (male!) exorcist was summoned into the birth room. The exorcist performed rituals to expel the demonic force causing the complications. Consider the following text from Mesopotamia, a prayer to the Sun-god offered by an exorcist: "This woman, daughter of her god— let her (womb's) knot be loosed before your godship; may this woman give birth safely; may she give birth and live; may her feotus come straight out; may she give birth safely and so sing your praises; may the sorcery (and) evil machinations be dispelled before your godship."[25] Here it seems that the complications in delivery are understood as a curse that needs to be revoked; thus, the exorcist appeals to the divine to open up the blocked womb.[26]

---

23. Scurlock, "Baby-Snatching Demons," 144. See too a full discussion of this text in Flynn, *Children in Ancient Israel*, 31–33. Note that the Palestinian Arabs pray to Noah as the saint for mothers in labor (Granqvist, *Birth and Childhood among the Arabs*, 64). It seems likely the choice of Noah reflects the same boating/birth metaphor.

24. The richness of the Mesopotamian literature starkly contrasts with the silence of the Hebrew Bible on this subject. Many studying ancient Israelite religion have noted that the official religion presented in the Bible does not match up with the archaeological picture, making one wonder if ancient Israelite women too used incantations and salves during labor. For a discussion of the nonofficial cult, see Susan Ackerman, "Household Religion, Family Religion, and Women's Religion in Ancient Israel," in Bodel and Olyan, *Household and Family Religion in Antiquity*, 127–58.

25. Scurlock, "Baby-Snatching Demons," 141.

26. Standardized prayers and incantations are also found in the Egyptian record in the New Kingdom "Magical Spells for Mother and Child" (P.Berlin 3027). These spells were uttered by a lector-priest or "magician of the nursery." Robert Ritner, "Magic: An Overview," *OEAE* 2:324.

2.3. A Baby Is Born: Ezekiel 16:4

Once the baby came out of the birth canal, the midwives sprang into action again. In describing young Jerusalem, Ezek 16:4 states: "As for your birth, on the day you were born, your cord was not cut, you were not washed with water to clean you, nor rubbed with salt, nor wrapped in wrapping (swaddled)." The care withheld from the infant Jerusalem provides a glimpse at the care that was normally given to a newborn. Unfortunately, this is all the information the biblical text provides—a glimpse. Egyptian and Mesopotamian sources on the other hand, go into more detail describing postpartum rituals.

2.3.1. Cutting the Umbilical Cord

The Egyptian birth wands, most often ascribed a protective function (see ch. 4), might in some cases also have served as the instrument for cutting the umbilical cord.[27] Mesopotamian evidence says the cord was cut with a special knife, or with part of a reed.[28] Slivers of reeds can be quite sharp and are inexpensive and readily available; therefore, each umbilical cord could be cut with a fresh reed.[29] Reeds also offer the advantage of being disposable, thus avoiding infections.[30] The birth ritual found in Enki and the World Order records that "Aruru, the sister of Enlil, Nintu, the Lady of Birth, she has received the pure brick of birth-giving sign of her office as *en*-priestess, she took with her the reed that cuts off the (umbilical cord), the stone *imam*, her leeks (…)."[31] In addition to referencing the reeds, the ritual also mentions leeks, which appear to be a remedy used to stop bleeding.

Cutting and tying the umbilical cord is a momentous moment: the baby becomes a totally separate life. The corpus of Mesopotamian litera-

---

27. The wands that have been discovered all have a dull edge (Janssen and Janssen, *Growing Up in Ancient Egypt*, 9). Whether they were once sharp enough to cut is unknown.

28. Knives made of sharp rocks are reported among Arab and Bedouin women who give birth out in the field (i.e., not at home) as they are traveling (Granqvist, *Birth and Childhood among the Arabs*, 52–56).

29. Scurlock, "Baby-Snatching Demons," 147.

30. Many thanks to Shawn Flynn for pointing this out (personal communication).

31. Stol, *Birth in Babylonia and the Bible*, 141–42.

ture provides many comments on this transition. As a new life, the baby was susceptible to demons.[32] Protective incantations warding off the various demons harmful to infants may have been recited when cutting the cord. More about these demons can be found in chapter 4. A hymn praising King Išme-Dagan of Isin states that the god Enlil "decreed for me a good fate, at my conception did he endow me with a good fate. Nintu even stood by at the birthing, as my umbilical cord was cut did he establish mastery for me. Enlil … gave me the shepherdship of Sumer as a gift."[33] While the hymn can be understood to give the king a divinely legitimized position, it also demonstrates the belief that a child's fate was determined when the umbilical cord was severed.[34] Iraqi practices in the early twentieth century retain this connection between the child's umbilical cord and his or her fate. Once the umbilical cord dries up and falls off, parents buried it in a place connected to the child's future. A boy's cord might be buried near a school to ensure he grows up studious. By the same token, a girl's might be buried in the house so that she would grow up to enjoy her household duties. Not only are the children's fates tied up in the cord, but so too are their genders. In addition to sealing a child's fate, ethnographic records also note the danger a child faced when the cord fell off. To ward off this danger, the cord might be placed under the child's pillow as a protective measure.[35]

Customs among the Palestinian Arabs attest to the continued importance the umbilical cord and stump held into the twentieth century.[36] When cutting the cord, a thread was tied to the child's navel. From this thread three finger-spaces were counted at which point the cord was cut. The stub was bound with a salted pad and tied with the same thread. A child's fate could be secured the moment the cord is cut. For a girl one might use the formula: "Who is this cord cut for? For Person X?" The

32. Belief in harmful jinn are behind the notion held among the Palestinian Arab women that the umbilical cord should not be cut at night (Granqvist, *Birth and Childhood among the Arabs*, 94).

33. Stol, *Birth in Babylonia and the Bible*, 143.

34. Like the king of Isin, the young prophet Jeremiah's fate was predestined. "Before I created you in the womb, I selected you; before you were born, I consecrated you; I appointed you a prophet concerning the nations" (Jer 1:5).

35. Drower, "Women and Taboo in Iraq," 110, especially n. 1.

36. On the customs listed in this section, see Granqvist, *Birth and Childhood among the Arabs*, 95–96. The reference to Karine is not explained, but it seems she might be related to Qārine, whom Iraqi women feared. See §2.6.4.

person named then has the ability to claim her (later in life) as a wife. The third day of life, when the stump generally falls off, is seen as a momentous occasion. Now the baby is completely separated from the mother. At this point a baby might be named or given a haircut. A special sacrifice for the new life might also occur at this time. While no longer attached to the child, the umbilical cord stump is still understood to hold protective powers. Some families rub the stump on the baby's eyelids as a medicine, and other families use it as an amulet to ward off Karine, an evil force.

2.3.2. Cleaning the Newborn

The second step listed in Ezek 16, washing the child with water, was necessary to remove blood and other fluids from the child. Like the list in Ezekiel, the myth of Enki and the World Order provides a list of items that were brought to the birth, including a water pail. The myth also includes two more steps in the cleaning ritual: rubbing the child with oil and inserting a finger into the child's mouth to clear it of amniotic fluid.[37] Rubbing or anointing the child with oil seems to be an alternative to the biblical reference of rubbing the child with salt.[38] Rubbing a child with either salt or oil might be compared to rubbing oil or lotion on a baby after a bath. Salt might have been used to exfoliate dried blood or the vernix that covers the baby at birth. Salt is also known to have antiseptic properties. However, it is unclear whether the whole baby was rubbed with oil and salt. For example, ethnographic parallels from early twentieth-century Iraq refer to salt and oil being used as a salve to bind up the navel after the cord is cut, rather than being slathered all over the infant.[39] Among the villages in Palestine, however, babies were rubbed all over with this mixture. Reference is even made to rubbing the eyes, ears, nose, and mouth with salt and oil. This mixture is left on for one whole day under the swaddling clothes.[40] In the following days the midwife would rub salt and oil on the baby in the morning and again at night. During this period of time a special garment referred to as

---

37. Scurlock, "Baby-Snatching Demons," 147.

38. However, ethnographic studies attest to a combination of salt and oil in Syria, Palestine and Iran (Meyers, *Rediscovering Eve*, 154).

39. Drower, "Women and Taboo in Iraq," 110.

40. Granqvist, *Birth and Childhood among the Arabs*, 95. In Jordan babies were rubbed with salt and oil on the first and seventeenth day after birth. At times buttermilk was also used to bathe the baby (Musil, *Arabia Petraea*, 215).

the "salt shirt" (and cap) was worn by the infant.[41] The "salt baths" appear to be understood as a safe alternative to water baths. A baby's first bath generally happened seven to fourteen days after birth and then again on day forty, at which point the mother was considered healed and both the mother and child were washed.[42] One wonders whether the observed antiseptic properties of salt led to the custom of bathing the vulnerable newborn in this manner.

The other practice referenced in Enki and the World Order, cleaning out the baby's mouth, is also of a practical nature. Today, one uses a bulb rather than a finger to clear the baby's mouth or nose.[43] Along with clearing out the child's mouth and nose, one might also clear out her lungs. Again, we find similarity between the practices described in Mesopotamia and modern practices. Holding a child upside down and smacking her seat is comparable to the midwife's duty in the Ninisinna hymn: once the baby is caught the midwife must cause the child to scream by putting "his abdomen towards the ground (i.e., to turn him over) (and) to make (him) exchange places with (his) head (i.e., to turn him upside down)."[44] It appears that this was a version of the modern Apgar score, meant to make sure the child has good reflexes and a set of healthy lungs. Note that a Hittite ritual text also attests to the practice of similar postbirth checkups.[45]

2.3.3. Swaddling

After cutting the cord, washing the infant, and clearing his lungs, nose, and mouth, the infant is ready to be wrapped up. The wrapping, or swaddling,

---

41. Musil, *Arabia Petraea*, 99.

42. Musil, *Arabia Petraea*, 101. Musil reports that a newborn would be washed daily in lukewarm water and then rubbed with salt. If this were not done, the child would be timid (Musil, *Arabia Petraea*, 215).

43. Sweeping the mouth with a finger is an old-fashioned way to remove any fluids, placental materials, etc. that may be stuck in the newborn's mouth (Lisa Stern, APRN, Planned Parenthood, personal communication).

44. Scurlock, "Baby-Snatching Demons," 148, especially n. 135.

45. Nick Wyatt, "Circumcision and Circumstance: Male Genital Mutilation in Ancient Israel and Ugarit," *JSOT* 33 (2009): 425. Granqvist notes that the Arabs also gave a postbirth checkup, although this checkup seemed more to do with physical appearance rather than the health of the baby. The midwife checked the shape of the nose and head and adjusted them if needed (Granqvist, *Birth and Childhood among the Arabs*, 73–74).

referenced in Ezek 16:4, is done via a long piece of cloth. The infant is placed in the middle, the two sides of the cloth are crisscrossed, and the ends of the cloth are tucked in to the swaddle, providing the baby with a snug little cocoon. Swaddling is particularly effective with newborns in the first three to four months of life, as it recreates the warm, cramped conditions of the womb.[46] While no remnants of ancient swaddling bandages have been identified, plenty of textual and iconographic materials attest to the practice. For example, the Mesopotamian reliefs and cylinder seals depict the wrappings as rather long pieces of cloth looped over a hook.[47] Both ends of the cloth are curled up so that they resemble an elongated omega shape. The cloths in this shape are associated with the birth goddess Ninhursag, protector of newborns. From the baby Jesus, wrapped in swaddling clothes and lying in a manger (Luke 2:7), to the ancient Greeks, to modern hospital rooms, the practice of swaddling can be found cross-culturally throughout history.[48] It should be noted that in ancient times, as in more modern ethnographic reports, swaddling clothes were old rags. In western Iran, a baby is swaddled, placed into a hammock, and "swung vigorously when he fusses."[49] Ethnographic reports from Palestine note that once the baby was swaddled, it was placed in a market basket or "on a plaited straw tray … such as the fellahin use for a table."[50] This would be akin to the modern practice of placing the infant in a "Moses basket."

---

46. Kirsten Linde, "Swaddling," *Encyclopedia of Children and Childhood in History and Society*, ed. Paula S. Fass, 3 vols. (New York: Macmillian, 2004), 3:802–3; Antonia Nelson, "Risks and Benefits of Swaddling Healthy Infants: An Integrative Review," *MCN American Journal of Maternal Child Nursing* 42 (2017): 216–25. Granqvist noted that practices differed in Palestine between the swaddling practice of the village and larger towns. Women in the villages swaddled their babies for forty days, while in Jerusalem babies were swaddled for four months if a summer birth or six months if a winter birth (Granqvist, *Birth and Childhood among the Arabs*, 100).

47. See §2.4. Egyptian iconography most often depicts naked infants, or infants riding in slings on their mother's hips or backs (Janssen and Janssen, *Growing Up in Ancient Egypt*, 20–21, and fig. 10). However, one image of a mother holding a baby suggests that the baby is swaddled. Steffen Wenig, *The Women in Egyptian Art* (Leipzig: Leipzig Edition, 1969), 47.

48. Lloyd deMause, *The History of Childhood* (New York: Harper & Row, 1974), 37–39.

49. Patty Jo Watson, *Archaeological Ethnography in Western Iran* (Tuscan: University of Arizona, 1979), 173.

50. Granqvist, *Marriage Conditions in a Palestinian Village*, 27, n. 2.

2.4. Visual Representations of Ezekiel's Birthing Rituals

The Mesopotamian rites pictured in figures 2.3 and 2.4 provide a visual reference for the rituals referred to in Ezek 16:4: cutting the umbilical cord, washing/anointing the newborn, and wrapping her in swaddling clothes. Figure 2.3 is a clay relief showing the goddess Ninhursag in the center. At her feet sit the crouched *kūbu* figurines discussed in chapter 4. The goddess appears to suckle a child at her breast. Two more disembodied heads peak out from behind her shoulders. The two elongated omega shapes flanking the goddess on both sides are worthy of mention. This same symbol can be found on the upper right-hand corner of a kudurru stone given by King Melishipak of Susa (fig. 2.4).[51] The image from the Ninhursag relief depicts this imagery in a more realistic fashion than the kudurru stone, which shows a more stylized image. In figure 2.4, the shape is rotated so that it looks more like the letter "U." It floats above a knife, which has been placed on something that looks like an altar. Based on its association with the goddess of childbirth, this image has been identified as the strips of cloth used for swaddling.[52]

The image on the kudurru stone is important for two additional reasons: it hints at a visual representation of the birth and shows what the knife that was used to cut the umbilical cord likely looked like. Note that the knife is not complicated, but rather resembles the simple copper knives found at Lagash and Kish.[53] A third image, found on a Neo-Babylonian cylinder seal, shows more of the birth rites (fig. 2.5).[54] A male and a female worshiper approach the altar of Ninhursag, identified as such by the symbol of the floating swaddling clothes. Each person holds a bowl in

---

51. Kudurru stones are markers of a land grant given by the royal family to a loyal subject. They are particular to the Kassites of Babylonia (ca. sixteenth to twelfth century BCE). The boundary stones include both images and words. The grants are given protection; hence, the signs or symbols of various gods and goddesses are found on the stones.

52. E. Douglas Van Buren, "Clay Relief in the Iraq Museum," *AfO* 9 (1933–1934): 165–71. The long pieces of material get their curlicues at the end from being consistently rolled up. For reference, one might think of the way an ACE bandage maintains its rolled shape even when laid out flat. The stylized U-shape then is a reference to the shape these bandages take when they are not in use, looped over hooks.

53. Van Buren, "Clay Relief in the Iraq Museum," 167, 171.

54. For a full discussion of the seal, see Van Buren, "Clay Relief in the Iraq Museum," 165–66, 168.

Fig. 2.3. Ninhursag with *Kūbu*, Eshnunna, circa Larsa period.

Fig. 2.4. Kudurru stone of Melishipak, Susa, Kassite, circa 1186–1172 BCE.

their hands. It may be that these bowls held water or oil to wash or anoint the infant, or alternatively, that the bowls held some sort of offering for Ninhursag. The object on top of the table or altar can be understood as the swaddled newborn. A third item, similar in shape to the one from the kudurru stone, appears floating to the left of the register. Since the scene is clearly related to birth, it is likely this item is meant to be the knife. Combining the clay relief, kudurru stone, and cylinder seal shows the story of the birth rites in pictures, rather than words.

Fig. 2.5. Cylinder seal, unknown, Neo-Babylonian.

2.5. Legal Symbolism

The actions found in Ezek 16:4 are not only practical; they symbolically describe a parent's legal claim to the infant. Once the infant's cord is cut, she is washed, cleaned, and swaddled. At this point the infant is a part of the family. Ezekiel goes on to imply that the reason young Jerusalem did not experience any of these actions was because she was not wanted; her "father" abandoned her. The Code of Hammurabi (§185) describes another unwanted infant, but there the infant is adopted, not abandoned. The adoption occurs while the infant is *ina mêšu*, "in its birth waters." While the law discusses whether the child can be reclaimed by his natal family, the fact that the infant is taken by the adoptive parents while still covered in amniotic fluid means that the new parents are the ones who claim the child. Washing the child was tantamount to the legal act of accepting the child as one's own.[55] The wording of some biblical narratives supports the idea that an adoptive mother could physically be in the room. Rachel and Sarah both hope that they will be built up through the birth of a child via their respective maidservants, meaning they would adopt the children born of the maidservants as their own (Gen 16:2; 30:3). When Rachel instructs Jacob to copulate with her servant Bilhah, her reasoning is that "she [Bilhah] may bear *on my knees*, and I will be built up through her" (Gen 30:3).[56] Given the discussion above, it could be quite possible that Bilhah might lean on Rachel for support in the birthing room. If this were the case, Rachel could be the one to wash the baby. In doing so, she would pledge legal ownership of the child. It is unknown if the adoptive mother was always in the birthing room, yet even if she were not, it is possible that this woman might be symbolically understood to wash and clean up the adopted baby.

2.6. Multiple Births: A Case Study

Since both ancient Israel and the cultures surrounding it provide multiple references to twins, this case study pauses to focus on twins. Twins are a unique example that can help shed light on the attitude and approaches

---

55. Claus Wilcke, "Noch einmal: Šilip rēmim und die Adoption *ina mēšu*; Neue und alte einschlägige Texte," *ZA* 71 (1981): 87–94.

56. Genesis 48:8–12 hints at the idea Jacob adopted Ephraim and Manasseh by putting them on his knees. Genesis 50:23 states quite literally that the children of Makir, Manasseh's son, were born upon his knees. Many translations understand this to mean the children were "recognized," "brought up," or "adopted" by Joseph in the same manner as Jacob adopted Joseph's children (NLT, ESV, KJV, ISV). Other translations retain the meaning of "were born" (NASB, ESV). Aside from the adoption issue, there is the problem of Joseph appearing in the birthing room. While most ancient and ethnographic sources referenced above state that men were not allowed in the birthing room, an account from Petra records a different practice: "Among the Ḥanâğre, the mother stands during birth. Two women support her under the arms and her husband kneels before her and receives the baby on his knee" (Musil, *Arabia Petraea*, 214; translation from German my own). Musil does not go into the legal ramifications for the man catching the child, but one wonders if by receiving the child *on his knees* the man is legally acknowledging the child.

toward children in the ancient Near East. Although each culture has different experiences with twins, some parallels can also be observed. To contextualize the discussion of multiple births in the ancient texts, it is helpful to understand how the occurrence of multiple births today might skew our understanding of the ancient texts. With the advent of reproductive technology, the birth rate of twins has reached a record high in developed countries. In 2014, the United States birth registry reported 33.9 twin births for every 1,000 births. Triplets and other multiple births registered in at 113.5 multiples per 1,000 births.[57] The 1990 census in China revealed the birth of 186,273 twins among 23,477,961 births. Low- to middle-income countries, however, tell a different tale. In a study collecting data from household surveys between the years 1987 and 2010, the global average was 13.1 twin births per 1,000 births. Of the areas examined, Asian and Latin American countries ranked lowest in twin births. This might suggest a relationship between a region's economic advancement and the number of twins born.[58] Yet the highest rate of twins is found in West and Central Africa. Western Nigeria has long been known as the "land of the twins," but has recently been displaced by the West African nation of Benin, which boasts 27.9 twin births per 1,000 births. Factoring out the twins born with the help of science, this means that Benin has almost four times more twins births than most higher income countries do.[59] What this data tells us is that, while good nutrition might help the health of the fetus, the conception of twins is not dependent upon a region's prosperity. The people of Central and Western Africa are, for the most part, pastoral subsistence farmers, not unlike some of the ancient Israelites. Knowing this helps the reader of ancient texts realize that a high number of twin births is not tied to the advanced medical knowledge of Western countries. It should also be noted that the data above relates specifically to fraternal, not identical twins, since identical twins, or monozygotic twinning, is understood to occur with the same frequency worldwide.[60]

---

57. C. Storrs and D. Goldenschmidt, "U.S. Twin Birth Rate Hits Record High," 23 December 2015, CNN, https://tinyurl.com/SBL1729j.

58. R. Harrington, "Twins Are Remarkably Common in One Area of the World," *Business Insider*. 17 September 2015. https://tinyurl.com/SBL1729e.

59. Data compiled by MeasureDHS (www.measuredhs.com); Jeroen Smits and Christiaan Monden, "Twinning across the Developing World," *PLOS ONE* (2011): http://doi.org/10.1371/journal.pone.0025239; R. Harrington, "Twins Are Remarkably Common."

60. Smits and Monden, "Twinning across the Developing World."

2.6.1. Twins in the Hebrew Bible and Ancient Israel

Most of the births recorded in the Hebrew Bible are single births, specifically single births of boys. However, twin births, again of boys, are mentioned. Of these, perhaps the most familiar are those born to Rebekah: Jacob and Esau. Tamar also births the twins Zerah and Peretz, and one can make the case that Ephraim and Manasseh were also twins.[61] Within the ancient Near East in general, births of twins were met with different attitudes: some were heralded with joy, others with fear, and others with ambivalence. The reaction to twins seems to be dictated by two factors: foreknowledge of a twin birth and the type of twins born. Consider, for example, the story of Jacob and Esau. Genesis relates that Rebekah becomes pregnant and then experiences the babies jostling and fighting within her (Gen 25:22). It is unclear how far along the pregnancy is when she experiences this. While quickening happens between gestational weeks sixteen to twenty-five, most first-time mothers experience this feeling closer to twenty to twenty-five weeks. Whether Rebekah knew she was pregnant with twins before she inquires of God is unknown. What she does know is that something about her pregnancy is unusual, so unusual that she is prompted to inquire of the Lord though an oracle (Gen 25:22).[62] Through this oracle, she learns she is pregnant with twins. She also learns the predestined fate of the children, which later guides her actions with respect to her children's birthright (Gen 27:1–45). The births of the other biblical twins are simply reported at the time of the birth.

Overall, the biblical text records neither outright fear nor bad omens accompanying the birth of twins. Instead, each account of twins stresses the birth order and includes some sort of mix-up, where the elder son is

---

61. Genesis does not record their births separately, but states that they were born (Gen 41:50). The reverse blessing, wherein Jacob blesses the younger Ephraim with the greater blessing, is also a common fate for the twins in the bible (Gen 48:19). The younger twin supplants the elder. Twins in ancient Near Eastern literature can be understood symbolically and have been read as a means to mediate conflict and bring together oppositions. Kuntzmann explores these themes throughout time, starting with the Hebrew Bible, and moving on to Mesopotamia, Ugarit, and Gnostic texts. Raymond Kuntzmann, *Le symbolism des jumeaux au Proche-Orient ancient: Naissance, function et evolution d'un symbole* (Beauchesne: Paris, 1983).

62. Susan Ackerman, "The Blind, the Lame and the Barren Shall Not Come into the House of the Lord," in Moss and Schipper, *Disability Studies and Biblical Literature*, 29–46.

displaced by the younger.[63] Jacob becomes the patriarch and carries on the covenant. Ephraim too receives the better blessing; while younger, he receives the blessing of the firstborn (Gen 48:17–20). Likewise, the younger twin Peretz, becomes greater than his elder brother; he is King David's progenitor (Gen 28:27–30; Ruth 4:18–22). The biggest issue for the biblical text is the disruption of the social order. In a kinship-based society, the birth of two people (especially sons) instead of one, interrupts the inheritance system and calls into question the place of the firstborn.[64]

While the birth of twins might not be a fortuitous event, the twins are by no means considered freaks of nature in the biblical text. The reason for this (lack of) reaction might well be dictated by the second factor referenced above: the type of twin. As in modern times, twins in the ancient world could be identical or fraternal. The details provided by Genesis leaves no doubt that Jacob and Esau were fraternal brothers. Esau's name reflects his appearance; he is hairy and red.[65] Later, Esau becomes the father of the Edomites, the red people. Esau is the skilled hunter, who prefers the outdoors. Jacob, on the other hand, is described as mild and preferring the indoors. The twins have opposite dispositions and look nothing alike. The names of the biblical twins are also instructive. The Ugaritic myth of The Gracious and Beautiful Gods describes the birth of the twin deities Shahar and Shalem/Shalim, whose names mean sunrise and sunset respectively.[66] "In the Bible, this motif may be reflected in the stories of Jacob and his twin Esau the Red, and of Jacob's grandsons Peretz ("break through") and Zerah ("Sunrise," wearing the red thread)."[67] The positive association

---

63. Cross-cultural data also finds cases of the younger twin supplanting the elder. In Yorba culture, the belief is that the older child has junior rank because she or he comes out of the womb first to test the waters, so to speak, for the younger child, who is in turn given senior rank in society. Taiwo Oruene, "Magical Powers of Twins in the Socio-Religious Beliefs of the Yoruba," *Folklore* 96 (1985): 211. In general, twins present a problem in kinship-based societies because they disrupt the normal order of lineage (Turner, *Ritual Process*, 45).

64. Sharon Roubach, "Two Who Donned the Veil: The Image of Twins in the Bible" [Hebrew], *Beit Mikra* 183 (2005): 366–90.

65. Gen 25:25: hairy (שֵׂעָר) and red (אַדְמוֹנִי).

66. In this myth, the boys have a common father (El) and a common nurse ("The Lady" likely Anat or Ashera). While mothered by two different women, the two are still considered twin deities and are perceived as fraternal twins (Herbert B. Huffmon, "Shalem שׁלם," *DDD*, 755–56).

67. Othniel Margalith, "A New Type of Ashera-Figurine?," *VT* 44 (1994): 113.

with deities, if only of a literary nature, alludes to a positive perception of fraternal twins; they are not considered doppelgangers or freaks of nature, but merely two children birthed at the same time.

Attitudes about identical twins are a little harder to discern. While the biblical text does not specifically reference any identical twins, an iconographic reference might attest to the occurrence of such twins. Within ancient Israel, three plaque figurines dating to the thirteenth century BCE depict the same scene: a woman about to give birth to twins.[68] The figurines are all identical and look almost like an ancient form of the person from the Hasbro game Operation. At first glance, one sees a figure of a woman with two babies, but looking closer it becomes clear that the torso is presented as a sonogram; the two babies appear as embryos about to be birthed. It is unclear whether the embryos are meant to be fraternal or identical twins. However, the artistic rendition of the embryos or fetuses is identical.

2.6.2. Twins in the Egyptian Record

The Egyptian record presents some cases that demonstrate various attitudes about twins. Prior to the Twenty-Fifth Dynasty, the official Egyptian attitude suggests that twins were an anomaly. As such, they were seen as a misfortune. This might be due to the fact Egyptians equated having a double of a person with bad luck, or that twin births were notoriously difficult and did not end well. With respect to the former idea, it should be noted that ancient Egyptians considered the placenta to be a double or twin of the child and gave it a special burial so that it did not come back and bother the living child.[69]

Despite the general distaste for twins in earlier periods, a few examples of Egyptian twins have found their way into the historic record. For example, the Eighteenth Dynasty stela of Suty and Hor says *pr.n.f m ḫt hnꜥ.i m hrw pn*, "he went forth with me from the womb on that day." The names Suty and Hor are derived from those of Seth and Horus, the archetypal brothers of Egyptian myth. In naming the twins after the divine beings, "Suty and Hor treat their [twin] birth in a fashion that both disguises and

68. The plaques and how they are used are discussed in depth in ch. 4.

69. Geraldine Pinch, *Magic in Ancient Egypt* (London: British Museum, 1994), 130; Lynn Meskell, *Archaeologies of Social Life* (Oxford: Blackwell, 1999), 163, 170–71.

celebrates it."[70] A second example comes by way of the double tomb of the royal manicurists Niankhkhnum and Khumtotep.[71] The men are carved as identical, given the same status, and their gestures suggest that the two were understood as a single unit. Without any inscriptions describing their relationship, Egyptologists have been left wondering how the two men were related. Suggestions, all based on comparisons with other tombs and Egyptian iconography in general, propose that the men are twins.[72] What is notable here is that the men appear to have had a single social being. Like the names Suty and Hor paralleling the divine world, the assignment of a single social being for Niankhkhnum and Khnumtotep seems to act as a general corrective to the status of twins, making them less of an anomaly by associating the twins with a known quantity: one person.[73]

From the textual record, an oracular amuletic decree of the Twenty-Second Dynasty states: "We shall fill her womb with male and female children. We shall save her from a Horus birth (?), from miscarrying (?), (and) from giving birth to twins."[74] Again, this decree echoes the misfortune of birthing twins. However, within two hundred years of this decree, the word for twin, ḫtr, became commonplace as a name, suggesting that the attitude towards twins changed. As Egypt became Hellenized, the Greek name Didyme (f.) or Didymus (m.) became common. Yet accounts as late as the 1930s find the pendulum swinging back; twins are again treated with suspicion. Ethnographic studies of Egyptians from this time-

---

70. John Baines, "Egyptian Twins," *Or* 2/54 (1985): 463.

71. The tomb is located at Saqqara.

72. Vera Vasiljević, like John Baines, argues they are twins. She notes they are depicted iconographically as each other's *ka* and their names include the name of the god Khnum, creator god of the ka/twins. Furthermore, they are buried together because they are doubles of each other and thus indispensable to each other in the afterlife. Vera Vasiljević, "Embracing His Double: Niankhkhnum and Khnumhotep," *Studien zur Altägyptischen Kultur* 37 (2008): 363–72. An intriguing case for understanding the men as gay lovers was made by reinterpreting the iconography within the tomb to show the embraces as sexual and the erasure of the wives as symbolic, the references to the song of the Two Divine Brothers as having homosexual undertones, and rereading the word *sn* not with the common meaning "brother," but as a generic term for friend, lover, or colleague. Greg Reeder, "Same-Sex Desire, Conjugal Constructs, and the Tomb of Nianhkhnum and Khnumhopte," *WA* 32 (2000): 193–208.

73. Baines, "Egyptian Twins," 480–81.

74. Baines, "Egyptian Twins," 470; I. E. S. Edwards, *Oracular Amuletic Decrees of the Late New Kingdom*, Hieratic Papyri in the British Museum 4th series (London: British Museum, 1960), 67–69, pl. 26.

period report a belief that when twins are born there is a chance that one twin's soul might leave his or her body at night and turn into a cat.[75] If it is a female twin, the ghost cat would be female, while a male twin's soul might present as a tomcat. The cats are attracted to the smell of food, and people would notice leftovers missing the next day. One must not wake a sleeping twin, for she would die if her soul were still in the form of a ghost cat. Feeding the twins breastmilk and camel milk for the first forty days lessened the possibility one of the twins' souls would befall the ghost-cat fate. If afflicted, the twin's soul would wander at night until he or she reached maturity, at which point the soul would no longer wander. As the varying Egyptian materials demonstrate, beliefs about twins can easily change over time.

2.6.3. Twins at Emar

An example of twin boys from Emar also deserves a note. Their case is unique in that multiple legal documents trace the course of these twins's lives. The first document records the sale of the boys, along with an older sister and a younger sister to a man named Baʾal-mālik, a local diviner.[76] The sum total for all four children was sixty shekels. Along with the sale tablet came three separate tablets, each imprinted with a single footprint.[77] The inscriptions next to the footprints said, "this is the footprint of (child's name)" and included the seals of the people witnessing the sale.[78] The parents were not selling the twins because they had malevolent feelings towards their children; rather, they were forced to sell them because of a crisis. Since the parents could not afford to take care of their children, selling the children presented a way to make the best of a difficult situation. The parents would be relieved of the financial burden, and the children would be provided for. While this might appear to be a sad story, other documents with the twins' names suggesting they did okay

---

75. Hans Alexander Winkler, *Ghost Riders of Upper Egypt*, trans. Nicholas Hopkins (Cairo: American University of Cairo Press, 2009), 26–27.

76. Sale document: R. 139. Footprints: Msk. 74.340, R. 78, and O.6766 (*Emar VI.2* and *Emar VI.3*).

77. There was no footprint tablet found for the youngest daughter. The price for all four children is low, but considering the parents' duress, not atypical. See Carlo Zaccagnini, "War and Famine at Emar," *Or* 64 (1995): 92–109.

78. Carlo Zaccagnini, "Feet of Clay at Emar and Elsewhere," *Or* 63 (1994): 3.

for themselves. One particular text refers to Išma'-Dagan and Ba'al-bēlu, the names of the two boys sold to the diviner Ba'al-mālik, as novice diviners. It appears possible that Ba'al-mālik took the boys in, reared them, and taught them his trade.[79]

Whether the Emar twins were identical or fraternal twins is unknown: it is possible to make a case each way based on the names of the twins and the way the parents treated the children. The boys were both named after divinities; Ba'al-bēlu includes the name of Ba'al and Išma'-Dagan, the name of Dagan. Fertility, of both land and people, is an attribute of both gods. Twins, and twin boys at that, are the definition of being blessed with fertility. If they were identical twins, it might be that the parents named them after Ba'al and Dagan both to disguise and to celebrate their births, like the Egyptian twins Suty and Hor. On the other hand, if they were identical twins and the parents were in such dire straits, they might have attributed their situation to the birth of identical twins in their family. Thus, the parents might have chosen not to sell the boys but instead to rid themselves and the city of the twins through exposure, or another, more drastic measure.The parents, however, did not try to kill the twins. In economic straits, they tried first to save themselves by selling their elder daughter. Only when that sale fell through, did they decide to sell all of their children. Their parents' actions seem to argue more on the side of fraternal twins. If they were fraternal twins, the names of the boys would then be a way to celebrate the parents' fertility, rather than to disguise the birth of identical twins. In either case, once born, the twins were allowed to live in Emar society and perhaps be educated and work as diviners.

2.6.4. Twins in the Mesopotamian Record

The Mesopotamian corpus also provides fluctuating attitudes on twins. The omen series called *Šumma izbu* ("if an anomaly") lists all kinds of strange birth defects or anomalies, both human and animal, and provides an interpretation for said anomaly. Any birth that was considered abnormal was an affront to the ordered nature of life and needed explaining and, at times, correction. The elaborate rituals to fix or eliminate the anomaly suggest that this list was meant for the elite or royal families.[80] The category

---

79. Yoram Cohen, "Feet of Clay at Emar: A Happy Ending?," *Or* 74 (2005): 165–70.

80. Leichty, *Šumma Izbu*, 11–13.

of identical twins features prominently in the tablets on human anomalies. At times, the issue is simply the birth of two identical babies, while at other times, the "monstrosity" tends a bit more to the grotesque, describing different anomalies (like the absence of a hand) on two boys who share an abdomen or share ribs. What is notable is that what we would consider today to be healthy and normal looking identical twins were included in the omen series. To the Mesopotamians, two people who looked alike were considered "double monsters."[81] A few omens mention the birth of multiples, from three babies all the way up to the birth of eight or nine children at a time. The overwhelming number of omens connected with twin and multiple birth anomalies affects the king or the populace, rather than the individual house where the twins were born, but here too there are exceptions.[82] Finally, as with the Egyptian materials, some of the omens seem contradictory.[83]

2.6.5. Twins in Ethnographic Literature

Well into the early twentieth century, ethnographers report the uneasy feelings about twins held by various peoples in Iraq. The demoness Qarīna is considered an invisible companion, or double of a human (she is always female, even if her human counterpart is male). Based on customs and beliefs attached to the placenta, Ethel S. Drower suggests this spirit was originally attached to the afterbirth.[84] The placenta too, is female, and called by the generic feminine name *jāra* throughout Iraq, but by the Assyrian (Nestorian) peoples as *jimma*, "twin," or *ḥawarta*, "female likeness/double." Customs surrounding the treatment of the placenta also make clear that the placenta was thought of as a kind of undeveloped double of the infant. For example, some women hope to trick Qarīna out of harming the baby by wrapping up the placenta with a black rooster or a

---

81. Leichty, *Šumma Izbu*, 17.

82. For example, the birth of triplets in general means the owner of the house (where they are born) will die (*Šumma izbu* tablet 1.101, 113, 114; Leichty, *Šumma Izbu*, 42–43).

83. For example, the birth of five children is understood to cause land to disappear, to be scattered, and to expand (*Šumma izbu* tablet 1.126–129; Leichty, *Šumma Izbu*, 44).

84. Drower, "Women and Taboo in Iraq," 108.

fish.[85] They are either trying to disguise the placenta as the animal or using the animal as tasty bait to draw Qarīna towards the placenta and away from the baby. In essence, the placenta is understood as the human infant's twin or double; Qarīna will not harm the baby because she is duped into harming the placenta instead.

Accounts from Palestinian Arab villages also reference the importance of the afterbirth. It was understood to be the baby's sister or comrade and was wrapped up and placed in the basket or tray with the baby lest a cat or dog find it. The villagers believed the child should stay connected to the afterbirth for twelve hours, during which time the baby would drink blood/power from the afterbirth. At the appointed time, but never at night, the cord was cut. The afterbirth was handled in one of two ways. The first option was for the midwife to bury it deep in the ground. If a dog or cat ate it or someone walked over it, then the birthmother might become barren. Another option was to preserve it with salt and hang it on the doorpost. This was done as an apotropaic measure to ward off Karine.[86] Notably, the latter practice was only done for the afterbirth of a boy.[87] While the omens of Šumma izbu were collected and arranged many years before the ethnographic reports, there remains one constant: any double of a human, be it in the form of a placenta or a live birth, requires "correction" so that evil will not befall the family or nation.[88]

As ethnographic parallels demonstrate, the reception of twins within a single society may also differ.[89] Thus, we must not expect the reception of

---

85. Drower, "Women and Taboo in Iraq," 109–10.

86. Karine seems to be the Palestinian counterpart to the Iranian Qarīna.

87. Granqvist, *Birth and Childhood among the Arabs*, 74, 93–94, 97. Granqvist does not comment on whether Karine only attacked boys, or if the villagers simply valued boys more than girls and chose only to protect the males.

88. It should be noted that identical twins were not an issue when it comes to the divine sphere. The constellation commonly known as Gemini was observed in the ancient world and found its way into Egyptian and Mesopotamian astronomy as the first created pair, Shu and Tefenet, and as the Great Twins (MUL.MASH.TAB. BA.GAL.GAL) respectively. The presence of divine twins seemed to be a way to help explain human twins and, in some cases, naming human twins after the divine twins was a way of "correcting" the problem identical twins presented (Baines, "Egyptian Twins," 476, 481).

89. In ancient times, Yorba saw twins as impure; a double birth meant woman had sex with two men or a man and an evil demon. Either way, the woman had committed adultery and brought impurity upon herself and her children (Oruene, "Magical

twins to be the same in ancient Israel as they were in Egypt, Syria, or Mesopotamia, or even expect the attitude towards twins to be the same within different time periods in ancient Israel.[90] Since the biblical narrative gives us three possible examples of twins, all reflecting the patriarchal period, we might infer that, like with the surrounding regions, attitudes towards twins changed over time and with exposure to a more cosmopolitan society. As people migrated into Israel, some of their beliefs regarding twins might have easily been transferred into the beliefs of the ancient Israelites.

2.7. Summary

The birth of a baby was a happy occasion in the life of the ancient Israelites. But before the celebrations could begin, many preparations had to happen. Proper preparations for birth were all done to insure the birth of a healthy baby. Stools, bricks, or stones were made, and rooms were prepared. Examining the practices of ancient Israel against those of surrounding cultures, we can see that the use of stones and bricks have both a practical and magicoreligious purpose. Each culture examined holds the belief that the time right before birth and during labor was precarious. Dangers lurked at every corner. A belief that supernatural forces were attracted to the birthing room sprung from the stark reality that many things could go wrong during birth.

It can be easy to get frustrated with the lack of information in the biblical texts regarding "the women's world," particularly when investigating birth. Yet, it should be remembered that men (the writers of the texts) were not allowed into the birthing chambers, so their knowledge of the process was limited. Little snippets about birth do appear, here and there, and in unexpected places. Where the biblical texts do offer some insight into the birthing room comes through poetic texts, which parallel the experience of labor to being in the middle of a battle. This imagery is powerful as the

---

Powers," 209). Other ethnographic studies show that societies adapt in multiple ways to deal with the presence of twins, from acceptance, to death, to deification, to seeing them as a mediator between the animal world (where births of multiples are common) and the human world (Turner, *Ritual Process*, 44–62).

90. As the example of the Yorba demonstrates, reception of twins within a single culture can change over time, from fear resulting in the death or expulsion of the twins (and their mother) to acceptance and reverence of the twins as representations of a god (Oruene, "Magical Powers of Twins," 208–16).

male writers are paralleling the male realm, the battlefield, with that of the female realm, the birthing room. While a modern reader might not equate battle with birth, it is notable that the writers used a metaphor that is gender balanced. Readers of Isaiah, Jeremiah, and Micah, regardless of their gender, would find something relatable in the metaphor as many men and women in ancient Israel experienced war and birth themselves.

For the lucky few, all the months of trying to successfully conceive and then carrying the baby to term were rewarded with the birth of a healthy child. In most cases, the birth produced a single child, but in a few cases, twins were born. As the Egyptian corpus showed, attitudes towards twins could change over time, moving from negative to positive. For the most part, the reaction to a twin birth in the ancient Near East seems dependent upon whether the twins were identical or fraternal. Identical twins challenged communities' beliefs, as they were understood as doubles, not as two individual persons. For this reason, fraternal twins posed much less of an issue, especially for kinship-based societies like ancient Israel.

Whether the birth was of one or two babies, once the baby was born one of the attending women would cut the umbilical cord and clean the baby with salt or oil. The infant would also be subject to an ancient Apgar test as the midwife would check the infant's lungs, skin color, and mouth. Provided everything went well, the mother would then immediately transition from birthing the baby to caring for the newborn. These three actions are seen not only in the biblical texts, but in other ancient Near Eastern cultures, with Mesopotamia offering some visual examples. What is quite amazing is that the postbirth activities have not drastically changed in over three thousand years, attesting to the fact that some things are not culturally bound.

3

The Newborn: Postpartum Rituals and Practices

Once the baby was born, the parents had a new life to protect, nurture, and care for. The magicoreligious ways parents did this are covered in the following chapter. This chapter explores more mundane things such as what to name a child, how to transport her, and ways to feed her. While such topics might be quotidian, they too carry undertones of the ever-present need to protect the valued, helpless infant whenever possible.

3.1. Naming the Baby

William Shakespeare penned the words, "What's in a name?," opining that names do not matter; the individual matters (*Romeo and Juliet* 2.2.47–48). While this might be true for star-crossed lovers, those in the ancient world believed that names really did matter.[1] Names recorded a parent's thoughts about the baby, as well as the child's legal and social status. Hence, there was a lot in the name. However, the naming process was not a uniform one; the time when a baby was named, as well as who named her, varied.

Over two-thirds of the birth narratives in the Hebrew Bible record women naming children.[2] For example, mothers or surrogate mothers name children in Gen 4:1; 29:32–35; 30:6–13, 22–24; 1 Sam 1:20; 4:21;

---

1. Granqvist provides a list of names from the Palestinian village of Artas, near Bethlehem, where family names were handed down from generation to generations. She notes the predilection for choosing names on the father's side of the family (*Child Problems among the Arabs*, 39). At times a child may be given a "fake" name that he uses temporarily. Temporary names are given to those thought to be in danger. Once the danger has passed, the child reverts to his given name (50, and §4.4).

2. Meyers, *Rediscovering Eve*, 158. On names and the naming process in general, see Karla Bohmbach, "Names and Naming in the Biblical World," in *Women in Scripture*, ed. Carol Meyers (Grand Rapids: Eerdmans, 2000), 33–39.

13:24. Nonfamily members could also name a child. Obed is not named by his biological mother (Ruth) or his foster mother (Naomi), but by the women of the town (Ruth 4:17).[3] Yet in almost every case the biblical text follows same the general pattern: she or he named the child X, because Y. The Y variable is an explanation of the child's name, which usually includes a pun. For example, Rachel names her child, Dan, via Bilhah, stating "God has vindicated me" (Gen 30:6). She links his name דן (Dan), with the verb meaning "to judge" (דין). Most biblical and ancient Near Eastern names express some sentiment, such as the feeling of the parents upon the birth of the child.[4] For example, Sarah and Abraham name their child Isaac, "laughter" (Gen 21:3–6). The two sons born to Zilpah are Asher, "happy/blessed," and Gad, "good fortune" (Gen 30:9–13).

Names also include God's name and reiterate that God is the opener of the womb.[5] In naming her children, Leah acknowledges that YHWH is the one who responds to requests for children (Gen 29:32–35; 30:17–20). Rachel names her firstborn child Joseph, with the hopes that God would "add," or grant her another [child] (Gen 30:22–24). Other theophoric names from the Bible and ancient Near East include: Nathaniel, "El (God) has given [a child]"; Shemaiah, "Yahweh has heard"; Nabu-apal-iddin, "Nabu has given an heir"; Išme-Dagan, "Dagan has heard [a plea for conception]"; Išmanni-ili, "My god has heard me"; and Amenhotep, "Amun has proved to be gracious."[6] Each name attests to the divine's role in the

---

3. Naomi's actions may be understood as a legal adoption or as a symbolic adoption. Edward Campbell, *Ruth: A New Translation with Introduction, Notes and Commentary*, AB 7 (Garden City, NY: Doubleday, 1975), 165. While unusual, this is not the only time that a nonfamily member names a child, the midwife named Perez and Zerah (Gen 38:29–30).

4. Ilana Pardes calls attention to the fact that many names reveal more about the parent's feelings and their character, than about the new born child. Ilana Pardes, *Countertraditions in the Bible: A Feminist Approach* (Cambridge: Harvard University, 1992), 41. Rainer Albertz's detailed treatment of names found in the Hebrew Bible, ancient Israel, and surrounding cultures breaks names down into the following six categories: names of thanksgiving, names of confession, praise names, equating names, birth names, and secular names. Rainer Albertz, "Names and Family Religion," in *Family and Household Religion in Ancient Israel and the Levant*, ed. Rainer Albertz and Rüdiger Schmitt (Winona Lake, IN: Eisenbrauns, 2012), 245–386, esp. 253.

5. Over sixteen hundred names from Iron Age Israelite inscriptions allude to birth and/or God's role in birth (Meyers, *Rediscovering Eve*, 158).

6. Janssen and Janssen, *Growing Up in Ancient Egypt*, 14; Ryan Byrne, "Lie Back and Think of Judah: The Reproductive Politics of Pillar Figurines," *NEA* 67 (2004):

child's conception and birth. Tricky labors are remembered with names like: Jephthah, "Let [Divine Name] open [the womb]"; and Iptaṭar-lišir, "[Divine Name] has loosened [the womb], let [the child] thrive/pass through."[7] Rachel's cry of "Ben-Oni," son of my affliction, encapsulates the drama she experienced in birthing her second son (Gen 35:18). Still other names are given based on characteristics noted at the time of birth, such as Jacob, "supplanter," or Esau, "hairy" (Gen 25:25–26). Whereas many biblical men are born, the only biblical woman to have a birth story is Dinah, whose name means "avenged." Notably, while Leah uttered an explanation of each of her sons' names, upon the birth of her daughter, the narrator simply records that her name was Dinah. The switch to a third-person narrator stating the name of a child is jarring. Perhaps it is meant to foreshadow the tragedy that will befall Dinah, thus creating suspense in the narrative. However, it also subtly highlights the preference for males and the preferential treatment that they received.[8]

A baby's name not only recorded circumstances surrounding his birth, or characteristics his family wanted to imbue him with, but also revealed a baby's social status. In addition to the biblical naming formula given above, we also find another naming formula in the ancient Near Eastern record. Mesopotamian sale documents and personal seals record a person's name as: PN (Personal Name) son/daughter of PN.[9] Linking a baby to his or her father/mother is a way to link generations together; knowing and pronouncing a person's name was of great importance as it was the way a person lived on after death.[10]

---

138. In ancient Egypt, children received names at birth. Names were given by mothers, fathers, or both parents. In addition to the theophoric names, babies were named after family numbers, attributes, animals, and numbers. Erika Feucht, "Childhood," *OEAE* 1:262.

7. Byrne, "Lie Back and Think of Judah," 138.

8. The male heirs carry on the family name, the family inheritance, and the cult of the ancestors. Ironically, they could not do this without the birth of female children who would in turn grow up to bear children.

9. Slave children names are written with a different pattern; babies are listed as an extension of the mother (PN mother and her little baby PN) or as an individual, simply PN (Garroway, *Children in the Ancient Near Eastern Household*, 141–49).

10. Karel van der Toorn, *Family Religion in Babylonia, Syria, and Israel: Continuity and Change in the Forms of Religious Life* (Leiden: Brill, 1995), 52–65. For more on remembering ancestors after death see Elizabeth Bloch-Smith, "The Cult of the Dead in Judah: Interpreting the Material Remains," *JBL* 111 (1992): 213–24.

Since a name had so much significance attached to it, receiving a name was a momentous occasion. The biblical text leads us to believe that a baby received a name upon birth. We often find the sequence: she conceived, bore a son, and named it (Gen 29–30). While many scholars hold that free children were named at birth, there is some leeway. A child might not be named until he or she was a few days old, or until after the period of mandated seclusion (Lev 12) was over. The book of Ruth seems to attest to a naming ceremony that coincided with Naomi holding Obed to her chest and thus being recognized as his foster mother (Ruth 4:16–17).[11] It is unclear if these events happened immediately after the birth (Ruth 4:13) or if some time, days or even weeks occurred between the birth and the adoption and naming ceremony.[12]

There are two other possibilities for the timing of the naming ceremony. Jewish tradition links naming to circumcision since God changed Abram's name to Abraham when he was circumcised (Gen 17:15). In Jewish tradition today, the circumcision takes place on the eighth day after birth at which time a child is named. Waiting until to name a child until he is circumcised is also linked to Jewish folklore. A *bobe-mayse* (old grandmother's tale of sorts) states that without a name, the angel of death cannot come and kill the boy before the *bris*.[13] Second, it is also possible that various kin groups or social groups had different customs for when the child was named. Within the censuses in the book of Numbers, the Levites are counted differently than the rest of Israel. While the general Israelite population was counted from the age of twenty, the Levites were counted from the age of one month (Num 1:2–3; 3:15). The general census was to list *by name* every male over the age of twenty. If the census

---

11. Albertz hypothesizes that a naming ritual occurred when the mother finished her period of postbirth seclusion (Albertz, "Names and Family Religion," 247).

12. Indeed, within a single ethnographic population one finds variation in when the child is named (Granqvist, *Child Problems among the Arabs*, 11–14; Musil, *Arabia Petraea*, 216–17). Many Arabs follow the custom of naming on the seventh day. This happens in conjunction with a ceremony where the hair is cut, and a sacrificial offering is made (Granqvist, *Child Problems among the Arabs*, 11 n. 1). Granqvist clearly states that no naming ceremony takes place in the village of Artas. However, Musil records a ceremony of transferring spit and bestowing a name on the child. "Nimm Speichel von meinem Speichel, und wandle meinen Weg, und du sollst heißen N.N." (Musil, *Arabia Petraea*, 217).

13. More about the implications of this *bobe-mayse* is covered in the section on gendering and circumcision below.

for the Levites was recorded in the same manner as the general census, then we can assume that the Levites were named by the time they were one month old.

As for slave children, it is possible that these children were not named for at least two to three years, until they were weaned and able to survive on their own.[14] Naming an individual gave him a place within society, a place in the household. For the slave child, this meant his or her own separate identity apart from the mother. Until the child had a name, the mother and child would have been considered one *unit* or one *item*, and any sale would have included them both.[15]

3.2. Gender(ing) and Impurity

The postpartum period today is understood as the time during which a woman experiences lochia discharge resulting from the childbirth, generally lasting four to six weeks. The Hebrew Bible also acknowledges a postpartum period during which the woman and child are separated from the larger community. The duration of the postpartum status is affected by the sex of the child. The purity laws in Lev 12 state that a woman giving birth has two stages of impurity, and the duration of each stage is directly related to the sex of the infant. The first stage of impurity puts the woman in the status of one who is *niddah*, experiencing her menses. It lasts seven days if she bears a boy; however, if she gives birth to a girl, stage one lasts fourteen days. The second stage of impurity is longer. If she bears a male child, her period of postpartum impurity is thirty-three days; if a female child, the woman is impure for sixty-six days (Lev 12:1–5). After this time, the mother shall provide the proper sacrifices to the priest, and she shall be made clean (Lev 12:6–8).[16]

The Levitical laws understand the postpartum period in terms of ritual purity rather than in a physiological sense, thus linking the sex of the child

---

14. H. D. Baker, "Degrees of Freedom: Slavery in Mid-First Millennium BC Babylonia," *WA* 33 (2001): 22.

15. Garroway, *Children in the Ancient Near Eastern Household*, 148–49.

16. Ethnographic studies also record a seclusion period, but on a slight different timeline. In early twentieth century Iraq a woman was considered impure for forty days if a son was born and for forty-five days if she birthed a daughter. While interval of impurity is shorter between a boy's birth and a girl's than it is in Leviticus, impurity is still based on the gender of the child (Drower, "Women and Taboo in Iraq," 107).

to how long a woman is considered impure. Impurity in turn, means that the woman must be separated from the community. A woman remains impure, and thus secluded for over two months after birthing a girl, but only about a month for bearing a son. From a purely physical standpoint, the period of a woman's lochia has nothing to do with the sex of the child; Israelite women did not automatically stop experiencing lochia on day thirty-three or sixty-six, respectively.[17] A woman still might have experienced some discharge after thirty-three days if she bore a son. We might wonder then why the law does not simply say "the woman shall remain impure for the entire time of her lochia," but rather makes a distinction based on the sex of the child. While a number of reasons could be behind the biblical childbirth laws, one suggestion, again based on sex, stands out. As previously mentioned, the birth of children was desired, especially the birth of a male child who could carry on the family line and work in the fields. Thus, a woman who bears a boy might feel elated and bond naturally with her child.[18] She might be encouraged to breastfeed, working through any difficulties that might arise with great determination. On the other hand, she might feel less excited if she bore a girl and might not put as much energy or effort into bonding with the child. Some scholars suggests that the Levitical laws acknowledge this and therefore enforce a longer period of impurity with the birth of female babies to give the mother extra time to bond with the child.[19] While the time of the mother's impurity differs for a boy and a girl, it is important to note that Leviticus prescribes the same sacrifices to be offered upon the birth of a newborn, regardless of the infant's sex (Lev 12:6).[20] One could read these laws as "indicating an

---

17. Thiessen looks to the Greek understanding of embryology to inform his understanding of Lev 12. He argues that the gendered impurity times are related to the Greek idea that male and female embryos develop at a different rate with females developing slower than males. Matthew Thiessen, "The Legislation of Leviticus 12 in Light of Ancient Embryology," *VT* 68 (2018): 1–23.

18. While not attesting to the mother's feelings, ethnographic reports do comment upon the general attitude surrounding the birth of a boy versus a girl. For example, Palestinian Arabs celebrate the birth of a boy and give a greater baksheesh, reward, to the one bringing news of a boy's birth. A father is greeted with "good tidings" upon the birth of a son, no such greeting exists for the birth of a girl (Granqvist, *Birth and Childhood Birth and Childhood among the Arabs*, 76–77).

19. Gruber, "Breast-Feeding Practices," 68 and references therein.

20. The Ugaritic record also mentions the need for postpartum purity offerings (*KTU* 1.23.54; Wyatt, "Circumcision and Circumstance," 425).

equivalency of male and female newborns," with respect to their sex.[21] It might also be that the offering has nothing to do with the newborn, but more to do with the status of the new mother.

Leviticus 12:3 says "on the eighth day, the flesh of his foreskin shall be circumcised." This comes as no surprise as it echoes God's commandment to Abraham in Gen 17:12. The context of Leviticus, however, demands a closer look at the relationship between impurity and circumcision in ancient Israel. The preceding verse, Lev 12:2, relays information about the mother's stage one impurity. One might wonder then, if Leviticus is also suggesting that during the seven days of stage one impurity, both the mother and the child are impure.[22] Circumcision, which ends the period of stage one impurity, can be understood as having purification properties.[23]

Looking beyond sex and issues of impurity, the period of separation in general can be understood as beneficial for both the mother and child. Newborns are vulnerable. They are both particularly susceptible to disease and sickness and dependent upon their mothers for sustenance. These vulnerabilities may have been part of the reason the *bobe-mayses* understood the Angle of Death to seek out newborns. Keeping the mother and child secluded from the general population has the practical effect of protecting the new mother and baby from any viral sickness, or "evil forces."[24]

Outside of the Hebrew Bible one finds a concern for purity and religious aspects, along with a medically centered approach in both the Hittite and ethnographic literature. Like the biblical laws, Hittite rituals tend to focus on the elite. One text with instructions for some prebirth rituals includes three offerings the mother must make.[25] After the various offerings she

---

21. Meyers, *Rediscovering Eve*, 159.

22. Later Jewish texts possibly understand the newborn male as purified by circumcision. Tzvi Novak notes that to this day, the Ethiopian custom is to treat the infant as having contracted impurity and to immerse it on the day of the mother's purification. Tzvi Novak, "Mother and Child Postpartum Defilement and Circumcision," thetorah.com. https://tinyurl.com/SBL1729g. The notion that both mother and child are impure can also be implied from the Hittite rituals referenced below.

23. The link between circumcision and purity can be seen in Egypt as well, where circumcision was one aspect of purification required of Egyptian priests. Herman Te Velde, "Theology, Priests, and Worships in Ancient Egypt," in Sasson, *Civilizations of the Ancient Near East*, 3:1733.

24. Avissar-Lewis, "Childhood and Children in Material Culture," 183.

25. Beckman, *Hittite Birth Rituals*, 16–17, text 7, referencing *KBo* 17.65.obv.1'–34'.

makes, "she bestows purity." On the next morning, the seer (a diviner) puri-
fies her mouth. After this purification, she is not allowed back in her house,
but must sit in a separate birthing hut until she gives birth. Seven days after
the baby is born, a *mala* offering (similar to the one the mother made prebirth) is made on behalf of the infant. The infant also requires purification;
presumably the birthing process bestowed some impurity upon the baby.
Again, we find two different timetables for the purification: a boy is purified
three months after his birth, while a girl must wait four months. Like the
biblical text, purifications and offerings happen in conjunction with birth;
however, the woman must do these things before, not after, the birth. After
the birth, "the infant must undergo purification and have offerings made on
his or her behalf."

The villages of Palestinian Arabs use slightly different purification rituals. While they did offer sacrifices, these were understood to have more
to do with warding off evil than with purification. A sheep was killed on
either the third, seventh, or eighth day after the birth in order that the baby
might live. In el-Karak, if a child was born on a Friday, a cock or male kid
was sacrificed to drive away evil spirits. Whereas one would expect purification via a sacrifice, purity comes instead through another ritual. As soon
as possible after the birth, a woman must hold the baby and walk three
times over the threshold, reciting "in the name of God, the Beneficent,
the Merciful," each time. Unlike the Levitical or Hittite texts, the sacrifice
and ritual walk were the same for both a boy and a girl. The primary ritual
actions related to a baby's sex had to do with what a mother ate postbirth.[26]

3.2.1. Gendering the Newborn

The gendering process is a long one and begins at birth. Unlike today,
where we make a distinction between sex and gender, the Hebrew Bible
understands these two as one and the same. Thus, a child with a penis is
a boy and will grow up to be gendered as an Israelite man; a child with
a vagina, likewise, is a girl who will grow up to be an Israelite woman.
Indeed, even the words used for female and male babies at the time of
birth suggest that a baby's sole gender marker is his or her genitalia. Leviticus 12:5 calls a female baby נקבה (*nəqēbāh*) a noun from the verb meaning "to bore [a hole]." A male baby is not called a בן (*bēn*) "son," but זכר

---

26. Granqvist, *Birth and Childhood among the Arabs*, 88 and 88 n. 22.

(*zākār*). The etymology of זכר is not as clear, but it is clearly related to the notion of masculinity. The Akkadian and Arabic cognates suggest זכר means testicles or the "male organ," again identifying the baby's gender first by means of his genitalia.[27] As the baby grows up, he or she will begin to acquire other gender markers. Children and other members of a society learn how to become male or female by watching others within their society act out these roles.[28] Adults perform actions demonstrating femaleness and maleness, which are then imitated by children.[29]

Gendering the newborn is different than gendering an older child who can take in information and repeat actions. When it comes to a newborn, gendering acts are done to not only establish the infant's gender, but also to confirm the infant's identity within his or her family and society. The different periods of impurity imposed on the mother for male and female babies serve as one of the first gender performances the child witnesses.[30] Other gender acts can be seen cross-culturally. Hittite birth rituals suggest that the baby receives gifts at birth according to its gender: baby boys receive "boy" gifts and baby girls receive "girl" gifts.[31] Similarly, a Sumerian tale about the bull of heaven impregnating a woman tells the story of a woman in hard labor.[32] The end of the tale states: "If it is a male, let him take a weapon, an axe, the fore of his manliness. If it is a female,

---

27. BDB, s.v. "זכר."

28. Judith Butler, *Gender Trouble: Feminism and the Subversion of Identity* (London: Routlege, 1990).

29. Since gendering is a process that takes place throughout a child's life, the discussion in this chapter is limited to gendering the newborn. Chapter 5 covers gendering the growing child.

30. Granqvist describes a belief among Palestinian Arabs that the foods served to a postpartum mother were directly linked securing the child's future. The foods were based on the baby's sex, thereby reinforcing and confirming the identity of the baby in the community. If a woman bears a boy, she is given hen soup, and if a girl, cock soup. This is done to insure the child will grow up and marry a woman or man respectively (Granqvist, *Birth and Childhood among the Arabs*, 88).

31. Beckman, *Hittite Birth Rituals*, 8–9, text 2, referencing *KBo* 18.62 + 63.obv.13′– 18′.

32. This tale was copied many times and some details in the folktale vary (Stol, *Birth in Babylonia and the Bible*, 61–63). Nick Wyatt notes similarities between the Akkadian tale of Sin seducing the heifer and the Ugaritic tale about the marriage of the goddess Nikkal and the moon god Kusuh (Hurrian)/Yarihu (West Semitic) found in *KTU* 1.24 (Wyatt, "Circumcision and Circumstance," 423–24).

let the spindle and the pin/distaff be in her hand."[33] The objects handed to or placed before the baby are meant to associate the boy baby with war and manliness and the girl baby with the domestic, female sphere. A variation of this tale says, "If it is a male, make him look at his weapon. If it is a female make her look at her [...] and her crucible."[34] While it is possible to read these quite literally, the possessive pronouns suggest these phrases are meant metaphorically: the boy must look at his penis and the girl at her vagina.[35] The latter variation speaks to the interconnectedness of gender and sex in the ancient world. It also emphasizes that an adult initiates the gendering process by having the baby gaze at his or her sexual organs. That men are associated with war and weapons and women with the home and household implements comes as no surprise.[36] Yet because the tale is written in poetry, one might also read the text with an eye to metaphor and parallelisms. The boy looks as his weapon, the thing that allows him to become the dominant sex in the ancient world. Like the boy, the girl looks at her weapon, her vagina, the thing that gives her power.

A female's sexual prowess is often referred to as a weapon in a metaphorical sense. In the Epic of Gilgamesh, the temple-prostitute Shamhat uses her best weapon, her sexuality, to tame Enkidu through a lovemaking session of epic proportions: six days and seven nights. Likewise, in "Inanna and the God of Wisdom," Inanna uses her feminine charms and convinces (seduces) Enki into giving her the keys to civilization— no small feat. At the start of the story, Inanna repeats the action of the female infant—she gazes at herself: "Her vulva was wondrous to behold. Rejoicing at her wondrous vulva, the young woman Inanna applauded herself."[37] The parallels with the gendering of the female infant here are clear. However, unlike the baby girl who is made to look at her "crucible," Inanna does so voluntarily. She has grown up and embodied the gender

---

33. Stol, *Birth in Babylonia and the Bible*, 61. Variants of this tale can be found in: MLC 1207, UM 29-15-367, VS 17 33, and AUAM 73.3094.

34. The variation is found in AUAM 73.3094.54–57. See Mark E. Cohen, "Literary Texts from the Andres University Archaeological Museum," *RA* 70 (1976): 133–39.

35. Following the suggestion by Martin Stol that *tukul.a.ni* = penis(?) and *ga.ri. im.ma.a.ni* = vagina (?) (Stol, *Birth in Babylonia and the Bible*, 63 n. 94).

36. Note that the primary characteristic of maleness in the biblical world is the ability to fight in war (Wilson, *Making Men*).

37. Diane Wolkenstein and Samuel Noah Kramer, *Inanna Queen of Heaven and Earth: Her Stories and Hymns from Sumer* (New York: Harper & Row, 1983), 12.

established for her at birth, and, like a warrior setting off to war, she takes stock of her weapons. While Inanna has agency as a young woman, in each of the other cases, gendering an infant imposes gender on a being who has, as of yet, no real agency.

3.3. Transporting and Feeding the Baby

Like the rest of the ancient Near East, Israelites nursed their infants.[38] Nursing was the most popular and practical way for a mother to feed her infant. Clay figurines depicting nursing mothers were popular in the ancient Near East, from Anatolia, to Syria, to Ugarit, Cyprus, Egypt, and Mesopotamia[39] (fig. 3.1). The illustration below comes from Egypt's Middle Kingdom (ca. 1981–1500 BCE). While many other images of nursing mothers are in the form of plaque figurines, this piece shows a three-dimensional depiction of a scene from daily life. One might imagine a similar scene taking place in ancient Israel.

Such depictions were less popular in Iron Age Israel, where the pillar figurine was favored. This figurine, while not showing the nursing act,

Fig. 3.1. Woman nursing, Egypt, Twelfth–Eighteenth Dynasties, circa 1981–1500 BCE.

---

38. Hebrew has multiple words to describe the nursing infant. Each word carries a connotation with respect to the child's vulnerability (Parker, *Valuable and Vulnerable*, 67–73).

39. Nakhai, "Mother-and-Child Figurines," 178–85.

highlighted the milk-giving breasts, attesting to the fact that there, too, breastfeeding was the normal course of action.

The Hebrew Bible describes infancy as a close, comforting relationship between the infant and the mother. The book of Isaiah describes the return of the exiled using the metaphor of one who gives birth; the returnees shall suck from Jerusalem's breast and find consolation in her bosom (Isa 66:11). Isaiah's imagery recalls the crying infant who is soothed by the mother's breast, finding joy in her mother's arms. We find the same suckling carried and dandled upon knees (Isa 66:12). While this could be a reference to games played with a toddler, when taken in the context of comfort being given (Isa 66:11–13), these terms convey the imagery of a mother implementing two of Harvey Karp's five S's to calm a fussy newborn: swaying/swinging (jiggling) and sucking.[40]

Many of the texts referencing nursing babes do so by saying they are at the mother's breast. In addition some of the texts seem to imply that the baby is being transported while nursing. Joel 2:16 says: "Gather the people, bid the congregation to purify themselves. Bring together the old, gather babes and the sucklings at the breast; let the bridegroom come out of his chamber, the bride from her canopied couch." Likewise, Deut 31:12 suggests that nursing mothers are to bring their little ones to hear the reading of the Torah.[41] How would a mother transport her baby? Carrying the child is one option and iconographic representations also suggest baby carriers as a hands-free option.

3.3.1. Baby Carriers

Most visual information regarding baby carriers comes from the Egyptian record. The tomb of Montemehet at Luxor (Twenty-Fifth Dynasty) shows a seated woman collecting figs from a tree with a baby strapped to her front (fig. 3.2). A textile wrap that appears to fit over one of the woman's shoulders supports the baby. It is akin to the slings produced by the modern company called Hot Sling.[42] Other similar wraps supporting a child on the woman's chest are seen in the Tomb of Neferhopte on Egyptian women of the Eighteenth Dynasty (fig. 3.3). The scene from Neferhopte's tomb shows

40. Harvey Karp, "The 5 S's for Soothing Babies," Happiestbaby.com, https://tinyurl.com/SBL1729f.

41. Gruber, "Breast-Feeding Practices," 68.

42. Hot Sling, "Homepage," https://www.hotslings.com/

Fig. 3.2. Woman and baby, Egypt, Luxor West Bank, TT 34, Tomb of Montemhet at Luxor, Twenty-Fifth Dynasty.

Fig. 3.3. Women and babies, Egypt, Thebes, TT 49, Neferhotep's Tomb, Eighteenth Dynasty.

children of many different ages being carried in different positions. Taller women carry the children on their front, while a shorter female carries a child on her back. If size represents age, it may be that the taller women are nursing mothers who use the sling to keep their infants near the breast. The shorter female carrying the baby on her back may be an older sister or other relative.

While many Egyptian representations of breastfeeding women show the mothers in a seated position, it is quite likely that this was not the only way to nurse a child.[43] In fact, as the contemporary attachment parenting movement argues, wearing your baby makes it easy for the child to nurse on demand. Women moving about the house might be able to stop what they were doing, sit, and nurse their child. Other women, making the trek to draw water, for example, might wear their infant. The same sling that made it easy for the infant to nurse would also be used to carry older infants on the woman's back. Between four and six months of age, infants gain enough neck muscles to support their heads while seated upright. Infants who have head control can then be transported on a mother's back. Again, note the female in figure 3.2 using the "hot sling" to transport an infant on her back. Foreigners, such as Nubians, Libyans, and Syrians, are shown holding a basket on their back to transport their infant (fig. 3.4). It appears that only the youngest children are carried in baskets. One can see older children walking next to their mothers and holding their hands. The depictions of these foreign mothers in the Tomb of Huy (Eighteenth Dynasty) show the women with colorful skirts, but naked from the waist up, suggesting that the nursing mothers would not be encumbered by tops when their infant needed to nurse.[44]

In addition to the explicit references to baby carriers found in the Egyptian record, the Mesopotamian corpus also attests to the possibility that baby carriers were used. There, we find three plaques depicting the birth goddess Ninhursag. She is nursing an infant and flanked by two *kūbu* figures. The plaques and the importance of the *kūbu* figures are discussed in chapter 2. Here it is important to draw attention to the object framing the goddess: an elongated horseshoe shape. Like an ACE bandage, the ends of

---

43. For Egyptian mothers sitting to nurse see, Janssen and Janssen, *Growing Up in Ancient Egypt*, 20 and fig. 7.

44. Granqvist refers to the ubiquitous site of women carrying babies: "Every morning she came as before with her milk-pitcher on her head, but now she had the child too, in a hammock, held fast to her forehead with a broad band as one can see any day in Jerusalem" (Granqvist, *Birth and Childhood among the Arabs*, 54). Elsewhere she states that a mother carries a portable hammock with her when she goes to the bizarre. From the description it seems like the child is swaddled into the hammock, which is then placed on the mother's back and secured to the mother's body by a band going from the hammock up around the mother's forehead. In a somewhat amusing fashion Granqvist notes the mothers take the hammocks off and hang them up while the mother shops or sells her wares (121). In general, babies are either carried in these hammocks or in the mother's arms. Older children ride on the mother's shoulders or neck (123–24).

the horseshoe curl around themselves giving the impression of a 1960s-style hairdo with a flip on the end. These two horseshoe-shaped objects on either side have garnered much attention. They have been identified as the symbol of the Sumerian goddess Ninhursag. The Egyptian birth goddess Hathor has a similar hairstyle, which became a shorthand symbol for writing the goddess' name. Unlike the Hathor wig, the horseshoe shapes on these plaques are elongated, representing something different than a wig. The objects were discussed in the previous chapter as swaddling clothes, which are hung on pegs when they are not in use.[45] I would suggest that the object might also function as a wrap used when the mother is nursing. Parents today might liken the long piece of cloth to the Moby Wrap, a single piece of

Fig. 3.4. Foreigners with children in baskets, Egypt, Thebes, TT 40, Tomb of Huy, Nubian Tribute, Eighteenth Dynasty.

cloth a little over 18 ft long (5.5 m) that is wrapped and crisscrossed over the parent to create a material web in which the baby is secured.[46] The wrap fits snuggly on the parent so that the baby is almost swaddled to the parent's body, rather than as a separate swaddled bundle. Proponents of the Moby Wrap note the easy transition between carrying and nursing the baby. There are even different wrapping techniques (from hug hold, to hip hold, to kangaroo hold) used for breastfeeding and carrying the child.[47] Since Mesopotamian art focuses on royal-political scenes rather than on family scenes, the information on these plaques offers important pictorial information for how babies were cared for. They were breastfed and swaddled. These were done separately if the horseshoe shape is merely swaddling clothes, or simultaneously if the horseshoe shape represents a swaddling wrap.

The link between breastfeeding and carrying an infant is supported by the texts as well. The Instruction of Any encourage a person as follows:

45. Van Buren, "Clay Relief in the Iraq Museum," 170.
46. Moby Wrap, "Home Page," http://mobywrap.com/
47. Moby Wrap, "Instructions," http://mobywrap.com/pages/instructions-the-moby-wrap.

Repay your mother for all her care. Give her as much bread as she needs,
then carry her as she carried you, for you were a heavy burden to her.
When you were finally born, she still carried you on her neck and for
three years she suckled you and kept you clean.[48]

Carrying the infant upon her neck, that is, in a sling, is immediately followed by a reference to breastfeeding.

Isaiah 66:11–13a presents another possible example linking breastfeeding and baby carriers.

That you may suck [תינק] from her breast consolation to the full, that you
may draw from her bosom glory to your delight. For thus said the Lord:
I will extend to her prosperity like a stream, the wealth of nations like a
wadi in flood; and you shall drink [lit., suckle, ינקתם] of it. You shall be
carried on shoulders and dandled upon knees. As a mother comforts her
son so I will comfort you. (JPS)

Discussing the birth and growth of the newly returned exiles, Isaiah lists
three actions, two of which are the same as in the Instruction of Any: they
will nurse/suckle, and they will be carried. The third action in the Instruction of Any is tantamount to "diaper changing"; here the third action is
described as "be[ing] dandled." In this passage, Isaiah uses two prepositional phrases "on the side/hip" and "on the knees." The second prepositional phrase "on the knees" is quite clearly linked to the last verb "shall
be dandled." However, the first prepositional phrase sits between the first
two verbs. Quite literally the text says: "and you shall suck/nurse upon
the side/hip you shall be carried." Most English translations connect the
prepositional phrase to the second verb so that the text reads: "you [the
infant nation] shall nurse/suckle *and* you will be carried on the [her] side/

---

48. I. Hasan et al., "History of Ancient Egyptian Obstetrics and Gynecology: A
Review," *Journal of Microbiology and Biotechnology Research* 1 (2011): 36. The passage
is translated with some slight differences by Lictheim "Double the food your mother
gave you, support her as she supported you; she had a heavy load in you, but she
did not abandon you. When you were born after your months, she was yet yoked
<to you>, her breast in your mouth for three years. As you grew and your excrement
disgusted, she was not disgusted, saying 'What shall I do!'" Miriam Lichtheim, *The
New Kingdom*, vol. 2 of *Ancient Egyptian Literature* (Berkeley: University of California
Press, 2006), 141.

hip and dandled upon the [her] knee."[49] In the Hebrew, the italicized "and" is absent; English translations include the word to make the sentence flow smoothly. In essence, the English translations make the first two verbs separate actions.[50] In fact, the awkward construction of this verse is recognized in the Septuagint and the Dead Sea Scroll, which eliminate "sucking" altogether, reading instead: "Their children/infants shall be carried on the hip."[51] Rather than dismissing the awkward nature of the verse, one can look to the available archaeological and ethnographical evidence to find a solution. As both Egyptian art and ethnographic studies demonstrate, it is not uncommon to nurse a baby while carrying him in a wrap or sling. As noted above, the freedom allowed through this practice is being reembraced in contemporary Western societies.[52] A new rendering of Isa 66:12b might envision the child being carried in a sling, thus connecting the two actions "nursing" and "being carried": "and they shall nurse (while) being carried upon the hip, and they shall be dandled upon the knee." The infant nation now engages in two quintessentially infant activities, both of which demonstrate the nurturing love of the parent for their little one. Indeed, the very next verse begins "As a mother comforts her son, so I will comfort you," linking the mother's breast and closeness of her body with comfort (Isa 66:13).

3.3.2. Nursing, Wet-Nursing, and Weaning

Psalm 22:10 (9) makes another reference to an infant at his mother's breast. Speaking in the first person, the psalmist identifies YHWH in the first half of the verse as the one who drew him from his mother's womb. In the second half of the verse, the psalmist states YHWH "made me secure/ trust in/on my mother's breast." The verse can be understood as saying that

---

49. Translation my own.

50. KJV, JPS, NIV, NASB.

51. According to Joseph Blenkinsopp, "MT *vînaqtem*, 'and you will nurse,' does not make good sense in the context; LXX *ta paidia autōn*, 'their children,' understood MT *vînaqtem* as a substantive *yônaqtām*, 'their infants' (literally, 'suckers'), and is supported by 1QIsaa; read *věyôněqôtêhem*, 'and your infants'" (*Isaiah 56–66: A New Translation with Introduction and Commentary*, AB 19B [New York: Doubleday, 2003], 304 n. i).

52. Many online boards include the question "which is the best baby carrier for nursing and walking?" Baby Center, "Best Baby Carriers for Nursing," https://tinyurl.com/SBL1729a.

the psalmist trusted in YHWH from the moment he was born. However, as a piece of poetry, the verse can also be understood as a metaphor. As the translation above tries to show, there are two words worthy of attention. When combined with the preposition עַל (ʿal), the verb "secure/trust" (בטח; bāṭaḥ) means to rely upon or trust in something. It is true the metaphor refers to a life stage in which an infant suckles at the mother's breast, but it is more than that. As many new mothers might know, nursing is not always an easy thing for the infant to learn.[53] Latching to the breast can be difficult for infants for a multitude of reasons including: cleft palates, wrong positioning, or mothers who have flat or inverted nipples. The psalmist was living in a world where infant mortality was high, where poor nutrition caused death. Not being able to latch properly or draw enough milk from the breast was a lethal prospect. The very fact that the psalmist could rely upon the milk provided from his mother, means the psalmist is also praising YHWH for his own life, for the ability to draw sustenance from the breast at the time when he needed it most: as a newborn.

As babies grow, their parents begin to introduce solid foods into the diet. For a period of time, the older baby both nurses from the mother and eats solid foods. The proportion of the baby's diet consumed in milk and food gradually shifts, so that at some point the baby draws less milk and consumes more solid food. At what point the baby is fully weaned is a good question. Some children wean themselves naturally and others need some encouragement to leave the breast. This said, infants in the ancient Near East on the whole nursed for a longer span of time than most infants in America today. A mother might have started nursing her offspring as a newborn infant, but weaned him as a young child. For example, the Instruction of Any mentions "the mother's breast in your mouth for three years" (7.19).[54] Consider too, the relief from the palace of Azitawadda (eighth century BCE) in modern day Karatepe that shows a child standing and nursing (fig. 3.5).[55] The child in question is most definitely not an infant held in the mother's arms, but a child almost tall

---

53. Mothers from around the world are supported by the nonprofit group La Leche League, which fields questions and offers support to mothers who desire to breastfeed. For La Leche League International, see https://www.llli.org/.

54. Lichtheim, *New Kingdom*, 141.

55. Gruber, "Breast-Feeding Practices," 64.

enough to reach the mother's breast while standing. A span of two or even three years is also found in Old Babylonian wet-nurse contracts.[56]

Wet-nurse contracts also attest to another reality, the fact that not all babies were nursed by their mothers. Reasons for this included the mother's inability to take care of the child or lactate, a particular social status, or her untimely death. In most cases, the person hiring the wet-nurse would be an adoptive parent or a woman who could not lactate properly.[57] However, there were times when the baby's own mother hired a wet-nurse even when she was perfectly capable of nursing the child herself. Since nursing, especially nursing on demand, brings on lactational amenorrhea causing the mother not to menstruate, upper class women trying to increase their fertility might hire a wet-nurse in order to begin trying to have children sooner. This

Fig. 3.5. Child nursing, Karatepe palace of Azitawadda, Tomb of Azitawadda, eighth century BCE.

might be the case, especially if the royal or wealthy family did not have a son or was hoping to have multiple sons. The narrative in 2 Kgs 11:2–3 gives an example of a royal infant Israelite (King Joash) being nursed by a wet-nurse, presumably so his mother could have more children.[58]

Exodus 2:5–10 tells an opposite tale, of a mother who had one too many sons. Baby Moses was cast away by his mother in a desperate act to

---

56. CT 48.70; BM 78812, Gruber, "Breast-Feeding Practices," 76–77.

57. Palestinian Arabs used wet-nurses only in the case when the mother died, or when the parents divorced. A child always belonged to the father and stayed with him in case of divorce (Granqvist, *Birth and Childhood among the Arabs*, 111, 125–26). Granqvist notes that family characteristics were understood to be inherited "very early influences received during suckling are supposed to set their stamp upon a child. All of these are factors of extreme importance in the final formation of a person's nature and are quite outside his won control. The power imbued upon breastmilk thus played a part in who is chosen to nurse the child should a wet-nurse be needed" (111).

58. The matriarch Rebekah, also from a wealthy family, had a wet-nurse. Her nurse became her companion, perhaps akin to a lady in waiting (Gen 24:59; 35:8).

save his life. The Pharaoh's daughter rescued him from the river and ironically ended up hiring his own mother to nurse him.[59] Exodus 2:9 specifies that the wet-nurse would be paid: "Take this child and nurse it for me, I will pay your wages." The Old Babylonian wet-nurse contracts provide some insight into what the wages cover. These specify that the payment to the wet-nurse was meant to cover the room and board, so to speak, of the infant while he nursed. The length of time Moses was nursed is not mentioned. All we know is that when the child "grew up," his mother returned him to the princess.

There are three more biblical narratives about nursing and weaning that are worthy of mention. A little comment in Gen 21:8 notes that Isaac grew up and was weaned. Again, the time is unspecified. The value in this text comes in the last part of the verse, where we learn that the end of the nursing period was cause for much celebration: "Abraham held a great feast on the day that Isaac was weaned." Whether or not there was a celebration on the day that a female child was weaned is not mentioned. Hosea 1:8 notes in passing that when Gomer had weaned Lo-Ruhamah, she conceived and gave birth to a son. Hosea makes no reference to a feast on the day she was weaned; rather the text seems more concerned with the birth of a son. This text is important because it mentions a female being breastfed, but here again, the biblical text does not state the specific amount of time that Lo-Ruhamah was nursed. Finally, 1 Samuel states that Hannah waits until Samuel is weaned before fulfilling her vow to bring him to reside at Shilo with Eli (1 Sam 1:20–24). Again, the text does not state outright how old Samuel is. Evidence presented from surrounding cultures suggests that children were weaned between two and three years old. The narrative details, however, allow us to draw some further conclusions concerning the time at which he was weaned and entered temple service. First Samuel tells us that Eli has two grown sons of his own (1 Sam 1:3). After Samuel's birth and dedication (1 Sam 1:19–2:11), the text notes that Eli's sons are horrible priests and worthless individuals (1 Sam 2:12–17). However, their actions somehow seem to occur without Eli noticing. Other people have to tell Eli about his sons' deeds (1 Sam 2:22) before he rebukes his sons. The text goes through great pains to paint an Eli who is going both literally and metaphorically blind to the things happening around him (1 Sam

---

59. For a new, child-centered treatment of this text, see Flynn, *Children in Ancient Israel*, 86–94.

3). Since Samuel becomes Eli's ward, it seems unlikely that Hannah would have given a young baby into his care; even a toddler of two seems like a lot of work for an elderly man to take care of. Based on the narrative, it seems possible that Hannah's motherly instincts might have kept Samuel at the breast for three or four years before she fully weaned him and sent him to the temple to serve under Eli (1 Sam 1:23, 24).

One final question remains: did women wean sons and daughters at a different time? Some have argued that Hos 1:8, which glossed over Lo-Ruhamah's weaning to relate the birth of her brother, presents evidence of weaning females earlier than males so that the mother could try for a son as soon as possible.[60] An Old Babylonian wet-nurse contract written up for an infant girl says she will be nursed for two years.[61] Other Old Babylonian contracts for boys list both two and three years as the contracted time for nursing.[62] While it seems possible that in some cases the gender of the baby might influence when a mother weaned the infant, it is hard to say that there was a definite gender divide in weaning akin to the gender divide seen in the seclusion period after birth. As many mothers today have experienced, sometimes it is not up to the mother when the infant stops nursing; sometimes the infant weans himself before the mother is ready to stop breastfeeding!

The ethnographic literature adds another dimension to this discussion. Among the Palestinian Arabs, the relationship between a child and nursing is very important. Time spent at the breast is thought to shape a child's character. Women nurse at the slightest fuss from the baby; however, girls are only nursed for one and a half years, whereas boys are nursed for another full year. It is said that one can never nurse a boy long enough. This does not mean boys were valued more than girls, but that by their very nature girls can quickly become too pampered. To combat this character (flaw?) a girl needs to learn from an early age how to control herself so that she does not bring shame to the family later in life.[63]

---

60. Gruber, "Breast-Feeding Practices," 68.

61. PBS 8/2.107; CT 48.70; MAH 15.951 (Garroway, *Children in the Ancient Near Eastern Household*, 260, 262–63).

62. Stol, *Birth in Babylonia and the Bible*, 181–83.

63. Granqvist, *Birth and Childhood among the Arabs*, 107. Granqvist also notes many cross-cultural studies differ in the age of weaning. Some list nursing up to four years of age, but that this is not usually done because a woman wished to get pregnant again (109 n. 4).

Unlike the biblical custom, Palestinian Arabs do not have a weaning cel- ebration. However, this transition in a person's life does not go unnoticed; a weaned baby is considered to have reached a new social age: "The baby- hood has past."[64]

3.3.3. Alternatives to Nursing

Although nursing was by far the most common means of providing food to the baby, it was certainly not the only method. It seems that at times babies, or perhaps even young children, were fed with the ancient equiva- lent of a sippy cup. Examples from ancient Egypt, while from a slightly ear- lier period than the Iron Age, attest to the possibility of using tiny cups.[65]

The most elaborate example of a sippy cup comes from the late Middle Kingdom Egypt (1850–1700 BCE) (fig 3.6). It is quite tiny, and at 3.5 cm high, 8 cm wide, and 4 cm deep, about the size of an apricot. The cup has an area to hold a little liquid, which would be poured out a tiny spout. Two lions, one standing on hind legs and one walking, a snake, a turtle, and another long-necked creature adorn the cup. These decorations are similar to the protective decorations on the wands discussed in chapter 4, suggesting that the cup or the liquid inside of it was protected and meant to benefit the baby. Rather than a simple clay vessel, this cup is made of faience, glazed with a bright blue color, and painted with decorations out- lined in black. Faience is composed of crushed sand or quartz, calcite lime, and various alkali compounds. A glaze containing copper pigments adds the blue or greenish color. The composition of the cup demonstrates that thought, time, and energy went into creating this baby cup. Whether or not it was used by an infant is unknown. It was found in a burial deposit along with some other items, suggesting that it was an offering meant to be used in the afterlife. A less elaborate version of an Egyptian feeding cup is seen in figure 3.7. Made of simple clay, devoid of decoration, this cup would have been less expensive to produce and perhaps available to more people. It too is small, measuring 5 cm x 7.8 cm, and was found in a cemetery burial deposit.

---

64. Granqvist, *Birth and Childhood among the Arabs*, 117. To mark the weaning a proverb is recited: "My first trouble is that of the teething, and my second trouble is the weaning" (117).

65. Avissar-Lewis also discusses the possibility of using cups and other vessels for feeding infants (Avissar-Lewis, "Childhood and Children in Material Culture," 54–55).

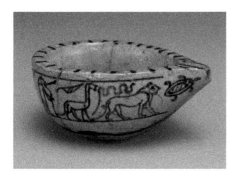

Fig. 3.6. Faience sippy cup, Egypt, Memphite, Lisht Northern Cemetery, Twelfth–Thirteenth Dynasty.

Fig. 3.7. Ceramic sippy cup, Egypt, Memphite, Lisht Northern Cemetery, Twelfth Dynasty.

Levantine excavations also found evidence of infant feeding cups, by way of juglets found in infant burials (fig. 3.8).[66] Juglets were common enough in Levantine households, but the way in which the juglets were placed in the burials demonstrates that juglets could provide another means of feeding the infant. In some burials the juglets were placed near the infant's head, and in a few cases, the juglet's spout seems to be pouring a now invisible substance into the infant's mouth.[67] Even though the juglets are small, the opening of the juglet would still allow liquid to quickly pour out. To make the juglet more bottle-like, cloth or another kind of other permeable covering may have once been affixed to the spout to act as a nipple of sorts.[68] So far, none of the excavation reports include detailed information as to what remains were found in the juglets. One might hypothesize goat's milk or water would have filled the bottles, or even breastmilk.[69] A final plausible option for feeding babies and children

66. Juglets accompanied a number of (mostly Middle Bronze II) infant burials at sites including: Tel Dan, Megiddo, Mevorakh, Tel Nesiba, Tel Qadish, Gaza, and Yokneam (Garroway, *Children in the Ancient Near Eastern Household*, 299–316).

67. Examples can be seen at Tel Qadish, Tel Nesiba, Tel Dan and Ashkelon (Garroway, *Children in the Ancient Near Eastern Household*, 314–15; Aaron J. Brody, "Late Bronze Age Intramural Tombs," in *Askhelon I: Introduction and Overview 1985–2000*, ed. Lawrence E. Stager, J. David Schloen, and Daniel M. Master (Winona Lake, IN: Eisenbrauns, 2008), 518, 528.

68. Avissar-Lewis, "Childhood and Children in Material Culture," 54–55, 184.

69. Egyptians had a special vessel dedicated to storing breast milk. With a capacity of a little over a hundred milliliters, the vessels could hold the amount of milk expressed at a single feeding (Janssen and Janssen, *Growing Up in Ancient Egypt*, 19).

Fig. 3.8. Jar burial, Tel Dan, Middle Bronze Age.

remains. Young individuals may have used the same drinking vessels that were used by adults. In much the same way as an adult today might hold a water bottle to a baby's mouth, skin bags, such as the ones seen on friezes from the Southwest Palace at Nineveh, held liquid that could presumably be poured into the infant or child's mouth.

3.4. Comforting and Quieting the Baby

Newborn infants have a lot to adjust to in life outside of the womb, and without the ability to speak, their main form of communication is crying.[70] Within the biblical text, the examples of Ishmael and Moses both demonstrate the power of an infant's wails to elicit a reaction from a caregiver (Gen 21: 9–23; Exod 2:1–10).[71] While much can be said for picking up the infant, holding her close or nursing her, there are times when the basic comforting maneuvers do not work. As will be seen in the next chapter, reasons for quieting a baby extend beyond the obvious desire to keep the caregiver's sanity intact.[72] This next section concentrates on different methods such as rattles and lullabies used to quiet and entertain the infant.

---

70. On infant crying as a means of communication, see Joseph Soltis, "The Signal Function of Early Infant Crying," *Behavioral and Brain Sciences* 27 (2004): 443–90; D. Out et al., "Physiological Reactivity to Infant Crying: A Behavioral Genetic Study," *Genes, Brains and Behavior* 9 (2020): 868–76. For an overview of scientific studies on crying and how it relates to infant abandonment or even infanticide, see Bosworth, *Infant Weeping*, 4–21.

71. Bosworth explores the relationship of these two texts in depth, noting the role crying plays in the outcome of each narrative (Bosworth, *Infant Weeping*, 67–92).

72. "The primary effect of infant cries on those who hear them is stress" (Bosworth, *Infant Weeping*, 18).

Crying is especially trying when it is night, and the family is attempting to sleep. One way to calm and quiet a child is through song. Both soothing words and a low-key, limping melody are used throughout the world to comfort the infant at night.[73] Turning to Mesopotamia, one finds many lullabies attempting to quiet crying infants that are both humorous and instructive. Whereas the later Old Babylonian lullabies have more of a ritual incantation flavor, some of the earliest Sumerian lullabies give off a soothing vibe. They are very simple and resemble something a parent might say today, such as "coo-coo" or "la-la." A lullaby written to quiet a Sumerian princess starts with the sounds: u_5.a, u_5.a, or "ooa, ooa."[74] Some Neo-Babylonian lullabies hush the baby by asking him to enjoy sleep like a fawn or gazelle, while one Old Babylonian lullaby adds some humor to the mix by wishing the child to be quite like one passed out drunk.[75] Eventually the lullaby form, through its combination of music and words, turns into a definable type of incantation meant to ward off evil. David Bosworth notes that "infant-directed speech has a more musical quality, with a more pronounced rhythm and melody."[76] Such speech fits well within the incantation genre, especially when incantations mask an adult's frustration with the inconsolable cries of a newborn.[77]

Like lullabies, rattles were used to hush the baby. Because they are a noisemaker, the rattles also served as a source of entertainment.[78] Any object that can be shaken or is easily grasped can serve this function. Indeed, the shape of modern baby rattles varies quite a bit. The biblical text does not mention rattles, but many rattles have been found in Egypt, Mesopotamia, Anatolia, and at various sites in ancient Israel, including

---

73. Bosworth, *Infant Weeping*, 22–33.

74. Stol, *Birth in Babylonia and the Bible*, 211 and n. 54.

75. Farber, *Schlaf, Kindchen Schlaf!*, 161–62, 164. Bosworth includes forty-six examples of Mesopotamian incantations directed at a crying baby (Bosworth, *Infant Weeping*, 39–52).

76. Bosworth, *Infant Weeping*, 26.

77. On the relationship between lullabies and incantations see, Bosworth, *Infant Weeping*, 23–27 and sources therein.

78. When it comes to archaeological objects that are small, unique, or otherwise puzzling they are often assigned to the generic category of "cultic object or toy." However, this witticism is being challenged with new attention being paid to where the objects were found and how they might have been used. Rona Avissar-Lewis notes the use of rattles to strengthen eye-hand coordination, as well as to entertain and quiet the child (Avissar-Lewis, "Childhood and Children in Material Culture," 56–57).

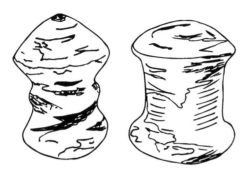

Fig. 3.9. Barrel-shaped rattle, Hazor and
Lachish, Iron Age.

Fig. 3.10. Anthropomorphic
rattle, Edom, Iron Age II.

among others: Megiddo, Gezer, Tel 'Ira, and Beth Shemesh (fig. 3.9).[79] As
with modern rattles, the shape and material of the rattles found in ancient
Israel also differs. Some are shaped like gourds with a solid handle, or a
loop handle, while others have holes through knob handles from which
they could be hung.[80] Most of the rattles with handles date to the Bronze
Age. A few unique rattles dating to both the Bronze and Iron Ages are
anthropomorphic in nature, resembling a female figure or stylized female
figure (fig 3.10).[81]

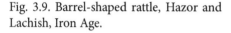

79. It is possible the Hebrew word מנענעים (root meaning to wave) found in
2 Sam 6:5 represents the rattle (Joachim Braun, *Music in Ancient Israel/Palestine*, trans.
Douglas W. Stott [Grand Rapids Eerdmans, 2002], 19). Rattles found in Egypt include
simple two ceramic rattles. The first comes from Thebes (ca. Thirteenth Dynasty) and
is decorated with white dots. See W. M. Flinders Petrie, *Objects of Daily Use* (London:
British School of Archaeology in Egypt, 1927), 59, LI:368. Five clay pieces inside con-
stitute the "noisemaker" aspect of the rattle. Interestingly, at Tel Amarna (ca. mid-
fourteenth century BCE) excavators state the ceramic rattle they discovered was made
especially for children. See Avissar-Lewis, "Childhood and Children in Material Culture," 57; Gwen White, *Antique Toys and Their Background* (New York: Arco, 1971),
34.

80. Nili Fox and Angela Roskop, "Of Rattles and Rituals: The Anthropomorphic
Rattle from the Nelson Glueck Collection at the Cincinnati Art Museum," *HUCA*
70–71 (1999–2000): 15–26; Braun, *Music in Ancient Israel/Palestine*, 100–104.

81. Braun gives two examples, one from Tell el-Far'ah [South], IAA I6936 and one
unprovenanced IAA P220 (Braun, *Music in Ancient Israel/Palestine*, 102–3); Fox and
Roskop, "Of Rattles and Rituals," 5–15.

Some of these rattles look like dipper juglets with a stylized anthropomorphic handle.[82] During the Iron Age, rattles that look like bells, and more often barrels or spools of thread, become popular.[83] Sometimes the barrels and bells have a perforation on one end suggesting that they may have been hung. The ceramic rattles, especially those with a barrel shape, are indigenous to ancient Israel and represent a style of rattle easy to mass produce and thus available to the masses.[84] Most barrel-shaped rattles are 4 to 7 cm in diameter. In part because of their size and weight and the fact they were made out of ceramic materials, scholars have dismissed the rattle as a child's toy.[85]

The main reason these closed form rattles have been disassociated from children concerns where they were found. Since most rattles were found in tombs and cultic settings, their use has been linked to the cult and funerary rites. However, in a 2000 study by Nili Fox and Angela Roskop of fifty-six rattles from clear contexts, they found sixteen were found in occupational areas.[86] To ignore these sixteen as aberrant and therefore unimportant dismisses them without asking what their use was. Since their study, other rattles have been found in nontomb settings. For example, three rattles were found at Tel Beth-Shemesh.[87] Two were used as part of a deliberate fill, and one was in an occupational setting. Despite the fact that none of the rattles were found with other cultic items, they are nonetheless listed in a table of "cult-related artifacts," attesting to the unchallenged view that

---

82. R. A. S. Macalister, *Excavation of Gezer* 1902–1905 and 1907–1909, vol 3 (London: Palestinian Exploration Fund, 2012), pl. LXVI, fig. 42; Olga Tufnell, *Lachish IV: The Bronze Age*, 2 vols. (London: Oxford University Press, 1958), pl. 28:24; and Fredrick Bliss, *A Mound of Many Cities, or Tel el-Hesy Excavated* (London: Palestinian Exploration Society, 1898), pl. 4 no.175.

83. Barrel and bell-shaped rattles were found at Hazor, Gezer, and Lachish. A gourd or fruit-shaped rattle was found at Megiddo. Those with grips or handles were found throughout ancient Israel (Braun, *Music in Ancient Israel/Palestine*, 100–104).

84. Braun, *Music in Ancient Israel/Palestine*, 106.

85. While some rattles may have been too large or heavy for infants, it is not impossible that older children may have used them, especially if tasked with the job of watching younger siblings.

86. Of the fifty-six rattles, thirty-one came from tombs, four from cultic areas, five from dump areas, and sixteen from occupational areas (Fox and Roskop, "Of Rattles and Rituals," 19).

87. Shlomo Bunimovitz and Zvi Lederman, *Tel Beth-Shemesh A Border Community in Judah: Renewed Excavations 1990–2000; The Iron Age*, vol. 2 (Tel Aviv: Yass Publications in Archaeology; Winona Lake, IN: Eisenbrauns, 2016), 596, fig. 16.14.

rattles must have been part of the cult.[88] However, it is possible that as a musical instrument, a rattle had many uses. The fact that rattles were both easily mass-produced and breakable could mean that the majority were found in tombs because they were in a context meant to preserve them. Shifting our perspective to the child, we might ask whether there was a relationship between the rattles and the children in the house. It seems logical that some rattles found in occupational settings could have been used to quiet infants. Further research into rattles and their location in the house is needed.

Other noisemaking instruments, sistra, are found throughout the ancient Near East, most notably in Egypt (fig 3.11).[89] They are associated with the goddess Hathor, divine patron of love, dance, and music, as well as the protector of women and childbirth.[90] Figure 3.11 shows a sistrum made of bronze or copper alloy belonging to the chantress Tapenu (1070–600 BCE). The Egyptian Tale of Sinuhe connects children to these open-form rattles in a significant way. When Sinuhe returns to Egypt, he is privy to a performance in the palace. Young children perform a ritual dance as they sing a song and

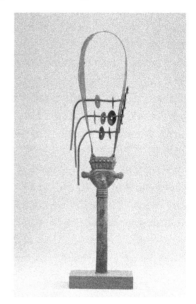

Fig. 3.11. Sistrum, Egypt, Third Intermediate Period.

---

88. Bunimovitz and Lederman, *Tel Beth-Shemesh*, 597, table 16.19.

89. Sistra have been found in Egypt, Sumeria, and Anatolia. William Foxwell Albright, "The Kyle Memorial Excavation at Bethel," *BASOR* 56 (1934): 8–9 and fig. 7.71; Tahsin Özgüc and Mahmut Alok, *Horoztepe: Eski Tunç Devri Mezarlig ve Iskân Yeri; An Early Bronze Age Settlement and Cemetery*, Turk Tarih Kurumu, Yayinlarindan 5/18 (Ankara: Turk Tarih Kurumu Basimevi, 1958), 42, 48–49, pl. xii; Henry G. Farmer, "The Music of Ancient Mesopotamia," in *The New Oxford History of Music*, 10 vols. (London: Oxford, 1957–1974), 1:239–40; Henry G. Farmer, "The Music of Ancient Egypt," in *New Oxford History of Music*, 1:258; Lawrence Stager, "The Fury of Babylon: Ashkelon and the Archaeology of Destruction," *BAR* 22.1 (1996): 62.

90. Hathor is often depicted using a sistrum to bestow good fortune on her patrons. Manfred Lurker, *The Gods and Symbols of Ancient Egypt* (London: Thames & Hudson, 1974), 11.

most importantly for this discussion, they shake sistra to appease the anger of the gods.[91] Here is a clear instance of rattles being used by children, presenting evidence against the notion that breakable items were not given to children.

3.5. Summary

During the infant's early days, the parents and caregivers became acquainted with the new little life. The infant was given a name that expressed praise and thanks. Names could include a theophoric element, like Nathaniel, "gift of God" or Shamash-ilu, "Shamash is god." They could also express an element of the infant's future, like Jacob, "supplanter," or Esau, "hairy." The exact moment of naming is not known. If some sort of public naming ceremony happened, such as suggested by Ruth 4:17, then naming would have to occur after the mother's period of postbirth impurity had ended. As discussed further in chapter 8, most infant deaths occurred in the first week after birth.[92] Waiting to see whether a child would survive this critical period and to hold off naming him or her could have been a coping measure. With a high rate of infant mortality, delayed naming might have been a way of not assigning the infant an identity. If naming represented an official "welcome to the family" moment, waiting to see whether the infant would be a viable member of the household would also make sense. Celebrating a little milestone, like making it through the first few weeks, could indeed be reason for a public celebration like the one mentioned in Ruth.

Mothers began to nurse their babies soon after birth, a process that lasted for at least two to three years. The ability to successfully nurse was not something to be taken for granted. In some cases, babies whose mothers who could not produce milk, who died in childbirth, or who could not keep their baby were nursed by a wet-nurse. The need for a wet-nurse could also be due to a mother's social class. The biblical text references

---

91. Fox and Roskop, "Of Rattles and Rituals," 18–19; Hellmut Brunner, "Das Besänftigungslied im Sinuhe (B 269–279)," *ZÄS* 80 (1955): 5–11.

92. For the purpose of statistical analysis, the World Health Organization has determined five and a half pounds to be the cutoff for low birth weight. They note that for clinical purposes an individual country may choose to use another number as the cutoff (World Health Organization, "Low Birthweight: Country, Regional and Global Estimates," 2004, https://tinyurl.com/SBL1729r).

Rebekah's nurse, Deborah, who not only suckled her, but then went on to be her companion for life (Gen 24:59; 35:8). Genesis tells us that Rebekah's family was well-off and able to provide her with a lifelong servant. Joash, the royal prince, also has a wet-nurse. In the case of the upper classes, wet-nurses were used as a way for mothers to avoid nursing and to become pregnant quicker than if they had to nurse a child for multiple years.

The majority of women, however, were not upper class and had to nurse their children while going about their daily chores. It appears that one way of navigating the difficulties of caring for an infant while needing to move about was to wear the baby in a wrap. Wearing the child was not only practical, but also allowed the infant easy access to the breast, something helpful for infants nursing on demand. The words of the psalmist attest to the close bond formed between the mother and infant during the early years: comfort was found on the breast. It is notable here that the male writers of the Bible turn to this bonding moment between a mother and infant to present the faithfulness of YHWH.[93] The discovery of "sippy cups" and juglets associated with infants in an archaeological context also suggests that infants may have been bottle-fed.

Without the words to express "I'm hungry, gassy, full, wet, soiled, constipated, unhappy, etc.," infants resort to crying. Parents sought to soothe their infants and may have done so with rattles. Found throughout the ancient Near East, and in abundance within ancient Israel, the musical rhythm of a rattle combined with the hand-eye movements, of a strange noisy object could quiet and entertain the infant. Given the nature of the rattles and where they were found, it seems quite possible that rattles had multiples uses, one of which was to hush babies. Whether or not little shakers were given to infants to hold and play with or handled solely by adults cannot be said for certain. However, considering the availability and the relative simplicity of the closed rattle's form, the concern with breakability should be revisited. Small infants today find great pleasure shaking everything from plastic Easter eggs filled with rice or dried beans to premanufactured rattles. With supervision, infants in ancient Israel might have enjoyed similar happiness shaking one of the many varieties of ancient rattles. At night, when sleep eluded the infant, tired parents the world over have sung lullabies to lull the infant to sleep. A calming tone of voice coupled with a soothing musical tune has put many an infant to

---

93. Many thanks to Shawn Flynn for pointing out this connection.

sleep. Early forms of lullabies consist of a few sounds "ooo" and "aaa." Not unlike the song "Rock-a-Bye Baby," later Old and Neo-Babylonian lullabies were expanded to include requests (sometimes a bit morbid) for the child to stop crying. Such lullabies might have been a part of the Israelite experience too.

From the moment the baby is born he or she begins the process of becoming part of his or her society. As seen in various parts of this chapter, in a world that by in large equated biological sex with gender, gendering was a part of many postbirth actions. Leviticus mandated seclusion with the mother for a period of time determined by the infant's sex. Female babies enjoyed more time alone with their mothers than their male counterparts. Whether this law was prompted by a need for ritual purity, or rooted in a more ethical reason, the infants in biblical Israel started their lives separated from most members of their community. Regardless of the reason, separation for any amount of time protected the infants from any disease and sickness that may have been in the community. If children in ancient Israel were named after the mother's initial period of impurity was complete, then male and female infants received names and were welcomed into the community at different times. Gendering appeared in other ways as well. Hittite culture bestowed gifts appropriate to the baby's sex upon him or her, and Mesopotamian literature states that adults placed items representative of the infant's gender in the baby's hand. Other texts state that the infants were simply to look at appropriate items, such as the weapon for a boy and the crucible for a girl. As poetic literature is prone to speaking in metaphors, it is possible that these items represent the penis and vagina respectively; the infant is forced to take stock of their "parts" and to recognize who he or she is.

Each of the topics covered in this chapter shows in small ways how vulnerable the little infant was; she could not feed herself, transport herself, or even express her needs through language. With a high rate of infant mortality, parents protected and nurtured the infant as best as they knew how. Life for the infant was precarious, and as the next chapter demonstrates, parents did all they could to protect their valuable little ones.

4

Inside Out:
How to Ward off Evil from Belly through Birth

Many mothers experience a desire to protect their children from the moment they find out they are pregnant. This urge spikes once the child is born and lasts through the nursing period. Research has demonstrated a link between the spike in this protective urge and the peptide corticotrophin-releasing hormone (CRH).[1] While women in the ancient world would have had the same physiological urge to protect their child, other factors also contributed to this desire. Since there was no end of possible maladies, mothers took precautionary steps to guard the child. Some of the objects and fears described in the first three chapters were put into artistic representations, often as a means of sympathetic magic by which the patron held, wore, or buried a symbolic representation of the being she wished to avoid during pregnancy. Other times figurines functioned as protective measures, warding off anything or anyone that might harm the pregnancy or child. This chapter explores many different physical objects used to protect the fetus, the infant, and the small child. The items examined fall into three broad categories: basic images and figures, objects with images and words, and objects with a quotidian use as well as a magicoreligious use.

4.1. Warding Off Dangers during Pregnancy

As mentioned in the first chapter, the Hebrew Bible does not provide an in-depth description of what occurs inside the womb during pregnancy.

---

1. Sarah Graham, "Hormone Found Linked to Mother's Protective Instincts," 2 August 2004, Scientific American, https://tinyurl.com/SBL1729d; S. C. Gammie, A. Negron, S. M. Newman, and J. S. Rhodes, "Corticotrophin-Releasing Factor Inhibits Maternal Aggression in Mice," *Behavioral Neuroscience* 118 (2004): 805–14.

Texts such as Ps 139:13–14 recognize YHWH's hand in conception and pregnancy, while others, such as Ps 35 or Ps 57 praise God as delivering the individual from great danger. Yet, there are no biblical texts that reference YHWH protecting the fetus from harm it might endure in the face of nefarious demons.[2] Nevertheless, as the adage goes, absence of evidence is not evidence of absence. Indeed, when the archaeological record is consulted, evidence of a belief in demonic forces harmful to pregnancies is found in ancient Israel and throughout the ancient Near East.

4.1.1. Pazuzu

During pregnancy, the demon Pazuzu was thought to attack the fetus. Women wore necklaces with his image as means of sympathetic magic used to ward off his attacks.[3] The demon is generally depicted with grotesque features and a large canine or leonine head, from which oversized eyes and horns protrude. The head is often two-faced, like the Greek god Janus, who is the guardian of gates, doors, beginnings, and transitions. Most amulets only depict his head (fig. 4.1). The two illustrations in figure 4.1 show the variation these amulets took.[4] Both amulets date to the same time period (ca. 800–600 BCE) and are made of bronze. The image on the left from Beth Shean is more stylized and human looking. On the other hand, the image on the right from Iraq is more feline in its detail. Figure 4.2 is based on a Neo-Assyrian amulet and shows Pazuzu's entire body, which is scorpion-like, with feathered wings and legs.[5] Amulets and other

---

2. It is possible that Jer 1:4–5 implies a world wherein danger could befall a pregnant woman. The lack of information in the danger-to-pregnant-woman category is not entirely surprising given the ideology and monotheistic white-washing of Israelite religion. Rainer Albertz, "Family Religion in Ancient Israel and Its Surroundings," in *Household and Family Religion in Antiquity*, ed. John P. Bodel and Saul M. Olyan (Oxford: Wiley-Blackwell, 2012), 89–93.

3. Traditional scholarship asserts the danger was from Pazuzu, but new scholarship assigns the danger to Lamaštu. Erle Lichty, "Demons and Population Control," *Expedition* (1971): 23.

4. The amulet on the left is housed in the Israel Museum (Registration number IAA 2009-926). The feline looking amulet, housed at the British Museum, comes from northern Iraq (Registration number 132964).

5. The piece from Iraq dates ca. 800–600 BCE. It is housed at the University of Chicago (Registration Number A25413).

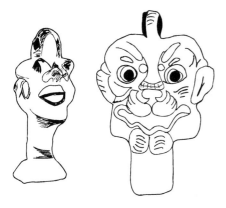 

Fig. 4.2. Pazuzu heads, Beth Shean, Iron   Fig. 4.2. Pazuzu full figure, Iraq, Neo-
Age II and northern Iraq, Neo-Assyrian.   Assyrian.

images of Pazuzu are found throughout Mesopotamia from the eighth to sixth century BCE.[6]

The demon figure also made his way to ancient Israel. Excavations at Beth Shean, Megiddo, and Horvat Qitmit all uncovered representations that were meant to be worn. The pendants from these sites belong to an Iron Age II context, corresponding to the influx of Assyrian and Babylonian culture into the land of Israel. Whether these were Mesopotamian women living in Israelite towns or Israelite women utilizing a foreign practice is difficult to determine. What is clear is that during the Iron Age II, the threat from Pazuzu was considered real and measures were taken to repel him.

4.1.2. Twin Pregnancy

The figurine depicted in figure 4.3 comes from Kibbutz Revadim, near the Philistine city of Tel Miqne/Ekron.[7] Its style belongs to that of the plaque figurines, familiar during the Late Bronze II–Iron Age. This particular piece dates to the mid-thirteenth century BCE. The woman is

---

6. Tal Oren, "An Amulet of the Demon Pazuzu," in *From the Late Bronze Age IIB to the Medieval Period*, vol. 1 of *Excavations at Tel Beth-Shean 1989–1996*, ed. Amihai Mazar (Jerusalem: Israel Exploration Society, 2006), 517–19; Ignacio Márquez Rowe, "Ceramic Stamp-Seal Amulets in the Shape of the Head of Pazuzu," *Iraq* 71 (2009): 151–55; Uri Gabbay, "A Collection of Pazuzu Objects in Jerusalem," *RA* 95 (2001): 149–51.

7. Margalith, "New Type of Ashera-Figurine?," *VT* 44 (1994): 109–10.

a nude female with long locks of hair, curling outwards at their ends and near her protruding navel.… She wears a closed crescent-shaped pendant on her neck, three bracelets on each wrist, and her hands hold open the deeply cut vagina above which is a ridge, presumably representing the pubic hair. Two nude babies with uplifted arms are accommodated in the area between the breasts, hair and arms, attached to the tips of the hair by a stroke. A tree and horned animals are modeled on each thigh.[8]

The symbols on her thighs are traditionally associated with life and fertility. Nakhai has interpreted the symbols (the bracelets, pendants on her neck, and designs on her thigh) as a unit meant to invoke divine protection for her delivery.[9] The crescent-shaped necklace is also worthy of note, as this item is frequently found on the top of figurines, both male and female, in the second millennium BCE. In some cases, the crescent is used as a symbol representing divinity.[10] If this is the case here, it argues for another link between the figurine and a goddess.

While the plaque-style figurine is quite common, the figurines almost never show the process of childbirth (parturition).[11] The method for making plaque figurines involves pressing wet clay into a mold. The front takes on the desired shape while the back of the figure is smoothed flat.[12] Four such parturition figurines have been discovered: the one pictured below from the vicinity of Tel Miqne/Ekron, one at nearby Tel Harassim/ Nahal Barkai, a third at Tel Aphek, and a fourth at Tel Burna.[13] Since parturition scenes are uncommon, one might wonder why these particular figures were made. Female plaque figurines as a corpus are understood as procreative talismans and usually depict the pregnant mother or a mother holding/nursing a single child.[14] The presence of two fetuses on these par-

---

8. P. Beck, "A New Type of Female Figurine," in *Insights through Images: Studies in Honor of Edith Porada*, ed. M. Kelly-Buccellati (Malibu, CA: Udena, 1986), 29–34.

9. Nakhai, "Mother-and-Child Figurines," 175.

10. Shmuel Givon, *The Fifth Season of Excavation at Tel Harasim (Nahal Barkai) 1994: Preliminary Report 5* [Hebrew] (Tel Aviv: Tel Aviv, 1995), 45.

11. Nakhai, "Mother-and-Child Figures," 175.

12. Raz Kletter, *The Judean Pillar Figurines and the Archaeology of Asherah*, BARIS 636 (Oxford: Tempus Reparatum, 1996), 50–52.

13. For an overview of each plaque and related bibliography, see Casey Sharp, Chris McKinny, and Itzahq Shai, "The Late Bronze Age Figurines from Tel Burna," *Strata* 33 (2015): 63–65.

14. Moorey, *Idols of the People*, 26; Nakhai, "Mother-and-Child Figurines," 170.

turition plaques is significant, and I would argue they can be understood as depicting a woman about to give birth to twins.[15] It goes without saying that birth is dangerous, but the birth of twins is even more dangerous. As discussed in chapter 2, twins historically have had a lower birth weight and are often premature. Chances of obstetric complications are also higher, leading to a mortality rate for twins that is four times that of a single birth.[16] If we understand the double fetus to represent the birth of twins, then the special nature of this figurine might go hand-in-hand with the special status and extra prayers needed for twin births.

If P. R. S. Moorey's conclusions are correct that plaque figurines in general act as protective talismans, this would mean that the figurines of pregnant women and women about to give birth would be made prior to the birth, for the women using them would be praying for protection during the pregnancy and birthing process. The creation and use of a plaque figurine showing two fetuses suggests that the women using

Fig. 4.3. "Twin Pregnancy" plaque, Revadim, Israel, mid-thirteenth century BCE.

them knew they were giving birth to twins ahead of time. Like Rebekah, the women might have experienced unusual discomfort during pregnancy, suggesting they were carrying twins, and used a plaque like the one seen in figure 4.3 to pray to a goddess, or to hold for good luck.

---

15. The identification of the figures on the plaque is debated. While Beck does not understand the female to be a goddess, Margalith identifies her as the goddess Athirat, the Great Lady, and the little babies as twins. He bases this on the Ugaritic myth that the divine twins Shahar and Shalem were nursed by The Great Lady (Margalith, "New of Ashera-Figurine Type," 109–15).

16. Jeroen Smits and Christiaan Monden, "Twinning across the Developing World," *PLOS ONE* (2011): http://doi.org/10.1371/journal.pone.0025239.

4.2. Warding Off Dangers during Childbirth

Chapter 2 discusses the practicalities of the birth process in depth. As was alluded to, some of the items in the birthing room were thought to aid in creating a safe place for the mother to give birth. These ritual items also had magical properties. Since extant realia is not available for ancient Israel, a feel for how ritual items might have been used, as well as what some looked like, can best be illustrated through the following examples used by Egyptians during and after the birthing process.[17]

4.2.1. The Egyptian Birthing Kit

The Egyptian birthing kit consisted of bricks, wands, and rods.[18] Each of these objects were decorated with figures that gave the objects an apotropaic, protective function. At the Middle Kingdom site of South Abydos, a brick with paintings on all sides related to birth was discovered.[19] Figure 4.4 shows the scene on the top of the brick depicting a woman sitting in a throne, holding a child. A woman kneels in front of her, while another woman stands behind her, supporting her shoulder. Flanking either side of the scene are two standards. The poles look like tree trunks and the tops have the heads of the goddess Hathor.[20] All the women in the scene look identical, with blue hair and white dresses.[21] The blue hair on the women

17. For an in-depth examination of the Egyptian birthing process, see Erika Feucht, *Das Kind im Alten Ägypten* (Frankfurt: Campus, 1995); Janssen and Janssen, *Growing Up in Ancient Egypt*, 1–13.

18. Josef Wegner, "A Decorated Birth-Brick from South Abydos: New Evidence on Childbirth and Birth Magic in the Middle Kingdom," in *Archaism and Innovation: Studies in the Culture of Middle Kingdom Egypt*, ed. David P. Silverman, William Kelley Simpson, and Josef William Wegner (New Haven: Yale University Press, 2009), 473–75.

19. Wegner, "Decorated Birth-Brick from South Abydos," 447–96.

20. Wegner suggests the tree trunks on the Hathor standards are meant to be sycamore trees, which are found linked to Hathor in the myth concerning the rebirth of Re (Wegner, "Decorated Birth-Brick from South Abydos," 460).

21. The colors blue and white also appear in the ethnographic literature. Reports from Arab Palestine noted that during delivery the mother wore a special blue dress, which was left ungirded. She also wore a white kerchief covering her head (Granqvist, *Birth and Childhood among the Arabs*, 68). While the similarity in colors is interesting, the literature does not explain whether the colors signified divinity or purity/newness like in the Egyptian corpus.

Fig. 4.4. Egyptian birth brick close-up, South Abydos, Thirteenth Dynasty.

signifies divinity, as does the throne the mother is sitting upon. The excavators identify this scene as a visual spell meant to invoke the presence of the goddess of childbirth, Hathor.[22] Various Egyptian spells from the Late Period support the idea that Hathor's presence was requested at the birth. "Rejoicing, rejoicing in heaven, birth giving is accelerated. Come to me Hathor my lady in my pavilion, in my happy hour."[23]

Due to poor preservation, only the bottom half of the figures on the sides of the brick are preserved (fig. 4.5). Despite missing the top of most of the figures, many figures are recognizable from parallels found on birth wands. The most complete figure is a striding wildcat. Other reconstructed figures include a nude goddess holding two snake standards. She conforms to the Mistress of the Animals iconography, a goddess type found throughout the ancient Near East, known as Anath, Qudshu, Astarte, and Ishtar-Inanna. Another image is an upright leonine figure, perhaps a female manifestation of the god Bes.[24] The presence of these figures along with the birth scene provides the brick with its apotropaic function.

The brick could have multiple uses, the most obvious of which would be as a part of the childbirth process.[25] Squatting over magically imbued bricks stacked on top of one another, the woman would find physical, if

---

22. Wegner, "Decorated Birth-Brick from South Abydos," 456–58.

23. Joris Borghouts, *Ancient Egyptian Magical Texts* (Leiden: Brill, 1978), 39–40, no 62.

24. Wegner, "Decorated Birth-Brick from South Abydos," 463–71.

25. Wegner, "Decorated Birth-Brick from South Abydos," 471–80.

Fig. 4.5. Egyptian birth brick, South Abydos, Thirteenth Dynasty.

not psychological support (if she believed the visual spells were at work) during the birth. Birth bricks were called *meskhenet*, which is also the name of a female deity often depicted with a human body and a brick atop her head.[26] Papyrus Westcar tells the story of princess Rudjedet and references placing the newborn on a brick during postpartum rituals. The excavators of the Abydos brick note that the dimensions of the extant brick are 35 x 17 cm, big enough to support either a baby in the fetal position or a swaddled baby.[27] Finally, there is the possibility that the brick might have simply served as an amulet, such that it provided much needed protection for the mother and newborn with its very presence.

Of the birthing-kit objects, wands are perhaps the most well studied, and a number of them have been discovered in good condition.[28] Many wands were found in burial contexts, pointing to the connection between death and the Egyptian belief in rebirth. All the wands have the same boomerang-type shape with one flat side and one convex side. Once considered magical knives, these objects are now understood as wands as they have no sharp edge. Etched into the face of the wand are pictures of the deities Bes and Taweret. The choice in deities is important as the Egyptian Bes was known as the protector of the newborn child,

---

26. Wegner, "Decorated Birth-Brick from South Abydos," 471. McGeough notes that *meskhenet* can also refer to the birth stool (McGeough, "Birth Bricks, Potter's Wheels," 314).

27. Wegner, "Decorated Birth-Brick from South Abydos," 478.

28. Around 150 wands dating to the Middle Kingdom and Second Intermediate Period have been discovered (Janssen and Janssen, *Growing Up in Ancient Egypt*, 9).

Fig. 4.6. Egyptian birth wand, Egypt, Twelfth–Thirteenth Dynasty.

and Taweret attended women in childbirth.[29] Accompanying the god and goddess are various kinds of animals. Based on the figures alone, the wands can be understood as having a connection to childbirth. The images on the wands means they were likely used in a ritual manner and possibly placed on the stomach of the laboring mother, or on the infant. Rough wear at a single end of the wands also suggests they might have been used to draw protective circles around the mother during the birth process, a practice also found in magical contexts of other parts of the ancient Near East.[30]

Many intact wands come from burials of the late Middle Kingdom. Figure 4.6 shows signs of wear on one tip, suggesting that it was used over a period of time before being placed in the tomb.[31] The wand is decorated on one side with the figures of protective deities most of whom carry knives to ward off evil spirits. Some wands also include inscriptions or

29. See below.

30. See the story of Honi the circle maker and circles drawn during the Maqlu ritual in Mesopotamia, as well as other examples from ancient Egypt. See b. Ta'an. 19a; Maqlû IX.95–98, 148–149; Tzvi Abusch, "Mesopotamian Anti-Witchcraft Literature: Texts and Studies Part I; The Nature of Maqlû: Its Character, Divisions, and Calendrical Setting," *JNES* 33 (1974): 253–54; Janssen and Janssen, *Growing Up in Ancient Egypt*, 9; Wegner, "Decorated Birth-Brick from South Abydos," 480–85.

31. This wand from the Middle Kingdom dates to the Twelfth to Thirteenth Dynasties (ca. 1981–1640 BCE). It is made of hippopotamus ivory and measures 5.2 cm in height by 34 cm in width. Metropolitan Museum of Art, "Atropaic Wand," http://www.metmuseum.org/art/collection/search/545740.

labels. Sayings such as: "protection by night and day," and "words spoken by these protective figures; we have come to spread protection over this child," support the conclusion that the wands were imbued with an apotropaic function.[32]

Another wand from the Metropolitan Museum of Art includes the inscription: "Recitation by the many protectors: We have come that we may extend our protection around the healthy child Minhotep, alive, sound, and healthy, born of the noblewoman Sitsobek, alive, sound, and healthy."[33] Notably, this wand includes the name of the mother and child, suggesting some measure of personalization. While dulled edges on some of the wands could suggest reuse, names suggest some wands were made for a specific birth. Names also present an interesting question as to when the wand was made and at what point the inscription was added. If the wands were meant to protect the mother during childbirth, then unless the child was named before birth, it seems that the inscription was added after the birth. If, on the other hand, the entire wand was made at one time, then it must have been made after the birth. In either case, the named wands point to a postbirth ritual utilizing the wand. Other wands exhibit an attempt at ancient repairs, again attesting to the importance the Egyptians placed on the wands.[34]

4.2.2. Bes

The figure of Bes is well known throughout the Levant.[35] A minor Egyptian deity, Bes was known from the Middle Bronze Age on as the protector of pregnant women, young children, and children's beds. The figure strikes a rather monstrous, yet jovial pose. His legs and arms are often akimbo, and he has a characteristic beard and scowl on his face.[36] Bes amulets are

---

32. Janssen and Janssen, *Growing Up in Ancient Israel*, 9. See also objects 15.3.197 and 30.8.218 in the Metropolitan Museum of Art.

33. Metropolitan Museum of Art 08.200.19.

34. BM EA24426.

35. Within Egypt, Bes seems to have been "an avatar of an ancient deity called Aha," who protected children. Bes's name is also associated with a premature child, and the word for "protect, or guard." Bes appears from the New Kingdom through the Ptolamic period. Michel Malaise, "Bes," *OEAE* 2:179–81.

36. For an overview of the iconographic progression of Bes, see Brian B. Schmidt, *The Materiality of Power: Explorations in the Social History of Early Israelite Magic*, FAT 105 (Tübingen: Mohr Siebeck, 2016), 87–89.

Fig. 4.7. Bes figures: (left) Egypt, thirteenth century BCE; (right) Tel Dan, third–second century BCE; (bottom) Gezer, tenth century BCE.

peppered throughout the Levant, especially in the Iron Age II period and into the Persian period, at major sites like Tell el-Far'ah [South], Lachish, Gezer, Tell en-Nasbeh, Beth Shean, Megiddo, Tell Mevorakh, and Tell el-Hesi.[37] He continues as a popular deity into the Greco-Roman period. Discoveries of molds used to make the figurines and amulets suggest that these Bes objects were locally made rather than imported from Egypt. Figure 4.7 shows three renditions of Bes. The top left shows how he appears in Egyptian scarabs from the thirteenth century BCE. The figure on the right, now housed in the Skirball Museum of Biblical Archaeology in Jerusalem, was found at Tel Dan (third–second centuries BCE). The bottom image is based on a faience amulet from the tenth century BCE levels at Gezer. Each of these images attests to Bes's long standing and wide-reaching popularity.

The tombs of Ketef Hinnom, best known for the two silver scrolls found within, also contained a Phoenician Bes head and a faience amulet

---

37. For further locations and references, see Othmar Keel and Christopher Uehlinger, *Gods, Goddesses, and Images of God in Ancient Israel* (Edinburgh: T&T Clark, 1998), 220–221; W. J. Bennett, Michael David Coogan, and Jeffrey A. Blakely, eds., *Tell el-Hesi: The Persian Period (Stratum V)*, ASOR 3 (Winona Lake, IN: Eisenbrauns, 1989), 216. Bes also appears in the personal name *qdbš*, "Bes has created" (Keel and Uehlinger, *Gods, Goddesses, and Images*, 205).

of the Egyptian goddess Bastet.[38] The collection seems to suggest that Bes was worshiped by the same people who venerated YHWH. Ketef Hinnom is not the only place where YHWH is seen along with Bes and Beset. The Kuntillet Ajrud pithos A contains an inscription to YHWH and Asherah, along with drawings of Bes-like figures. Mixing worship of YHWH and non-YHWHistic deities is the sort of thing that the prophets Jeremiah and Ezekiel rail against (Jer 7, 44; Ezek 7:20). Yet, as many excavations have demonstrated, an Israel who worshiped only YHWH was more of a prophetic ideal. In examining the multiple instances where an inscription is accompanied by an image, Brian Schmidt argues that some Israelites may have gone one step further, converging YHWH/Asherah with Bes/Beset. "The one pair was conveyed in writing (YHWH and Asherah) and the other portrayed in image (Bes and Beset) in order singularly to harness and enhance their combined international, regional, and local apotropaic powers."[39] Bes remained a popular protective figure for Israelites through the end of the Iron Age.

4.3. Postpartum Dangers

4.3.1. Kūbu

Despite all of these protective measures, miscarriage did occur, and stillborn babies were born. As mentioned in §1.2, the biblical literature calls a miscarriage a נפל (nēpel) "something that has fallen [out]," but does not associate any supernatural powers with it. In Mesopotamian art, however, we find a demon associated with the netherworld called the kūbu (fig. 4.8). While the word kūbu does not mean "stillborn" per se, depending on the context, it can be translated as such. Associated with the earth and the netherworld, these pitiful beings are both harmful and helpful to the living. One can suffer from the "hand of the kūbu," but also reap the benefits of a peaceful harvest given by them.[40] To draw a modern analogy, the kūbu look and act a bit like the figure of Gollum from the Lord of the Rings trilogy.

---

38. On the scrolls as apotropaic see: Jeremy Smoak, "Amuletic Inscriptions and the Background of YWHW as Guardian and Protector in Psalm 12," *VT* 60 (2010): 421–32. For information on the Bes and Bastet pieces see Keel and Uehlinger, *Gods, Goddesses, and Images*, 366, and Gabriel Barkay, *Ketef Hinnom: A Treasure Facing Jerusalem's Walls*, Israel Museum Catalogue 274 (Jerusalem: Israel Museum, 1986), 7.

39. Schmidt, *Materiality of Power*, 204–5.

40. Stol, *Birth in Babylonia and the Bible*, 20 n. 34.

The *kūbu* beings are represented in terracotta as emaciated, shrunken looking
figures, or "like the foetus in the womb
in an advanced stage of development."[41]
They are crouched in the fetal position,
their elbows resting on their knees, with
their hands on the side of their heads.
Whatever powers the *kūbu* might have,
its form can only be explained as a representation of a fetus, close to full term.
The link between the figures and birth is
further strengthened by a plaque found at
Kish, a city 12 km east of Babylon.[42] Created sometime between 1850–1650 BCE,
the plaque depicts the birth goddess Ninhursag nursing a child. Flanking her on
either side are two *kūbu* figures.

Fig. 4.8. *Kūbu* figures, Iraq,
Larsa (?).

Two other plaques were found at Eshnunna and date to the Larsa period
(ca. 1868–1699 BCE).[43] These two plaques show a complete scene with a
goddess in the center surrounded by five figures. Like the Kish plaque, two
emaciated figures flank the goddess's feet. The goddess cradles a child in her
arms, while two floating heads peak out behind each of her shoulders. On
either side of the heads, there is an elongated horseshoe shape that curls at
each end.[44] The goddess wears atypical headgear; instead of the customary
horned crown signifying divinity, she wears a shrine. Based on the crown
and other symbols on the plaque, the goddess is identified as the Great
Mother Goddess, Ninhursag. While one can easily identify the beings on
the bottom as *kūbu* figures, identifying the other three heads is harder. The
two beings flanking the goddess could be twins, and she could be nursing
the baby she is holding. An early interpretation sees the five as "potential
human beings who have not yet materialized and whom the goddess had
power to call into corporate existence."[45] While possible, I think one might

41. Stol, *Birth in Babylonia and the Bible*, 29.

42. P. R. S. Moorey, "Terracotta Plaques from Kish and Hursagkalama," *Iraq* 37
(1975): 87; and pl. XXe.

43. One plaque is housed in the Iraq Museum and the other is in the Louvre.

44. For a discussion of the horseshoe shapes on the plaques see, §2.3.3.

45. E. Douglas Van Buren, "A Clay Relief in the Iraq Museum," *AfO* 9 (1933–

also understand the plaque to represent an ancient understanding of fetal development with the two heads at the top representing the fetus. Moving down the plaque, one sees two options: a viable birth represented by the baby cradled in the goddess's arms or the stillborn/ miscarried baby represented by the *kūbu* figures. While not much is known about the use of these plaques and figurines, based on their content and the locations in which they were found, it seems quite possible that they were used in home rituals as sympathetic magic to protect against untimely births. Interestingly, no "person" comparable to the *kūbu* is found in Levantine art.

The figure seen in figure 4.9 is unique. It was a gift to the Cincinnati Art Museum, and many have commented upon it. Noting the clear similarities to the *kūbu* figures seen throughout the ancient world, Edith Porada's investigation into the piece is the most thorough to date. She concludes that "the artist of the figurine in Cincinnati was the first to give form to the demon."[46] The close detail given to the body, its posture, and the pedestal it sits upon elicits a feeling of hopelessness when looking at it. This is a form that no parent would wish a child to have.

Fig. 4.9. *Kūbu* bronze figure, provenance unknown.

4.4. Protecting Newborn Babies

Parents knew infants were susceptible to diseases and other potentially lethal maladies. One such particularly frightening occurrence is known today as SIDS: Sudden Infant Death Syndrome. This is the name given to deaths that occur at night, usually between midnight and nine in the morning. It occurs in babies under one year old, with infants between two

---

1934): 170. She suggests that the doubling of all the objects on the right and left was done for aesthetic purposes as ancient art values symmetry.

46. Edith Porada, "An Emaciated Male Figure of Bronze in the Cincinnati Art Museum," in *Studies Presented to A. Leo Oppenheim*, ed. Robert D. Biggs and John A. Brinkman (Chicago: University of Chicago Press, 1964), 166.

to four months of age at the highest risk.[47] Other factors contributing to SIDS include sleeping in a room that is too hot, bed sharing, exposure to tobacco smoke, and putting a baby to sleep on his or her stomach.[48] Recent studies have also shown that the risk of SIDS is highest in young mothers.[49] All these risk factors were present in the ancient Near East. Women were encouraged to marry young and have children early and often. Families slept together on mats in the same room.[50] As the advent of the "Back to Sleep" campaign of the 1990s demonstrates, infants historically slept on their stomachs. The odds were not stacked in favor of infants in the ancient Near East. For societies like those of the ancient Near East who prized male heirs, the toll of SIDS was particularly damaging; 51–60 percent of all infants who die of SIDS are male.[51]

Understandably, ancient Israelites felt trepidation concerning sleep. For example, Ps 4:9 (8) reassures the sleeper: "Safe and sound, I lie down and sleep, for you alone, O Lord keep me secure" (JPS). It was a real possibility that this night might be the last night. We still find residual notions

---

47. Infants at this age do not have a fully mature self-waking mechanism and therefore physically cannot waken themselves or turn over if they feel something obstructing their airway. See Hannah Kinney and Bradley Thach, "The Sudden Infant Death Syndrome," *New England Journal of Medicine* 361 (2009): 799–801; Rosemary Horne, Fern Hauck, and Rachel Moon, "Sudden Infant Death Syndrome and Advice for Safe Sleeping," *The BMJ*, 28 April 2015, https://doi.org/10.1136/bmj.h1989.

48. Kinney and Thach, "Sudden Infant Death Syndrome," 800; Horne, Hauck, and Moon, "Sudden Infant Death Syndrome"; Peter Blair et al., "Hazardous Co-sleeping Environments and Risk Factors Amenable to Change: Case-Control Study of SIDS in South West England," *The BMJ*, 13 October 2009, http://dx.doi.org/10.1136/bmj. b3666.

49. Frank Sullivan and Susan Barlow, "Review of Risk Factors for Sudden Infant Death Syndrome," *Paediatric and Perinatal Epidemiology* 15 (2001): 146.

50. Non-Western bed sharing differs from Western bed sharing. Whereas Western cultures generally sleep on raised mattresses with pillows and comfortable bedding, many non-Western cultures sleep without pillows on mats placed on hard floors. A study undertaken to determine if non-Western bed sharing decreased SIDS found that there was no difference in the level of SIDS. The study used breastfed infants whose mothers did not smoke or drink as a control variable; the only difference was the method of bed sharing. E. A. Nelson et al., "International Child Care Practices Study: Infant Sleeping Environment," *Early Human Development* 62 (2001): 43–55. While the difference in bed-sharing styles is important to consider, other variables contributing to SIDS were still present in the ancient Near East.

51. Sullivan and Barlow, "Review of Risk Factors," 147.

of a nighttime attack (like SIDS) in simple childhood prayers: "Now I lay me down to sleep, the Lord I pray my soul keep. Guide me through the starry night, wake me to the morning light. If I die before I wake, I pray the Lord my soul to take."

For those in the ancient world, infant and childhood death in the night was thought to be caused by a demon or a demoness. Nighttime jinn came to attack not just young children, but anyone who was weak and vulnerable.[52] The most famous nighttime demon in the Hebrew Bible is the destroyer of Exod 12:23 who does YHWH's bidding, striking down firstborn while they slept.[53] There were two quite logical ways to avoid such nighttime visitors: guarding one's house and not drawing attention to the house.

Means of guarding the house could take many different forms. For example, one might turn to apotropaic, magicoreligious rituals meant to protect the household. In the case of the destroyer, sacrificial blood smeared on the doorpost protects the house and stops the destroyer from entering (Exod 12:23).[54] Jealous of a new baby, neighbors or villagers might invoke the evil eye to harm the infant.[55] Positive eye charms, such as the *wedjat* eye, served as a symbol of protection for those in the household.

---

52. Granqvist makes reference to the jinn and demons that live under the earth who are always ready to attack. Arabs are incredibly careful not to bother them and are constantly uttering a protective formula "God's name over thee!" To this end, mothers say the name of God every time they interact with their child (Granqvist, *Child Problems among the Arabs*, 101–4).

53. The same destroyer makes another appearance in 1 Chr 21:15–20, where he seeks to kill the inhabitants of Jerusalem. Destroying deities are found throughout the ancient Near East such as Erra in Mesopotamia, and Reshep in Ugarit and Northwest Semitic areas. See Samuel A. Meier, "Destroyer משחית," *DDD*, 242.

54. Many scholars have commented on the Passover ritual as a protective ritual brought to Israel by semi-nomadic shepherds from Mesopotamia: Leonhard Rost, "Weidewechsel und altisraelischer Festkalender," *ZDPV* 66 (1943): 205–15; Noth, *Exodus*; Childs, *Exodus*. Recently, Thomas Schneider has presented the possibility that the Israelite ritual drew upon well-known Egyptian protection rituals ("God's Infanticide in the Night of Passover: Exodus 12 in the Light of Egyptian Rituals," in *Not Sparing the Child: Human Sacrifice in the Ancient World and Beyond*, ed. Vita Daphna Arbel, Paul C. Burns, J. R. C. Cousland, Richard Menkis, and Dietmar Neufeld [London: T&T Clark, 2016], 52–76).

55. The evil eye is understood to come from a place of envy. For the barren mother or childless couple next door, the presence of a baby nearby brings jealous feelings to the surface. If the baby is crying and drawing attention to himself, this resentment is

Fig. 4.10. Faience *wedjat*-eye amulet, Egypt, Third Intermediate Period, ca. 1090–900 BCE.

Small representations of the *wedjat* eye were found at many sites in ancient Israel during the Iron Age, including Jericho, Gezer, Gerar, and Beersheba.[56] Figure 4.10 is an example of this ubiquitous symbol from the Third Intermediate Period in Egypt (ca. 1090–900 BCE). Guard dogs, albeit of the miniature clay variety, were another way to repel unwanted visitors. Various sites in Mesopotamia had small figurines of dogs buried under the door or threshold of houses (fig. 4.11).[57] The dogs were inscribed with names in order to drive away the evil: "Don't hesitate, bark!"; "Don't hesitate, bite!"; "Dispatch him!"; "His bark is loud"; "The one who drives away the *asakku-demon*"; "The one who repulses evil"; and so forth.[58] Little dogs were also found in ancient Israel during the early excavations of Gerar.[59] These dogs belong to a period of "Eastern influence" (i.e., Mesopo-

---

magnified. See Fiona Bowie, *The Anthropology of Religion* (Oxford: Blackwell, 2000), 235–40.

56. W. M. Flinders Petrie, *Gerar* (Jerusalem: British School of Archaeology, 1928), 12, 20, pl. XLV; Kathleen Kenyon, *Excavations at Jericho II: The Tombs Excavated in 1955–58* (Jerusalem: British School of Archaeology, 1965), 513; William Dever. H. Darrell Lance, and Reuben G. Bullard, *Gezer IV: The 1969–71 Seasons in Field VI, the "Acropolis"* (Jerusalem: Keter Press, 1986), 4.2: pl. 56; Deborah Sweeney, "Egyptian Objects," in *Beer-Sheba III: The Early Iron IIA Enclosed Settlement and the Late Iron IIA=Iron IIB Cities*, ed. Ze'ev Herzog and Lily Singer-Avitz (Winona Lake, IN: Eisenbrauns, 2016), 1063–64. Meyers discusses the use of the *wedjat* eye as a symbol of protection and not a belief in Horus (Meyers, *Rediscovering Eve*, 155).

57. (British Museum) Nimrud, Nineveh, Kish, AN1924.304, AN 1924.303, AN1924.302.

58. Lichty, "Demons and Population Control," 24.

59. Petrie, *Gerar*, 18 and pl. 38:3–7.

Fig. 4.11. Guard dog, Kish, Neo-Babylonian.

tamian) and are listed with other small clay animals found at the site. While not much is said about the location of the Gerar dogs, it is tantalizing to think that this practice of using "guard dogs" made its way to ancient Israel.

Fear of the evil eye can still be seen today and is prevalent in reports from early twentieth-century Palestine. "The belief in the eye greatly dominates the imagination of the people, plays a part in daily life, and has a paralyzing effect on them."[60] The evil eye was given as the cause of death for two-thirds of all deaths in the Palestinian village of Artas. Fortunately, the power of the eye can be averted by drawing its first glance to something other than the intended victim. New things, such as newborn babies, are particularly susceptible to the eye. Shiny amulets are thus fastened to the infant to attract the first glance of the eye. Blue eyes are considered very dangerous, and sympathetic magic explains the reason blue dots adorn a baby's forehead and blue beads are strung around the necks. The evil eye is also attracted to beauty; therefore, one of the simplest ways to avoid the eye was to keep a newborn child dirty. This superstition explains why infants are not bathed with water at birth, but rather rubbed with salt and oil—one would not want the infant looking too beautiful. Along the same lines, a mother must not dote too much over her baby lest she attract the attention of the eye.[61]

---

60. Granqvist, *Childhood Problems among the Arabs*, 107–11, esp. 108.

61. As to this last point, one account goes so far as to state "So kann z. B. der bewundernde Blick der Mutter ihrem Kinde Schaden bringen; deshalb soll man ein

Since harm came in the dark, lighting the room where the child slept was another measure parents could take to ward off demons. Pointing to various biblical texts, Meyers notes that light was understood as divine protection, the earthly form of which was produced by clay lamps.[62] While lamps have been discovered scattered throughout many sites and are not specifically limited to sleeping areas, this does not negate the idea that light provided protection at night. Lamps were portable and moved along with an individual. Ethnographic studies from Baghdad in the mid-twentieth century show that a light next to the mother and child is kept burning through the night to ward off the evil *chesba* spirit.[63] The correlation between lamps and divine protection is also supported by the presence of many lamps within tombs throughout ancient Israel.[64] Lamps seem to have been used for both practical and protective reasons during the funerary rites as well as the deceased's journey in the afterlife. Mesopotamian texts take the connection between light and divinity one step further. In some Old Babylonian texts, the lamp itself is understood as the embodiment of the god Nusku or Girra, whereas some texts from Nuzi refer to the lamp itself as divine, placing the determinative for god before the word for lamp (${}^{d}nuru$).[65]

Another means of guarding the sleeping chambers is to call upon a protective deity to counteract the malevolent forces trying to attack the

---

schlafendes Kind nich bewundern oder küssen" (Lydia Einsler, *Mosaik aus dem heiligen Lande: Schilderung einiger Gebräuche und Anschauungen der arabischen Bevölkerung Palästinas* [Jerusalem: Druck des Syrischen Waisenhauses, 1898], 24).

62. Job 29:4 and Prov 6:20–23 speak to this understanding (Meyers, *Rediscovering Eve*, 154).

63. Other cultures, such as Albanian Muslims and Moroccan Berbers, also keep a child's room lit. Talmudic and medieval Jewish sources report the use of light to fight off demons seeking to harm newborns (Meyers, *Rediscovering Eve*, 154–55). The Baghdad accounts also state that additional protection is provided by a dagger or knife placed beneath the pillow or bedding of both the mother and child (Drower "Women and Taboo in Iraq," 110).

64. Lamps with soot showing evidence of use were found inter alia in the tombs of Ketef Hinnom, Lahav, and Tell 'Eitun. Barkay, *Ketef Hinnom*, 28; David Ussishkin, "Tombs from the Israelite Period at Tel 'Eton," *TA* 1 (1974): 109–27, esp. 125; Oded Borowski, *Lahav III: The Iron Age II Cemetery at Tell Halif (Site 72)* (Winona Lake, IN: Eisenbrauns, 2013), 8.

65. Karel van der Toorn, "Family Religion in Second Millennium west Asia (Mesopotamia, Emar, Nuzi)," in Bodel and Olyan, *Household and Family Religion in Antiquity*, 27.

infant. The various psalms attesting to YHWH's protective power also fall into the category of guarding the house. Understood in this light, the statement in Ps 121:4, "See, the guardian of Israel neither slumbers nor sleeps" (JPS), becomes a powerful mantra. In addition to lamps and protective deities, a third kind of guardian is found via the cult of the ancestors. Maintaining the cult of the ancestors was an important job as the ancestors were thought to protect the inhabitants of the household, both living and unborn.[66] Vestiges of a cult of the ancestors has been identified in texts and archaeological remains from the first and second millennium BCE in ancient Israel, Mesopotamia, Ugarit, and Emar.[67] As will be seen, disturbing the ancestors was a dangerous prospect.

4.4.1. Lamaštu

Mesopotamians were very concerned with keeping the house quiet in order to both keep the nighttime demons away and to keep the household ancestors (or gods) happy and protecting the house. With respect to infants, their cries at night were thought to do two things. First, the cries drew the attention of the demoness Lamaštu, a figure with notable similarities to Lilith of Jewish lore (fig. 4.12).[68] This demoness has been described early on as having two heads and terrible claws (late third to early second

---

66. Dianne Bergant, "An Anthropological Approach to Biblical Interpretation: The Passover Supper In Exodus 12:1–20 as a Case Study," *Semeia* 67 (1994): 43–62; Brian B. Schmidt, *Israel's Beneficent Dead: Ancestor Cult and Necromancy in Ancient Israelite Religion and Tradition* (Tübingen: Mohr Siebeck, 1994); Elizabeth Bloch-Smith, *Judahite Burial Practices and Beliefs about the Dead*, JSOT Supp (Sheffield: Sheffield Academic, 1992); Naomi Steinberg, "Exodus 12 in Light of Ancestral Cult Practices," in *The Family in Life and in Death*, ed. Patricia Dutcher-Walls (New York: T&T Clark, 2009), 89–90.

67. van der Toorn, "Family Religion in Second Millennium West Asia," 25–27; Daniel Fleming, "The Integration of Household and Community Religion in Ancient Syria," in Bodel and Olyan, *Household and Family Religion in Antiquity*, 40–42; Theodore Lewis, "Family, Household, and Local Religion at Late Bronze Age Ugarit," in Bodel and Olyan, *Household and Family Religion in Antiquity*, 61; Albertz, "Family Religion," 99; Saul Olyan, "Family Religion in Israel and the Wider Levant of the First Millennium BCE," in Bodel and Olyan, *Household and Family Religion in Antiquity*, 119.

68. Figure 4.12 is taken from a bronze amulet dating to the Neo-Assyrian period. This amulet is shaped like a rectangle, with Pazuzu's head peeking over the top. Below his head are five registers of symbols, spirits, and a bedroom scene into which Lamaštu

Fig. 4.12. Lamaštu, northern Syria, Neo-Assyrian.

millennia BCE) and later on as the personification of evil, with a "lion's head, a furry or scaly animal's body with big human-like breasts, human hands, and big bird-of-prey feet."[69] Depictions of her are found in various amulets, which are thought to have been used apotropaically.[70] The daughter of the primordial gods Anu and Antu, Lamaštu was very likely an addition to the Mesopotamian pantheon and understood to have been around since the beginning of time. Her evil character caused her parents to kick her out of the heavens. Left to roam with the mortals, she snuck in through open windows or doors to suckle children with her own poisonous milk.[71] She was the reason babies died in their sleep. Lamaštu also attacked pregnant women, causing stillborn births and failed pregnancies. All in all, she was a force to be reckoned with. A series of incantations against this most wicked of demons has been found in areas spanning from Mesopotamia to Syria, a testament to her sphere of influence.[72]

has burst to do her evil. Pazuzu is chasing her out. For more on the piece, see Wiggermann, "Lamaštu," 236–49, esp. 244.

69. Walter Farber, *Lamaštu: An Edition of the Canonical Series of Lamaštu Incantations and Rituals and Related Texts from the Second and First Millennia B.C.*, Mesopotamian Civilizations 17 (Winona Lake, IN: Eisenbrauns, 2014), 3–4.

70. F. A. M. Wiggerman, "Lamaštu, Daughter of Anu, a Profile," in *Birth in Babylonia and the Bible, Its Mediterranean Setting*, ed. Martin Stol (Groningen: Styx, 2000), 217–52.

71. Wiggerman, "Lamaštu," 230; Farber, *Lamaštu*, 3.

72. Farber has compiled a full edition of these texts. See Farber, *Lamaštu*.

In addition to alerting Lamaštu, the infant's wailing could cause the ancestors to wake up and leave the house unprotected. To avoid this, parents turned to lullabies to help their newborns fall asleep and keep quiet.[73] A quiet, sleeping infant would then be protected by the ancestors. The following Old Babylonian lullaby comes from Tel Duweihes in southern Babylon.

> Little one, who dwelt in the house of darkness—
> Well, you are outside now, have seen the light of the sun.
> Why are you crying, why are you yelling?
>   Why didn't you cry in there?
> You have roused the god of the house, the *kusarikkum* has woken up:
> "Who roused me? Who startled me?"
> The little one has roused you, the little one has startled you!
> "As onto drinkers of wine, as onto tipplers,
>   may sleep fall on him!"[74]

Lullabies such as this express the exasperation of the exhausted new parent. The parent wishes the child would go to sleep and that the sleep would be as heavy as that of a person passed out drunk.[75] The infant's cries are grating on the nerves of a parent. The lullaby rhetorically asks why the infant is crying now when she is already outside the womb and has parental caretakers. Not only should the baby quiet down and sleep for the parent's sake, but she should be silent for her own sake as well. Her crying might wake the house god or her ancestor. Underlying this lullaby is the notion that the dead do not like to be awakened from the grave. First Samuel 28 offers a clear example of this. Saul asks the woman of Endor to raise up Samuel from the dead. Upon coming up Samuel's first grumpy words are: "Why have you disturbed me and brought me up?" (1 Sam

---

73. Lullabies, like most folk songs, were not often written down, as they belong to the corpus of oral literature. In a few cases, they were included in magicoreligious incantations. Identifying lullabies as actual lullabies and not original incantations is based on the pattern of the rhyme and rhythm and parallelisms, as well as the pool of motifs they draw from. Walter Farber, "Magic at the Cradle. Babylonian and Assyrian Lullabies," *Anthropos* 85 (1990): 139–48. See §3.4.

74. The translation comes from Walter Farber. He notes that the *kusarikkum* refers to a beneficent spirit who protects the house. The spirit has the head of a human and the body of a bison (Farber, "Magic at the Cradle," 140). A German translation can be found in Farber's earlier work (Farber, *Schlaf, Kindchen Schlaf!*, 161).

75. See the discussion in §3.4.

28:15 JPS). Samuel's subsequent words are not ones of comfort or protection, but ones of rebuke and doom. Waking up the ancestors or gods is not a good thing.[76] On the other hand, keeping the ancestors and household gods happy secures their protection over the family.

Demons who crept in the night were also found in Egypt. Papyrus Berlin 3027 contains many spells meant to kept mothers and children safe. Text C refers to a demon whose intents seem similar to that of Lamaštu.

> Run away, you who enters in darkness, who has a nose behind a face, who misses what he has come for. Run away, you who enters in darkness, whose nose is behind and face is reversed, who misses what he has come for. Did you come to kiss the child? I will not let you kiss it. Did you come to reassure? I will not let you give reassurance. Did you come to take it away? I will not let you take him away from me. I have made this potion against you from the X-herb that does ... from garlic (?)…. Who harms you, from honey—who is sweet against men, and terrible to the deceased, out of the ... of the X-fish, from the jawbone of—from the back of the perch.[77]

The recitation of words accompanied by a prophylactic potion is meant to keep the baby safe from the terrors that come in the night. The intended actions of the demon appear to be sickness and death, meant to take away the child from the parent; kissing the child might be similar to the "kiss of death," while "reassurance" might be a metaphor for quieting a crying baby, permanently.

Noisemakers such as the rattles mentioned as entertainment in the previous chapter have many uses, one of which was to drive off evil spirits.[78] Considering rattles are found in numerous excavations throughout ancient

---

76. Note that the dead Samuel is identified as an Elohim, literally, a god (1 Sam 28:13). Samuel and Saul have an adopted father-son relationship, thus making Samuel a quasi-ancestor. David Jobling, *I Samuel*, ed. David Cotter, Berit Olam (Collegeville, MN: Liturgical Press, 1998), 253–54.

77. Adolf Erman, *Zaubersprüche für Mutter und Kind: Aus dem Papyrus 3027 des Berliner Museums* (Berlin: Akademie der Wissenschaften, 1901), 12. Translation from the German is my own. Ritner identifies the demon as a "vampiric" male or female demon, and reads "garlic" as "onion" (Ritner, "Magic," 2:332).

78. Fox and Roskop, "Of Rattles and Rituals," 24. Rattles depicted on Late Aegean geometric vases (eighth to seventh century BCE), are also interpreted to be driving away evil spirits. Eva Rystedt, "Notes on the Rattle Scenes on Attic Geometric Pottery," *Opuscul a Atheniensia* 19 (1992): 125–33.

Israel, it might be that they, like the Mesopotamian lullabies, served a dual purpose of quieting infants for both the family's sake and the infant's sake. Rattles shaken by or for the infant quieted him, thus keeping not only him safe, but the family safe as well. Maybe ancient Israelites also sung lullabies or employed chants of a more ritualistic nature. Taking into consideration that much of the biblical text does not focus on the daily practices found in domestic religion, we should not discredit the possibility that lullabies existed and were perhaps used in combination with rattles.[79]

The demoness *Karine* (Palestine) or *Qārine* (Iraq) appears in the ethnographic literature. She seems to be the more recent appellation of Lamaštu. *Karine* is described as a female demon who cannot tolerate the happiness of a woman. The best way to steal a woman's happiness is to steal her joy, her children. To ward off *Karine*, mothers resorted to amulets, scare tactics, and trickery.[80] Amulets, by far the most common deterrent, consisted of written words of power invoking the divine name. One might also frighten the demoness with a pouch full of disgusting items (a crushed newborn dog or pig snout), or with the scent of aloe. For a boy baby, the afterbirth could be preserved in salt and then hung above the door. *Karine* would be attracted to the scent and tricked into attacking something other than the baby. A mother might even give her child a temporary name or change the child's name for the first few years of life. This way if *Karine* was searching for a specific person, she would not find him.[81] In one case, a mother even dressed her child as a girl (with long braids and a dress!) for seven years. Then, satisfied the danger had passed, the mother cut the boy's hair and let him wear boy clothing. A final, common method of warding off *Karine* was to intentionally keep the children dirty. Like the evil eye, *Karine*, in search of beautiful children, would pass over the unkempt children. Granqvist is careful to note that this last method of trickery might seem repulsive to the Western mind, but was meant as a means of welfare by those employing them.

---

79. Unlike Mesopotamia and other surrounding lands, excavations on the land of ancient Israel have not produced large quantities of written documents. Of those found, the majority are of a political nature, meaning that lullabies may have only existed as oral literature. On the nature of which texts get recorded, see Farber in n. 73 above.

80. The following examples and further discussion can be found in Granqvist, *Birth and Childhood among the Arabs*, 112–14.

81. Substituting a name seems to be done more for sons than daughters.

4.5. Summary

The world of ancient Israel was filled with dangerous spirits waiting to attack infants and children. A parent responded to this reality for both physiological and practical reasons. Flooded with the hormone CRH, a mother or mother-to-be felt a close bond with her baby, so much so that she would do anything to protect the new life. Practically, this meant taking measures to ward off attacks from the spirit world from pregnancy through the birth of the baby. These attacks were thought to either originate with the demons or to be spurred on by human action. While demons like Lamaštu or Lilith might seek to claim the baby for their own, women jealous of the mother's pregnancy or new child might prompt harm to the baby by casting the evil eye on it. In such cases women used sympathetic magic as a means of defense, wearing or hanging amulets of the *wadjet* or Lamaštu. Other forms of sympathetic magic included wearing amulets of Pazuzu or keeping plaques or representations of the *kūbu* figure nearby. Evil forces could also be repelled via apotropaic methods, such as drawing protective boundaries around the house or birthing room. Protective talismans, like the plaque with the twin embryos, offered another possible way for mothers to safeguard their pregnancies. Finally, amulets, drawings, or other visual representations of protective gods and goddesses, like Bes or Hathor could be used to invoke divine protection.

In addition to the more straightforward images and figures, we find two other classes of objects. The first includes objects with images and words, and the second, objects with both a practical use and a magicoreligious use. In the former category, we can place the miniature guard dogs buried under the thresholds whose very names were meant to frighten away unwanted visitors. Egyptian birth wands containing spells, and at times the name of the child, again attest to the power of the written and spoken word. While the lullabies and the later set of incantations which they become a part of are not necessarily found written on a visual representation of Lamaštu, one might imagine them being used in conjunction with an amulet of Lamaštu.

The last class of objects is perhaps the most intriguing because it emphasizes the fact that material culture is a complex set of symbols. This category includes items that are both easily identifiable as having a protective use, as well as items for which that function might be overlooked. The Egyptian birthing brick, for example, is readily associated with both a protective and practical use. A sturdy object, it might provide support for the mother during birth and act as a resting place for the infant after the birth. But the images of the deities on the brick give it another function, transforming it into a protective visual spell. Finally, the more quotidian objects, the lamps and rattles, highlight, first and foremost, their everyday use. Lamps provide light and rattles are noisemakers. But they also shield the newborn from harm; lamps embody divine protection and rattles keep the protective ancestors at peace.

In each of their different ways, the items in this chapter, used either alone or in conjunction with other protective items, provided the mother with a multitude of ways to harness her protective instincts. While the exact ritual or use of each object might be a bit murky to the contemporary reader, what should be clear is that the much-desired baby was not left to fend for itself.

The chapter highlights both the fact that parents desired to keep the child alive and that demons or jinn sought to kill them. The connecting link between the two is that children were desired by all, which emphasizes the importance of the child in the household. Chapter 5 continues to explore the value of the child as he or she is gendered into his or her place within the household economic system.

5
Gendering, Engendering, and Educating the Growing Child

Being a part of a society means knowing what actions are proper and expected. Children learn these actions through the process of enculturation and socialization. Passing on culture to the next generation has important implications for the continuity of a society. To study the transfer of culture to the child requires first understanding the world in which the child lives.[1] This world consists of the way a child relates to his environment and the people, adults and other children, with whom he interacts.[2] Manipulation of material culture also plays a part in socialization and in engendering the child.[3] Sometimes a child may actively embrace the socialization process by engaging in activities. Other times a child's actions may be passive, as he learns through observing and internalizing the lessons his parents impart. As will be seen in this chapter, uncovering a child's world and the way a child grows up in that world is directly related to the adult's world.

5.1. Gendering and Engendering

Within an archaeological discussion, the process of engendering means "to consider something with a focus on gender or gender issues."[4] The

---

1. Lillehammer, "Child Is Born," 89–90; Kristine Garroway, "Children and Religion in the Archaeological Record of Ancient Israel," *JANER* 17 (2017): 119–21.

2. Lillehammer, "Child is Born," 90.

3. Joanna S. Derevenski, "Engendering Children, Engendering Archaeology," in *Invisible People and Processes: Writing Gender and Childhood into European Archaeology*, ed. Jennie Moore and Eleanor Scott (London: Leicester University Press, 1997), 196.

4. Carol Meyers, "Engendering Syro-Palestinian Archaeology: Reasons and Resources," *NEA* 66 (2003): 190.

next chapter will consider how gender affected the socialization process and the way a child grew up. Children born biologically male were
understood as men *in potentia*, and likewise babies displaying biological
female parts were understood to be women *in potentia*. The process of
becoming a man or woman, or gendering the growing child, is a con-
tinuation of the process started at birth.[5] At times gender is imposed
upon the child by an adult, but at other times, a child takes part in the
process of gendering as he or she mirrors the actions modeled by the
adults in his or her community. Gender is therefore best understood as
a performance.[6] Children and other members of a society learn how to
become male or female by watching others within their society repeatedly act out female and male roles. Successful gendering and enculturation is key to producing adults who can contribute to society and in turn
reproduce society.[7]

Part and parcel of gendering is enculturation. Just as maleness and
femaleness are passed on through repeated performances, so too is culture. All areas of enculturation are learned, and all parts of society, from
parents, to peers, to siblings, model the desired cultural behavior for the
child.[8] Children, in turn, as "active participants in the economic, social,
political, and religious aspects of cultures" repeat the learned information
for future generations.[9] Recognizing the place of a child as the receptacle
of culture is one way of engendering and one way of understanding how
children were educated.

---

5. See the ritual of looking at the spindle or weapon, described in ch. 3.

6. Judith Butler, *Gender Trouble: Feminism and the Subversion of Identity*
(London: Routledge, 1990). Many of the recent studies conducted on gender from
a historical perspective come from those archaeologists utilizing aspects of anthro-
pology and sociology. Derevenski, *Children and Material Culture*; Judith Baxter, *The
Archaeology of Childhood: Children, Gender, and Material Culture* (Walnut Creek, CA:
AltaMira, 2005); Sarah Nelson, ed., *Handbook of Gender in Archaeology* (Lanham:
Alta Mira, 2006); Sara Crawley, Lara Foley, and Constance Shehan, eds., *Gendering
Bodies* (Lanham: Rowman & Littlefield, 2008).

7. David Gilmore, *Manhood in the Making: Cultural Concepts of Masculinity* (New
Haven: Yale University Press, 1990), 29.

8. Jennifer Dornan presents an overview of the relationship between individual
agency and the larger social structure in which an individual exists (Dornan, "Agency
and Archaeology," 303–29).

9. Baxter, *Archaeology of Childhood*, 11.

Everyday children did not go to a formal schoolhouse.[10] Instead, learning how to re-create their culture, how to be male and female in their society, provides what we might call today "formal education."[11] The things taught to everyday ancient Israelite children were less reading, writing, and math and more how to provide for the family.[12] For a boy, this meant learning what a proper man did for the family, and for a girl, it meant learning a woman's role.[13] Each child had to learn not only how to become a man/woman, but also how to master the tasks that were vital to the survival of the family and ancient Israelite culture.[14] The child's schoolroom was life, and the teachers, their elders.[15] Proverbs 1:8 states, "My son, heed the discipline of your father, and do not forsake the instruction of your mother" (JPS). Both father and mother played a role in the child's educa-

10. Crenshaw examines the possibility of formal education in ancient Israel, providing a review of the scholarship addressing schooling in the Hebrew Bible, Palestinian inscriptions, and ancient Near East parallels. James Crenshaw, "Education in Ancient Israel," *JBL* 104 (1985): 601–15. He concludes there is no clear picture of formal school in ancient Israel. Instead, he argues most education occurred in a family setting, "where practical instruction in daily life was provided for boys and girls according to the opportunities available to them" (614).

11. Young men such as Daniel and his compatriots or Jeremiah's scribe Baruch attest to the fact that some boys of a certain class were given formal education (Dan 1:4–6; Jer 45). Egyptian sources contain lots of information about the scribal, elite class and the way they were trained (Janssen and Janssen, *Growing Up in Ancient Egypt*, 67–89). Mesopotamian sources also suggest that elite families educated children, even daughters. Konrad Volk, "Kinderkrankheiten nach der Darstellung babylonisch-assyrischer Keilschrifttexte," *Or* 2/68 (1999): 7. But, as Dever notes regarding ancient Israel, "Few people were educated, except in the school of hard knocks" (Dever, *Lives of Ordinary People in Ancient Israel*, 204).

12. Parents both managed and educated children at the same time, teaching them labor skills and information about family history, land claims, and ethics. Carol Meyers, "The Family in Early Israel," in *Families in Ancient Israel*, ed. Leo Perdue, Joseph Blenkinsopp, John J. Collins, and Carol Meyers (Louisville: Westminster John Knox, 1997), 31.

13. The relationship between the adult and the child, as well as the environment the adults built for their children, played a big role in their education (Lillehammer, "Child Is Born," 91–100). Among Palestinian Arabs, "the father trains the boy and the mother trains the girl" (Granqvist, *Marriage Conditions in a Palestinian Village*, 140).

14. For an example of education in Greek culture, see Specht, "Girl's Education in Ancient Greece," 125–36.

15. Roland de Vaux, *Ancient Israel*, trans. John McHugh (London: Darton, Longman & Todd, 1961), 48–50.

tion, and, as Exod 20:12 commands, children were to honor their parents. The child would learn not only by observation and imitation, but also through asking questions (Exod 13:8; Deut 6:7, 20). Cross-cultural studies demonstrate that children living in a culture where women were important contributors to the subsistence base were expected to help contribute to the family economic system.[16] To do so, children were educated in those life skills (such as baking bread, herding animals) needed to contribute to the family and to reproduce their society.

5.2. Boying the Boy

It is well attested that infants and children belong to the realm of women.[17] As direct care providers, women have different responsibilities than men. In an agriculturally based life, this means women are tied to the homestead so that they may care for the infants and children. Their share of labor is not less than their male counterparts, but different. While the men are in the fields or with the flocks, the women take on the domestic chores of running the household and tending the gardens closer to home.[18] As boys

---

16. Lillehammer, "Child Is Born," 93–94.

17. In recent history, the shift from boy child in the house as "girly" to postcircumcised boy as man can be seen in the circumcision ceremonies found in Moslem Egypt (Janssen and Janssen, *Growing Up in Ancient Egypt*, 97–98).

18. Meyers, *Rediscovering Eve*. Whether a family lived in a village or city, division of labor remained along gender lines. In such cases, boys would have gone on to learn the trade of their fathers, rather than learn how to tend flocks. Passing on the family trade can be seen as early as the third millennium in Babylon where records use "sons of potters" as a title for children who are learning the family trade. Piotr Steinkeller, "The Organization of Crafts in Third Millennium Babylonia: The Case of Potters," *AoF* 23 (1996): 23–53. Ceramics in particular can be a trade the entire family engages in. Darby hypothesizes that ceramic workshops producing JPFs were run by families. Here the trade was separated by gender and age; the men did the main production and were aided by women and children. Erin Darby, *Interpreting Judean Pillar Figurines: Gender and Empire in Judean Apotropaic Ritual*, FAT 2/69 (Tübingen: Mohr Siebeck, 2014), 211. Ethnographic research in Palestine, Syria, and Jordan noted that women produced handmade ceramics, whereas men produced wheel-made objects. Hamed Salem, "Implications of Cultural Tradition: The Case of Palestinian Traditional Pottery," in *Archaeology, History, and Culture in Palestine and the Near East: Essays in Memory of Albert E. Glock*, ed. Tomis Kapitan, ASOR Books 3 (Atlanta: Scholars Press, 1999), 69–73; Cathy Lynne Costin, "Use of Ethnoarchaeology for the Archaeological Study of Ceramic Production," *Journal of Archaeological Method and Theory* 7 (2000):

begin to grow up, they separate from their mothers and start to emulate the men in their lives, traveling away from the safety of the house to the wilds of the flocks and fields.[19] The separation of older, teenage boys and girls in the Lachish reliefs (ch. 6), "implies the existence of a social structure which dictated that, once having obtained a certain age, boys were considered part of the male population and could no longer remain with the female members of the family in public."[20] Learning how to make this transition meant that a boy had to recognize himself as a different entity and gender than his mother.[21] He had to grow up, putting away the childish things that would tie him to an infantile period. Some of these actions were done voluntarily, while others were imposed upon the boy.

5.2.1. Circumcision

For the Israelite boy, the most notable act of gendering comes through circumcision. The moment of circumcision serves as a separation from the women's sphere of influence. Israelite women were not circumcised. Therefore, the circumcision cut transported the boy into the male sphere, separating female from male. Leviticus 12:3 states that the male child should be circumcised on the eighth day. This law is in accordance with the practice continued into the present wherein Jews circumcise their sons on the eighth day. Earlier in the Bible, God commands Abraham to cir-

---

395; Darby, *Interpreting Judean Pillar Figurines*, 196. Here again, the production of ceramics carried out on a gender divide.

19. Among Bedouin Arabs boys and girls stay with their mothers until the age of seven or eight years. Then the boys go with their fathers and connect with them, while the girls stay under their mothers' care until their marriage. Josef Henniger, *Die Familie bei den heutigen Beduinen Arabiens: Und seiner Randgebiete; Ein Beitrag zur Frage der ursprünglichen Familienform der Semiten* (Leiden: Brill, 1943), 103.

20. Pauline Albenda, "Western Asiatic Women in the Iron Age: Their Image Recorded," *BA* 46 (1983): 85. Gendered separation is also seen in a royal family procession from Carchemish. The king leads the procession, followed by the male children, eight subsequent children, and finally the queen (86). However, Schwyn notes that the gender separation in Judean depictions is much less rigid than that of people in the Zagros mountain region (Schwyn, "Kinderbetreuung im 9.–7. Jahrhundert," 7).

21. Nancy Chodorow, "Family Structure and Feminine Personality," in *Woman, Culture, and Society*, ed. Michelle Rosaldo and Louise Lamphere (Stanford: Stanford University Press, 1974), 43–66. Stephen Wilson points out that this understanding of male gendering contradicts Freud's longstanding hypothesis that male gender is present at birth, resulting in a latent Oedipal complex (*Making Men*, 165 n. 28).

Fig. 5.1. Judean man, Lachish relief, Nineveh, Southwest
Palace Room XXXVI, panels
8–10, 700–681 BCE.

cumcise himself, his household, and his son Ishmael. God also commands
Abraham that every other child throughout the generations to come
should be circumcised on the eighth day (Gen 17:9–14, 23–27). Both these
commandments describe circumcision as integral to the covenantal relationship between God and Israel. As such, circumcision not only engen-
ders the boy child as a male Israelite, but also enculturates the boy child as
a member of the Israelite people from a very early age. The Lachish Relief,
discussed further in the next chapter, provides extrabiblical evidence of
circumcision among the Israelites. One portion of the relief shows naked
Judeans about to be slaughtered by the Assyrian army. As seen in figure 5.1
the Judean men were clearly circumcised.[22]

Circumcision is both an ethnic and religious practice, one that identifies the member as an Israelite to his own people (inward identification) and
to other people (outward identification).[23] Because circumcision is highlighted as *the* identity marker of a male Israelite, it is important to understand the function of circumcision within the ancient Near East broadly.

Other ancient Near Eastern cultures also practiced circumcision, but,
unlike the Israelites, this circumcision was not attached to a covenant.
Jeremiah 9:25–26 suggests the following West Semitic peoples circumcised: Canaanites, Ammonites, Moabites, Edomites, Phoenicians, and
Arameans. No East Semitic people, such as the Akkadians, Assyrians,
and Babylonians are listed.[24] Extrabiblical evidence of Canaanites prac-

---

22. The drawing was made from photographs taken using the RTI technology.
A description of RTI and its importance for interpreting monumental reliefs can be
found in ch. 6.

23. In arguing against the mutual exclusivity of circumcision as an internal Israelite marker, Avraham Faust includes a comprehensive discussion of scholarship in both
camps. Avraham Faust, "The Bible, Archaeology, and the Practice of Circumcision in
Israelite and Philistine Societies," *JBL* 134 (2015): 273–90.

24. Philip King, "Gezer and Circumcision," in *Confronting the Past: Archaeologi-*

ticing circumcision is suggested based on a find from the Gezer excavations. A terracotta phallus was found in a stratum dating to the period when Gezer was inhabited by Canaanites but ruled by Egyptians (ca. late twelfth to mid-eleventh century BCE) (fig. 5.2). The phallus was handmade and clearly circumcised.[25] The site of Tel Miqne-

Fig. 5.2. Ceramic phallus, Gezer, Late Bronze Age II/Iron Age I.

Ekron also produced a clearly circumcised ceramic phallus from the same time period. As Ekron is known from the Bible to be a Philistine site, the presence of such an item raised many questions. The excavators attribute its presence to a time of Egyptian or Phoenician influence over the site, two cultures that did circumcise.[26]

At Ashkelon, one of the Philistine pentapolis cities, a cache of seven *situlae* was found.[27] The *situale*, all under 12 cm long, are hollow bronze vessels with reliefs of Egyptian-style deities processing around exterior. The god Min or Amen-Re, commonly found on Egyptian *situlae*, holds his member and "raises his right hand in a gesture of joy or pleasure."[28] The shape of the vessel is phallic, keeping in line with the depiction of Min, and suggests that the shape might be related to the vessel's cultic use. Unlike the object found at Gezer, the Ashkelon objects appear to be uncircumcised phalli.[29] Other such phallus-shaped objects have been found at Tell es-Safi/Gath, another Philistine city (ca. late ninth to early eighth century BCE). According to the excavators, the *situlae* appear to be erect, and therefore

---

cal and Historical Essays on Ancient Israel in Honor of William G. Dever, ed. Seymour Gitin, J. Edward Wright, J. P. Dessel (Winona Lake, IN: Eisenbrauns, 2006), 334.

25. King, "Gezer and Circumcision," 333, 338–39.

26. Trude Dothan and Dalit Regev, "Iron Age I Limestone Phallus," in *Tel Miqne-Ekron Excavations 1985–1988, 1990, 1992–1995: Field IV Lower, The Elite Zone*, ed. Seymour Gitin, Trude Dothan, and Yosef Garfinkel, Harvard Semitic Museum (Winona Lake, IN: Eisenbrauns, 1996), 469–70.

27. Lawrence Stager, "Ashkelon and the Archaeology of Destruction: Kislev 604 BCE" [Hebrew], *ErIsr* 25 (1996): 68–70*. These objects are now on display at the Rockefeller Museum in Jerusalem.

28. Stager, "Ashkelon and the Archaeology of Destruction," 69*.

29. Aren Maeir, "A New Interpretation of the Term ʿopalim (עפלים) in the Light of Recent Archaeological Finds from Philistia," *JSOT* 32 (2007): 26.

one cannot tell if they were circumcised.[30] While the latter example is not conclusive, both Gath and Ashkelon are Philistine sites, and the Philistines are known as the "uncircumcised" *par excellence* of the biblical text (1 Sam 17:26, 36; 18:25–27).[31]

The purpose of circumcision for non-Israelites seems to be a kind of rite of passage, probably linked to puberty and the transition from childhood to manhood. Both ancient sources and modern ethnographic sources attest to a group of initiates participating in the rite.[32] Since not every child undergoes puberty at the same time, the puberty rites are not always associated with physiological puberty. Rather, such rites, especially if they are done in a group setting, fall more into the concept of social puberty, when a society declares the child ready for transition into adulthood and mysteries of adulthood.[33] Indeed, the depictions of circumcision in the Egyptian materials show a range of physical ages. The individuals

---

30. Maeir, "New Interpretation of the Term ʿopalim," 28. These objects are found throughout ancient Israel, suggesting perhaps something of a cultic nature to them, reminding one of the items left in the various temples of Asclepius throughout the Greco-Roman world. A ceramic phallus shaped object was found in a cultic context at Tel Malḥata in the Negev, a site demonstrating a mix of Judean culture and Edomite culture. Again, the object appears erect making difficult to tell whether it is circumcised. Seventeen such phallic objects were found at Hellenistic Maresha, in the Shephelah/ Judean lowlands. Izhaq Beit-Arieh, "A Phallus-Shaped Clay Object," in *Tel Malḥata: A Central City in the Biblical Negev*, ed. Itzhaq Beit-Arieh and Liroa Freud (Winona Lake, IN: Eisenbrauns, 2015), 580.

31. Avraham Faust points out that the biblical references naming the Philistines as uncircumcised all reflect an Iron Age I world, the time period in which distinctive Philistine culture is well attested. Prophetic and other later texts, reflecting an Iron Age II world stop referring to the Philistines as uncircumcised. In this period, the distinction between Philistine material culture and that of the Israelites/Canaanites becomes less marked. Faust suggests that in Iron Age II the Philistines began circumcising (Faust, "Bible, Archaeology, and the Practice of Circumcision," 273–90).

32. Egyptian reliefs suggest group circumcision. See the discussion surrounding fig. 5.3. African tribes also hold group circumcision. Turner, *Ritual Process*, 17, 65; Howard Eilberg-Schwartz, *The Savage in Judaism: An Anthropology of Israelite Religion and Ancient Judaism* (Bloomington, IN: Indiana University, 1990), 141–76.

33. For further exploration of physiological versus social puberty see the discussion by Arnold van Gennep, *The Rites of Passage* (Chicago: University of Chicago, 1960), 65–74. Consider, too, the modern practice of the bar mitzvah. A Jewish child will become bar mitzvah, a legal Jewish adult, on his thirteenth birthday, but the social recognition of the transition marked by the religious ceremony and subsequent party do not often align.

in Ankh-mahor's tomb (discussed below) do not have the characteristic sidelocks of Egyptian children, but imagery from royal tombs envisions circumcision occurring when the king still has his sidelocks.[34] Like the first acts of gendering discussed in chapter 2, puberty rituals are driven by the adults in society. The boy might have some say in whether he is willing or complicit, but the ceremonies are inductions driven and conducted by adults. Without going through the process of *communitas* for a specific ritual, the boy is missing a link to others in his society. *Communitas*, or "communion of equal individuals" can only be "acquired by the incumbents of positions during the *rites de passage*, through which they changed positions."[35] To opt out of a ceremony is tantamount to opting out of society. Foregoing a rite like circumcision, the boy remains set apart from other members of his society. Physiologically the boy will become a man, but socially the boy might not be recognized as a man. With such social pressures, it hardly seems plausible that the boy would opt out of the ritual, even if he did have the choice.

The Bible does not record the actual details of the procedure. The most information we get is that circumcision was performed with a flint knife (Exod 4:25; Josh 5:2–3). Egyptian materials offer a little more information on how the procedure was executed in Egypt, but much remains unknown. For example, it is not known whether the practice belonged solely to the upper echelons of society or if it was a practice that all classes engaged in.[36] Reference to men undergoing circumcision first comes from a tomb dating to the Sixth Dynasty. The tomb, located at Saqqara, belongs to a man named Ankh-mahor (ca. 2355–2343 BCE). It includes two references to the circumcision of five initiates, two of whom were Ankh-mahor's sons, into the rank of *ka*-priest of Ankh-mahor's mortuary cult. Not unlike Israelite priests, Egyptian priests held purity in high regard and underwent various rites to cleanse themselves. Circumcision was one of these rites, required for priests of all types. Tucked away in a storeroom of Ankh-mahor's tomb, a presentation scene depicts men bringing special cloth and goods needed for the circumcision ceremony.

The ceremony itself appears on a doorway (fig. 5.3). Two unnamed initiates, perhaps Ankh-mahor's sons, are shown standing. On the left, a

---

34. Janssen and Janssen, *Growing Up in Ancient Egypt*, 91–92.

35. Turner, *Ritual Process*, 96–97.

36. Some mummies even show evidence of circumcision in late puberty (Nunn, *Ancient Egyptian Medicine*, 171).

Fig. 5.3. Circumci-
sion scene, Saqqara,
Egypt, Ankh-more's
Tomb, Sixth Dynasty.

man stands behind the initiate in a restraining position. Before the initiate, another man kneels. This man holds a knife and is shown in the act
of circumcising the initiate. The second initiate stands erect with his hand
on the head of the man kneeling in front of him. The caption above the
two reads: "Rub off everything" and the reply "I will do it sweetly."[37] While
some interpret this to mean an anesthetic was used in the ceremony, others
have argued that the second scene on the right does not depict circumcision, but rather the ritual shaving of pubic hair, also necessary for purity.[38]

The next piece of important evidence comes over one thousand years
later, from a stela recording the biography of Uha (ca. 2011 BCE). Between
statements about having a loving childhood and establishing his own
household comes a description about his circumcision. He claims to have
been circumcised along with a hundred and twenty other men, suggesting that circumcision was done in a group setting. He also boasts that he
neither hit nor scratched, nor was he hit or scratched by anyone else.[39] In
other words, he took his circumcision "like a man." It seems reasonable

37. Ann Macy Roth, *Egyptian Phyles in the Old Kingdom: The Evolution of a
System of Social Organization*, Studies in Ancient Oriental Civilization 48 (Chicago:
University of Chicago Press, 1991), 66.

38. Roth, *Egyptian Phyles in the Old Kindgom*, 68. Other scholars understand the
hieroglyphs to refer to analgesia used during the operation (Nunn, *Ancient Egyptian
Medicine*, 169; Janssen and Janssen, *Growing Up in Ancient Egypt*, 90–91).

39. Roth, *Egyptian Phyles in the Old Kindgom*, 71; James B. Pritchard, ed. *Ancient*

that since his circumcision was momentous enough to make it into his biography, it was an important event. Based on the placement between being loved by his family and running his own house, the record of his circumcision marks his transition from childhood to manhood. As such, his circumcision acts as a pubescent coming of age ritual. Depictions of young men or children engaging in sport have also been linked to circumcision and the puberty rites. The tomb of *Mrrw-kȝ* includes two familiar scenes: the shaving scene and *ka*-priests. It also includes young men participating in games, poking fun at a bound captive, and taunting other participants by saying their team (perhaps referring to a group of initiates) was stronger.[40] A third scene is badly damaged but seems to fit stylistically with the circumcision scenes in Ankh-mahor's tomb. If the damaged area did include a circumcision scene, then the whole scene can be interpreted as a puberty rite.

A few other texts from the Upper Egyptian site of Dendra reference a single person sponsoring the circumcision of a larger group of people. One text compares sponsoring circumcision ceremonies to sponsoring someone's tomb, an act of great prestige.[41] As the relief from Ankh-mahor's tomb shows, the ceremony was expensive, requiring special clothes and goods, and if the interpretation of the *Mrrw-kȝ* tomb scene is correct, it could have required hosting athletic competitions as well.

Upon completing puberty or manhood rituals, many cultures recognize the participant as ready for marriage. Historically, some groups have believed that circumcision aids in fertility and therefore understood puberty rituals that incorporated circumcision as a way to enhance virility in the man's married life. The virile man is a desired man, and the relationship between fertility and manhood is well established in the ancient world. For example, Ps 127:3–5 uses the metaphor of a quiver full of arrows, a quintessential weapon of the successful warrior, to represent virility and children.[42] Two Ugaritic texts demonstrate this connection

---

Near Eastern Texts relating to the Old Testament with Supplement, 3rd ed. (Princeton, NJ: Princeton University Press, 1969), 326.

40. Roth, *Egyptian Phyles in the Old Kindgom*, 70–71.

41. Roth, *Egyptian Phyles in the Old Kindgom*, 71–72.

42. Josephus claimed that the pre-Islamic Arabians circumcised at thirteen because Ishmael, the founder of their people, was circumcised at thirteen (Josephus, *A.J.* 1.12.2). The indigenous Southeast Asian Malays also conduct circumcision at puberty. For females, the process of childbirth makes her a woman. Carol Laderman,

as well. Both texts describe mythological marriages, which include references to circumcision in the context of puberty and marriage. In one text,
the goddess Nikkal marries the moon god (*KTU* 1.24). The text includes
the familiar Semitic root *ḥtn* to describe the wedding/marriage, as well as
the more common cognate *ʿḥz*, which means, "to marry." Most interesting
for this discussion is the word *qz*, found in parallel to the word *agtz* (marriage). While "summer" is a common meaning for the word, if one understands the Ugaritic *qz* with the less common meaning, "cutting," then one
can interpret *qz* here in a marriage context as "circumcision."[43] One needs
to be cut before he is married. The second Ugaritic text includes a more
metaphorical reference to circumcision. Using agricultural imagery, the
male figure is described as one seated with a staff in his hand. The staff is
then described as a vine that is pruned (*KTU* 1.23).[44] This act is done as
a puberty rite, one that must be done before the male could be betrothed.

The ethnographic literature from Arab Palestine provides fascinating
remnants of a tradition that attests to the continued connection between
circumcision and marriage. Villagers do not hold to a specific age for circumcision, but rather hold ceremonies for multiple children at once. This
is done so the family can save costs. Granqvist records two ceremonies
with boys ranging between eight months old to five years old. The only
guiding principle is that circumcision must be completed before marriage.[45] Among Bedouins in Transjordan it happens that as soon as the cut
is healed the male is married. Taamre Bedouin in particular have a tradition that a gift, such as money, is given to the boy who is circumcised. At
other times it appears that the circumciser himself offers a present to the
boy. In the cases where a marriage is to be contracted, the circumciser is
the boy's paternal uncle. The boy's uncle says "Speak my son! Thou shalt

---

"Symbolic and Empirical Reality: A New Approach to the Analysis of Food Avoidances," *American Ethnologist* 8 (1981): 484–86. Various African tribes also practice
circumcision at puberty. Van Gennep, *Rites of Passage*, 70–71; Victor Turner, *The
Forest of Symbols: Aspects of Ndembu Ritual* (Ithaca: Cornell University Press, 1967),
151–279; Hodder, *Symbols in Action*, 116–17.

43. The Ugaritic term *ḥatnu* is found in *KTU* 1.24.32. Alternatively, *qz* could
mean summer. Robert Allan, "Now that Summer's Gone: Understanding *qz* in *KTU*
1.24," *SEL* 16 (1999): 19–25; Wyatt, "Circumcision and Circumstance," 424.

44. Wyatt, "Circumcision and Circumstance," 423. See too, Eilberg-Schwartz's
discussion on uncircumcised fruit trees (Eilberg-Schwartz, *Savage in Judaism*, 149–
54).

45. Granqvist, *Birth and Childhood among the Arabs*, 201.

have my daughter! Be witnesses ye who are present, that my daughter is to be for him!"[46] Since cousin marriage is considered particularly desirable among agnatic kinship groups, it makes sense that the paternal uncle would offer his daughter.[47] The circumcision itself involved a week-long ceremony, much like a wedding, full of celebrations, singing and feasting. The boys were given festive new clothes to wear with ostrich feathers and coins sewn on. To counteract the attention of the evil eye that the new clothing might draw, boys were also given special amulets and necklaces of blue. A big blue dot was also placed over the eyes.[48] Fear of the evil eye was sometimes so great that a fake bride, held up on a pitchfork, led the procession to the circumciser's house. The hope was that the fake bride would distract the evil eye from the boy, and his circumcision would take place without complications.[49]

It is possible that at one point the Israelites might also have understood circumcision as a puberty or marriage/fertility rite. Not only do biblical texts reference circumcision in conjunction with marriage, but the Hebrew terms, as well as those in cognate languages, recognize a link between the two. Since marriage and betrothal took place at a much earlier age, the two might have been synonymous in some cases. The Bible reports that Shechem must be circumcised before he marries Dinah (Gen 34:14–17).[50] While Gen 34 might be a story about who counts as a real Israelite, the narrative nonetheless requires circumcision as a precursor to marriage. The older association between circumcision and marriage is also seen in the David narratives; Saul asks David for one hundred Philistine

---

46. Granqvist, *Birth and Childhood among the Arabs*, 201.

47. Naomi Steinberg, *Kinship and Marriage in Genesis: A Household Economics Perspective* (Minneapolis: Fortress Press, 1993). The practice of the father-in-law (to be) acting as the circumciser seems to be similar to the traditions by the word *hoten*, discussed below.

48. Granqvist, *Birth and Childhood among the Arabs*, 189–94.

49. Granqvist, *Birth and Childhood among the Arabs*, 199.

50. The passage in Gen 34 is open to many different interpretations; it has been decried by feminists, and upheld as a polemic against intermarriage. Phyllis Trible, *Texts of Terror: Literary-Feminist Readings of Biblical Narratives* (Philadelphia: Fortress, 1984); Danna Nolan Fewell and David Gunn, "Tipping the Balance: Sternberg's Reader and the Rape of Dinah," *JBL* 110 (1991): 193–211; Lyn Bechtel, "What If Dinah Is Not Raped? (Genesis 34)," *JSOT* 62 (1994): 19–26. Wyatt includes a mythic reading of Gen 34 incorporating the Akkadian, Ugaritic and Vedic traditions (Wyatt, "Circumcision and Circumstance," 417–21).

foreskins as the bride price to marry his daughter Michal (1 Sam 18:25). Finally, the strange story in Exod 4:24–26 also refers to circumcision and the bridegroom. While riddled with ambiguities, Zipporah's main actions are clear. She circumcises her son with a flint knife, touches the foreskin to his (her son's or Moses's) leg/genitals and proclaims: "You (Moses?) are a bridegroom of blood/ bloody bridegroom to me." In verse 26 she again states "A bridegroom of blood because of the circumcision." As the phrasing here demonstrates, there is a known relationship between marriage and circumcision.[51] The Hebrew word for "daughter's husband" is *ḥātān*, which etymologically means "the one who undergoes circumcision."[52] Additionally, the word *ḥōtēn*, "wife's father" is the circumciser. Many scholars have pointed out the same root in cognate languages.[53] Arabic *ḥātin* means wife's father from the word *ḥatana*, "to circumcise." The same root is found in Akkadian: *ḥatnūtu* means "marriage," while *ḥatanu(m)* means "in-law, relative by marriage." Even though the Eastern Semites did not circumcise, the link between these two words suggests that the root *ḥtn* originally meant both circumcise and marriage.[54]

Returning to the Israelite practice of infant circumcision, one might wonder how, based on the surrounding cultural norms and probable historical roots as a puberty rite, it became displaced to the eighth day after birth. In considering this question, Gen 17 is key.[55] It is another rendition of the covenant between God and Abram, this time sealed by a name change and the command to circumcise. Consider Abraham's family as a case study for the etiology of infant circumcision.[56] He is circumcised when he became fertile—granted he was ninety-nine years old (Gen 17:24). Ishmael, on the other hand, is circumcised when he is thirteen, pubescent and ready to become a man (Gen 17:25). All future children are to be circumcised on the eighth day, and indeed some chapters later

---

51. William Propp suggests that if this text belongs to the E source, then it could be the Elohist's way of explaining circumcision. William Propp, "Origins of Infant Circumcision in Israel," *HAR* 11 (1987): 358–59.

52. Milgrom, *Leviticus 1–16*, 747.

53. Wyatt, "Circumcision and Circumstance," 420–21; Milgrom, *Leviticus*, 747; King, "Gezer and Circumcision," 335.

54. William Propp, *Exodus 1–18*, AB 2 (New York: Doubleday, 1998), 237.

55. Since infant circumcision appears in Gen 17 and Lev 12, scholars credit P with the advent of infant circumcision (Propp, "Origins of Infant Circumcision in Israel," 356–57).

56. Wyatt, "Circumcision and Circumstance," 411–12.

Isaac becomes the model for infant circumcision (Gen 21:4). Circumcision "symbolized the fertility of the initiate as well as his entrance into and ability to perpetuate a lineage of male descendants."[57] For the Israelites, circumcision was transformed from a ceremony marking social maturity and virility to a ceremony quite literally marking the member as part of a fertile covenantal line.[58] Circumcision became equivalent to the covenant.

Reasons for the shift are unknown, but many suggestions have been proposed. For one, an adolescent might choose not to be circumcised, but infants have no choice. While this might be the least likely reason for the shift, it does bring up an important point. Infants have no choice in the matter; the enculturation and gendering moment happens without their consent. Since many infants and children died before reaching adolescence, it might also have been a shift born out of practicality. This would mean that the Israelite community believed circumcision before death was important. To be sure, this idea finds some support in biblical and early Jewish texts that suggest the circumcised were allotted a more pleasant afterlife.[59] A second possibility is that circumcision was moved to coincide with an older eighth-day naming ritual.[60] The timing of the eighth day corresponds with the length of a woman's initial impurity after bearing a male child. The eighth day after birth would be the first time the mother could participate in any rituals to celebrate the boy's birth. While this accounts for the timing of the eighth day, there is still the question of when the shift to infant circumcision was made. If one takes the Levitical materials to be written in the exile, then the need for infant circumcision can be understood as one way the Israelites coped with the loss of a nation and the loss of a centralized peoplehood.[61] Facing the reality that their ethnicity was no longer bound up in the land, infant circumcision became a way for Israelites to separate themselves from the people they were living among. If the unthinkable happened, a child was separated from the parents before coming of age (through slavery, death of a parent, separation from parents

---

57. Eilberg-Schwartz, *Savage in Judaism*, 143.

58. Eilberg-Schwartz, *Savage in Judaism*, 174–76.

59. See Ezek 32 for biblical examples. For Jewish texts see, Propp, "Origins of Infant Circumcision in Israel," 363–65.

60. Albertz, "Names and Family Religion," 247.

61. Wyatt, "Circumcision and Circumstance," 409–10.

via further wars, and so forth), the child would carry with him the marker of the Israelite people and his status as a member of the covenant.

5.2.2. Circumcision as a Gendering Moment

No matter what the timing, circumcision acts as a gendering moment. This might be inferred from the previous discussion, but it deserves a little more fleshing out. A cut at puberty makes more sense from a gendering perspective; it serves as the sign that a boy has moved out of the female domestic sphere and into the male sphere. The fact that the father is commanded to circumcise his son makes this all the more poignant. With this act, the father publicly states that the boy child is welcomed into his realm of influence. In a primarily agrarian society, this means a shift in jobs. The boy will take on more manly tasks, some of which he might have been previously prepped for. If before the child played pretend war with his friends, now he is ready to train for real warfare. If he helped his mother tend the fruits and vegetable gardens close to the house, now he is ready to expand his agricultural education to tend a field of his own, away from the house and the domestic sphere. Infant circumcision transfers the gender distinction to a much earlier age. In terms of engendering the child, infant circumcision hints at the idea that the child carries with it its mother's impurity from childbirth. Infant circumcision, again by the father, causes the child to leave behind "his mother's ritually polluting female birth blood."[62] The residual female impurity clinging to the infant changes into the pure blood of the covenant, the covenant carried on by Israelite males.

5.2.3. Education, Labor, and War

A boy's journey toward full gendering continued as he learned other ways of becoming male. As a little one, boys, like girls, would spend most of their time in the house or close to their mother. As they grew and were weaned, boys would start to separate physically from their mothers, leaving the house, which for many boys meant heading to the fields.[63] Young

---

62. Elizabeth Wyner Mark, "Wounds, Vows, Emanations: A Phallic Trope in the Patriarchal Narrative," in *The Covenant of Circumcision*, ed. Elizabeth Wyner Mark (Lebanon, NH: Brandeis University Press, 2003), 7.

63. The discussion here assumes an agricultural lifestyle common to a majority of the Israelite population. This said, there were, of course, children who grew up in cities

children, girls and boys alike, might be put in charge of the family flock. Young David almost misses his anointing as he is out tending sheep (1 Sam 16:11–13).[64] Egyptian tombs from the Old Kingdom depict boys watching over flocks, and ethnographic studies from Iran attest to boys as young as five years old helping their fathers with the flock and then going off to play.[65]

Other ethnographic studies also document many jobs related to tending animals as jobs suitable for young boys.[66] For example, a boy of eight or nine years old might be placed in charge of watching over a flock co-op, called a *riyehn*, comprised of up to 144 sheep/goats. His payment consists of food, money, and a new set of clothing. During the spring, care for newborn animals is also needed. Boys are hired to watch over groups of calves, lambs, and kids. Duties for this job include protecting the animals, making sure they did not try to run away to nurse, and keeping them from eating any of the nearby crops. Spring also means sheep shearing time. While the men shear, the boys immobilize the sheep by tying together their legs. One can imagine young Israelite boys engaging in similar activities as they learned how to become men and provide for a family.

Like the ancient Near Eastern method of using social age categories, the Palestinian Arabs assigned boys jobs according to their social age. Granqvist gives examples of occupational social ages, listed here from youngest to oldest: he who chases animals, goat herder, shepherd, plough man, he who can bear arms. A case study of a boy thought to be eight or nine years old listed the following duties: he watched the garden, took

---

that would learn their fathers' trade. For a discussion on what these trades might have been and the education provided to a more elite class of children, see the discussion in Flynn, *Children in Ancient Israel*, 94–109.

64. Young David's sling and stones were very popular among Palestinian Arab boys. Older boys would teach younger boys how to make a sling out of scraps of material. The children would practice with the sling so that they could make the stone drop right in front of the wayward sheep and make it turn back (Granqvist, *Birth and Childhood among the Arabs*, 127–28). This example shows how older children, not just adults, could teach younger children. It also attests to the skill needed to be a shepherd and makes David's accurate shot to Goliath's head a little more believable.

65. Janssen and Janssen, *Growing Up in Ancient Egypt*, 51; Watson, *Archaeological Ethnography in Western Iran*, 205.

66. Watson, *Archaeological Ethnography in Western Iran*, 105–12. Note that in the biblical narratives where girls are tending flocks they do not have brothers (Rachel and Zipporah).

trips into Bethlehem for his father, delivered things, watched over younger siblings when the mother was gone, delivered bread to the father at work, and took a four-hour round-trip journey to fetch dung and grass for the cows when his father was ill.[67] As this example demonstrates, children were given a lot of responsibility at a young age. Here too we might infer that children in ancient Israel, who also lived in an agrarian society, were tasked with many of the same responsibilities.

While the biblical text remains relatively silent on such everyday chores, it nonetheless provides an explicit description of what it means to be a man, and within this context, we can glean some information on the process of engenderment and becoming a man. A man was to be strong, independent, intelligent, and virile. A child, by contrast, was weak and clung to his family, looking to them for direction in all he did. A man wore his hair long and possessed facial hair, which demonstrated his fertility; to lack these was considered laughable and babyish (2 Sam 10:4–5).[68]

Manly traits are best seen in the context of the battlefield, and it comes as no surprise that coming of age narratives can be linked to battlefield imagery.[69] For example, 1 Sam 17 tells the story of David's coming of age during war. Like Joseph, he is a messenger boy, going out from the homestead to bring news of his older brothers (Gen 37:2, 12–14; 1 Sam 17:17–18). On one of these days, David decides to "man up" and do something none of the other Israelite men have volunteered to do; he offers to fight the Philistine champion Goliath. At the start of the battle, he is a boy who does not know how to wear armor or wield a sword. In place of manly weapons, he chooses the weapons of his childhood: his staff, a slingshot, and stones (1 Sam 17:40). Upon killing the giant, David is almost magically transformed into a man. Putting aside the things of his youth, David raises the champion's sword and chops off his head (1 Sam 17:51). Moreover, he now has strength enough to own not one, but two coats of armor (1 Sam 17:54; 18:4). In the ultimate marker of manhood, David is also eligible to marry a princess (1 Sam 17:25).

Contrasting David's engenderment into an Israelite on the battlefield is the story of young Jether (Judg 8:19–21). Whereas David is self-motivated to participate in a military coming of age ritual, Jether's father,

---

67. Granqvist, *Birth and Childhood among the Arabs*, 130.

68. Susan Niditch, *My Brother Esau Is a Hairy Man: Hair and Identity in Ancient Israel* (New York: Oxford University Press, 2008), 79; Wilson, *Making Men*, 135.

69. Chapter 2 notes the parallels between virility and battlefield imagery.

the judge Gideon, commands him to kill two kings taken as prisoners of war. If Jether can do this, he will demonstrate his prowess in war, defend his family's honor, and show kinship solidarity.[70] However, while Gideon clearly thought his son was ready to cross into manhood, Jether had different thoughts on the matter. Judges 8:20 reports that Jether did not draw his sword because he was afraid, for he was still a youth. Placed in the position to cross the threshold into manhood, Jether remains on the side marked "boy." The proverb uttered by the prisoners of war, "As the man is, so too is his manly strength," confirms this. He might have the intellect and self-control associated with a man, but without a display of strength, he is no man. Jether's failure to pass into manhood meant that his gendering process was not complete.

In both narratives, David and Jether are both called נער (> na'ar) Much has been written on how to define a נער, but little consensus has been reached regarding the age parameters of the term.[71] It is clear, however, that this is a stage in life associated with youth; it is not a term for a man. For David and Jether, being a נער meant that they were old enough to test out their abilities on the battlefield, but for both it also meant that heroic feats of strength were not expected. Both David and Jether needed the consent and encouragement of an Israelite man to engage in a military killing. While David's kill is heralded, it should be noted that Jether suffers no ill consequences from failing to kill. Gideon does not disinherit the boy on the spot or taunt him. Some נערים were ready to make the transition to manhood, while others needed more time.

The contrast between the battlefield killings of David and Jether is reminiscent of the way in which puberty rites of passage were described above. While these are stories of individuals and not groups, and concern shows of physical strength and not stoic strength in the face of circumcision, there are some similarities. Comparing the narratives reinforces the notion that puberty rites were not necessarily associated with physiological puberty. Consider the possibility that willingness to kill a man was a rite of passage for the ancient Israelite boy. Such a rite of passage might have replaced circumcision as a puberty ritual. David and Jether, both described as the same social age, were thought ready to go through social puberty. The adult men in their lives encouraged them to see whether

---

70. Wilson, *Making Men*, 130.

71. For a recent overview of scholarship on the term נער, see Parker, *Valuable and Vulnerable*, 60–64.

they had the guts to kill. This sort of test, focused on a demonstration of strength and nerves of steel, is the way in which a society decides a child is ready for transition into manhood. Once the adults have declared the boys ready, they allow the initiates to undergo the rite of passage and then to join them as adults in society

5.3. Girling the Girl

Unlike her male counterpart, the ancient Israelite female did not undergo a specific ceremony to mark her as an Israelite female. There is no reference to female circumcision either in infancy or at puberty and no reason to think that this was a common practice. The only reference to a puberty ritual comes at the end of the story about Jephthah's daughter, when a communal practice of pubescent girls heading to the hills for four days is established (Judg 11:40). What took place during the four days wandering is left out of the narrative.[72] If this was indeed a common ritual for ancient Israelite girls, then presumably the rites involved were taught to them prior to departure. Notable in the story is the emphasis on sisterhood, community, and a connection with other women.[73] The primacy placed on rituals undertaken in community with other women is not limited to shadowy puberty rites, but can be found clearly modeled in the household and through the practice of household religion, discussed below.

5.3.1. Education

As previously mentioned, small children of both genders spent their early years with their mothers, learning how to carry out various household jobs.[74] Education first took place through observation while the mother toted her children around as she carried out her tasks. Ethnographic stud-

---

72. Peggy Day has compared the story of Jephthah's daughter to that of Iphigenia and Kore as a means of trying to uncover what occurred during these puberty related hillside wanderings. Peggy Day, "From the Child Is Born the Woman: The Story of Jephthah's Daughter," in *Gender and Difference in Ancient Israel*, ed. Peggy Day (Minneapolis: Fortress, 1989), 58–74. Day also references a body of ethnographic literature on female rites of passage (68 n. 7, 70 n. 16).

73. Many thanks to Rabbi Sarah Joselow for pointing this out.

74. Division of labor based on sex has long been acknowledged as a phenomenon found in preindustrial societies. Inter alia, Judith K. Brown, "A Note on the Division of Labor by Sex," *AA* 72 (1970): 1074–78. Meyers refers to this positively in ancient

ies from western Iran find that infants are strapped to the mother's back and carried about as needed until age of two.[75] This practice makes sense seeing as how other childcare providers (aunties, grandmothers, and older sisters) might not always be available, as they would have their own work to complete. When a mother's chore was stationary and safe, perhaps during food preparation as opposed to collecting water at a well, the child could be placed on the ground to crawl around and observe.

One can imagine children sweeping floors, collecting kindling for the fires, watching younger siblings, setting the table, and so forth. Small orchards and gardens located near the house would need watering and tending as they grew. A child could be taught when a vegetable or fruit was ripe enough to pick and then harvest the crop. They might help during the milking process by holding an animal's head in place, or like Rachel and David, even act as shepherds for the family flock (Gen 29:9; 1 Sam 16:11).[76] Any number of small jobs might easily have been passed on to the young labor force. Indeed, a popular New Kingdom Egyptian proverb states: "You shall not spare your body when you are young; food comes about by the hands, provisions by the feet."[77]

Ethnographic studies show that young girls especially face a conundrum. Starting around age seven girls are encouraged to stay close to home and stop going off with friends to play. If she obeys her mother she will be given work to do, something young children would rather avoid.[78] Studies of Palestinian Arab girls noted that girls had less time to play as they were quickly given odd jobs to do.[79] Granqvist notes three broad categories of social ages for girls and lists the activities associated with each group. The first group was girls aged zero to seven. They chase chickens from the sitting place, hand things to the mother, cannot comb her own hair, cannot girl herself, and cannot bake (because she is too short to lean over the oven). Between the ages of seven and puberty a girl was a

---

Israelite culture with her understanding of society as heterarchy (Meyers, *Rediscovering Eve*, 196–99).

75. Watson, *Archaeological Ethnography in Western Iran*, 205.

76. The expectation that children would work and help in the household are the same in ancient Egypt. Charlotte Booth, *Lost Voices of the Nile: Everyday Life in Ancient Egypt* (Glouchestershire: Amberley, 2015).

77. Booth, *Lost Voices of the Nile*, 128.

78. Erika Friedl, *Children of Deh Koh: Young Life in an Iranian Village* (Syracuse, NY: Syracuse University Press, 1997), 221.

79. Granqvist, *Birth and Childhood among the Arabs*, 135–66.

goat herd and guardian of the fig tree. Presumably she could also do the things a younger girl could not. At puberty a girl was a wood gatherer and drawer of water.[80] As these examples demonstrate, children, both ancient and more modern, were expected to work hard and participate in the household economic system.

While the biblical text does not provide much information about a young girl's education, ethnographic studies help provide details about what young girls learned. A study of villages in western Iran found that young children, especially girls, are encouraged to imitate adult activities.[81] Little girls are found playing house with dolls made from sticks and mud and pretending to fetch water with rocks representing water containers.[82] Even infants are given a stick and told to "churn" the milk. Notably, the chores that the girls imitated are those associated with women. We know from the Human Relations Area Files (HRAF), which examined activities in 185 agricultural societies, that female dominated activities included food preparation and weaving. Based on these studies, one can also expect to find young Israelite girls learning how to bake and weave.[83]

Most houses in ancient Israel had a hearth, as well as a tabun oven.[84] The latter was often found in the central courtyard area, while the more portable hearths could be placed in various rooms of the house or on the roof. It is estimated that women spend up to three hours a day grinding grain into flour to prepare bread for a family of six.[85] Often done in the com-

---

80. Granqvist, *Birth and Childhood among the Arabs*, 137–38.

81. Watson, *Archaeological Ethnography in Western Iran*, 268.

82. Granqvist also records Palestinian Arab girls playing with homemade dolls, and playing make-believe "house" (Granqvist, *Birth and Childhood among the Arabs*, 135–36).

83. For evidence of ancient Israelite women as primary food producers, see Carol Meyers, "Material Remains and Social Relations: Women's Culture in Agrarian Households of the Iron Age," in *Symbiosis, Symbolism, and the Power of the Past: Canaan, Ancient Israel, and Their Neighbors, form the Late Bronze Age through Roman Palaestina*, ed. William G. Dever and Seymour Gitin (Winona Lake, IN: Eisenbrauns, 2003), 430–31.

84. Ovens like this are found throughout the Levant. Nabil Ali, "Ethnographic Study of Clay Ovens in Northern Jordan," in *Modesty and Patience, Studies and Memories in Honour of Nabil Qadi, "Abu Salim,"* ed. Hans Georg Gebel, Zeidan Abdel-Kafi Kafafi, and Omar Al-Ghul (Jordan: Yarmuk University, 2009), 9–18. Granqvist reports that such ovens are the center of activity and need much attention (Granqvist, *Birth and Childhood among the Arabs*, 156).

85. Carol Meyers, "From Household to House of Yahweh: Women's Religious

pany of women from other neighboring houses, this was a way for women to connect and talk about their households. Little girls would watch the women, learning what properly ground grain looked like.[86] They would also overhear the daily gossip, passively partaking in this sort of female culture. In western Iran, some contemporary villages have milk co-ops, where women put a little of their daily milking yield into a group pot. Each woman takes a turn claiming the group pot. The milk collected in it is more than she would be able to produce from her own flock and allows her to periodically make some special treats for the family.[87] Sharing in this way builds community and furthers kinship ties. It seems reasonable that co-ops such as this might have existed for milk and other products, like grain, in ancient Israel. One can speculate little girls watched these exchanges take place and would learn the rotation and how much extra was to be deposited in the group pot.

Textile weaving was another subject that could be learned at an early age.[88] In order to be used for clothing, wool must be shorn from the sheep and then beaten and spun into threads. Other types of woven items included nets and mats made of willow branches and reeds. Using looms, women could create any number of items the family needed. As for clothing, iconography suggests that there was not much variation on the general shape of the tunic.[89] In the modern Iranian village of Hasanabad, dressmaking is described as follows: "No patterns are needed because there is only one way to make a woman's gown or a pair of *shawal* (trousers), and the girls learn the correct method."[90] Evidence of textile making is abundant in sites from ancient Israel. Spindle whorls, needles, and loom weights are the most commonly found items (fig. 5.4).

Culture in Ancient Israel," in *Congress Volume Basel 2001*, ed. André Lemaire, VTSup 92 (Leiden: Brill, 2002), 21. For an overview on theories and methods used to reconstruct archaeological populations, see Chamberlain's manual. Andrew Chamberlain, *Demography in Archaeology* (Cambridge: Cambridge University Press, 2006).

86. "The girl by copying her mother, learns how to do it [bake bread]" (Granqvist, *Birth and Childhood among the Arabs*, 156).

87. Watson, *Archaeological Ethnography in Western Iran*, 98–99.

88. Again, ethnographic reports show older girls imitating these activities with a stick spindle and pretend wool (Watson, *Archaeological Ethnography in Western Iran*, 176–77, 268).

89. The tomb painting from Beni Hasan and the Assyrian reliefs depicting the siege of Lachish show Semites wearing tunics of varying lengths.

90. Watson, *Archaeological Ethnography in Western Iran*, 188.

Fig. 5.4. Whorls and loom weights, from left to right: Gezer, thirteenth–twelfth century BCE; Gezer, twelfth century BCE; Gezer, twelfth century BCE.

In the Bible, women are associated with weaving and identified as skilled workers in the temple and Mishkan. Judges 16:13–14 suggests that Delilah was skilled with a loom in her own house. Texts from Ugarit, Egypt, and Mesopotamia also link women to weaving.[91] Based on the material culture and texts, it seems likely that as ethnographic studies suggest, learning how to weave would be an integral part of a young girl's education.

5.3.2. Household Religion

While men and women may both have participated in household religion, many of the rites were focused on issues concerning women's health and women's reproductive issues such as fertility, pregnancy, lactation, and infant survival.[92] Women carried out religious activities on a daily basis in

---

91. Meyers, "Material Remains and Social Relations," 433.

92. Ethnographic reports from southwestern Iran demonstrate that family household religion continues to play an important role in health and reproductive beliefs. Erika Friedl, "Islam and Tribal Women in a Village in Iran," in *Unspoken Worlds: Women's Religious Lives in Non-Western Cultures*, ed. Nancy Falk and Rita Gross (San Francisco: Harper & Row, 1980), 163–64. Yet, in a later study of a village called Deh Koh, when discussing troubles surrounding fertility, Friedl states that only "dumb, lazy, or desperate women blame all troubles on the will of God." It seems that for some villages, herbal and folkloric tradition were understood as separate from the modern Islamic religion (Friedl, *Children of Deh Koh*, 43).

order to secure divine favor in matters concerning the household.[93] In a society that believed the divine acted favorably upon those who knew how to enact proper religious rites, learning these rituals then became another important part of a girl's education. The discussion below looks at three different kinds of religious activities: protecting the young, manipulating cultic objects, and daily mealtime rites.

Danger lurked around every corner, threatening to harm infants and children. The previous chapters explored ways in which mothers combatted these malevolent forces. As an infant, the Israelite child was a passive participant in religious rituals meant to protect her. But as the child grew, she would become more cognizant of these rituals. Witnessing protection rituals for her siblings or cousins, she would begin to piece together how to protect a newborn. She would learn that the multiple lamps left lit throughout the night in the sleeping quarters were meant to repel more than darkness. Amulets hung on her mother or her sibling would be understood as more than just a piece of decoration, and lullabies sung to the child did more than provide quiet so the rest of the household could slumber. Through repetition, the young girl might even learn to sing the lullabies to her little sister or brother and unwittingly start to take a more active role in the household religion.

A girl might also learn through observation how to manipulate cultic objects in the house. Many households had anthropomorphic figurines. The Hebrew Bible calls these some of these figures תרפים (tərāpîm).

What and who these objects are has been debated, with the two most prevalent ideas being household gods or ancestor figures.[94] A third possibility is that they were figures used for consulting a particular deity.[95]

---

93. Scholars have been quick to point out that religion is a modern construct; what we in a modern society might qualify as a "religious ritual" was to the ancient Israelite simply a part of everyday life. Jonathan Z. Smith, *Imagining Religion* (Chicago: University of Chicago Press, 1982), xi. For a discussion of Israelite children and religion through the lens of enculturation, see Garroway, "Children and Religion," 116–39.

94. See the comprehensive review of scholarship regarding household gods versus ancestor figures in: Shawn Flynn, "The Teraphim in Light of Mesopotamian and Egyptian Evidence," *CBQ* 74 (2012): 694–711.

95. Flynn proposes this idea based on a review of Mesopotamian and Egyptian figurines. He posits that just as the shabti figurines of Egypt underwent a radical change in use, the תרפים of the biblical text may have changed in function and use as well (Flynn, "Teraphim," 705).

Genesis 31:30–35 states that Rachel stole her father's תרפים, found in many translations as "gods."[96] She hides the תרפים by placing them in her saddlebag, leading the reader to conclude that these objects were small. First Samuel 19:11–17 provides a different picture of a תרפים. In this passage, Michal buys David some time to escape from their house by placing a dummy in David's bed. This dummy is a תרפים, translated as "idol," that she covers with a wig of goat's hair and clothing. The ruse works for a little while, suggesting that this תרפים was human sized. Judges 17 makes the case for תרפים as a legitimate or at least an accepted part of the Israelite cultic repertoire, but as evidenced by 2 Kgs 23:24, at a later date תרפים become nonsanctioned cult objects. Based on parallels with ancient Near East texts from Nuzi and Emar, it seems that the תרפים were likely physical representations of ancestors.[97] As the previous chapter discussed, the ancestors needed proper care so that they would protect the household. However they were used, one thing remains clear: they had an anthropomorphic shape and came in different sizes. Figures 5.5 and 5.6 come from Tel Gezer (ca. twelfth to eleventh century BCE) and represent what the excavators call "chalk figurines." Found in a domestic context, these tiny figurines are not unique in the archaeological record; variations of them are found throughout the Levant.[98] While we cannot know for sure what a תרפים looked like, the figures from Gezer (ca. twelfth–eleventh century BCE) offer one possibility. They are anthropomorphic, are small enough to be carried, and were found in domestic areas on the acropolis. As such they may be considered images belonging to elite houses, similar to the houses where תרפים are said to be found in many of the biblical passages.

Another type of image attested to by the archaeological data is that of the terracotta female figurine. Female figurines have a long tradition in the ancient Near East and are generally associated with goddesses of one type or another.[99] Within ancient Israel, the most popular of these female figurines were the iconic Judean Pillar Figurines (JPF), which appeared

---

96. For examples: KJV "gods"; NRSV "gods"; NASB "gods"; JPS "gods."

97. Karel van der Toorn, *From Her Cradle to Her Grave*, trans. Sara Denning-Bolle (Sheffield: JSOT 1994), 39; van der Toorn, "Family Religion in Second Millennium west Asia," 27. The ancestors were also important to the family and household in Syria (Fleming, "Household and Community Religion," 40–43).

98. For example, figures similar to those at Gezer have been found at Beth Pelet (Gerar) and in Syria at Tell Afis.

99. Nakhai, "Mother-and-Child Figurines," 165–98. Figurines were also wide-

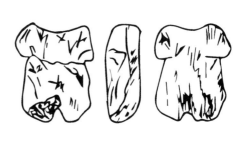

Fig. 5.5. Gezer "snow man," Gezer, Late Bronze Age II/Iron Age I.

Fig. 5.6. Gezer "chalk figure," Gezer, Late Bronze Age II/Iron Age I.

from the tenth century BCE onward.[100] These figurines can have a hand-made, pinched face, bird-like in appearance. JPFs can also have a stylized, molded head wherein distinct facial features are surrounded by a braided crown. Both types feature large breasts that are sometimes supported by the hands (fig. 5.7). Understood as everything from a fertility goddess, to a mediatrix of YHWH, to instruments used for apotropaic purposes, these figurines permeate the archaeological record.[101] Studies examining the distribution of cultic items with domestic contexts found that most houses in ancient Israel had one JPF within it.[102] JPFs were found inside of small cultic assemblages, as well as on their own, meaning that they were not kept in a certain place, but might have been moved throughout the house.

Archaeological excavations of houses have revealed several possible places where children might have seen JPFs and begun their religious

spread throughout the entire site of Israel's northern neighbor, Ugarit (Theodore Lewis, "Family, Household, and Local Religion," 79.

100. Kletter, *Judean Pillar Figurines and the Archaeology of Ashera*; Darby, *Interpreting Judean Pillar Figurines*, 2014.

101. For an overview of the different positions, see Garroway, "Children and Religion," 129; Ian Wilson, "Judean Pillar Figurines and Ethnic Identity in the Shadow of Assyria," *JSOT* 36 (2012): 259.

102. John Holladay, "Religion in Israel and Judah under the Monarchy," in *Ancient Israelite Religion: Essays in Honor of Frank Moore Cross*, ed. Patrick D. Miller, Paul D. Hanson, and S. Dean McBride (Philadelphia: Fortress, 1987), 276.

education: cultic niches, stands, or in a specific cultic assemblage within the courtyard or dining area.[103] With the case of terracotta figurines or JPFs, one can imagine that a child witnessed them being used daily. Children might see their mothers offer prayers or votive offerings to the figurines. Alternatively, mothers might have touched the figurines for good luck or waved the JPFs around in an apotropaic act to ward off evil and garner protection for the family.[104] However the JPFs were used, in observing the ritual, small girls would be passively enculturated into their family's religious practice on a regular basis. A more active enculturation might take place if the girls started to "play religion" as they might play house. Like the girls from the Iranian village of Hasanabad created dolls with stick bodies and mud heads, little Israelite girls might have created their own JPF "dolls" with sticks and pinched mud faces.[105] Made of sticks and dried clay, evidence of such "dolls" would not be found in the archaeological record. As discussed in chapter 7, many nonpermanent objects can function as objects of play. The idea of JPFs as playthings has often been raised and summarily dismissed.[106] Yet the idea of imitation

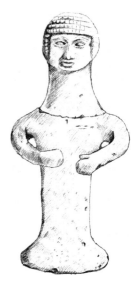

Fig. 5.7. Judean Pillar Figurine, Tel Duweir, Iron Age II.

---

103. The question of larger cultic spaces like a family shrine is harder to envision. Older interpretations regarding family cultic areas understand them as partitioned off from the main house to serve the extended family, rather than the nuclear family. Ziony Zevit, *The Religions of Ancient Israel: A Synthesis of Parallactic Approaches* (London: Continuum, 2001), 123–24, 248–54; Avraham Faust, "The Archaeology of the Israelite Cult: Questioning the Consensus," *BASOR* 360 (2010): 23–35. Other scholars call into question the ubiquity of the family shrine, arguing that permanent household shrines were not common. Rudiger Schmitt, "Typology of Iron Age Cult Places," in Albertz and R. Schmitt, *Family and Household Religion in Ancient Israel and the Levant*, 228. Depending on the family, children might be aware of such family shrines, but their usual interaction with the images would have been primarily in domestic spaces that they frequented.

104. Darby, *Interpreting Judean Pillar Figurines*, 369–82 and 393–94.

105. Watson, *Archaeological Ethnography in Western Iran*, 202.

106. Raz Kletter includes a comprehensive overview of the arguments for and

JPFs has not been raised. With the combination of a mother's desire to pass on knowledge to her children, the necessity of giving a girl a proper religious education, and the fact that children learn through example, the idea that a girl would create an imitation JPF cannot be proven but seems a likely possibility.[107]

Mealtime rites are the third aspect of religion that a girl would learn. Meals were more than just a means of filling one's belly; they were a way to communicate with the divine or the ancestors. In Mesopotamian texts, part of preparing the daily bread included portioning off some of the bread and offering it back to the ancestors. This rite, called *kispu*, was elaborated upon once a month during the festival of the New Moon.[108] The Bible refers to this feast in 1 Sam 20 wherein David takes leave of Saul's court under the ruse of going home to celebrate and make a special sacrifice with his family during the New Moon. The tradition carries on into rabbinic times where women are commanded to offer back to the Lord a portion of the weekly challah (m. Shabb. 2:6). Daily meals also provided a context in which to thank the gods for their provision.[109] Karel van der Toorn draws attention to the repetitiveness of daily offerings and meal rituals, stating that "the young girl saw her mother do this all the time, and because of that, the importance of the daily food offering dawned on her at a young age."[110] While there is no explicit evidence for this, van der Toorn's conclusion does seem reasonable.

---

against understanding JPFs as toys and the scholars who make those arguments. Reasons to reject them as toys include: find spots, one-sided decoration, fragility, uniform shape, and the fact they are not placed in children's graves (Kletter, *Judean Pillar Figurines and the Archaeology of Ashera*, 73). Julie Parker recently argued for a reconsideration of JPFs as things used by children. Julie Parker, "I Bless You by YHWH of Samaria and His Barbie: A Case for Viewing Judean Pillar Figurines as Children's Toys" (paper presented at the Annual Meeting of the Society of Biblical Literature, Boston, MA, 18 November 2017).

107. Scholars such as Holladay push back against the idea that any small objects belonged to children, and in doing so they seem to dismiss the notion that a child could make a religious object (Holladay, "Religion in Israel and Judah under the Monarchy," 291 n. 109).

108. Van der Toorn, "Family Religion in Second Millennium West Asia," 25–26; Van der Toorn, *From Her Cradle to Her Grave*, 35–36.

109. One should also acknowledge the possible role that males played in blessing the meal and the way that boys would learn from their fathers (Garroway, "Children and Religion," 126–27).

110. Van der Toorn, *From Her Cradle to Her Grave*, 37.

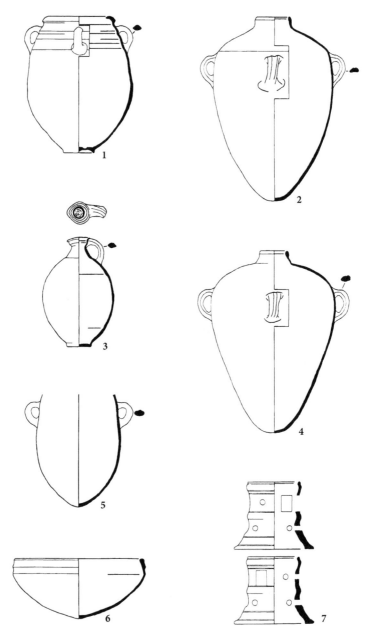

Fig. 5.8. Ceramics Associated with Meals: Tell Halif, Iron Age II. Reproduced from James Hardin, *Lahav II: Households and the Use of Domestic Space at Iron II Tell Halif; An Archaeology of Destruction*, Reports of the Lahav Research Project (Winona Lake, IN: Eisenbrauns, 2010), pl. 4. © 2010 Eisenbrauns.

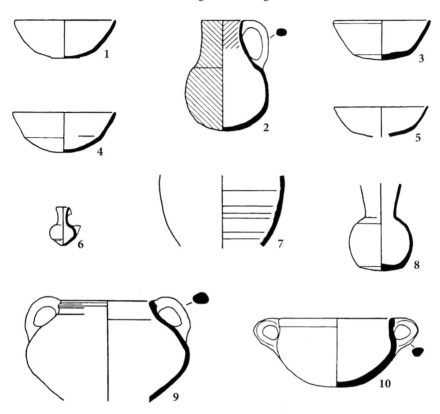

Fig. 5.9. Ceramics Associated with Meals, Tell Halif, Iron Age II. Reproduced from James Hardin, *Lahav II: Households and the Use of Domestic Space at Iron II Tell Halif; An Archaeology of Destruction*, Reports of the Lahav Research Project (Winona Lake, IN: Eisenbrauns, 2010), pl. 5. © 2010 Eisenbrauns.

Evidence of meals exists in the archaeological record in the form of items used for food storage, consumption, and preparation. Tabuns, hearths and ceramic jars, jugs, juglets, bowls, plates, as well as items fashioned out of stone, such as grinding stones, querns, and mortar and pestles, all contribute to the picture of an ancient Israelite meal (figs. 5.8 and 5.9). Special offerings made as a part of the meal would use these everyday objects, meaning that some quotidian objects doubled as ritual objects. Other times the quotidian items were intermingled with specific cultic objects such as figurines, incense stands, standing stones, and astragali. Good examples of this are the collection of items found in two different Iron Age II domestic settings. The first example comes from the

Ammonite site Tel Jawa, where Paulette M. Michèle Daviau offers the following reconstruction:

> The range of activities that can be deduced from such a corpus comprises the setting up of a figurine or symbolic stone in a particular area on the roof or upper storey, food and drink offerings, use of scented materials, lighting of lamps, sprinkling the figurine, the badetyl, or the sacred area itself, offerings in small or miniature vessels, casting of lots or divination, and libations.[111]

The scene painted by Daviau is similar to the one seen at the Israelite site of Tell Halif, which is reconstructed in figure 5.10. Such a scene could be easily witnessed by children before or after the meal. The book of Jeremiah even suggests that children did more than witness domestic cult rituals; they participated in them. Jeremiah 7:18 states: "The children gather wood, the fathers kindle fire, the women knead the dough to make cakes for the Queen of Heaven, and to pour out drink offerings to other gods."[112] Ethnographic studies from the mid-twentieth century in western Iran find that both women and children gather brush for firewood, which is used to prepare the daily meal. In these villages women prepared regular bread by mixing flour, water and salt and flapping it between their hands until it looked like a tortilla. This bread was placed on a pan and cooked over a hearth.[113] The daily bread prepared in ancient Israel might have looked much the same. However, the cakes that Jeremiah speaks of are a bit fancier. These cakes are identified with the Hebrew loan word *kawān*, which has etymological links to the Akkadian word for sweet cake

---

111. P.M. Michèle Daviau, "Family Religion: Evidence for the Paraphernalia of the Domestic Cult," in *The World of the Arameans II: Studies in History and Archaeology in Honor of Paul-Eugène Dion*, ed. Paul-Eugène Dion, JSOT Supp 325 (Sheffield: Sheffield Academic, 2001), 221.

112. Who exactly the Queen of Heaven was remains unknown. She could be anyone from Ištar, to Ashtoreth, to Anat. Philip Schmitz, "Queen of Heaven," *ABD* 5:586–88. For alternate readings see the suggestions offered by William Holladay, *Jeremiah 1: A Commentary on the Book of the Prophet Jeremiah Chapters 1–25*, ed. Paul Hanson, Hermeneia (Philadelphia: Fortress, 1986), 251. On the ritual as a family activity see Jack Lundbom, *Jeremiah 1–20*, AB 21A (New York: Doubleday, 1999), 475; Holladay, *Jeremiah 1*, 254.

113. Watson, *Archaeological Ethnography in Western Iran*, 205–6.

kamānu.[114] Such cakes involved a sweetener, like raisins or honey, and were baked on a special pan.

TELL HALIF, FIELD IV
Isometric Reconstruction of
Area of Cultic Activity (AREA B)

0m   3m

Fig. 5.10. Area B, Area of Cultic Activity, Tell Halif, Iron Age II. Reproduced from James Hardin, *Lahav II: Households and the Use of Domestic Space at Iron II Tell Halif; An Archaeology of Destruction*, Reports of the Lahav Research Project (Winona Lake, IN: Eisenbrauns, 2010), fig. 5.12. © 2010 Eisenbrauns.

---

114. See, Holladay, *Jeremiah 1*, 254; *CAD* 8:110–11.

Watching their mothers and other women in the house prepare the daily bread along with the special cakes was a vital part of a young girl's education. She learned how much flour must be prepared to provide food for her family, as well as for offerings to the gods. In learning these things, the girl internalized the proper recipes, ingredients, and steps needed to enact different rituals. If the family had more than one god it venerated or provided offerings to their ancestors, daughters would need to learn how to do these other meal-based rituals as well so that when it was their turn, they were able to make offerings that provided efficacious outcomes.

5.4. Summary

This chapter explores the child's world and the way in which parents helped to shape that world. From an early age parents began socializing, enculturating, and educating their children. Socialization and enculturation can be seen through acts of gendering. Sometimes parents actively gendered their children, and other times the children were passively gendered through observing what adult males and females did in Israelite society. For example, parents actively gendered their sons by circumcising them. Once a puberty rite, in ancient Israel, the rite was displaced to infancy. Infant boys did not have a choice in the matter; the parents took it upon themselves to gender their infant in this way. Little girls did not have an early physical gendering marker in the same way as little boys. The yearly ritual referred to in Judg 11 gives some evidence of a puberty rite for girls. Recalling the journey of Jephthah's daughter, pubescent females would go to the hills and perform a ceremony where they mourned their virginity. Both male and female children were actively taught how to become proper Israelite men and women. This teaching did not happen at a school desk, but happened through modeling proper gender performances. For a child, time spent passively observing adults was soon turned into active participation in their own education. Gender performances on the part of the adult provided a child with an education, one that would allow a child to successfully reproduce Israelite culture.

The child's activities within their world can be considered gendered in as much as girls carried out female activities and boys, male activities. For male children, these gender performances first took the shape of learning how to work in the fields and tend to the flocks. Leaving his mother's side, a boy would venture out to do "boy" tasks, such as helping with sheep shearing or keeping watch over a co-op of baby animals. He learned how to do these by accompanying his father, older brothers, or other men in the village. Becoming an Israelite man also meant learning self-control, wearing his hair long, becoming self-sufficient, and most importantly undergoing feats of strength. For young boys, this would begin as it did for David, in the field, keeping the flocks safe from animals such as lions, bears, and hyenas. The cunning and wit gained there could then be transferred to the battlefield where the boy could show his readiness to become a man by proving his military prowess.

Female children began to mirror their mother's performances first in small ways and later in more active ways. Little girls might watch a mother go about her daily household chores and then imitate them as she played house. As the girl grew, she would be given age appropriate tasks. She might help with milking sheep or goats or collecting water from the spring. Some tasks could be learned gradually. For example, the production of textiles, clothes, mats, and other woven items required many hands and was a process that took time to master. Learning how to grind grain to the proper consistency and make it into the bread eaten at every meal also required time. A girl would also learn the ritual acts surrounding the meal, such as separating some dough for an offering, or making special cakes for a goddess. In each of these different ways, parents passed on important information to their children as they socialized and enculturated them as proper Israelites.

As children began to grow and become enculturated, they started to manipulate material culture. Some of the discussions above hint at this. For example, tasks that a child carried out required a child to touch and change the world in which she lived. A girl would learn how to make bread or weave, which would include using such things as a grinding stone, mortar and pestle, loom weights, and spindles and whorls. Boys would learn how to use implements needed for farming and herding, or possibly tools used in the family trade. However, before children were ready to pick up the real objects and engage in such work it is possible that children in ancient Israel, like children in the modern ethnographic studies, began to learn through play. Chapter 7 touches upon enculturation as one avenue for understanding the function of play. However, material culture is more than just something a child uses for work or play; material culture is also a way a society can broadcast their culture to others. Chapter 6 discusses material culture and the role it plays via the use of dress and adornment in a child's life.

6

Dressing Up

Playing dress up is a fun pastime for many children. In putting on clothing that belongs to another person or profession, a child enters a world of make-believe. While it is unlikely that ancient Israelite children dressed up as princesses or policemen, their clothes did say something about who they were and the status they held. Yet even dressed in regular clothing, through play, a child could pretend to be someone or something else. The next two chapters explore the categories of physical appearance and leisure activities associated with playing, two elements that comprised what an Israelite child might have looked like to the outside observer.

6.1. Introducing Clothes

The Hebrew Bible states the first clothing ever donned by humans was a pair of fig leaves (Gen 3:7). Arguably not the most durable form of clothing, God provided humans with cloaks of animal skins to cover their bodies (Gen 3:21). While the account in Genesis does not reference children, it is a coming-of-age story. The preadolescent, innocent Adam and Eve mature into sexual beings after eating the forbidden fruit. Both recognize that they are naked and that they should cover their nakedness (Gen 3:10–11). A similar coming-of-age story is found in the Epic of Gilgamesh with the character of Enkidu. When he first enters the story, he is a wild man who lives among the animals, an ancient Tarzan, as it were. Like Adam and Eve, he is naked and unashamed. Upon sexual congress with Shamat Harmitu, he undergoes a change and becomes humanized. As a sign of his change, he enters the civilized world where he must wear clothing. Clothing in these stories represents the thing that makes these characters human, the thing that differentiates them from the animals they have lived among.[1] While clothing can take on social and cultural symbols, it can also indicate age.[2] Clothing in these myths also signifies the difference between a child and an adult. The clothes make the (wo)man, as it were.

Eventually clothing shifted from animal skins to woven garments, with wool being the most popular textile. The invention of the two-beam vertical loom in Syria, around 1450 BCE allowed patterns to be added to the textiles.[3] Loom weights, spindle whorls, and even loom frames have been discovered at almost every archaeological site and attest to the production of textiles on both a domestic and industrial scale. Because of the landscape and weather patterns in the land of Israel, textiles have not been preserved, and one must rely upon textual clues, iconographic evidence, and the ethnographic literature to reconstruct children's clothing.

6.1.1. Anthropology of Clothing and Adornment

Interpreting the clothing and adornments in the various sources requires an understanding of what clothing means. One way of thinking about this is to ask what practical uses clothing provides. For example, clothing and adornments can protect one from the elements, provide warmth and/or serve as a way to carry objects necessary to daily life (such as an ax or javelin). However, clothing goes beyond the practical function, providing an unspoken means of communication. This discourse is a way of conveying meaning through clothing and adornment. Clothes with different designs, fringes, materials, or shapes may have some aesthetic meaning to the wearer, but often these choices are driven by something else. For example, clothing can also be understood as divine protection. Genesis 2–3 develops the concept of clothing as a literal symbol of God's protection (Gen 3:21). Ethnographic studies of children's clothing in western Iran attest to

---

1. Clothing can also be understood as cultural progress and a mark of civilization in these myths. See M. E. Vogelzang and W. J. van Bekkum, "Meaning and Symbolism of Clothing in Ancient Near Eastern Texts," in *Scripta Signa Vocis: Studies about Scripts, Scriptures, Scribes and Languages in the Near East Presented to J. H. Hospers* (Groningen: E. Forsten, 1986), 268, 273.

2. For social and cultural aspects of clothing, see Bryan Turner, *The Body and Society: Explorations in Social Theory* (Los Angeles: SAGE, 2008), 5–6.

3. Dominique Collon, "Clothing and Grooms in Ancient Western Asia," in Sasson, *Civilizations of the Ancient Near East*, 1:503–4.

this belief as well; children are bedecked with many items meant to protect them and ward off evil.[4]

The emotional component behind clothes is something a contemporary reader might resonate with: the feeling of opening the closet and picking out an ensembled based on how one "feels" that day. One might dress based on an upcoming activity. For example, sneakers are easier to play sports in than dress shoes. Furthermore, one might choose tennis sneakers for tennis or soccer cleats for soccer. Dressed in full tennis gear, as opposed to old sneakers and jeans helps one feel more like a tennis player, while at the same time presenting oneself as such to the opponent. Within the category of clothing and emotion, clothing displays mood and the power to execute social roles, at the same time clothing can also display attraction or shame.[5] Both attraction and shame are related to clothing's ability to proclaim a person's social standing. Attraction to power and wealth might be initiated by seeing a person dressed nicely, for "all members of a society can recognize what that society defines as 'fine' dress or a 'fine' appearance; there is no difficulty in recognizing those with wealth and political status by means of their attire."[6] As the adage "dress for success" suggests, dressing nicely affects how people perceive you and the level of attraction they have towards you.

Shame has a strong relationship with the lack of clothing, whether it be too few clothes, inappropriate clothing, or total lack of clothing. Nudity, in specific, is important for this discussion because the nudity of children is recognized as distinct from the nudity of adults. Whereas nudity for adults is considered shameful and uncivilized by the ancient world, nudity of (small) children is devoid of these associations.[7] The anthropological literature states by in large that nakedness in children is okay because they know no shame. Older anthropological thought understood modesty and the covering of the body as an impulse; how-

---

4. Watson, *Archaeological Ethnography in Western Iran*, 233, 270.

5. Ronald A. Schwarz, "Uncovering the Secret Vice: Towards an Anthropology of Clothing and Adornment," in *The Fabrics of Culture: The Anthropology of Clothing and Adornment*, ed. Justine M. Cordwell and Ronald A. Schwarz (The Hague: Mouton, 1979), 23–46.

6. Heather McKay, "Gendering the Discourse of Display," in *On Reading Prophetic Texts: Gender Specific and Related Studies in Memory of Fokkelien van Dijk-Hemmes*, ed. Bob Becking and Mindert Dijkstra (Brill: Leiden, 1996), 173.

7. Vogelzang and van Bekkum, "Meaning and Symbolism of Clothing," 273 n. 45; McKay, "Gendering the Discourse of Display," 190–91.

ever, more recent understandings associate clothing with social control. Anthropologists note that: "The shame occasioned by nakedness, and the corresponding need for conforming citizens to be decently clad, is taught to the young of each society as an appropriate internalization of every adult's responsibility to their community."[8] Just as Adam and Eve knew they were naked after experiencing a sexual awakening, the presence of clothing acts as a sign of social and sexual control in a society. Properly covering up and presenting one's body in a socially acceptable way is something seen even today, where the debate rages on between feminists who assert women should be able to dress how they wish without garnering unwanted male attention, and others who suggest that a scantily or suggestively dressed woman is presenting—via her clothing—a specific type of sexualized message.

6.2. Clothing in the Biblical Text

In addition to the functions identified by anthropologists, adornment in the biblical text has been shown to serve three other roles: affirming or reinforcing social norms, enhancing a person who is important or attractive, and/or showing the role or status of a character.[9] These conclusions are based on studies of adult clothing in the Bible.[10] We can ask whether clothing functions in the same way for children in the text or whether clothing functions differently. The stories of Samuel, Joseph, and David include well-known scenes where clothing plays an important role. A brief examination of these narratives shows how the clothing in each story portrays a specific social status.

---

8. McKay, "Gendering the Discourse of Display," 190–91, and bibliography in her n. 72.

9. McKay, "Gendering the Discourse of Display," 181–82; Nelly Furman, "History Versus Her Story: Male Genealogy and Female Strategy in the Jacob Cycle," in *Feminist Perspectives on Biblical Scholarship*, ed. Adele Collins (Atlanta: Scholars Press, 1985), 107–16.

10. Mayer Gruber, "Private Life in Ancient Israel," in Sasson, *Civilizations of the Ancient Near East*, 1:641; Albenda, "Western Asiatic Women in the Iron Age," 82–88. For an overview of clothing and adornment spanning the ancient Near East through to Christian times, see Alicia Batten, "Clothing and Adornment," *Biblical Theology Bulletin* 40.3 (2010): 148–59.

6.2.1. מעיל קטן "Little Robe"

Samuel is the youngest of the children mentioned in the biblical text who receives special clothing. His story begins with his mother, Hannah, dedicating him to a life of service before he is even born (1 Sam 1:11). A few verses later, the reader sees Hannah struggling with her vow. She will not go up to the yearly sacrifice as is her custom but will remain behind to tend her newborn baby. In fact, she will not attend the sacrifice until Samuel is weaned because if she brings her nursing child along with her, she will have to leave him there in fulfillment of the vow (1 Sam 1:21–23). When Samuel finally enters into the Lord's service, Hannah visits her beloved child each year and brings him a "little robe" (מעיל קטן > maʿîl qāṭōn) that she has made (1 Sam 2:19). This kind of garment is worn over the inner tunic and denotes the special status of the person wearing it. Other people to wear a מעיל include men of rank, the daughters of David, and the high priest.[11] Viewing clothing as having an emotional component, one might understand this article of clothing as a way for Samuel to "feel priestly" and to present his high-ranking office to the lay people. The text does not state how long it took to make, or what it looked like, but Samuel's little robe is special because his mother made it for him and because it signifies his social status. As he grows, Samuel no longer wears a מעיל קטן, but a full sized מעיל. Samuel's garment is so distinctive that his robe comes to be synonymous with his status as a man of God (1 Sam 28:14).

Notable here is that his *mother* makes the garment and presents it to him on a yearly basis. Heather McKay makes the point that in the Bible "adornments are provided by one type of giver only—males."[12] This statement is generally true for the biblical text, and technically true if one considers everything within a house to be the property of the (male) owner of the house. Since women are the main textile producers, the reader expects that Hannah would make the garment out of wool or other materials provided to her by her husband. However, whereas other biblical texts make a point of male characters being the ones to give the adorning items, it seems significant that here a female character is doing the giving. First Samuel 2:19 states specifically that Hannah would bring it (the garment) up to him every year when she accompanied Elkanah

---

11. BDB, s.v. "מעיל." Exod 28:33–34; 1 Sam 18:4; 2 Sam 13:18; Ezek 26:16.
12. McKay, "Gendering the Discourse of Display," 199.

to make the annual sacrifice. Given McKay's conclusions, there seems to me three possible ways of understanding this exchange. First, it might be that regular everyday clothing was not considered a gift. We know that at this point Samuel had entered the Lord's service and was wearing a linen ephod symbolic of that position (1 Sam 2:18). This solution to female gift-giving is plausible but seems unlikely. The text seems to go out of its way to mention this special tradition Hannah had in bringing the garment to Samuel. The second possibility is that Hannah represents an exception to the rule. A third possibility is that it was acceptable for females to give male children adornments until a certain age when a child no longer was a child but was wearing adult clothing. Granted, Samuel was wearing the linen ephod associated with temple service, but this does not mean he was an adult; 1 Sam 1:21 seems to imply that Samuel was still a young child. The issue here is the word נער describing Samuel. The NJPS translates this as "young Samuel, meanwhile grew up in the service of the Lord." Other versions translate נער as "the child Samuel" (KJV, JPS 1917, ASV, ERV) and "the boy Samuel" (NIV, ESV, NASB). The picture here is of a young boy in the process of growing up. After this verse, Hannah leaves the narrative.[13] While the text does not give a cut-off date for Hannah's yearly gift, the fact we hear nothing more of such gifts confines their significance to the initial years of Samuel's service before the Lord. Those writing from a social-scientific perspective argue that Samuel was abandoned by his mother; Hannah had voluntarily given up control of her son to another person/institution.[14] Yet Hannah's yearly visit and the מעיל קטן play a very important role in understanding her actions. For it was not as we might think today, a total abandonment where all ties are cut off. Rather, the מעיל קטן functions both as a marker of Samuel's special status and as a symbol of the unbroken bond between mother and son.

---

13. The next set of narratives in 1 Sam 2–3 take place in the tent of meeting and describe Samuel's ascendancy to the priesthood and the downfall of Eli's family.

14. "Abandonment … refers to the voluntary relinquishing of control over their children by their natal parents or guardians, whether by leaving them somewhere, selling them, or legally consigning them to some other person or institution." John Boswell, *The Kindness of Strangers: The Abandonment of Children in Western Europe from Late Antiquity to the Renaissance* (New York: Pantheon, 1988), 24. This is the approach explored by Naomi Steinberg in *World of the Child in the Hebrew Bible*, 98–105. In this, Steinberg provides a comprehensive bibliography of scholarship approaching the Samuel birth narrative as an annunciation-type scene and barren woman motif, as well as scholarship examining theological and composition history.

6.2.2. כתנת פסים "Long-Sleeved Tunic"

Joseph also receives a special piece of clothing from a parent.[15] To signify his status as the favored child, Jacob gives Joseph a כתנת פסים (*kətōnet passîm*), usually translated as "coat of many colors" (Gen 37:3). A כתנת is more accurately a tunic worn next to the skin, not a coat. Moreover, the description פסים literally means "flat of the hand/foot," so that the tunic given to Joseph seems to be long-sleeved and long-skirted.[16] The phrase כתנת פסים is also used to describe the dress worn by unmarried princesses of marriageable age (2 Sam 13:18). In 2 Sam 13, the כתנת פסים functions as an outward marker that Tamar is one of the virgin daughters of King David. As such, it should afford her that protection. On the one hand, the dress declares she is her father's property, and, on the other hand, it protects her by prohibiting advances based on her royal status.[17] Tamar tears her כתנת פסים when she is defiled by her brother (2 Sam 13:19). The symbolic protection provided to her by that garment has failed her, a failure that she exposes to the public by symbolically ripping the dress.[18] At seventeen years old, Joseph, like Tamar is unmarried and of marriageable age (Gen 37:2). Joseph's כתנת פסים does not necessarily proclaim that his sexuality is his father's property, but it does function as a marker of his status within the family, and as such, should have provided him some protection. Rather, Joseph is stripped of his tunic, and once it is removed, he is thrown into a pit and sold (Gen 37:23–28). The removal of the tunic symbolically removes him from the family. Notably, in both stories the כתנת פסים is worn by teenagers of an elevated status (a favored son and a daughter of the king). The garment, in turn, is torn when they experience a symbolic death: eaten by a wild animal (Gen 37:33) and sexually violated (2 Sam 13:11–19).

---

15. McKay understands Jacob's gift as a gift of honor from one male to another male ("Gendering the Discourse of Display," 187).

16. BDB, s.v. "כתנת"; BDB, s.v. "פסס." There is, however, no consensus on what exactly the phrase means. For a discussion of possible meanings including "ornamented tunic" see Nahum Sarna, *The JPS Torah Commentary: Genesis* (Philadelphia: Jewish Publication Society, 1989), 255–56.

17. McKay, "Gendering the Discourse of Display," 195.

18. McKay, "Gendering the Discourse of Display," 195.

6.2.3. מד "Outer Garment"

David too removes clothing in what could be construed as a near-death scene. The young shepherd boy comes before King Saul offering to face the Philistine hero Goliath (1 Sam 17:31–37). King Saul accepts David's offer and clothes David with his own kingly garb (1 Sam 17:38–39). David puts on the king's מד (*mad*), a generic word for "outer garment" along with the king's bronze helmet, breastplate, and sword.[19] The king's clothing proves too awkward for David to move in, so he removes them and takes up his usual shepherding adornments: his stick, sling, and shepherd's bag (1 Sam 17:40). The text emphasizes David's lack of battle armor to highlight his youth and innocent trust in God. In much the same way as the Adam and Eve narrative uses clothing to present a condensed coming-of-age narrative, so too does the David and Goliath story. After the battle, David is now strong enough to wield Goliath's own heavy sword and chop off his head (1 Sam 17:50–51). Not only does David gain the status of a warrior, but he also gains the respect of Saul, Jonathan, the army, and the people Israel (1 Sam 18:1–7). He grows into a man.[20]

6.2.4. חתלה "Swaddling Band"

Another reference to child's clothing that deserves mention is that of the swaddling band or swaddling blanket. In recounting the creation of the earth, God uses the term חתלה (*ḥătullāh*), "swaddling band," to describe how dense clouds bound up the seas when it gushed forth from the womb (Job 38:8–9).[21] While this reference describes the clothing item in poetic terms, it also attests to an awareness that infants were wrapped in swaddling bands. Such imagery recalls the discussion in chapter 2 of the long pieces of cloth associated with the goddess Ninhursag and the lack of swaddling bestowed upon the infant Jerusalem in Ezek 16:4.

The textual examples from the Hebrew Bible include some memorable references to clothing worn by children and even hint at the possibility that social status was portrayed through dress. Yet none of the narratives give a detailed description of the clothing. We are left to wonder how age

---

19. BDB, s.v. "מד."
20. Wilson, *Making Men*, 126–28.
21. BDB, s.v. "חתלה."

and gender might have affected a child's dress and adornment. Here the archaeological record can be helpful.

6.3. Clothing in Monumental Art: The Lachish Reliefs

Monumental art provides the first resource for examining children's dress. Children are most readily found in deportation scenes of the Neo-Assyrians. They are integral to the artist's rendition of deportation as children symbolize that entire families and population groups were deported.[22] Neo-Assyrian reliefs make it easy to define younger children, but more difficult to determine who is an adolescent and who is an adult. It is only possible to distinguish the adolescent/older child from an adult through a careful examination of height, dress, and adornment in comparison with that of the other individuals, both younger and older.

The reliefs in Sennacherib's Southwest Palace at Nineveh present an excellent case study for examining ancient Israelite, specifically Judean, children. These reliefs depict the deportation of Judean families from the city of Lachish in 701 BCE. When examining the clothing shown here, it is important to keep in mind the class of people being deported. The Assyrians had a policy of mixing populations, so that they deported the more elite members of a population and replaced them with a similar class of Assyrians. This mixing can be seen in the biblical text in 2 Kgs 17:24. The deported people brought to Assyria could become land tenants, raising crops and vineyards and producing wine, oil, and honey (2 Kgs 18:28–32). They might also become craftsmen for the state of Assyria or even high-ranking officials in the Assyrian administration.[23] Based on the depictions of the people depicted on the Lachish reliefs, we might conclude the deported individuals are wearing clothing typical of the upper classes.

Since the Judeans march out by families, we may assume that children shown next to an adult are closely related to that adult. Through these

---

22. In her examination of Neo-Assyrian reliefs, Schwyn places the depiction of children into various categories, including: child on an adult's shoulders, child holding the garment of a caregiver, child self-standing accompanied by a caregiver, child sitting with an adult caregiver in a wagon or on a pack animal, and child sitting alone with other children in a wagon or on a pack animal (Schwyn, "Kinderbetreuung im 9.–7. Jahrhundert," 1–14).

23. Gershon Galil, "Israelite Exiles in Media: A New Look at ND 2443+," *VT* 59 (2009): 71–79.

scenes, the viewer is presented with a glimpse of children from infancy through adolescence. The cluster of children by families indicates that the relative age of the child is shown primarily through height differentiation and secondarily through clothing and adornment. As will be shown in the analysis of the relief, clothing and adornment are gender specific; there is a "male costume," and "female costume." There also appears a third category, that of "gender indeterminate," meaning gender is difficult to ascertain based on the relief.[24]

The drawings in figures 6.1–6.5 are based on photographs of the Lachish reliefs housed in the British Museum.[25] These photographs are unique because they were taken using Reflective Transferring Imaging [RTI] technology provided by the University of Southern California which allows the "researcher to use a no-cost, easily downloadable viewer to examine a given target from any light angle (or with a combination of two virtual light angles) or boost the reflectivity/contrast of a surface to bring out optimal details in an easy and intuitive manner…. RTI can be of decisive value for analyzing any text or artifact where a clear view of the textures supplies crucial information for interpretation and analysis."[26] The textures in reliefs can sometimes obscure crucial details that even a lens closely zoomed-in can miss. The following analysis of the drawings comes from the viewing the photographs with a variety of different lighting angles.

6.3.1. The Littlest Children

The very youngest Judeans can be seen riding on two different carts (figs. 6.1 and 6.5). Each cart is manned by a female figure, identified as such by her clothing. Both carts have a woman at the font driving the pack animal. In figure 6.1, a second woman sits behind the driver, holding an infant in her lap. The infant (Infant A) is naked, which is to be expected, and the gender of the child is not immediately marked in any way. Infant A's hair

---

24. Schwyn notes that the gender and hairstyle of children is not always depicted and that gender identification based on naked bodies is also not always possible. In her analysis so far, she found 2.5 times as many boys as girls identifiable on Neo-Assyrian reliefs (Schwyn, "Kinderbetreuung im 9.–7. Jahrhundert," 4).

25. Photographs were taken by Jason Riley and used with his permission.

26. University of Southern California West Semitic Research Project, "Training Program," https://tinyurl.com/SBL1729m.

Figs. 6.1–6.5 (below and following page). Lachish relief, Nineveh, 700–681 BCE, Southwest Palace Room XXXVI, panels 8–10.

and perspective, however, is unexpected. Unlike the other figurines in the deportation scenes, Infant A faces backward, showing the left side of the head. All other infants and children face forward in the Lachish relief and show the right side of their head. Infant A most definitely has something on his or her head as can be seen in figure 6.2. One option is that this is a head covering of some sort. However, this seems unlikely because no other Judean infants, walking or seated, in the Lachish relief or other, have a head covering like this.[27] A second, more intriguing option is to understand this as hair. If it is hair, then it is shoulder length hair that has a little wave or curl towards the end. While hair does not help too much in determining gender, it might show a Levantine tradition of a sidelock or the influence of Egyptian hairstyles on some portion of Israelites.[28] This possibility is explored further below. A second child (Child A) sits behind mother and baby, holding on to the female adult for support. Child A wears a short-sleeved ankle-length tunic that is unbelted. Child A appears to have short, wavy or curly hair, similar to the texture of hair seen in the adult male seen leading the pack animal further to the right in figure 6.1.[29]

In the second cart, a young child (Child B) sits behind the woman, holding onto her for support (fig. 6.5). Three little ribs are apparent, demonstrating that Child B is naked. While Child B appears rather large in proportion to the woman, the lack of clothing and the fact that the child is riding, not walking, shows the child's relatively young age. It is difficult to tell whether it is a male or female child, since the genitalia are not shown. However, the child has well defined arm and calf muscles, similar to how a grown man's arms and legs are carved.[30] A grown women's legs, while mostly covered by her dress, nonetheless do not show any indica-

---

27. Schwyn, "Kinderbetreuung im 9.–7. Jahrhundert."

28. Schwyn notes that most hairstyles on infants are ambiguous (Schwyn, "Kinderbetreuung im 9.–7. Jahrhundert," 4). Examples of children in Egyptian victory reliefs, similar in nature to the Neo-Assyrian reliefs, can be found in Keel's discussion of the various Egyptian depiction of Canaanite "atonement" scenes. Othmar Keel, "Kanaanäische Sühneriten auf ägyptischen Tempelreliefs," VT 25 (1975): 448 = Abb. 15–17, 457 = Abb. 21, 22. A third possibility is that this shows an Assyrian tradition of an infant's hairstyle. However, since the rest of the relief takes pains to identify an individual's ethnicity through clothing and adornment this third possibility seems the least likely reason for the infant's hairstyle.

29. A second possibility is that Child A wears a stripped head covering or hat of some sort, but this is unprecedented in the relief.

30. Based on the attention given to the musculature and the fact that this child

tion of developed leg or calf muscles. Neither does one find definition in a female's arms. One wonders if the muscle development shown on Child B is a way of indicating (from a side view where genitalia would not be easily seen) that it is a boy.

The similarity in size and pose between the two young children riding on carts suggest that they are the same age; however, the difference in clothing suggests they might be two different genders. Ethnographic parallels support the idea that male children went naked for a longer period than their female counterparts.[31] In a part of the Lachish relief not photographed in RTI but copied by R. D. Barnett, one sees another small, naked child with no hair.[32] Rather than riding in a cart, this child is walking, which lends support to the idea that perhaps male children went naked longer in ancient Israel too. Nakedness might also be an artistic convention meant to show very young age or simply a way of distinguishing young males and females.

Egyptian temple reliefs at Karnak, Luxor, and Medinet Habu provide an interesting parallel to the depiction of infants in the Lachish reliefs. Here again the subject is the destruction of a city in the land of Israel by a foreign ruler. While the reliefs come from a slightly earlier period (1550–1077 BCE) and show the destruction of Canaanite, rather than Judean or Israelite cities, the children are all naked and wear a sidelock of hair. The age of the Canaanite children in these reliefs is not known, but as Othmar Keel notes, it has been argued that they held a high status, perhaps even that of crowned prince.[33] Since elite Egyptian children of both genders were often depicted nude and wearing their hair in a sidelock it is difficult to know whether the Canaanite children also looked this way or if nudity with a sidelock was an Egyptian iconographic convention to depict chil-

---

is sitting and not being held, I am identifying the individual as a young child, rather than an infant.

31. According to one ethnographic study, in southern India, boys went naked until age seven and girls until age five. Paul Hockings, "Badaga Apparel: Protection and Symbol," in Cordell and Schwarz, *Fabrics of Culture*, 152. See also the discussion of nakedness among children in the Yorba tribe in Henry John Drewal, "Pageantry and Power in Yorba Costuming," in Cordell and Schwarz, *Fabrics of Culture*, 190.

32. R. D. Barnett et al., *Sculptures from the Southwest Palace of Sennacherib at Nineveh* (London: British Museum Press, 1998), 338. This particular section of the relief was at an angle and height too difficult to photograph using RTI.

33. Keel, "Kanaanäische Sühneriten auf ägyptischen Tempelreliefs," *VT* 25 (1975): 436–42.

dren in any geographical region.[34] The fact that both the Egyptian record and the Assyrian record use nudity to depict children in the land of Israel could, however, point to an actual custom. It should also be noted that if the hair on Infant A represents a sidelock, then it is possible the other nude children in the relief may also have sported this haircut. Because Infant A is the only nude infant/child depicted facing backwards, the other naked children facing forwards could have had a sidelock on the side of their head hidden to the viewer.

Analyzing the group of youngest children, we can make the following observations. The youngest child appears to be Infant A, sitting on his or her mother's lap (figs. 6.1 and 6.2). It is possible that very young children wore their hair gathered in a sidelock on the left. Infants were depicted without clothing, a practice that seems to last until they could sit supported on their own and even walk on their own (fig. 6.4). Children who were too young to walk long distances rode on carts. Of the three young children on carts, a comparison of the two children who could sit up by themselves provides some preliminary insights into the differences between male and female children. Child A in figure 6.1 appears to be a female child. Whereas each of the young boys in the Lachish reliefs have short tunic with belts, this young child is dressed like an older female, in an ankle length tunic.[35] In addition, she wears her head uncovered and her short, curly hair exposed. If head covering is linked to puberty like it is in many conservative Middle Eastern cultures today, the uncovered head of Child A might demonstrate the desexualized nature of prepubescent females.[36] Some scholars have identified the covering worn by older

---

34. Notably, during the Old Kingdom, Middle Kingdom, and New Kingdom, infants, and at times some older children, are depicted in the nude as a way of showing they were prepubescent (Janssen and Janssen, *Growing Up in Ancient Egypt*, 26–27; Feucht, "Childhood," 1:262). The sidelock became a symbol of male and female children alike from the Fifth Dynasty on. The lock was either braided or had the end rolled up, perhaps similar to what is seen in with Infant A. Notably, Egyptian children retain the sidelock of youth seemingly for their entire childhood (Feucht, "Childhood," 1:262).

35. Alternatively, all young children might wear long dresses. However, this seems to be unsupported both by the relief itself and the anthropological reports.

36. Ethnographic studies in Arab-Muslim countries, like Egypt, find that women donned the veil as an act of resistance against Westernization. They embraced the veil as a feminist symbol of group identity. Fadwa el Guindi, *Veil: Modesty, Privacy, and Resistance* (Oxford: Berg, 1999). In Turkish society, covering the head is related

females as an outer mantle worn like a hood: "The long rectangle cloth worn by the women of Lachish served as both an outer coat and head covering."[37] It is possible females are wearing their outer mantles for the purpose of traveling, but it seems equally as possible that this portion of the Judean female population covered their heads. Whatever the case may be, Child A is not donning this particular adornment.

On the other hand, Child B, sitting behind the female in figure 6.5 is naked, without any hair depicted. A similarly depicted child (naked without hair) is shown walking in front of two women.[38] I would tentatively suggest that the two naked children without hair showing are male. In the case of the child in figure 6.5, careful work was done to show the musculature in the legs and arms, similar to the way the muscles of adult males, and as will be shown later, younger males, were carved.[39] The infant with the proposed sidelock, however, does not have such detail on the legs or arms, keeping this infant in the "ambiguous gender" category.

6.3.2. Younger Children

Younger boys are about one-third of the height of the adults (figs. 6.3 and 6.4). The clothing worn by these boys is not as elaborate as the older boys. While they have the same short-sleeved, knee-length tunic, there is no decorative band on the skirt. One man has two younger boys flanking him (fig 6.4). The one on the right is slightly taller, coming up to the highest

---

to a complex understanding of hair and what it symbolizes (sexuality being one of those symbols). Carol Delaney, "Untangling the Meanings of Hair in Turkish Society," *Anthropological Quarterly* 67.4 (1994): 159–72. Unbound and uncovered hair has many meanings within the Greco-Roman world as well, where again there is an association with sexuality. Charles Cosgrove, "A Woman's Unbound Hair in the Greco-Roman World, with Special Reference to the Story of the 'Sinful Woman' in Luke 7:36–50," *JBL* 124 (2005): 675–92.

37. Albenda, "Western Asiatic Women in the Iron Age," 84; King and Stager, *Life in Biblical Israel*, 272. Neither publication gives a reason for understanding these "long clothes" as an outer mantle as opposed to a specific head covering.

38. This child is very difficult to photograph due to the positioning of the relief in the British Museum. Jason Riley was not able to take a photo using RTI, so my conclusions here are based on Barnett's drawings of the child (Barnett et al., *Sculptures from the Southwest Palace*, pl. 338).

39. According to Barnett's drawing, this same nonmuscular depiction may be true of the child walking in front of the two women.

decorative band on his skirt. The boy on the left is slightly shorter; the top of his head reaches the second band on the man's skirt. Both boys wear the short tunic and belt. The taller boy has a braided or twisted belt that resembles that of the older boys and men. However, this younger boy's belt is not quite the same; it does not include the length that hangs past his waist. The shorter boy has an even simpler belt. It appears to be a plain sash, devoid of decoration, that circles his waist. Both younger boys have uncovered, smooth heads. The young boy in figure 6.4 also has a short tunic, a simple belt, and a smooth head (see also fig. 6.3 top). Men with uncovered heads on the other hand, are shown with curly hair, which might suggest that boys of this young age had shaved heads or wore a skull cap of some sort.

6.3.3. Older Children

Regardless of gender, older children are shown as reaching a height just above an adult's waist (figs. 6.3 and 6.5). Older boys are dressed like their fathers in a short-sleeved, knee-length tunic, which has a horizontal band around the bottom and midway up the skirt. The tunic is held in place, like an adult man's, with a belt that appears either braided or twisted, the length of which hangs down between his legs (fig. 6.5). Both adult men and older boys wear a rounded head covering that appears to have fringed earflaps of some sort (fig. 6.5). Individuals of this slightly shorter stature do not have facial hair like some of the grown men they accompany. Older girls are depicted wearing clothes like their mothers's: an unbelted ankle length tunic with short-sleeves (fig. 6.3). They also wear the same head covering as grown women. The female costume was much simpler than the male costume. There is little degree of variation between adults and adolescents. If Child A is indeed a female, the only difference in the female costume for the young is the lack of a head covering.

The male costume, while similar, is not the same for the different ages. Once a boy is old enough to don clothing, he puts on the short tunic worn by males of all ages in the relief. Just as clothing is used to show status in other ancient Near Eastern cultures, it appears clothing shows status in this group of deportees.[40] Belt decoration specifically seems linked to

---

40. For example, in ancient Egypt, the length of the triangle in a man's skirt is related to his position in society. The longer the point, the more elite the individual. Blanche Payne, *History of Costume: From the Ancient Egyptians to the Twentieth Century* (New York: Harper & Row, 1965), 9–14.

social age; the older a boy becomes, the more elaborate the belt becomes. The shortest (and presumably the youngest) male children with clothing have a plain belt (figs. 6.3 and 6.4). The slightly older boy, standing to the right of his male caregiver and standing a little taller than the boy behind him, wears a decorated belt (fig. 6.4). The oldest boy (fig. 6.5) wears a decorated belt like that of an adult male, with the extra length falling between his legs. The use of the belt to show social ages is significant, for it is how males gird their loins. Katherine Low has linked the relationship between gender and loin girding to the display of strength and power in the Hebrew Bible.[41] If Low's observations regarding loin girding in the Hebrew Bible as displays of social power correlate to dress, then it is possible the progression in the length and ornamentation of the boys' belts were used to signify their rank in the social order. Perhaps as boys reached different social ages or passed rites of passage within their family and/or society, they were given new belts.[42]

6.4. Adorning Children in Ancient Israel

6.4.1. Burials

Looking at clothing and adornment in the reliefs provides a second-hand, or outsider's, perspective on how children in ancient Israel dressed. The burials of infants and children, on the other hand, provide a first-hand set of data. While burials present the deceased in an idealized manner, the personal items found in infant and child burials often correspond to adornment items associated with these ages in other sources, making burials a valuable source to investigate.[43]

An investigation of over 450 individual infant and child burials from the Early Bronze Age through Iron Age II (3600–539 BCE) found examples of toggle pins, rings, earrings, bracelets, anklets, beads, bones and shells, scarabs, faience and alabaster items, and knives buried with these little

---

41. Katherine Low, "Implications Surrounding Girding the Loins in Light of Gender, Body, and Power," *JSOT* 36 (2011): 3–30.

42. Marking a movement from one stage in life to another is reminiscent of the belting ceremonies used in various martial arts to distinguish ranks.

43. Baxter, *Archaeology of Childhood*, 97; Michael Parker Pearson, *The Archaeology of Death and Burial* (College Station: Texas A&M Press, 2000), 102–4; Garroway, *Children in the Ancient Near Eastern Household*, 24 n. 43.

ones.[44] Of those interments with personal grave goods, bracelets, beads and scarabs were by far the most common items. Bracelets and anklets were made from bronze and iron and at times were even found still circling the leg or arm bones. Beads were made from carnelian, bone, glass, and in some cases, precious metals. Some beads appeared to be strung in a necklace, but sometimes only a solitary bead or two was placed with the body. Shiny objects, like beads and metal jewelry would reflect light and could also be used to scare away demons and other maladies.[45] Ethnographic reports from Iran detail an almost comical picture in which the clothing of little children is bedecked with items meant to shun the Evil Eye.[46] Little children's jackets are laden with blue and white beads, cowry shells, rooster bones, old coins, and colorful buttons. In some cases, even swaddling blankets have shells and beads sewn on for protection.

Two sites from Israel stand as testament to the variety of adornments associated with children. The first example comes from Beth-Pelet (Tell el-Farʿah [South]). There three Iron Age I (1200–1000 BCE) child burials contained a rich array of personal grave goods including many such metal jewelry items and beads.[47] Tomb 204–205 contained fifteen gold beads, a set of gold earrings, and the remains of a child. Tomb 222 contained two children buried with carnelian beads, bronze anklets, toe rings, and gold, silver, and electrum earrings. No infants were buried at the site with such elaborate grave goods, which is not surprising considering that infants in general are buried with even fewer examples of personal grave goods. However, at a second site, Dothan, a group of three Iron Age II infant jar burials were found clustered together. Two of them contained iron bracelets, anklets, beads, and earrings. The report states "layers of small beads and two metal earrings" were in one jar, and in a second, a skull and "two leg bones with an anklet on each and what seems to be a bracelet encircling two small arm bones."[48] No other ceramic grave goods, such as a

44. Garroway, *Children in the Ancient Near Eastern Household*, 218–44, 295–98.

45. Carol Meyers discusses the use of light to fend off demons (*Rediscovering Eve*, 154–55), as does ch. 4 above.

46. Watson, *Archaeological Ethnography in Western Iran*, 233, 270.

47. Olga Tufnell, "Burials in Cemeteries 100 and 200," in *Beth-Pelet I*, ed. W. F. Petrie (London: British School of Archaeology in Egypt, 1930), 11–13.

48. Daniel Master et al., *Dothan I: Remains from the Tell (1953–1964)* (Winona Lake, IN: Eisenbrauns, 2005), 113.

bottle, were mentioned.[49] As a group, most infants and children at other sites throughout Israel were buried without personal grave goods, leading one to hypothesize that the items in these graves just mentioned might be indicators of social status. With Dothan in the hill country and Beth-Pelet located on a major trade route in the south, geography and the local economy might also factor into the results, showing the way in which local burial practices differed.

Moving slightly to the east, to the center of the Jordan Valley and the site of Tell es-Sa'idiyeh (biblical Zarethan, Josh 3:16; 1 Kgs 7:45–46), one finds an even more intriguing interpretation of personal grave goods. The burials here contained many Egyptian style amulets. During the Late Bronze Age, Egyptian amulets were worn as status symbols by adults, but by the Iron Age, these same items were worn by children as protective amulets. Furthermore, the metal ornaments and beads that were popular in the child and infant burials from Israel, are here associated specifically with infants, children, and female adults. Males did not have any of these items in their graves.[50] A separate study of anklets found within the Early Iron Age burials at the site revealed further information regarding the use of ornamentation to display gender and status.[51] While anklets (and bracelets) are found at many different sites, the size of the cemetery, age distribution of individuals, and relatively intact nature of burials at Tel es-Sa'idiyeh provided a significant number of burials to analyze.[52] Anklets

---

49. However, a fourth Iron Age II jar burial was found in Area A112 (Master, *Dothan I*, 112). This jar burial contained no jewelry but did have an Assyrian bottle jar associated with it. The presence of multiple jar burials at a single site and from the same period but containing different items demonstrates that burials and the goods with them were not uniform. Whether jewelry signaled a higher status infant is difficult to say.

50. See John Green's discussion of Tel es-Sa'idiyeh and the conclusions drawn from the burials in John Green, "Social Identity in the Jordan Valley during the Late Bronze and Early Iron Ages: Evidence from the Tall as-Sa'idiyya Cemetery," in *Studies in the History and Archaeology of Jordan XI*, ed. Fares al-Hmoud (Amman: Department of Antiquities, 2013), 419–29.

51. John Green, "Anklets and the Social Construction of Gender and Age in the Late Bronze and Early Iron Age Southern Levant," in *Archaeology and Women: Ancient and Modern Issues*, ed. Sue Hamilton, Ruth D. Whitehouse, and Katherine I. Wright (Walnut Creek, CA: Left Coast Press, 2007), 283–311.

52. Further work on ornamentation and the relationship between genders and ages will help determine whether the patterns found at Tel es-Sa'idiyeh are indicative of a local custom or a wider custom. Notably, no decorations were seen on the

were found in pairs on women, infants, and children. Burials of men on the other hand, rarely had anklets, and when they did it was a single anklet and the individual was of high status. However, the discovery of ornaments on female skeletons is well documented, and might correlated to the idea of "jewelry as money."[53] The practice of adorning children and infants with anklets has been linked anthropologically to rites of passage or protection from evil forces.[54] The interpretation of the amulets and anklets from Tel es-Saʿidiyeh supports the idea that gender and age determined the kinds of adornment worn by an individual at the site.

6.4.2. Ethnography

The ethnographic literature suggests that clothing in various villages is both gender and age specific, and relatively uniform. For example, in the western Iranian village of Hasanabad, children ages five to ten years old wear child-sized versions of adult clothing. Boys wear black or striped pants and an old shirt, and girls wear trousers and a gown, like their mothers.[55] Girls and women wear their hair in braids, bound with lightweight braided cords of yarn. Older girls and women line their inner eyes with black eye soot made from burned fat.[56] Kohl and other eyeliners were used throughout the ancient world and some cosmetic dishes have even been identified in the archaeological record. The interesting part here is that girls wear the makeup as well as the women; we might consider the possibility that this was the case too in the ancient world. Younger children at Hasanabad, of both sexes, ages one year to five years old, wear a knee length gown with no underpants, while infants are wrapped in swaddling clothes and wear a tiny little skull cap with a chin strap, like the women wear.[57] So too in Palestinian Arab villages, the children's appearance mimics that of adults. Girls wear their hair braided like older women, a belted dress and a

---

deportees in the Lachish Relief. Perhaps any items of value had been confiscated by the Assyrians.

53. Green, "Anklets and the Social Construction of Gender and Age," 286.

54. Hockings, "Badaga Apparel," 152; Schwarz, "Uncovering the Secret Vice," 25–26; Watson, *Archaeological Ethnography in Western Iran*, 233, 270.

55. Watson, *Archaeological Ethnography in Western Iran*, 27.

56. Watson, *Archaeological Ethnography in Western Iran*, 197.

57. Watson, *Archaeological Ethnography in Western Iran*, 27.

headcloth. A boy has a tuft of hair on the crown of forehead, a striped shirt with a leather belt and a knit cap.[58]

6.5. Summary

Clothing can have many different functions. From a literary perspective, donning clothing can be understood as symbolic of a coming-of-age moment. Anthropologists, on the other hand, note that clothes have both a practical and social function. For example, clothing can be used to regulate body temperature and to communicates certain social messages. Different types of clothing show power, status, and attraction. The presence or absence of clothing can also be a means of social control. Nudity in small children is accepted, while nudity in adults is considered shameful and a condition to be avoided.

Within the Hebrew Bible children's clothing presents social status. Little Samuel wears a special מעיל קטן given to him by his mother. This garment symbolizes not only his place of service in the temple, but also symbolizes the bond between the child and his mother. As Samuel grows up and becomes independent, his mother ceases to bring him this little garment. Older children, such as the teenage Joseph and Tamar each are identified as having a כתנת פסים. This piece of clothing was a tunic that reached to the ankles and wrists. The כתנת פסים symbolized one's special status within their family; it identified Joseph as the favorite son and Tamar as a virginal princess. The status outwardly presented by the clothing was meant to protect the wearer. However, for both Joseph and Tamar, the garment attracted unwanted attention. Ironically, instead of protecting them, the garment became the symbolic vehicle of their demise. The instant Tamar and Joseph experience "death," each כתנת פסים is symbolically torn. Clothing is also an integral part of another teenager's life. Like the coming-of-age stories with Adam and Eve and Enkidu, David's narrative also uses a change in clothing to signify his maturity. Before slaying the giant Goliath, David is not ready to wear the king's מד, which can be understood as a symbolic "mantle of kingship." After he proves himself a man of war, David is able to don the appropriate clothing of a warrior and eventually even the robes of a king. Because there are not many stories about female children, it is difficult to make any conclusions regarding

---

58. Granqvist, *Birth and Childhood among the Arabs*, 124–25.

the Bible's presentation of clothing and gender. However, from the stories that we do have, it is possible to see a thread of value woven through them. Each child, Samuel, David, Tamar, and Joseph has a special place within their family, and the clothing they wear defines them as valuable to their family in a particular way.

The iconographic record adds more to our understanding of clothing in ancient Israel and provide a snapshot of how children were gendered through their clothing. The Lachish relief suggests that clothing for Judeans was gendered and differed according to age. The basic uniform was simple: a tunic or dress with an overcoat added for warmth. Older females wore a long dress and covered their hair with a long mantle, while men wore a short tunic with a long, braided belt. Young girls appear as miniatures of the adult women; their clothing is the same, only their height belies their age. Boys, in contrast wore a short, belted tunic with age shown not only by height, but perhaps also by small additions to their dress. These additions could also demonstrate social ages or social stages achieved as the boys grew. For example, a correlation can be seen between the height of the boys and the decoration and length of their belts. The younger the child, the shorter and less ornate his belt. In the youngest children it is difficult to determine gender based on clothing alone. Infants are naked and may wear a sidelock. Older toddlers seem to wear a simple dress similar to that discussed in the ethnographic literature.

Ethnographic literature states that children ages one to five years old did not wear pants under the dress, which was most likely for the purposes of toilet training. It also finds that while young children wore fewer clothes, their dress may have been a bit more decorative as amulets of protection were sewn on their tops. The inclusion of beads, scarabs/amulets, and shiny objects in Iron Age burials may also have indicated a small child or infant's status as vulnerable and in need of protection. Because the inclusion of jewelry in infant and child burials of the Iron Age was not common, the items might also be evidence of a particular social status. In some cases, such as Tel es-Sa'idiyeh, which has an extensive and well-preserved cemetery, the appearance of anklets and bracelets on a skeleton can even be used to determine gender and age.

With respect to ancient Israel in general, some attention has been given to adult clothing: how clothing reinforces social norms, enhances the importance of a person, and shows the status and role of an individual or character in the Bible. However, little has been done with children's dress. Building on the studies of adult clothing and assessing how children's dress either fits or does not fit the conclusions drawn for adults is an important step forward. With respect to the evidence above, it seems likely that a child's clothing was related to his or her status and perhaps even their social age. Reexamining iconographic sources and the adornments in child burials is also important for looking at the relationship between adults and children and another way of bringing the discussion of dress into the realm of child centered interpretation. Further interpretation of previously published burials, as well as the current excavation reports will hopefully yield more information regarding children and dress.

7
Playtime

The desire to play and interact playfully cuts across cultures. Pretend play in particular has been established as a human universal, making play an important part of a child's life experience and a worthy, if not sometimes elusive subject of investigation.[1] Pretend play happens at all ages via objects, storytelling, or symbolic and imaginative play.

Caregivers in the West use repetitive games such as peek-a-boo, songs, and facial expressions to teach the infant. A cross-cultural examination of play among toddlers found that children begin imitative play between twelve to fifteen months of age. Boys play with objects, while girls are more likely to engage in symbolic play.[2] Anthropologists have noted that as the infant grows older the interaction between adults and the infant shifts: adults move from coach, to playmate, to spectator. While these general cultural patterns are similar, the time spent playing and the kind of play is culturally specific. For example, in some cultures with high infant mortality rates, extensive face-to-face time with young infants is relatively unheard of.[3] A low-investment parenting style is thought to be a coping strategy for dealing with the real possibility the infant might die. Less time spent bonding with the infant translates into a reduced sense of loss. Interaction between caregivers and infants also varies according to the subsistence method of a society. Studies from Central Africa found

---

1. Mark Nielsen, "Pretend Play and Cognitive Development," *International Encyclopedia of the Social and Behavioral Sciences*, ed. James D. Wright, 2nd ed. (Amsterdam: Elsevier, 2015), 870–87.

2. Hui-Chin Hsu, "Play during Infancy and Early Childhood: Cultural Similarities and Variations," in Wright, *International Encyclopedia of the Social and Behavioral Sciences*, 218–25.

3. David Lancy, "Accounting for Variability in Mother-Child Play," *AA* 1092 (2007): 273–84.

hunter-gathers spent more face-to-face time with infants, while farmers did so to a lesser degree.[4] As will be demonstrated below, cultural differences also determine the kinds of games children play and how long they are allowed to play before they are brought into the full-time workforce.

7.1. What Does It Mean to Play?

7.1.1. Case Study: Isaac and Ishmael

Genesis 21:9 states: "And Sarah saw the son whom Hagar the Egyptian had borne to Abraham מצחק [maṣaḥēq]." While the final word is a pun on Isaac's name (Yitzkhak) meaning laughter, מצחק is often translated as "mocking."[5] In the context of Gen 21 it appears that young Ishmael and young Isaac were engaged in some sort of activity wherein Ishmael was making fun of Isaac. The nature of the activity is debated.[6] Many commentaries understand the word with the most innocent meaning; Ishmael was in some way amusing his little brother.[7] The JPS translation says the two boys were "making sport," that is, playing together. Indeed, plenty of ethnographic materials report older siblings playing with smaller siblings. In many cases, boys are reportedly sent away to play more often than girls and are allowed to play for more years than girls. Girls are expected at a younger age to be helping their mothers with work around the house. In the Iranian village of Deh Koh, a mother reportedly scolded her eleven-year-old daughter for ripping her skirt while playing, insisting she should have been at home, helping. The girl's twelve-year-old brother, on the

---

4. Barry Hewlett et al., "Culture and Early Infancy among Central African Foragers and Farmers," *Developmental Psychology* 344 (1998): 653–61.

5. NIV, KJV, ASV, NASB.

6. Based on Gen 26:8, Richard Elliot Freidman translates מצחק as Ishmael was "fooling around." Richard Elliot Freidman, *Commentary on the Torah* (San Francisco: HarperSanFrancisco, 2001), 71. It is possible to understand Ishmael as mocking Isaac or abusing him, though this negative meaning need not be inserted into the text for Sarah to want secure Isaac's status; so Gerhard von Rad, *Genesis*, OTL (Philadelphia: Westminster, 1972), 232. The rabbinic commentators pick up on the word play between Isaac's name (Yitzkhak) and the participle (*mitzachak*) and see Ishmael "Isaac-ing," that is, trying to assert his claim to the birthright (t. Sotah 6:6; b. Rosh Hash 18b; Gen. Rab. 53:13).

7. Early translations of the Hebrew translating "playing" include the LXX, Vulgate, Jub. 17.4.

other hand, was sent away to play with his friends.[8] As young boys, Isaac and Ishmael might have simply been fooling around, playing outside.

7.1.2. Developmental Theories of Play

While we may not be able to answer exactly what it was that Ishmael was doing, Gen 21:9 raises an important question: What does it mean for a child to play, and how do we define play in ancient Israel? Engaging this question is necessary to set up how one might think about play in the context of a society such as ancient Israel.

From a theoretical stance, play can be understood in many ways. Play can be understood as having a biological function; it trains young people for work, offers an exercise in restraint, provides a safe space to exercise the desire for competition and domination, functions as an outlet for harmful impulses, and fulfills wishes.[9] Play in this way addresses the real-life skills needed for survival.[10] For example, Palestinian Arab boys were observed watching the men load and unload camels. The boys then made heaps of clay and pretended these were camels to load and unload.[11] Play can also be thought of as simply imitating adults, or, in a slightly more complex way, as learning socialization.[12] Recent research addressing the relationship between child play and development has found a clear link between the two, but defining the direction of the relationship is the same as the chicken and the egg conundrum.[13]

7.1.3. Identifying Types of Play and Playthings

Identifying toys in the archaeological record is a tricky enterprise. For one, there is overlap with objects used for play and ritual. For exam-

---

8. Friedl, *Children of Deh Koh*, 218–19, 220–27.

9. Joshua Huizinga, *Homo Ludens: A Study of the Play Element in Culture* (London: Routledge & Paul, 1980), 2. In Jewish terms, play as the outlet for harmful impulses might be understood as a way to safely express the *yetzer ha-ra*'.

10. Brian Sutton-Smith, *The Ambiguity of Play* (Cambridge: Harvard University, 2001), 50.

11. Granqvist, *Birth and Childhood among the Arabs*, 129.

12. Bronislaw Malinowski, *A Scientific Theory of Culture* (New York: Oxford University Press, 1944); Robert White, "Motivation Reconsidered: The Concept of Competence," *Psychological Review* 66 (1959): 197–333.

13. Sutton-Smith, *Ambiguity of Play*, 38–42.

ple, a sistrum might be understood as a noisemaker, thus an object of play, or as a ritual item used in a ritual dance. The same can be said for astragali, which could be used for gaming or ritual purposes.[14] Indeed, the presence of children in ritual and the relationship between sport and ritual is a topic needing further research.[15] Another potential barrier to determining what qualifies as a toy is one's own preconceived notions of what toys look like and how objects are used. Studying a culture so far removed from the Western world initially led archaeologists to identify toys according to their type, size, and form. Often objects that were small or seemed to have no immediate utilitarian purpose were identified as toys.[16] However, the identification of such objects can often be uncertain and based on assumptions concerning size, shape, and location.[17] To help overcome such barriers, it is useful to think about the subject from a child's perspective. As acknowledged above and in chapter 5, children learn from their environment as they are socialized and enculturated to become the next generation of Israelites. To determine if something is a toy we might think about objects as follows: "If children's play is a vehicle for learning to adjust to the adult world, then children of past societies had the same basic need for playing as do modern children."[18] Objects of play might therefore include musical instruments, like the sistra and rattles previously discussed, daily work objects, game pieces, and other objects used for amusement.

---

14. Ulrich Hübner, *Spiele und Spielzeug in antiken Palästina* (Universitätsverlag Freiburg Schweiz: Vandenhoeck & Ruprecht Göttingen, 1992), 51–52 nn. 57–58.

15. The overlap between objects used in play and ritual, as well as the presence of sport within ritual can be seen in the Egyptian record. As various scenes demonstrate, the difference between sport and ritual is difficult to define. Ceremonies for the dead king, the *sed* festival, and the ritual throwing of balls seemingly mix the two categories. For a full treatment of sport and play in Egypt, see Wolfgang Decker and Michael Herb, *Bildatlas zum Sport im alten Ägypten Corpus der bildlichen Quellen zu Leibesülangen, Spiel, Tanz, und verwandten Themen*, 2 vols. (Leiden: Brill, 1994).

16. For difficulty determining whether small objects were used as toys, see Lillehammer, "Child Is Born," 99–100.

17. Joanna R. Sofaer Derevenski, "Where Are the Children? Accessing Children in the Past," *ARC* 13.2 (1994): 10.

18. Lillehammer, "Child Is Born," 100.

7.2. Play in Ancient Israel

The following categories, borrowed from the field of anthropology of play, will help facilitate a discussion of play in ancient Israel.[19] The diversity of child play can be seen in the many different forms it takes. Play can be in the mind (daydreaming), solitary play (with toys of some sort), behavioral (acting playful), informal (joking, tricking), performance (playing an instrument or dancing), celebrations and festivals (parties or rituals), contests (games and sports), or risk taking (rock climbing or other extreme sports). The ancient record provides examples of a few of these categories: informal play, celebrations and festivals, solitary play, and contests. Within these categories the biblical text provides us with examples of some of the non-object-centric types of child play, while the archaeological record provides examples of object-centered play.

7.2.1. Informal

Informal play, such as joking or playing, is best exemplified by the trickster motif found throughout the Torah. While the tricks and jokes are more of a literary nature, there is no denying the fact that the ancient Israelites enjoyed a good joke. Consider the Jacob narratives—a young boy who lives up to his name by tricking his older brother, not once, but twice, out of his inheritance. Esau is so famished he cannot think straight and is tricked into giving up his birthright for a tasty bowl of soup. Then, Jacob tricks his father by dressing up in animal hair and imitating his brother, so stealing his brother's blessing. One might frown upon Esau's troglodyte nature and the dishonor Jacob shows his father. But the genius of the farce is that it works! Jacob, the younger son, tricks his way into the status of the firstborn son. With poetic justice, Jacob is then tricked by Laban into marrying the wrong daughter and having to work extra time to marry the daughter of his choice. Passed on through oral tradition, children might hear and laugh along with stories like this.

7.2.2. Celebrations and Festivals

Many biblical texts discuss festivals and celebrations such as Passover, Sukkot, and Shavuot. Whether in their early form, or their later incarna-

---

19. Sutton-Smith, *Ambiguity of Play*, 4–5.

tion as pilgrimage festivals to Jerusalem, these would have been occasions to celebrate. Judges 21:19–21 describes an annual festival at Shiloh during which young maidens would come out of the vineyards to dance. Such a festival may have been a grape harvesting or treading party like the one at Shechem referenced in Judg 9:27. The dancing in these cases may be jovial and informal, or perhaps, as with Egyptian festivals and parties, the dancing may have been more of a formal, religious performance.[20] Pictorial evidence from Egypt depicts males and females dancing in the same gender groups. Often these groups are accompanied by woodwind or percussive instrumentalists. The dancers themselves hold sistra or other such noisemakers to accompany their dances.[21] While the biblical text does not reference instruments in the Judges passages, one might imagine singing or drumming to be a part of festival celebrations as they are in other passages. Indeed, Miriam took a timbral in her hand and led other women in song (Exod 15:20). Other texts, such as Ps 150 suggest that instruments of all types were used in religious celebrations, again attesting to the interwoven nature of play, music, and ritual.

7.2.3. Solitary Play: Figurines and Miniature Objects

7.2.3.1. Figurines

A wide variety of figurines exist in the archaeological record. In the Iron Age I–II period in particular, we find four-legged animals (solid and hollow), JPFs, horse and riders, beds and other furniture models, chariots, birds/snakes, and other anthropomorphic figures. These items were all identified

---

20. The Egyptians also had harvest festival dancing as witnessed in grave paintings from Giza and Saqqara (Decker and Herb, *Bildatlas zum Sport im alten Ägypten Corpus*, 840–41). The Egyptian record is replete with examples of different kinds of dancing: the funerary dance of the *mmw*, pair dancing, formation dancing, free style dancing, mirror dances, dances for entertainment, etc. (723–853). Other activities associated with the cult can be categorized as "ritual play," such as throwing balls and running races (21–138).

21. Dimitri Meeks, "Dance," *OEAE* 1:356–60. Note, too, the discussion of Egyptian children, sistra, and dancing in §3.4. As mentioned in ch. 3, both sistra and rattles have been found in ancient Israel; however, unlike their ancient Egyptian counterparts, these objects were not found with iconographic or textual explanations. Therefore, information regarding their usage remains unclear. Researchers do not know whether they were used by adults *or* children, or by adults *for* children.

in early days as toys due to their small size. When the study of domestic religion became the topic de jour, these objects were reassigned to the category of cultic items.[22] There is the possibility that ritual objects could become broken or defiled, in which case they might have been thrown away in a dump, buried, or discarded.[23] Here one should note that objects often enjoy an expanded life with a second use. Cross-cultural studies, as well as early sources like the Talmud show that local garbage pits are popular spaces for children to play.[24] If children picked up objects from the local dumping area, or picked up discarded models or figurines from the house, they might imbue them with a new meaning as toys. Ethnographic evidence provides examples of this, citing the reuse of magical figurines (in the category of a JPF) as recycled children's playthings.[25] As more work is done on these cultic objects, it is important to keep in mind that objects also do not have one singular meaning. Archaeologists and anthropologists alike recognize that objects have multiple meanings, and furthermore, that the

---

22. For example, William Albright (Tell Beit Mirsim) and Kathleen Kenyon (Jerusalem and Jericho) both identified these items as toys. See William F. Albright, *The Excavation of Tell Beit Mirsim (Joint Expedition of the Pittsburgh-Xenia Theological Seminary and the American School of Oriental Research in Jerusalem)*, 3 vols., AASOR 12–13, 17, 21–22 (New Haven: American Schools of Oriental Research, 1932–1943), 3:142; Kathleen Kenyon, *Digging Up Jericho* (London: Ernst Benn, 1957), 142. Olga Tufnell states that "city deposits and tombs in Judah contain many broken pottery models which are but crude playthings or homely symbols of no intrinsic worth." Olga Tufnell, *Lachish III (Tell ed. Duwier) The Iron Age* (London: Oxford University, 1953), 374. Raz Kletter argued against JPFs as toys because of where they were found, their uniform shape, their crude manufacturing, their breakability, and the fact they are not found in children's graves (*Judean Pillar Figurines and the Archaeology of Ashera*, 73).

23. Most of the JPFs, animals, and models were found broken and disposed of in a manner similar to other discarded domestic items. See Raz Kletter, "Clay Figurines," in *Beersheba III: The Early Iron Age IIA Enclosed Settlement and the Late Iron IIA–Iron IIB Cities*, ed. Zev Herzog and Lily Singer-Avitz (Winona Lake, IN: Eisenbrauns, 2016), 1130.

24. Children are known to play in garbage heaps. This location as a place of play is taken for granted in b. Shabb. 121b. See also Watson, *Archaeological Ethnography in Western Iran*, 299.

25. Moorey, *Idols of the People*, 8; Mary Voigt, "Çatal Höyük in Context: Ritual at Early Neolithic Sites in Central and Eastern Turkey," in *Life in Neolithic Farming Communities: Social Organization, Identity and Differentiation*, ed. Ian Kuijt (New York: Kluwer Academic/Plenum, 2000), 267. For a counter-argument, see Meyers, "Terracottas without a Text," 115–30.

people who use the objects bestow meaning on them.[26] It is also significant
to note that objects which were originally created as one thing might have
been reworked to use as something else. For example, the sherds from a
broken clay vessel could be refashioned into disks used as stoppers, game
pieces, spindle whorls, or buttons (buzzes).[27]

In listing the following items under solitary play, I am not arguing that
every clay figurine was used as a toy or "doll."[28] Rather, in thinking about
the child's world, a child-centered interpretation of the objects revisits the
possibility that the original designation of these objects as toys might be
accurate after all. While perhaps not originally intended as toys, *some* of
the clay objects might indeed have enjoyed use as toys *at some point* in
their lifetime. Such a view keeps in mind that items can be used differently by different people at different times, so that an item no longer used
by an adult in its primary function might be used differently by a child.[29]
It also acknowledges that the figurines are often found in occupational
settings, either inside houses or in refuse pits. These places are part of a
child's world, where children might have an impact on the material culture. At the same time, it acknowledges the caution of archaeologists who
note the lack of usage marks on the figurines, which leads them to say that
the figurines are not toys because they do not show any evidence of being
played with.[30] Which is to say that not every figurine needs to have found

---

26. Ian Hodder, *The Present Past: An Introduction to Anthropology for Archaeologists* (London: Batsford, 1982), 206–9.

27. Trude Dothan and Baruch Brandl, *Deir el-Balaḥ: Excavations in 1977–82 in
the Cemetery and Settlement*, Qedem 50 (Jerusalem: Institute of Archaeology, Hebrew
University, 2010), 239–46; Kristine Garroway, "Childist Archaeology: Children, Toys,
and Skill Transmission in Ancient Israel" (paper presented at the Annual Meeting of
American Schools of Oriental Research, Boston, 18 November 2017).

28. The view held here differs from Hübner's view, which is that terracotta figurines of males and females alike definitively functioned as "dolls" (*Spiele und Spielzeug
in antiken Palästina*, 92–93). His view that every little girl would have dreamed of a
teraphim (albeit in doll size) akin to the one Michal used to fool Saul's guards (1 Sam
19:13) seems a bit over the top (*Spiele und Spielzeug in antiken Palästina*, 93).

29. The possibility of ceramic objects used as toys is gaining some traction in the
archaeological community. Objects once thought of as having a single use are being
reexamined. See Dale Manor, "Toys 'R' Us at Tel Beth-Shemesh" (paper presented at the
Annual Meeting of American School of Oriental Research, Boston, 16 November 2017).

30. Carol Meyers has investigated the JPFs from an anthropological perspective,
seeking to determine whether the categories for figurines developed by Ucko could
be used to identify how the JPFs were used. She argues that while that JPFs are small

reuse as a toy in order for some to have been used as such. As Julie Parker has pointed out, many of the arguments made for interpreting ceramic figurines, especially the JPFs are being called into question.[31] With this in mind, the following figures are meant as representative examples of the kinds of human and animal forms found in ancient Israel.[32]

Figures 7.1–7.9 represent examples of the various categories of human, animal, and inanimate objects. Figures 7.1 and 7.2 are JPFs. These female figurines are perhaps the most hotly contested items when it comes to interpreting the corpus of figurines.[33] They have their source in the North, but were found throughout ancient Israel and gain their name *Judean*

---

and found near domestic settings (two of Ucko's criteria for identifying a figurine as a toy), they are not found in conjunction with an array of other figurines. Peter Ucko, "The Interpretation of Prehistoric Anthropomorphic Figurines," *The Journal of Royal Anthropological Institute of Great Britain and Ireland* 92 (1962): 44, 47; Meyers, "Terracottas without Texts," 119–20. "The expected diversity of human and animal figurines is lacking for both human and animal terracottas" (120 n. 10). However, such a diverse grouping of animal or human figurines is not seen at all in ancient Israel. It is possible that children in ancient Israel did not have access to multiple animals and anthropomorphic figures with which to play. On the other hand, sites such as Beth Shemesh show evidence of groups of figurines from occupational debris being used as fill. The groupings of these figurines include a wide variety of human and animal forms together. Raz Kletter, "Anthropomorphic and Zoomorphic Figurines and Hollow Vessels," in *Tel Beth-Shemesh A Border Community in Judah: Renewed Excavations 1990–2000: The Iron Age*, vol. 2, Emery and Claire Yass Publications in Archaeology (Winona Lake, IN: Eisenbrauns, 2016), 546–57.

31. Parker, "I Bless You by YHWH of Samaria and His Barbie."

32. For a catalogue of figurines organized by types and subtypes, see Thomas Holland, *A Typological and Archaeological Study of Human and Animal Representations in the Plastic Art of Palestine during the Iron Age* (PhD diss., Proefschrift Oxford, All Souls College, 1975); Holladay, "Religion in Israel and Judah under the Monarchy," 249–99).

33. She has been understood as the goddess Asherah, a magical fertility aide, a cultural status symbol, and an apotropaic guardian. Fymer-Kensky, *In the Wake of the Goddesses*, 159; Raz Kletter, "Between Archaeology and Theology: The Pillar Figurines from Judah and the Asherah," in *Studies in the Archeology of the Iron Age in Israel and Jordan*, ed. Amihai Mazar, JSOTSup 331 (Sheffield: Sheffield Academic, 2001), 205; van der Toorn, "Israelite Figurines," 62; William G. Dever, *Did God Have a Wife? Archaeology and Folk Religion in Ancient Israel* (Grand Rapids: Eerdmans, 2005), 194–95; Carol Meyers, *Household and Holiness: The Religious Culture of Israelite Women* (Minneapolis: Fortress, 2005), 31; Ian D. Wilson, "Judean Pillar Figurines and the Ethnic Identity in the Shadow of Assyria," *JSOT* 36 (2012): 259–78; Darby, *Interpreting Judean Pillar Figurines*, 34–50.

because they predominate in Judea during the eighth to seventh century BCE. As mentioned in the discussion of JPFs in chapter 5, they either have a standardized, molded head or a stylized face, with a pinched nose and hollow eyes.[34]

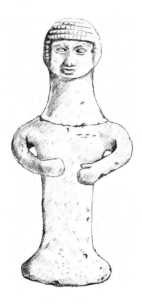

Fig. 7.1. Judean Pillar Figurine, molded head, Tel Duweir, Iron Age II.

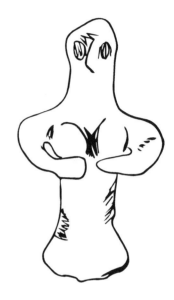

Fig. 7.2. Judean Pillar Figurine, pinched face, Beer-Sheba/Tel Erani, Iron Age II.

The horse and rider figures are also common figures in the Iron Age and appear throughout the ancient Near East.[35] The examples here show the

34. While the relatively cheap production value and cost of materials lends support to the idea JPFs were used as toys, their uniform production in form and technique suggest their original use was as something else (Avissar-Lewis, "Childhood and Children in the Material Culture," 119*). As Kletter argued, we should not expect handmade toys to be uniformly produced and a uniform shape widely distributed (*Pillar Figurines*, 73). We might apply this same theory to the horse and rider figurines as well.

35. Like with the JPFs, scholars have tried to identify the horse and riders as representing divinities, either a warrior or sun god. The case for this identification, as well as arguments against it are summarized by Cornelius. He suggests that the horse and rider pieces are more likely representations of ordinary people who are part of a cavalry, a military unit well known in the Iron Age. He even entertains the idea that these figurines may have been toys. Izak Cornelius, "A Terracotta Horse in Stellenbosch and

stylistic variety that these figures could take. The riders fall into two main types, those with a pillar body and those with crescent-shaped bodies. Like the JPFs, they are often crudely made and whitewashed.[36] Figure 7.3 is that of a rider, separated from his horse. In many cases the riders are separated from their horse through breakage. Sometimes, however, one can still see the hands of a rider attached to the neck of a horse.[37] Figure 7.4, from the northern Levant, shows a horse with a rider still attached. Similar figures appear in southern Iraq during the Kassite/Neo-Babylonian Periods and in the Levant into the Persian Period, attesting to a long history of use.[38]

Fig. 7.3. Rider figurine, Tel Beth Shemesh, Iron Age.

Fig. 7.4. Horse and rider figurine, Deve Hüyük, ca. 1150–350 BCE.

Chariots were another popular ceramic form and wheels from them have found in various periods at Tel Beth Shemesh, Gerar, Gezer, Tel Jemmeh, Lachish, and Megiddo. The chariot seen in figure 7.5 belongs to

---

the Iconography and Function of Palestinian Horse Figurines," *ZDPV* (2007): 28–36. See also Kletter's discussion and references throughout, Kletter, *Pillar Figurines*.

36. Kletter, "Anthropomorphic and Zoomorphic Figurines and Hollow Vessels," 543.

37. See, for example, the piece at the Ashmolean, AN1968.1392.

38. Tel Dor and Kish.

Fig. 7.5. Chariot model, Kish, Akkadian to UR III.

an earlier period (Bronze Age) and comes from the Mesopotamian site of
Kish. It is included here as an example of what the model wheels might
have once been attached to.

Figure 7.6 includes three chariot wheels and an example of a chariot
fitting. The ivory chariot fitting seen in figure 7.6 was found in a domestic
setting at Gezer (Late Bronze Age or Iron Age I). The fitting is consistent
with other Egyptian style chariot models found at Beth Shean in the Late
Bronze Age. The fragmentary ceramic wheels in figure 7.6 are again from
Gezer. The one on the left dates to the Middle Bronze Age II and serves
as one of the earliest wheels of its type found in the land of ancient Israel.[39] The wheel to the left of center comes from a Late Bronze II or Early
Iron Age I stratum of Gezer. The last wheel, on the far right, comes from
Beth Shemesh. It was identified as a handmade wheel from the eleventh
century BCE. The excavators noted that the hole in the wheel was made
with a stick.[40]

The small zoomorphic figurines found at almost every site include
lions, oxen, sheep, goats, rams, birds, ducks, bulls, and the ambiguous

---

39. See Dever's discussion for further information on the two chariot items from
Gezer (Dever, Lance, and Bullard, *Gezer IV*, 19, 115).

40. Examples of crudely made Iron Age chariot wheels were found at Beth Shemesh (Kletter, "Anthropomorphic and Zoomorphic Figurines and Hollow Vessels," 540
and fig. 15.8A:8, 9).

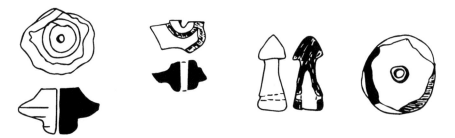

Fig. 7.6. Chariot wheels and fitting, from left to right: Gezer, Middle Bronze II; Gezer, Late Bronze II/Iron Age I; Gezer; early eleventh century BCE; Beth Shemesh; eleventh century BCE.

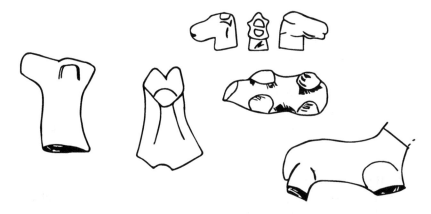

Fig. 7.7. Terracotta animal figurines: clockwise, Tel Beth-Shemesh, Iron Age; Tel Beth-Shemesh, Iron Age; Gezer, thirteenth–twelfth century BCE; Tel Beth-Shemesh, Iron Age; Tel Beth-Shemesh, Iron Age.

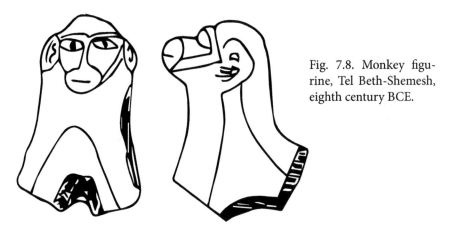

Fig. 7.8. Monkey figurine, Tel Beth-Shemesh, eighth century BCE.

quadruped. Figure 7.7 shows an array of solid animal heads typical of those found throughout the Iron Age. Most of the animals are handmade and fall into the ambiguous quadruped shape, showing a head with ears or horns. Again, while it might be true that these objects were used as cultic items, some figurines appear secular in nature. Consider figure 7.8. This figure was found at Beth Shemesh and has the head of a monkey on the body of a quadruped. Monkeys are not native to ancient Israel, and the piece itself is unique in the archaeological record. Exploring the significance of monkeys, Kletter states, "it seems that the Beth Shemesh figure has no religious significance, but should rather be explained as a whimsical creation, which sees the monkey in the role of an exotic, pet animal, or as an animal representation of human behavior (related to sex, music, ugliness, lack of intelligence, etc.)."[41] Animal figurines may have had cultic or secular uses, or even been used by children as toys; it is simply difficult to determine. Archaeologists maintain that objects crudely made, fired at a low temperature, and miniature in size represent objects that were made for or by children as toys.[42] Take, for example, the torso of what appears to be a crouching lion found at Beth Shean. The excavators state that "such a small and crudely made figure could have been a toy."[43] Many of the animal figurines found in the archaeological record of ancient Israel meet these criteria.

In addition to the small figurines commonly identified as cultic in nature, there are figurines and pieces of figures that are not so quickly identified as part of a cultic assemblage. These objects may be dolls, or figures of play used by children.[44] For example, crudely made chalk "snowman" figurines found at Gezer and Gerar fall into the category of things

---

41. Raz Kletter, "A Monkey Figurine from Tel Beth Shemesh," *Oxford Journal of Archaeology* 21 (2002): 150.

42. Avissar-Lewis, "Childhood and Children in Material Culture," 97*, 115*. A wide variety of animal figurines identified as toys has been found at El-Lahun in Egypt. Hippos, pigs, donkeys, crocodiles, and apes are among the animals (Booth, *Lost Voices of the Nile*, 135).

43. Naama Yahalom-Mack and Amihai Mazar, "Various Finds from the Iron Age II Strata in Areas P and S," in *Excavations at Tel Beth-Shean 1989–1996*, ed. Amihai Mazar, vol. 1 (Jerusalem: Israel Exploration Society, 2006), 468, fig. 13.1.2.

44. They might also be so called teraphim, or ancestor figurines, referred to in the biblical text. Vestiges of a cult of the ancestors has been identified in texts such as the Bible, and in archaeological remains from the first and second millennium BCE Mesopotamia, Ugarit, and ancient Israel (van der Toorn, "Family Religion in Second Millennium West Asia," 25–27; Fleming, "Household and Community Religion," 40–42;

not usually identifiable as cult objects.[45] At Gerar, W. M. Flinders Petrie even identified one object as a doll's leg.[46] Dolls are referenced in the Akkadian literature (passu) and also in ancient Egypt.[47] Egypt in particular offers many examples of dolls made from pottery and wood. Some of the examples come from tombs of little girls, solidifying their identification as favored toys.[48] Cross-cultural studies attest to imaginative games such as "playing house" as a popular past time for little girls. They made dolls of sticks and mud and created houses out of other things they gathered up.[49] References to playing house and the "play of girls" abound in the Mesopotamian record as well.[50] The gendered usage of figurines is also found cross-culturally at the Iron Age site of Deve Hüyük, near Carchemish. There, horse and rider figurines (fig. 7.4) were found on boys's graves, while female figurines were found on girls' graves.[51]

7.2.3.2. Case Study: Miniature Vessels

In determining whether an object used in the daily routine was a toy related to a child's development, archaeologists sometimes find size and

---

Lewis, "Family, Household, and Local Religion," 61; Olyan, "Family Religion in Israel and the Wider Levant," 119).

45. Dever, *Gezer IV*, pl. 59.4; 60.5.

46. Petrie, *Gerar*, 18.

47. Petrie, *Objects of Daily Use*, 59–60; Avissar-Lewis, "Childhood and Children in Material Culture," 118*; Booth, *Lost Voices of the Nile*, 136. It seems that some of the game pieces (*passu*) referenced in the Akkadian literature were shaped like dolls or miniature humans (*CAD* 12:224–25).

48. "That these figures (no. 365–73) were used as toys is shown by a similar wooden figure ... found with a model couch in the grave of a girl, thus removing these from the class of concubine figures" (Petrie, *Objects of Daily Use*, 59).

49. Playthings made from various objects found around the house and yard are used and then discarded; toys are not expected to last long (Friedl, *Children of Deh Koh*, 233).

50. The Game Text and the Elevation of Ištar. Anne Kilmer, "An Oration on Babylon," *AoF* 18 (1991): 10–11, 13.

51. P. R. S. Moorey, *Cemeteries of the First Millennium BC at Deve Hüyük, Near Carchemish, Salvaged by T. E. Lawrence and C. L. Woolley in 1913 (with a Catalogue Raisonné of the Objects in Berlin, Cambridge, Liverpool, London and Oxford*, BARIS 87 (Oxford: British Archaeological Reports, 1980), 100–104. Whether the figures represent toys or deities remains debated; what is not debated is the gendered distribution of the figurines (Hübner, *Spiele und Spielzeug in antiken Palästina*, 92).

quality to be helpful factors. Miniature vessels offer an interesting case study. Some, like those appearing in the domestic setting at places like Timnah or Tell Beit Mirsim, were not handmade but show signs of careful, skillful crafting.[52] However, other miniature vessels, like those from Tel Nagila are handmade and include the fingerprints of their creators (fig. 7.9). Through a fingerprint analysis, archaeologists determined that the handmade miniatures from Tel Nagila were made by children, demonstrating that children were playing by imitating the actions of their caretakers—essentially, "playing house." These miniature vessels of Tel Nagila have been described as bringing "socializing values, educational, cultural, religious and functional aspects to the child."[53] Archeologists reached similar conclusions regarding two miniature vessels from Megiddo Room 98/K/70. The two vessels there were crudely made and permeable, suggesting that they were nonfunctioning vessels. However, a closer inspection revealed that those particular vessels had been fired and painted with a red slip. The excavators suggest that "they may represent a socialization attempt by a child to create a red slipped vessel," which was "met with consent and appreciation."[54] If the child was indeed attempting to replicate the pottery production process, the miniature vessels are good examples of play as both developing skills needed for life and play as a form of socialization.

---

52. The miniature vessels at these sites have not undergone fingerprint analysis: Amihai Mazar and Nava Panitz-Cohen, *Timnah (Tel Batash) II: The Finds from the First Millennium BCE*, vol. 1 (Jerusalem: The Institute of Archaeology, Hebrew University, 2001), 135–37; Sara Ben-Arieh, *Bronze and Iron Age Tombs at Tell Beit Mirsim* (Jerusalem: Israel Antiquities Authority, 2004), 23 and fig. 2.55:60. Miniaturized sketches of two dipper juglets from the tombs at Gezer might indicate the presence of miniature vessels within tombs. Whether or not these were graves with infants or children is unknown, as the relationship between the grave good and skeletons was not always clear: Maeir and Panitz-Cohen, *Bronze and Iron Age Tombs at Tel Gezer, Israel: Finds from Raymond-Charles Weill's Excavation in 1914 and 1932* (Oxford: Archaeopress, 2004), 22.

53. Uziel and Avissar-Lewis, "Tel Nagila Middle Bronze Age Homes," 290.

54. Yuval Gadot and Assaf Yasur-Landau, "Beyond Finds: Reconstructing Life in the Courtyard Building of Level K-4," in *Megiddo IV: The 1998–2002 Seasons*, ed. Israel Finkelstein, David Ussishkin, and Baruch Halpern (Tel Aviv: Emery and Claire Yass Publications in Archaeology, 2006), 595.

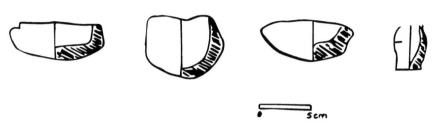

Fig. 7.9. Miniature vessels, Tel Nagila, Middle Bronze Age II.

7.2.4. Contests

The archaeological record attests to a variety of games being played in ancient Israel. For example, the popular Egyptian game, *senet*, or 3 x 10, has been found in many sites throughout ancient Israel.[55] *Senet* was played with a game board, dice, and game pieces.[56] Based on Egyptian tomb paintings and the position of the games in tombs, it appears that the game was played by two people who moved their pieces from one end of the board to the other by positioning, mixing, and segregating their pieces. There were no captured pieces. Games such as this fall into the category of "racing games."[57] Players moved their pieces by rolling or tossing knucklebones or dice. Game pieces ranged from simple conical shapes to more elaborately carved animals. The ancient Near East record attests to similar game pieces and similar games, differing according to the number of playing

---

55. Examples were found at Gerar, Megiddo, Hazor, Gezer, and Beth Shean (Petrie, *Gerar*, 19, pl. 42:8; P. S. Vermaak, "A New Interpretation of the Playing Objects in the Gilgamesh Epic," *Journal for Semitics* 20 (2011): 113–18. A rather early example from the EB IB–II was found in the Beersheba Valley at the site of Abu Qurinat, attesting to the popularity of this game throughout history. Svetlana Talis, "An Early Bronze Age IB–II Settlement at Abu Qurinat" [Hebrew], *ʿAtiqot* 85 (2016): 53*, 107.

56. Hübner, *Spiele und Speilzeug in antiken Palästina*, 67–69; Decker and Herb, *Bildatlas zum Sport im alten Ägypten Corpus*, 642–81. Egypt had a rich tradition of board games in addition to *s[e]n[e]t* (Decker and Herb, *Bildatlas zum Sport im alten Ägypten Corpus*, 633–42, 682–88).

57. For an overview of racing games and game boards in general, as well as an analysis of a mobile gaming board discovered in the Iron Age levels at Beth Shemesh, see the bibliography and article by Michael Sebbane, "ḥnn Gaming Board Section A: Two-Sided Gaming Board Fragment Bearing and Ownership Inscription," in *Tel Beth-Shemesh A Border Community in Judah: Renewed Excavations 1990–2000: The Iron Age*, vol. 2, Emery and Claire Yass Publications in Archaeology (Winona Lake, IN: Eisenbrauns, 2016), 639–46.

spaces used.[58] For example, a game found at Knossos had eighteen fields, while the so-called Royal Game of Ur contained twenty. Anthropologists studying games cross-culturally note how "traditions and games cross geographic and time boundaries, and while the rules might vary (think modern day 'house rules'), the basic structure and morphology of games changed very slowly over time."[59] Thus, it is not surprising that we find similar games in ancient Egypt, Greece, Mesopotamia, and ancient Israel.[60] Board games could also be found on more permanent surfaces, such as rocks or stone slabs.[61] Unfortunately, the archaeological record does not provide a game box with a list of ages that the games were appropriate for, so it is hard to say whether these games were for adults, children, or both. The game board in figure 7.10 comes from Egypt and is an excellent example of what a complete board with game pieces looked like.

Many other popular games in the ancient Near East were played with dice or knucklebones. The dice found at Tell Beit Mirsim and Gaza were four-sided pyramids with a range of one to four dots. At Ashkelon, cube-shaped bone dice (astragali) were found with the pattern of dots we are familiar with today.[62] Such astragali were most commonly made by grinding the protruding edges, and then polishing the sides. Animal bones used to create astragali include sheep and goats, and less frequently pigs, gazelles, and other wild animals.[63] Astragali have been found in sites throughout the Levant and Near East.[64] For example, the site of Lachish produced over one hundred such bone dice, some of which were polished and perforated, others of which were left unworked. The groupings of worked and unworked dice together suggest a game that required both

---

58. Petrie, *Objects of Daily Use*, 51–57; Petrie, *Gerar*, 19, pl. 42:8; Dever, *Gezer IV*, 4.1:126 and n. 240; *CAD* 12: 224–25.

59. Joshua Schwartz, "Play and Games," in *The Oxford Handbook of Jewish Daily Life* (Oxford: Oxford University Press, 2012), 643.

60. Schwartz, "Play and Games," 643; Scwartz, "Ball Play in Jewish Society in the Second Temple and Mishnah Periods," *Zion* 60 (1995): 247–76.

61. Hübner, *Spiele und Spielzeug in antiken Palästina*, 67.

62. William Hallo, "Games in the Biblical World" [Hebrew], *EI* 24 (1993): 83–84*.

63. Hübner, *Spiele und Spielzeug in antiken Palästina*, 43–45.

64. Levantine sites include, inter alia, Megiddo, Tanaach, Tell Qasile, Tell el-Hammah, Tel el-Ajjul, Beth Shean, Ekron. Astragali were also found at sites in Anatolia, Cyprus, the Aegean, Mesopotamia, and Egypt. Garth Gilmour, "The Nature and Function of Astragalus Bones from Archaeological Contexts in the Levant and Eastern Mediterranean," *Oxford Journal of Archaeology* 16 (1997): 167–75.

Fig. 7.10. Game board, Abydos, Egypt, Eighteenth Dynasty.

plain and marked dice.[65] Dice made of clay were also found in various Mesopotamian sites and referred to in the literature with the term *kiṣallu*.[66] Ethnographic reports from western Iran find that knucklebones are still a popular pastime for children. These knucklebones have four sides and each side is named. Like in the game of dreidel, the side that lands face up determines what move the player makes.[67]

7.2.5. Other Play and Playthings

Other forms of play include games that require a toy and games of imagination. For example, ethnographers working in different parts of Iran during the 1960s through the 1990s report that children throw pebbles on the ground and then throw a small ball or stone and scoop up the pebbles, akin to the way one plays jacks.[68] Make-believe games like "shepherd,

---

65. Paul Kraft, "Worked Bone," in *Lachish V*, ed. David Ussishkin (Tel Aviv: Yass Publications in Archaeology, 2004), 2434–2440.

66. Hallo, "Games in the Biblical World," 83–84; *CAD* 8:434–35.

67. Watson, *Archaeological Ethnography in Western Iran*, 199.

68. Friedl, *Children of Deh Koh*, 232; Watson, *Archaeological Ethnography in Western Iran*, 199l; Ganqvist, *Birth and Childhood among the Arabs*, 129.

sheep, wolf" imitate events in daily life. In this game played by both girls and boys, one child is the wolf, another the shepherd, and the others the sheep. The wolf tries to steal the sheep, while the shepherd tries to protect them.[69] The events represented in this game recall the actions taken by David, when as a young shepherd boy, he protected his father's flock from the mouth of bears and lions (1 Sam 17:34–35). Later rabbinic sources also highlight the connection between animals and child's play.[70] The Talmud, and perhaps also the book of Job, reference children playing with birds, and a passage from the Mishnah states that carrying around a grasshopper on Shabbat qualifies as breaking Shabbat because people store grasshoppers as toys for children (b. B. Bat. 20a; Job 4:29; m. Shabb. 9:7). Finally, in a discussion listing the reason a person might cut off the head of an animal it is revealed that one commonly does this to give to a child to play with![71] Like games involving imagination, play involving animals would not leave a mark in the archaeological record.

The adventures of Gilgamesh involve two words, *pukku u mekkû*, which are widely understood to be a reference to playthings of some sort.[72] With *pukku* meaning "drum" and *mekkû*, "drumstick," scholars originally thought that that these objects were literal drums and drumsticks used within the context of games.[73] More popularly, these objects have been defined as a hoop and driving stick. There is also a possibility that these two items are words for game and game piece.[74] These words have also been understood as a puck and mallet, akin to playthings in a game involving a stick and an object of play such as polo or hockey.[75]

---

69. This kind of game seems widespread throughout Iran (Friedl, *Children of Deh Koh*, 237; Watson, *Archaeological Ethnography in Western Iran*, 199). For make-believe games in Egypt, see Booth, *Lost Voices of the Nile*, 137–38.

70. Note, Isa 11:6–8 speaks of a time when children will be able to safely play with the viper and the cobra.

71. Maimonides, *Mishneh Torah*, Zemanim, Shabbat 1:6. Maimonides may have been commenting on the source from b. B. Bat. 20a. (Many thanks to Zev Farber for pointing out these talmudic and later sources.)

72. The Ugaritic version states that Gilgamesh kept besting the men of Uruk (presumably in a game) on a daily basis (Hit Gilg I, I 11b–13a).

73. *CAD* 12:502, 10.2:7.

74. P. S. Vermaak, "New Interpretation of the Playing Objects," 109–38; Benno Landsberger, "Einige unerkannt gebliebene oder verkannte Nomina des Akkadiaschen," *Wiener Zeitschrift für die Kunde des Morgenlandes* 56 (1960): 109–29.

75. The Elevation of Ishtar Tablet IV B compares the *pukku u mekkû* to a confron-

While the interpretation of the objects remains uncertain, their function is clear: they are toys. The concept of playing in general and a list of children's games is treated in the so-called Games Text, a Middle Babylonian text from Nippur.[76] The Mesopotamian corpus also includes references to jump ropes, wrestling, running races, and games of hide and seek.[77] Looking forward in time to the Greco-Roman period and Talmudic eras, we find references to piggy back rides, tug-of-war, pulling/pushing games, throwing stones on water vases or trees, splashing, swimming, watching reflections in mirrors/water, stealing fruit from a neighbor, and breaking vessels. All of these might be continuations of games played in ancient Israel and surrounding lands.

Tops and other spinning items were also popular in the ancient world, evidence of which has been found in archaeological contexts from many time periods.[78] Spinning disks were usually made from potsherds, demonstrating again the reuse and refashioning of objects. The edges would be roughly chipped away to form a circle. Some of these toys show signs of further filing, likely done by using a rock as a smoothing stone. The disks identified as tops had a single hole bored through the center.[79] One would place a wooden rod into the hole and spin the rod between

---

tation in battle knocking around (Kilmer, "Oration on Babylon," 13–15). Granqvist makes note of little boys playing a stick and stone game, much like golf (Granqvist, *Birth and Childhood among the Arabs*, 129).

76. While the concepts in the "Games Text" describe play, the text in general belongs to a cultic hymn praising Inanna/Ištar (Kilmer, "Oration on Babylon," 9–22).

77. Respectively, *keppû* (*CAD* 8:312), *kitpulu* (*CAD* 8:467), *lāsamu* (*CAD* 9:104–5), *napāgu u buruburu* (*CAD* 11.1:263) (Kilmer, "Oration on Babylon," 10). See Hübner, *Spiele und Speilzeug in antiken Palästina*, 13–14.

78. For more information on the creation, worldwide locations, time periods, and identification of spinning toys, like the buzz, see the discussion by van Beek. Gus van Beek, "The Buzz: A Simple Toy from Antiquity," *BASOR* 275 (1989): 53–58. Avissar-Lewis discusses the use of the buzz, as well as the spinning top (Avissar-Lewis, "Childhood and Children in Material Culture," 127*).

79. Pottery chipped away into disks and then rubbed round are given the generic designation "disks" in the archaeological literature. This is done by way of acknowledging that a disk might have been used for various purposes. For example, many archaeologists identify disks with a single hole as spindle whorls, or possibly flywheels in bow drills (inter alia, Dothan and Brandl, *Deir El-Balaḥ*, 246; Shlomo Bunimovitz and Zvi Lederman "Iron Age Artifacts," in Bunimovitz and Lederman, *Tel Beth-Shemesh A Border Community in Judah* 2:583).

the thumb and middle finger.[80] Evidence of spinning tops is found in ethnographic reports across the globe, including the Palestinian village of Bir-Zet: "Spinning tops were made in Bir-Zet like so, children cut out a round piece from a pomegranate and suck a stick in it to make a spinning top."[81]

Disks with two holes look very similar to ceramic buttons and were even referred to as such in some of the early archaeological literature (fig. 7.11).[82] These buttons are not to be confused with loom weights that are similar in appearance but have distinguishing features; most notably, the loom weights are a slightly different shape (rounded trapezoids) and their holes are narrower and were made before firing.[83] The two-holed disks were identified early on as toys, as excavators found them reminiscent of a wooden toy produced in America at the turn of the twentieth century called a buzz.[84] Operating the buzz, or button-toy, required a length of string to be threaded through the two holes and then knotted together. One then twisted one end of the thread around and then pulled it taught, causing the disk to travel up and down the length of the string. Double-pierced disks have been found at many sites in Israel including Beth Shean, Hazor, Megiddo, Bethel, Gezer, Tel el-Ajjûl, Tell el-Far'ah, and Tell Jemmeh. Another possibility was to thread two of the buzz toys together, wind them up, and then hold the thread while releasing the disks, causing the disks to travel up and down the string like a yo-yo.[85] A study of these double holed disks from sites across Israel shows that some of the disks appear to be made by a skilled artisan, while other disks appear less

---

80. Avissar-Lewis, "Childhood and Children in Material Culture," 127*.

81. H. Schmidt and P. Kahle, *Volkserzählungen aus Palästina I–II* (Göttingen: Vandenhoeck & Ruprecht, 1918–1930), 76. Quoted in Hübner, *Spiele und Speilzeug in antiken Palästina*, 86. Translation from the German my own. For a bibliography of spinning tops worldwide, see Hübner, *Spiele und Speilzeug in antiken Palästina*, 86–88.

82. R. A. S. Macalister, *The Excavation of Gezer 1902–1905 and 1907–1909* (London: Palestine Exploration Fund, 1912), 1:95 = v. 3 pl. 24:33; 2:90 = v. 3 pl. 132:37–38. The disks in fig. 7.11 all come from a single site, Tell Jemmeh, and demonstrate the wide variety of disks.

83. Dothan and Brandl, *Deir El-Balaḥ*, 263.

84. Petrie, *Gerar*, 18, pl. 39:24–25; O. R. Sellers et al., *The 1957 Excavation at Beth- Zur*, ASOR 38 (Cambridge, MA: ASOR, 1968), 83; Herschel Shanks, "Buzz or Button?," *BAR* 17.3 (1991): 62–63; Beek, "Buzz," 53–58.

85. Avissar-Lewis, "Childhood and Children in Material Culture," 128*.

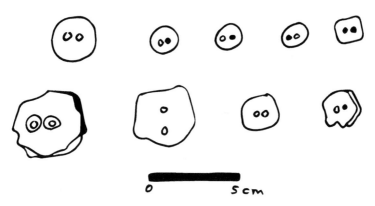

Fig. 7.11. Buzz, Tel Jemmeh, Late Bronze Age II–Iron Age II.

skilled.[86] Disks in the latter category have rougher edges, nonsymmetrical holes, or holes that are not all the way complete. Such technical errors are often associated with children and suggests the possibility that children were creating their own toys.

7.3. Summary

The subject of play is perhaps best understood through an anthropological lens. Cross-cultural studies demonstrate that play can be gendered, with boys preferring object play and girls symbolic play. The type of play and the time spent playing is culturally specific. An agrarian based household, such as the ancient Israelite בת אב (*bēt ʾāb*), would have a much different approach to play than a household in an industrialized nation. Agrarian societies spend much of their time tending fields and flocks and preparing daily necessities for the house.[87] Despite the vast differences in social structures, anthropologists point out that play serves a specific function cross-culturally. Whether understood biologically, as a means of developing life-skills, or on a related note as a means of socialization, play fosters a child's development as he moves into the adult world. Understood in these

---

86. Garroway, "Childist Archaeology."

87. For example, a woman would spend upward of three hours a day grinding enough grain to make bread for an average household of six people (Meyers, "From Household to House of Yahweh," 21).

ways, play has a valuable place in society as it can be understood to serve as a means of engendering the child in to adult society.

Identifying what constitutes play and toys is a complex issue. Engaging in this query asks us to move beyond our own notions of how we identify toys and to think about objects having multiple uses. Consider, for example, the relationship of music and ritual to play. Anthropology again offers a means of moving forward, providing helpful categories for identifying play and what it may have looked like in ancient Israel. The discussion above addressed: informal play, celebrations and festivals, solitary play, contests, and miscellaneous types of play. While the biblical text does not abound with references to toys, it does include descriptions of informal play by way of the trickster motif evidenced in the characters of Jacob and Laban. The dancing of the young girls at Shiloh represents play within celebrations and festivals, as does the song of Miriam (Exod 15:21–21; Judg 21:21). As presented in the Bible, festival music, instruments, and celebrations are sometimes similar in nature to the way these elements appear in Egyptian festivals. Again, dissecting the religious elements apart from the play elements in ritual is not an easy task, as the two categories are often intertwined. At times, however, it is possible to distinguish between the two. One can distinguish instrument playing, such as young David is known for, as performance playing.

The archaeological record adds to our knowledge of solitary play and contest play in ancient Israel with the discovery of objects, games, game pieces, dice, and figurines. Yet, despite their unanimous identification as toys, the games and game pieces are not without their issues. It is impossible to tell the minimum age for games like *senet* and whether they were meant for individuals of all ages. Game pieces, such as the astragali, again attest to the relationship between ritual objects and play; not only can astragali be thrown in a game of knuckle-bones, but they can also be used in divination. While the former objects are more readily identified as toys, other objects, like figurines, are highly contested as toys. Reasons for dismissing anthropomorphic and zoomorphic figurines as toys include: toys will show signs of wear, toys will be broken, they should appear in areas frequented by children, be of a wide typological variety, and be made of child-friendly materials. Further arguments against figurines, such as the JPFs and horse and rider figurines, as religious or magical objects state that one cannot reuse an object because it would defile the object. Arguments against JPFs in specific as toys include: they are too uniform in shape, they were not decorated on the back side, they are breakable, and there is no archaeological evidence they were used by children.[88] Yet the conclusions drawn all beg the question. As referenced above, most figurines are found broken (hence signs of wear), found in areas trafficked by children and made of clay (a common, child-friendly substance).[89] As for the argument that objects would be defiled if used improperly, there is no reason that children could not have played with the items after they were "decommissioned" from their original use, or broken. Found in quotidian domestic waste and not in *favissae*, broken JPFs seem to argue for themselves that they needed no special disposal treatment.[90] The argument regarding the uniform shape of many zoomorphic and anthropomorphic objects has recently been addressed by Julie Parker, who noted that toys like Barbies all have a uniform shape.[91] Because the objects discussed here could have more than one use, there needs to be a better argument for how all the objects were used.[92] It seems time for a rapprochement to occur between the current, popular opinions on figurines and the older opinions, which allowed for the possibility the objects were toys; these items might have been multiple things to multiple people.

Looking at other kinds of play, we find they are not so easily categorized. The word used to describe actions by Isaac and Ishmael is "play," yet, the text does not elaborate on what they were doing. Perhaps they were engaging in imaginary play, such as a game of "shepherd, sheep, wolf," or were involved in a more physical form of play, such as wrestling. Finally,

---

88. Kletter, *Judean Pillar-Figurines and the Archaeology of Asherah*, 73; Philip Johnston, "Figuring out Figurines," *TynBul* 54 (2003): 99.

89. While children may not have been present in some of the public buildings where JPFs were discovered, children were present in and around the domicile. It has long been accepted by European archaeologists that toys were made of "simple and organic materials, and they were often discarded thrown away" [when the child was through with them] (Lillehammer, "Child Is Born," 98-99).

90. In contrast to the disposal of JPFs see the disposal of figurines showing Greek influence at Tel Dor, where multiple favissae were discovered. Ephraim Stern, "The Beginnings of Greek Settlement in Palestine in Light of the Excavations at Tel Dor," in *Recent Excavations in Israel: Studies in Iron Age Archaeology*, ed. S. Gitin and W. Dever, AASOR 49 (Winona Lake, IN: Eisenbrauns, 1989), 107–24.

91. Parker, "I Bless You by YHWH of Samaria and His Barbie."

92. Fowler's description of the so-called Astarte plaque figurines applies to the JPFs as well: "The truth is we simply do not know what these figurines were, nor, for that matter, what purpose they might have served." Mervyn Fowler, "Excavated Figurines: A Case for Identifying a Site as Sacred?," *ZAW* 97 (1985): 335.

looking cross-culturally to ancient Israel's neighbors, one can find hints of gendered play. The Mesopotamian Game Text and the Elevation of Ishtar, present the idea that play could be gendered. The play of girls was equated with dolls, while boy-play included running, wrestling, and *puku u mekkû*. Some play, like jump rope and throwing astragali, was undertaken by both girls and boys.

As the study of toys in the ancient Israel moves forward, attention to gendered play could be a possible avenue of research. Other kinds of research might use fingerprint analysis on the miniature objects and figurines as a means of identifying objects made by children. Finally, one must not discount the objects of play that do not leave a mark in the archaeological record. Play with objects that disintegrate as ethnographic sources suggest (mud and stick dolls) and play with animals both fall into this category.

8

Till Death Do Us Part

Isaiah 11:8 envisions a time when "A suckling shall play over a viper's hole, and a weaned one pass his hand over an adder's den."[1] This stanza is situated in a description of an idyllic future, an eschatological prophecy (Isa 11:1–12:10) of a world at peace. Isaiah 11:6–9 describes this peace through harmony in nature. Practically speaking, this verse reflects on the daily dangers faced by infants and children. Chapter 4 discusses potential dangers and the ways parents protected their children. This chapter faces the reality that death happened and investigates some of the reasons behind infant and child death. Following the model presented for studies of the Greco-Roman world, the chapter presents evidence from various genres (law, narrative, correspondences, burials, and ethnography) examining children of varying age ranges, and then investigates attitudes toward infant and child death.[2]

The infant mortality rate in ancient Israel was extremely high, estimated to have reached 50 percent in an infant's first year.[3] Compared with the United States, which had a rate of 5.82 percent in 2014, infant death in ancient Israel was a reality for every family.[4] Most infant deaths in the

---

1. The term used for suckling is יונק and the term for a weaned one גמול.

2. Mark Golden, "Did the Ancients Care When Their Children Died?," *Greece and Rome* 35 (1988): 152–63.

3. Patricia Smith and Gal Avishai, "The Use of Dental Criteria for Estimating Postnatal Survival in Skeletal Remains of Infants," *Journal of Archaeological Science* 32 (2005): 86; Patricia Smith and Marina Faerman, "Has Society Changed Its Attitude to Infants and Children? Evidence from Archaeological Sites in the Southern Levant," *Servei D'investigacions Arqueològiques Prehistòriques* (2008): 211. As late as the 1990s some developing countries still saw such high mortality rates. Douglas Ewbank and James N. Gribble, *Effects of Health Programs on Child Mortality in Sub-Saharan Africa* (Washington DC: National Academy Press, 1993).

4. Center for Disease Control, "Infant Health," https://tinyurl.com/SBL1729b.

ancient world happened during the perinatal period (zero to seven days after birth) and were caused by a low birth weight.[5] Birth weight in turn was related to the mother's age, genetics, health, and previous number of pregnancies.[6] Based on population projections from burial sites, archaeologists estimate another 50 percent of children died before the age of fifteen years.[7] Most of the time the deaths not occurring from low birth weight can be attributed to other causes, wherein the death was not intentionally meant. Accidents, disease, epidemic, sickness, and malnutrition fall into this category. Other times, the deaths take a more sinister turn and can be categorized as deaths caused intentionally by war, cannibalism, infanticide, and sacrifice. Both kinds of deaths are recorded in the textual and archaeological data, and both kinds of deaths demonstrate the extreme fragility of a young one's life.

8.1. Deaths Caused by Human Hands

The deaths discussed in this section are those caused directly by human intention. The Hebrew Bible records many such deaths. The most fantastical of these deaths is perhaps those of the children in 2 Kgs 2:23–25.[8] A group of נערים קטנים (naʿărîm qəṭannîm) "young youths," repeatedly shout the insult "Be off, baldy!" at the prophet Elisha. Elisha, not taking

---

Within a single Palestinian village the mortality rate was as follows: 0.86 percent die at birth; 30.48 percent die "in infancy" (between birth to seven years of age); 3.74 percent die "while growing up" (ages seven to twelve years); 1.82 percent die as "youths" (those who are twelve years and up but not year married) (Granqvist, *Child Problems among the Arabs*, 83).

5. For the purpose of statistical analysis, the World Health Organization has determined five and a half pounds to be the cutoff for low birth weight. They note that for clinical purposes an individual country may choose to use another number as the cutoff. ("Low Birthweight").

6. Smith and Avishai, "Use of Dental Criteria," 83–84.

7. Smith and Avishai, "Use of Dental Criteria," 86. Life expectancy was not that long. For example, studies of burial populations in Bronze Age Lachish, Kabri, and ʿEn Esur found adults died between thirty to forty years old. Yossi Nagar, "Human Skeletal Remains from T. 80 in the ʿEn Esur Cemetery," *Atiqot* 64 (2010): 121–24; Marina Faerman et al., "The Bioarchaeology of the Human Remains," in *Tel Kabri: The 1986–1993 Excavation Seasons*, ed. Aharon Kempenski (Tel Aviv: Yass Publications in Archaeology, 2002), 283–94; Meyers, *Rediscovering Eve*, 98–99.

8. Some have tried to argue these are not children; however, Parker presents a strong case for reading them as none other than children (*Valuable and Vulnerable*, 92).

kindly to this, curses the name of Adonai. Upon his words, two she-bears emerge from the woods and maul forty-two ילדים (yəlādîm), "children." Parker notes that the both words for children are masculine plural and has suggested that we might read this as either a group of boys or as a mixed group of boys and girls.[9] Whether boys, or boys and girls, Elisha appears to cause the death of many children (via she-bears). This vignette showcases Elisha's powers and his ability to manipulate the name of God.[10] It has also been interpreted as a tale of warning; children are to respect their elders.[11] In this way, it is linked to a set of laws regarding the child who is a rebellious and stubborn son, a drunkard and glutton (Deut 21:18–21).[12] The individual in question is specifically called a בן (bēn) "son." He is identified as a child since he appears to still be living under his parent's roof, and therefore the expectation is that he is subject to their rules.[13] The parents bring this child to the judges, stating that they have reproved him, but he has not listened and reformed his ways; they have tried to work it out at home, but he has such disregard for his parents that the legal system must step in.[14] The son, found guilty of these charges,

---

9. Parker, *Valuable and Vulnerable*, 93; Cogan and Tadmor point out that the number forty-two might be a figure of speech for "large group." Mordechai Cogan and Hayim Tadmor, *II Kings: A New Translation with Introduction and Commentary*, AB 11 (New York: Doubleday, 1988), 38.

10. The magical manipulation of God's name is well established by the Second Temple period. Amulets, stories, exhortations of angles, and written spells all include the name of YHWH. Gideon Bohak, *Ancient Jewish Magic* (Cambridge: Cambridge University, 2008), 22, 119, 127, 305–7. "The aggressive use of the power inherent in God's name is extremely important, because it probably is the oldest, longest-continuing practice in the history of Jewish magic" (127).

11. Cogan and Tadmor, *II Kings*, 39, and sources within.

12. Fleishman provides an overview of the scholarship on the relationship between these verses and their relationship to other ancient Near Eastern laws, and he provides his own suggestion that these verses represent a case of inner biblical exegesis. Joseph Fleishman, "Legal Innovation in Deuteronomy XXI 18–20," *VT* 3 (2003): 311–27.

13. Based on the accusations at hand, it seems that this son must be nearing adulthood. Mark Biddle, *Deuteronomy*, Smyth and Helwys Bible Commentary (Macon, GA: Smyth & Helwys, 2003), 325.

14. In ancient Israel and the ancient Near East in general, honoring one's parents was part of the social fabric (Exod 20:12; Lev 19:3; Deut 5:16; Fleishman, "Legal Innovation," 311–27). For more on parent-child contractual obligations and the possibility of them being broken in 2 Kgs 2, see Flynn, *Children in Ancient Israel*, 156–63.

is then stoned to death so that the evil will be swept away from within Israel.[15]

8.1.1. Cannibalism and Sacrifice

Other cases whereby children could die by the hand of another human include cannibalism and sacrifice. As to the former, 2 Kgs 6:24–30 narrates a tale so incredible it rivals that of she-bears eating children; in this story two mothers eat a child.[16] The city is under siege and food is scarce. To fill their empty bellies, two mothers agree the best thing to do is eat their children: Son A one day, and Son B the next day. The key to the narrative rests in verse 29. The mother of Son A cries out to the king that he must intercede on her behalf because they ate her son, but the mother of son B has had the gall to hide her son! This is clearly an extraordinary situation. Society has run so amok that parents are eating children. The curses in Deut 28:52–57 and Jer 19:9 warn of such times wherein Israelites will be at war and forced to eat their children in secret.[17] Such curses are not unusual, but rather part of the standard litany of curses such as those found in the Vassal Treaties of Esarhaddon. Section 47 of these treaties adjures Adad to curse the treaty-breaker with famine so severe that parents and children will end up eating each other. One of the curses closely resembles those of the biblical texts: "In your hunger, eat the flesh of your

---

15. This law was less than popular, and we might question how often it was put into practice. The very notion that the torah allowed parents to stone their children was curtailed early on. By the time of the Mishnah (200 CE), the rabbis felt very uncomfortable with the laws of the בן סרר (m. Sanh. 8:1) In good rabbinic fashion, they argued that these laws could only apply to a boy over the age of thirteen years and one day. In doing so, they set a legal precedent for who can be charged as a "child" for a crime.

16. For a reading of this text as one of sacrifice and not cannibalism, see Kristine Garroway, "2 Kings 6: 24–30: A Case of Unintentional Elimination Killing," *JBL* 31 (2018): 51–68.

17. University of Pennsylvania, "Essarhaddon's Succession Treaty," ORACC, https://tinyurl.com/SBL1729n. Michel notes the similarities and differences between the Neo-Assyrian and Neo-Babylonian imperial rhetoric of eating children and that of the biblical text. Andres Michel, *Gott und Gewalt gegen Kinder im Alten Testament*, FAT 37 (Tübingen: Mohr Siebeck, 2003), 213–20. He concludes that most of the biblical texts follow the Neo-Assyrian rhetoric. The only exception is that of 2 Kgs 6:28–29, which reflects the actual Neo-Babylonian siege of Jerusalem in 587/86 BCE (Michel, *Gott gegen Gewalt*, 219–20).

sons!"[18] While the practice appears to be rhetorical in nature (there is no evidence for people eating children), it is a scary prospect.[19] Times are so bad that the existing members of society must eat, and therefore obliterate, the future members of society.[20]

These narratives are not the only time that parents cause their own child's demise. Parental sacrifice of children is scattered throughout various books of the Hebrew Bible, and much has been written on the topic.[21] The most well-known attempt at sacrificing a child is probably the Akedah, the binding of Isaac, found in Gen 22. Abraham is asked to sacrifice "his son, his only son, the son whom he loves" (Gen 22:2). His story has a happy ending; a ram, not a human child is sacrificed.[22]

---

18. Section 47, line 449: *ina bu-ri-ku-nu UZU-MEŠ DUMU-MEŠ-ku-nu ak-la* (University of Pennsylvania, "Essarhaddon's Succession Treaty"). For a discussion of the Mesopotamian texts referring to the cannibalism of children during times of crisis, see Michel, *Gott und Gewalt*, 202–13.

19. A Ninth Dynasty Egyptian grave (ca. 2100 BCE) of the individual Anchtifi includes the following "note" attesting to a horrific event wherein children were eaten because everyone was starving from hunger: *während ganz Oberägypten Hungers starb und jedermann seine Kinder eins nach dem anderen auffrass*. Michel, *Gott und Gewalt*, 202 n. 8; W. Schenkel, *Memphis—Herakleopolis—Theben: Die epigraphischen Zeugnisse der 7.–11. Dynastie Ägyptens*, ÄAT 12 (Weisbaden: Harrassowitz, 1965), 64.

20. For children as future members of society, see Garroway, *Children in the Ancient Near Eastern Household*, 245–46. The rhetoric of war and children can also be seen in various prophetic texts (Hos 9:10–17; Isa 54; 66:7; Koepf-Taylor, *Give Me Children or I Shall Die*, 55–63).

21. The discussion here provides an overview of sacrifice from an objective perspective, pointing out where it appears in the biblical text. For scholarship and bibliography of those examining child sacrifice from a theological, polemical, or ideological perspective, see the recent works, inter alia, Michaela Bauks, "L'enjeu théologique du sacrifice d'enfants dans le milieu biblique et son dépassement en Genèse 22," *Études théologiques et religieuses* 76.4 (2001): 529–42; Francesca Stavrakopoulou, *King Manasseh and Child Sacrifice: Biblical Distortions of Historical Realities* (Berlin: de Gruyter, 2004); Heath Dewrell, *Child Sacrifice in Ancient Israel* (Winona Lake, IN: Eisenbrauns, 2017).

22. Scholars have pointed out that the original form of the story appears to have had a less satisfying ending, one in which Isaac meets his fate at the hand of his father. They point to an insertion bookmarked by the phrase "And an angel of the Lord called to him/Abraham" in verses 11 and 15, and note that Abraham and Isaac go up to Moriah together (v. 5), but only Abraham comes down (v. 19). See Howard Moltz, "God and Abraham in the Binding of Isaac," *JSOT* 96 (2001): 59–69, esp. 64; Stavrakopoulou, *King Manasseh*, 192–93. Other scholars see this request as repugnant, a trou-

Jephthah, in fulfillment of his vow to YHWH (Judg 11:30–31), sacrifices his own daughter (Judg 11:34–40).[23] Whereas Abraham replaces Isaac with an animal, Jephthah is said to have gone through with the action (Judg 11:30). Yet the act is not described in detail. In fact, the text only says, "he did to her as he had vowed." This circumlocution for sacrifice perhaps hints at this author's discomfort with child sacrifice.

Discomfort with child sacrifice is not limited to these narratives but is seen throughout the biblical text, most explicitly in the texts coming from the late monarchic period onwards. These texts attempt to distance child sacrifice from Israel, a reaction suggesting that at one time YHWH did desire child sacrifice. One method of distancing was to put cases describing intentional child sacrifice in the hands of foreigners. For example, during the Assyrian resettlement of Samaria, the Sepharvim are noted as ones who burn their children as offerings to their gods (2 Kgs 17:31). None of the other people listed along with the Sepharvim are said to do so, making the practice a defining characteristic of this people group (2 Kgs 17:30–31).[24] So, too, 2 Kgs 3 tells of the Moabite King Mesha sacrificing his son on the city wall so that the siege of the Israelites would end. Here the text suggests during times of extreme duress, (foreign) children could be sacrificed.[25] Another means of distancing was to offer redemption as an alternative and state that child sacrifice was "no command of mine."[26]

The need for distance is also a reaction to texts describing two regular kinds of child sacrifice. The first type is typified by Exod 22:28b–29 (Eng. 29b–30), which according to Heath Dewrell describes a regular practice

---

bling text of violence against children perpetrated by the very Being meant to protect children (Michel, *Gott und Gewalt*, 246–314).

23. Much has been written on the troubling nature of this text, but perhaps most memorable is Trible's treatment (Trible, *Texts of Terror*, 92–116). Day points out similarities between Jephthah's daughter's status and her actions as a *betulah* with female characters in Greek narratives (Day, "From the Child Is Born the Woman," 58–74). For an overview of sources treating the story as an etiology and a folktale, see Dewrell, *Child Sacrifice in Ancient Israel*, 112–15.

24. For literature on the Sepharvim and child sacrifice, see Dewrell, *Child Sacrifice in Ancient Israel*, 117–19.

25. The use of children as an intermediary between the human realm and the divine is well attested to in archaeological and anthropological literature (Garroway, "2 Kings 6:24–30," 58–59).

26. Jer 19:5; Garroway, *Children in the Ancient Near Eastern Household*, 186–87; Dewrell, *Child Sacrifice in Ancient Israel*, 107, 148–90.

wherein the "giving" (i.e., sacrifice) of the firstborn to YHWH was routinely expected: "The firstborn of your children/sons you shall give to
me ... on the eighth day you shall give him to me."[27] Separation from the
mother on the eighth day seems to imply nothing short of infant sacrifice.[28]
The second category of sacrifice found in the biblical text is the *mlk* sacrifice, referenced in Lev 18:21, 20:3; Deut 12:30–31, 18:10; Isa 30:27–33;
Jer 7:31, 19:5, 32:35; and Ezek 20:25–26. An exhaustive examination of
the texts has led scholars to the conclusion that the exact nature of this
sacrifice is unknown, but it seems to have some correlation (although the
exact link is not known) to the *mlk* offerings found in the Punic tradition.[29] Dewrell states, "Admittedly, it is difficult to determine the purpose
of the *mlk* sacrifice solely on the basis of biblical evidence; the biblical
text is more interested in condemning the rite than expounding on the
logic underlying it."[30] The Punic tradition offers more information on the
purpose of the *mlk* sacrifice within their society. Based on the steles that
accompany many of the sacrifices, it appears that they were done in fulfillment of a vow. The expectation was that upon completion of the sacrifice,
a positive divine answer would ensue.[31] Unlike in Punic lands, there is no

---

27. Other variations of this decree appear in Exod 13:2, 11–13; 34:19–20; Num
3:11–13, 8:1–20, and 18:13–18. For a review of scholarship and the most recent treatment of the topic of child sacrifice in these laws, see Dewrell, *Child Sacrifice in Ancient
Israel*, 72–90.

28. Based on other texts that allow for the redemption of the firstborn, some
scholars see a progression: infant sacrifice, to redemption (of firstborn males), to the
Levites taking the place of the firstborn. See Michael Fishbane, *Biblical Interpretation in Ancient Israel* (Oxford: Oxford University Press, 1985), 181–87; Karin Finsterbusch, "The Firstborn between Sacrifice and Redemption in the Hebrew Bible," in
Human Sacrifice in the Jewish and Christian Tradition, ed. Karin Finsterbusch, Armin
Lange, and Diethard Römheld (Leiden: Brill, 2007), 87–108; Garroway, *Children in
the Ancient Near Eastern Household*, 185–86. Another possible understanding of these
texts is that firstborn children were routinely sacrificed, but only by a small portion of
YHWHist worshipers (Dewrell, *Child Sacrifice in Ancient Israel*, 88–90).

29. Dewrell provides a full bibliography and discussion of *mlk* as a diety (or not),
the Punic evidence, and the biblical texts that reference parents "giving" their children/
"crossing their children over" למלך (Dewrell, *Child Sacrifice in Ancient Israel*, 4–36,
44–50; see also, Garroway, *Children in the Ancient Near Eastern Household*, 183–86).

30. Dewrell, *Child Sacrifice in Ancient Israel*, 122.

31. Mosca provides a comprehensive look at the Punic stele and the issue of vows.
P. G. Mosca, "Child Sacrifice in Canaanite and Israelite Religion: A Study in *Mulk* and
מלך" (PhD diss., Harvard, 1975), 61–97. Classical authors, most notably Kleitarchos,

archaeological evidence for the presence of a Tophet within ancient Israel: no urns, no bones, and no stele. Therefore, whether a vow fulfillment was the purpose of the biblical *mlk* sacrifice is simply not known.

8.1.2. Infanticide

Infanticide, the killing of a child less than one year of age, is the last subject to investigate in this section on deaths caused by humans.[32] Socioanthropological studies find that female infanticide was much more common than male infanticide.[33] Their conclusions are based on economics; sons were deemed more economically beneficial than daughters. This seems especially true in patrilocal agrarian societies, war-ridden places, and societies that depended heavily upon sons for eldercare.[34] In these societies, daughters were not only another mouth to feed, but also a financial burden as a dowry was needed to marry them off.[35] In Roman times, the *paterfamilias* had the right to decide if the family would keep the infant.[36]

---

also assert that Punic children were sacrificed in relation to vows. See *FGrHist* 137 F 9; John Day, *Molech: A God of Human Sacrifice in the Old Testament*, University of Cambridge Oriental Publications 41 (Cambridge: Cambridge University, 1989), 86–91.

32. For an anthropological overview of infanticide in societies throughout the world, see Michael Tooley, *Abortion and Infanticide* (Oxford: Clarendon, 1983), 309–22.

33. Female infanticide occurred in Scandinavia, India, and China: Eleanor Scott, "Killing the Female? Archaeological Narratives of Infanticide," in *Gender and the Archaeology of Death*, ed. Bettina Arnold and Nancy L. Wicker (New York: AltaMira Press, 2001), 5–7.

34. Beth A. Nakhai, "Female Infanticide in Iron II Israel and Judah," in *Sacred History, Sacred Literature: Essays on Ancient Israel, the Bible, and Religion in Honor of Richard Elliott Friedman*, ed. Shawna Dolansky (Winona Lake, IN: Eisenbrauns, 2008), 258; A. L. Hughes, "Female Infanticide: Sex Ratio Manipulation in Humans," *Ethology and Sociobiology* 2 (1981): 109–11; Scott, "Killing the Female?," 7; Susan Scott and Christopher J. Duncan, *Demography and Nutrition: Evidence from Historical and Contemporary Populations* (Oxford: Blackwell Science, 2002), 271. Granqvist notes times in which a child might be subject to infanticide. It is said there is an old practice to bury newborn baby girls in the sand alive (Granqvist, *Child Problems among the Arabs*, 44 n. 55).

35. Steinberg, *Kinship and Marriage in Genesis*, 27; King and Stager, *Life in Biblical Israel*, 36–40; Dever, *Lives of Ordinary People in Ancient Israel*, 180–81.

36. W. V. Harris, "Child Exposure in the Roman Empire," *Journal of Roman Studies* 84 (1994): 1–22; C. Laes, *Children in the Roman Empire: Outsiders Within* (Cambridge, UK: Cambridge University Press, 2011).

From Roman Egypt comes a letter from a man named Hilarion. In the letter, dated June 17, 1 BCE, he says: "If you are delivered of a child [before I get home] if it is a boy keep it, a girl discard it."[37] This letter supports the idea that a father might decide to dispose of a child based solely on the sex of the infant, health notwithstanding.

The biblical text offers two clear examples of infanticide. The first comes from the narrative surrounding baby Moses. Pharaoh decrees the Hebrew midwives are to dispose of male infants but keep female infants (Exod 1:5–16, 22).[38] Second, the metaphorical child "Israel," discussed in chapter 2, is left to die as an infant (Ezek 16). To these two we might add the fact that Hagar too appears to attempt the exposure of the baby Ishmael, placing him under a bush to die in the wilderness (Gen 21:14–16).[39] Within the limited number of examples from Hebrew Bible two of the three two biblical texts concern males. While this may seem at odds with the anthropological and textual records, which favor female infanticide, the reason for the male infanticide is specifically linked to the socioeconomic role boys had in continuing a lineage.[40] The concern in Exodus was that baby Israelites would grow up into adult Israelites, thereby increasing Israelite population—something Pharaoh wished to avoid (Exod 1:8). For his part, Ishmael presented a danger to the covenantal line of Abraham through Isaac (Gen 21:10).[41] The reasons behind the attempted biblical

---

37. P.Oxy. 744; Naphtali Lewis, *Life in Egypt under Roman Rule* (Oxford: Clarendon, 1985), 54.

38. Moses's mother, in accordance with the Pharaoh's decree, does not keep her son but attempts to save him. She follows Pharaoh's orders to put the child in the Nile, but rather than tossing him in, places the baby in a basket (Exod 2:1–10).

39. Genesis 21:14–21 seems to be a separate vignette, chronologically out of place. Genesis 17:24 states that Ishmael is thirteen years old. However, this age is inappropriate for the child in Gen 21, who is first placed on his mother's shoulder (perhaps in a sling [?]), and then left under a bush (vv. 14–15). Ishmael is referred to as an object, not as an independent actor. Hagar moves away from the boy so she may not watch as he dies (v. 16), and the Lord hears Ishmael's cries and responds (v. 17). If Ishmael were anything other than a small baby, he would crawl or walk back to his mother. E. A. Speiser, *Genesis*, AB 1 (Garden City, NY: Doubleday, 1964), 155; von Rad, *Genesis*, 233.

40. For example, Ishmael threatened the covenantal lineage established in Isaac, so he was cast off along with his mother. When Hagar could not provide for the boy, she chose to try and save herself. Pharaoh's decree, on the other hand, was motivated by his desire to get rid of an entire nation.

41. For a reading of the Akedah as a polemic, see Yariah Amit, *Hidden Polemics in Biblical Narrative*, trans. Jonathan Chipman (Leiden: Brill, 2000), 66–70.

infanticides of males underscore the need to look at the context in which the infanticides were undertaken.

Sex preference was not the only reason behind infanticide. Population control also appears to have been a factor. Indeed, Pliny argued population regulation was a real concern and defended the use of infanticide.[42] In the Athenian world, the elite were concerned with maintaining the proper number of people to inhabit the *oikos*. Too many heirs meant the depletion of property.[43] So too in Rome, a father might also desire to keep the family size small and the land intact, a concern that would also be present in ancient Israel.[44] At the site of Carthage, the many burials of neonates in urns (referenced above with regard to the *mlk* sacrifices) has made for a lively debate, currently at an impasse, in the archaeological community. Suggestions behind these burials include: sacrifices to Punic gods, an infant cemetery, and infanticide as population control.[45] The reason the debate cannot be settled is due partly to the issues with dating the bones

---

42. Simon Mays, "Infanticide in Roman Britain," *Antiquity* 67 (1993): 887.

43. Scott, "Killing the Female?," 8. On the lives of Athenian children in general, see Mark Golden, *Children and Childhood in Classical Athens* (Baltimore: Johns Hopkins University Press, 1990). In Melanesia, Polynesia, and other parts of the South Sea, as well as among Australian aborigines, controlling family size was of utmost importance. Infanticide was used as a means to an end (Tooley, *Abortion and Infanticide*, 315).

44. Mays, "Infanticide in Roman Britain," 887; Raymond Westbrook, *Property and the Family in Biblical Law* (Sheffield: JSOT Press, 2009).

45. Stager and Wolf address the possibility of population control. Lawrence Stager and Sam Wolf, "Child Sacrifice at Carthage—Religious Rite or Population Control?," *BAR* 10 (1984): 31–51. A debate as to whether the site and other Punic sites like it throughout the Mediterranean Rim (seventh to first century BCE) represent sacrifices of infants or infant cemeteries remains deadlocked as scholars continue to debate how to age the bones. Those understanding the bones to include those of fetuses argue that fetuses cannot be sacrificed. J. H. Schwartz, *What the Bones Tell Us* (New York: Holt, 1993), 52–53; Jeffrey H. Schwartz et al., "Skeletal Remains from Punic Carthage Do Not Support Systematic Sacrifice of Infants," *PLoS ONE* 5 (2010): e9177, https://doi.org/10.1371/journal.pone.0009177; Schwartz, "Bones, Teeth and Estimating Age of Perinates: Carthaginian Infant Sacrifice Revisited," *Antiquity* 86 (2012): 738–45. Other physical anthropologists estimate the age of the bones and teeth to be those of neonates, who were intentionally sacrificed. Patricia Smith et al., "Aging Cremated Infants: The Problem of Sacrifice at the Tophet at Carthage," *Antiquity* 85 (2011): 859–74; Smith et al., "Age Estimations Attest to the Practice of Infant Sacrifice at the Carthage Tophet," *Antiquity* 87 (2013): 1991–99.

and partly because scholars do not agree on how to reconstruct the Punic cultural attitudes toward infants.[46]

There are many other possible reasons for infanticide. For example, parents may not have wished to keep a disfigured child.[47] The Roman laws of the Twelve Tablets (ca. 450/449 BCE) stated that healthy children who could become citizens were kept, but unhealthy children or those with disabilities should be exposed (Plato, *Resp.* 5.459–461; Plutarch, *Lyc.* 16). Illegitimacy could also factor into the decision to keep a child. Ethnographic reports of Arabs at Petra describe what happens when a child was born out of wedlock; the child was buried in the sand as soon as the umbilical cord was cut: "Wenn eine ledige Person oder eine verheiratete Frau ein eheliches Kind gebiert, wird diesem gleich nach der Geburt die Nabelschnur herausgezogen und man versharrt es im Sand."[48] Granqvist reports that in former times both the woman and the child were killed.[49] The rationale

---

46. The classical writers note the Punics offer their children to the god (Porphyrius, *Abst.* 2.56 = Eusebius, *Praep. ev.* 16.6; for translation and commentary, see Carl Clem, *Die Phönikische Religion* [Leipzig: Hinrichs, 1939]). For example, Diodorus Siculus wrote that "there was in their city a bronze image of Cronus extending its hands, palms up and sloping toward the ground, so that each of the children when placed thereon rolled down and fell into a sort of gaping pit filled with fire" (*Bib. hist.* 20.6–7). There are those who understand the classical writers to be polemical, describing the barbaric practices of the Punics, and others who see no polemical undertone in what was written. P. Xella et al., "Phoenician Bones of Contention," *Antiquity* 87 (2013): 1202–3.

47. The Mesopotamian omen series *Šumma izbu* provides portents for many kinds of (to them, strange) births including: albinos, half-human forms, one who looks like Humbaba, cripples, dwarfs, and idiots (Leichty, *Šumma Izbu*, 36–39). The texts only prophecy what will happen to the family or the city; they do not mention what will happen to the infant.

48. Musil, *Arabia Petraea*, 215. I consulted with two native German speakers on the translation here, and all agreed that the phrase "man versharrt es im Sand" is most troubling. Each confirmed that the closest referent for *es* would be *die Nabelschnur*, meaning the umbilical cord would be buried in the sand. *Nabelschnur*, however, is feminine, and one would expect it to take a feminine pronoun, not a neuter pronoun. Grammatically, *es* seems to refer back to *das Kind*, meaning the child was buried in the sand. While disturbing, the practice seems akin to the older tradition regarding female infants referenced above (Granqvist, *Child Problems among the Arabs*, 44 n. 55).

In the village of Artas, illegitimate children were unknown as the parents took great care to marry their daughters off young, thus shortening any time she might have to couple outside of marriage (Granqvist, *Child Problems among the Arabs*, 65).

49. Granqvist, *Child Problems among the Arabs*, 66.

for killing the child or child and mother was both social and moral; the mother had shamed her family and dishonored herself.

One wonders whether the infant in Ezek 16 was discarded for this reason. Ezekiel 16 allegorically describes the adoption and marriage of Jerusalem to God.[50] Jerusalem is born of non-Israelite (identified in the text as Canaanite) parents: her father was an Amorite and her mother a Hittite (Ezek 16:3). Upon birth, she is immediately subjected to infanticide by being placed in a field and abandoned (Ezek 16:4–5). The description of Jerusalem's sisters as Samaria and Sodom secure her in a family tree of undesirables (Ezek 16:46). After her adoption by God, Jerusalem grows up and, like her sisters, plays the harlot (Ezek 16:15–53).[51] Steeped in language of idolatry, harlotry, and foreign nations, one can but wonder if Ezekiel is suggesting Jerusalem herself was a product of an illegitimate union.[52]

---

50. Foundlings, those who were cast out and then adopted, are prevalent in the ancient world. The practice seems to be a "happy ending" to some cases of infanticide. In many cases (especially in the Greco-Roman world) the foundlings were brought into a family as slaves. Maier Malul, "Adoptions of Foundlings in the Bible and Mesopotamian Documents: A Study of Some Legal Metaphors in Ezekiel 16:1–7," *JSOT* 46 (1990): 97–126; Garroway, *Children in the Ancient Near Eastern Household*, 101–8; Boswell, *Kindness of Strangers*, 53–179; Sarah Pomeroy, "Infanticide in Hellenistic Greece," in *Images of Women in Antiquity*, ed. Averil Cameron and Amélie Kuhrt (Detroit, MI: Wayne State University Press, 1985), 207–22. On the allegorical nature of the text, see Walther Zimmerli, *Ezekiel 1: A Commentary on the Book of the Prophet Ezekiel, Chapters 1–24*, trans. Ronald E. Clements, Hermeneia (Philadelphia: Fortress, 1969), 336–39. Shawn Flynn recently offered a new reading of the metaphorical relationship between Israel and YHWH using the langue of Mesopotamian exposure and adoption documents. In this case one can read God and Israel retaining the father-daughter, not the husband-wife, metaphor throughout Ezekiel (Flynn, *Children in Ancient Israel*, 185–90).

51. After Gen 19, Sodom becomes a code word for all that is sinful and wrong. Samaria is best known for her idolatry, which according to the biblical text, caused the fall of Samaria, i.e., the Northern Kingdom (1 Kgs 12:25–33; 16:31; 2 Kgs 17:7–9). For an analysis of the father-daughter relationship in Ezek 16 see, Johanna Stiebert, *Fathers and Daughters in the Hebrew Bible* (Oxford: Oxford University Press, 2013), 196–202.

52. If the origins of the Israelites are to be found within the land of Israel, and not (as those ascribing to the conquest model suggest) from outside of Canaan, then Ezekiel can be understood as speaking to a historical reality. Benjamin Mazar, *Jerusalem through the Ages* [Hebrew] (Jerusalem: Israel Exploration Society, 1968), 4*; Moshe Greenberg, *Ezekiel 1–20*, AB 22 (Garden City, NY: Doubleday, 1983), 274; Margaret Odell, *Ezekiel* (Macon, GA: Smyth & Helwys, 2005), 186–89. Various models for the

While the biblical text gives many examples of ways a child could die by the hands of another human, there is no extant archaeological evidence of child sacrifice, infanticide, or cannibalism (or death by bears) within ancient Israel.[53] However, there is evidence of the infanticide of illegitimate children at a slightly later date.[54] While excavating the bathhouse at Roman Ashkelon (fourth to sixth century CE), archaeologists discovered a sewer full of animal bones, trash, and human neonate bones. These neonates were judged to have been one to two days old, and their burial context suggests that they were simply discarded, rather than buried.[55] The excavators surmise that the bathhouse, the "red light district" of the ancient world, was home to courtesans who discarded their illegitimate infants. Moreover, DNA analysis discovered that the majority of the neonates were boys,

---

emergence of Israel have been proposed including: conquest, peasant revolt, peaceful infiltration, and different understandings of internal political and ethnic creations within Canaan. Inter alia, Alt, *Die Landnahme der Israeliten in Palästina*; William F. Albright, "The Israelite Conquest of Canaan in the Light of Archaeology," *BASOR* 74 (1939): 11–23; Noth, *History of Israel*; Mendenhall, "Hebrew Conquest of Palestine," 65–87; Gottwald, *Tribes of Yahweh*; Israel Finkelstein, "The Emergence of Israel in Canaan: Consensus, Mainstream and Dispute," *SJOT* 5 (1991): 47–59; Israel Finkelstein and Nadav Na'aman, *From Nomadism to Monarchy: Archaeological and Historical Aspects of Early Israel* (Jerusalem: Yad Izhak Ben-Zvi: Israel Exploration Society, 1994); Dever, *Who Were the Early Israelites and Where Did They Come From?*

53. As the biblical and ancient Near Eastern texts hint, children would be vulnerable during warfare. The prophetic texts use violence against children as a metaphor to express responses of disgust, fear and repentance. Jason Anthony Riley, "The Motif of Children as Victims of War" (paper presented at the Annual Meeting of the Southwestern Region of the Society of Biblical Literature, Irving, TX, March 11, 2017). The archaeological record is rife with evidence of violence against children during war. For children in war reliefs, see Schwyn, "Kinderbetreuung im 9.–7. Jahrhundert," 1–14. Remains of children can also be seen in Iron Age destruction conflagrations at sites such as Megiddo and Lachish. Yossi Nagar, "Human Skeletal Remains," in *Megiddo IV: The 1998–2002 Seasons*, ed. Israel Finkelstein, David Ussishkin, and Baruch Halpern (Tel Aviv: Yass Publications in Archaeology, 2006), 471–72; Patricia Smith, "Skeletal Remains from Level VI," in *The Renewed Archaeological Excavations at Lachish (1973–1994)*, ed. David Ussishkin (Tel Aviv: Yass Publications in Archaeology, 2004), 2504–7.

54. The example from Roman Ashkelon is significant because it is rare to find evidence of infanticide in the archaeological record. Infants who were exposed or abandoned were either picked up by another party and adopted or died and their remains left to the elements (Garroway, *Children in the Ancient Near Eastern Household*, 188).

55. The same conclusions were reached at different sites in Roman Britain (Mays, "Infanticide in Roman Britain," 883–88).

not girls. Based on the ratio of male to female neonates, they posit that some female infants were kept and raised as future courtesans, rather than subjected to infanticide.[56] This example from the archaeological record again demonstrates the importance of considering the find location and re-creating the sociohistorical background when drawing conclusions as to why infanticide was practiced.

8.2. Other Deaths

As treated here, other deaths are those that are not intentionally forced upon a child by another human. Many times, the underlying causes of a child's death as described in the biblical and ancient Near Eastern texts are not always straightforward, leaving the cause the death open to speculation. The archaeological record can be helpful in trying to determine what ailments befell children, as skeletal and microbial analyses have revealed numerous illnesses a child might have succumbed to.

8.2.1. Biblical Sources

Three biblical narratives present themselves as case studies of children's deaths. The first case is found in 1 Kgs 17. The boy there is the only child of a widow who can barely make ends meet, making this small family unit the embodiment of the poor and destitute class in ancient Israel.[57] Right after Elijah brings economic prosperity to the household through the miracle of the bottomless jars of flour and oil, the son falls ill. In a single verse, the son becomes sick, then very, very sick, and finally his breath leaves him (1 Kgs 17:17). The rapid succession of events describes a child who over the course of a short while goes from being healthy to dead.[58]

---

56. Marina Faerman et al., "Determining the Sex of Infanticide Victims from the Late Roman Era through Ancient DNA Analysis," *Journal of Archaeological Sciences* 25 (1998): 861–65.

57. F. Charles Fensham, "Widow, Orphan, and Poor in Ancient Near Eastern Legal and Wisdom Literature," *JNES* 21 (1962): 129–39; Jonathan Ben-Dov, "The Poor's Curse: Exodus XXII 20–26 and Curse Literature in the Ancient World," *VT* 56 (2006): 431–51, esp. 432–33. Throughout the narrative the boy is called בֵּן, "son." The term has no age limitations but rather highlights familial connections (Parker, *Valuable and Vulnerable*, 46–49).

58. Brueggemann points out that the text refrains from using the verb "to die," thus leaving open the possibility that the boy was not actually dead, rather close to

Without more details, one is left to wonder what affliction came over the child. In choosing to reference the breath, rather than simply state the child died, one might imagine some sort of respiratory episode taking place.[59] In developing countries, acute respiratory infections (ARI) have an extremely high mortality rate for children under the age of five.[60] A 2000 study found 1.9 million children died of ARIs, with 70 percent of those deaths coming from developing countries.[61] ARIs cover everything from pneumonia, pharyngitis, bronchitis, to the common cold, and today are treated with vaccines. Without the availability of vaccines, people in the ancient world turned to other cures, such as calling on men of God, like Elijah, to work miracles.

The case in 2 Kgs 4:17–20 also recalls a child being revived by a wonder worker, this time it is Elisha. Unlike the parallel story in 1 Kings, we know a little more about the child. He was born to a woman who had no son. She was in this predicament because her husband was old (2 Kgs 4:14).[62] Elisha predicts she will bear a son in one year, and indeed she does (v. 17). The boy is then described as growing up (v. 18), meaning that he was not an infant at the time of his death. In fact, he is old enough to go to the fields by himself where his father was reaping, and it is here that the boy takes ill (v. 18). Ethnographic parallels find that boys joined their father in the fields as young as five years old, and Joseph and David act as messengers to men in the field as teenagers (Gen 37:12–14; 1 Sam 16:11).[63] However, the boy here is still young enough to be carried and held on his mother's knees (2 Kgs 4:19–20), suggesting that he is a younger child.

---

death. Walter Brueggemann, *1 and 2 Kings*, Smyth and Helwys Bible Commentary (Macon, GA: Smyth & Helwys, 2000), 212.

59. Gray also notes the link to breath and suggests that ground floor of the house was full of debris and the boy's death may have been "a simple matter of hygiene." John Gray, *1 and 2 Kings*, OTL (Philadelphia: Westminster, 1963), 342.

60. Eric A. F. Simoes et al., "Acute Respiratory Infections in Children," in *Disease Control Priorities in Developing Countries*, ed. Dean T. Jamison et al. (New York: Oxford University Press, 2006), 483–98.

61. B. G. Williams et al., "Estimates of Worldwide Distribution of Child Deaths from Acute Respiratory Infections," *Lancet Infectious Diseases* 2 (2002): 25–32.

62. Parker, *Valuable and Vulnerable*, 150. Note general the similarities to Gen 18:1–15.

63. A boy of eight or nine years old is old enough to run errands for the family. A boy of ten years might start to shepherd a field and care for a flock (Granqvist, *Birth and Childhood among the Arabs*, 132–35).

The cause of the child's death appears to be related to his head, for he shouts, "my head, my head," and then dies. Head pain can be due to many different things. What happened to the child to precipitate him holding his head and crying out is unknown, and it is difficult to hypothesize what illness could have such an immediate effect other than (sun) stroke, or head trauma.[64] The narrative is more interested in curing the ailment than explaining what it was.

To these two narratives we can add a third: the death of Bathsheba and David's illegitimate son. In 2 Sam 12:13–24 we read of the death of David's first son with Bathsheba and the couple's reaction to the child's death. Verse 14 suggests that the death of the child will be caused by God as David's punishment for killing Uriah: "However, since you have spurned the enemies of the Lord by this deed, even the child about to be born to you shall die" (JPS).[65] The following verse says, "The Lord afflicted the child that Uriah's wife had born to David, and it became critically ill" (JPS).[66] The context suggests that the child here is a newborn who dies within seven days of becoming ill (2 Sam 12:18). Note that the

---

64. Thenius suggests that the boy experienced sunstroke. Otto Thenius, *Bücher der Könige* (Leipzig: Weidermann, 1849), 281. Sunstroke is a serious condition that needs to be treated immediately. Among other symptoms, a throbbing headache, disorientation, and fainting can occur. United Kingdom, Government, "Conditions of Heat Exhaustion and Heatstroke," NHS.uk, https://tinyurl.com/SBL1729k. If the boy was hit on the head, a trephination may have been a medical option in Elisha's absence. Trephinations, which relieve pressure on the brain due to blood pooling among other things, have been found on crania in the land of Israel from prepottery Neolithic Jericho (8350 BCE) through the Arab period (eighth century CE). Joe Zias, "Health and Healing in the Land of Israel—A Paleopathological Perspective," in *Illness and Healing in Ancient Times* (Haifa: University of Haifa, 1996), 16.

65. The phrase "this deed" is ambiguous. David's sin is understood by Josephus to be the "very grievous sin" of adultery (Josephus, *A.J.* 17.7; 13.1 [Whiston]). The Talmudic sages too follow suit (b. Sanh. 107a and b. Shabb. 56a). The biblical text, on the other hand, implies David's sin was murder, the sin *par excellence* in the biblical text. Taking a woman to bed was understood as par for the course if you were a king. Shulamit Valler, "King David and 'His' Women," in *A Feminist Companion to Samuel and Kings*, ed. Athalya Brenner (Sheffield: Sheffield Academic Press, 1994), 140–41.

66. The word here comes from the root אנשׁ, which generally means to become weak or sick. However, in this context a more intense meaning, such as incurable sickness is a better understanding of the word. While ילד (*yeled*) is often translated as "child," in many contexts, such as here, it refers to a newborn (Parker, *Valuable and Vulnerable*, 64–65).

reader is led to believe the infant takes ill immediately after his birth, but the text does not specifically say the child was born and became ill.[67] Precious little information is given textually regarding the illness with which the infant is afflicted. However, knowing the rate of infant mortality in ancient Israel, it is not unreasonable to wonder if this death, understood as a consequence meted out by God, could be a way to understand why infants died soon after birth.[68] It was noted above that babies who die within the first week of life usually die due to low birth weight. Young, first-time mothers such as Bathsheba, are likely to have babies with low-birth weights, who are susceptible to low oxygen levels, difficulty feeding and gaining weight, infection, breathing problems leading to respiratory distress syndrome, intraventricular bleeding, gastrointestinal problems, and sudden infant death syndrome.[69] Any one of these complicating issues could lead to an infant's death.

---

67. Depending on how one reads the timing of the events in 2 Sam 11 and 12, it is possible to read the child as being older than seven days. Note 2 Sam 11:27 uses a syntactical structure similar to the start of 2 Sam 11, wherein actions move rapidly, and the subject of the verbs changes. When the mourning period ended *David* (again) *sent* for Bathsheba, and *he brought* her into his house, and *he took* her as a wife, and *she bore* a son. Assuming David and Bathsheba had ceased extramarital relations, the verse spans at the very least, nine months' time. Before we hear of the child again, a lengthy interview between Nathan and David ensues (2 Sam 12:1–14) and ends with the prophecy David's son, not he, shall die (2 Sam 11:4). Verse 15 picks up the rapid pace of the narrative chain seen previously in 2 Sam 11 and 12: And *Nathan returned* to his house, and *YHWH smote* the child whom the wife of Uriah had born to David, and *it (sickness/ child) was incurable*. How much telescoping has gone on in the text, and how much time passed between the time the child was born, David and Nathan met, and God smote the child is not made explicitly clear. The child is a ילד, which can carry a broad range of meanings (Flynn, *Children in Ancient Israel*, 15–16). I follow Flynn and think we are meant to understand the child is an infant and that this was a horrible fate (151–56).

68. For those texts ascribing to a Deuteronomistic theology, deeds and actions have real consequences. Furthermore, there was the belief that the sins of the fathers could be visited upon the children (Exod 20:5–6, 34:6–7; Num 14:18; Deut 5:9–19, 7:9–10). Cross-generational retribution is present in the Hittite literature and Mari contracts as well (*ANET*, 207–8, 395d; ARM 8.1).

69. Stanford University, "Low Birthweight," Standford Children's Health, https://tinyurl.com/SBL1729i.

8.2.2. Ancient Near Eastern Sources

Texts outside the Hebrew Bible attest to many potentially lethal causes of infant and child death. Fevers, epilepsy, pertussis, typhoid fever, infectious diseases of an unknown kind, open fontanelle, spina bifida, tracheomalacia, jaundice, and the mysterious *būsānu*-sickness were all things that trained doctors (*asû*) and herbalists (*ašipu*) were called upon to treat.[70] Cramps due to "bitter breast milk," coughs, vomiting, and constipation are also attested to in the textual record.[71] Lists of the sicknesses, their supposed origins, and the cures are found throughout the medical and omen literature.[72] The intersection of medical and omen literature in the ancient world means that "medical care was a religious activity."[73] While observation and logic could help one administer preventative care, there were plenty of cases in which a child became sick and needed professional care.

One curious text from Mari is worthy of mention.[74] This text speaks of "the three children of Baṭaḫrum, […], all died at one time. One day they were not sick; then Baṭaḫrum wrote [to fetch] a LÚ.MAŠ.ŠU.GÍD.GÍD, so I sent a LÚ.MAŠ.ŠU.GÍD.GÍD. Afterwards, during the night they all died

---

70. Scurlock and Andersen provide an overview of the Assyria and Babylonian corpus and correlate the symptoms found there with diseases and illnesses known today (Scurlock and Andersen, *Diagnoses in Assyrian and Babylonian Medicine*).

71. Volk investigates various ailments and source texts from Old Babylonian Mari (Volk, "Kinderkrankheiten nach der Darstellung babylonisch-assyrischer Keilschrifttexte," 1–30). The fortieth tablet of the omen series *Traité akkadien de diagnostics et prognostics médicaux* includes a list of maladies affecting babies and the subsequent measures taken by the diviner/exorcists. Notably, most of this tablet references observations about babies and notes sicknesses or abnormalities in their development and the preventative measures (rather than cures) to keep the baby in good health. René Labat, *Traité akkadien de diagnostics et prognostics médicaux* (Paris: International Academy for the History of Science, 1951); D. Cadelli, "Lorsque l'enfant paraît … malade," in *Ktèma: Civilisations de l'Orient, de la Grèce et de Rome antiques, 1997*, Ktèma 22, Centre de recherche sur le Proche-Orient et la Grèce antiques (Strasbourg: Université Marc Bloch, 1998), 11–34. Farber also discusses other Mesopotamian omen texts related to infants and sickness (Farber, *Schlaf Kindchen, Schalf!*).

72. See SA.GIG.ME. The texts starting *šumma šerru*, "if a baby," are particularly interesting as they discuss things affecting infants who are not weaned (roughly zero to three years), the same group of individuals that are known to die young, and who are also "missing" from many of the burial contexts.

73. Meyers, *Rediscovering Eve*, 151.

74. M 6319 (AEM 1.1:280).

at one time."[75] The Mari letter is intriguingly vague because it describes the sudden death of multiple children with no suggestion of a sickness or epidemic.[76] Konrad Volk suggests that the death of the children may be related to a later part of the letter in which one learns that a man (presumably Batahrum) has stolen temple property. The death of the children may therefore be understood as divine punishment.[77] Divine punishment in turn was often understood in terms of plagues or pestilence.[78]

8.2.3. Archaeological Sources

An analysis of human remains provides a helpful portal into the lives of ancient children. The first thing to note is that studies of skeletal remains from various periods find many of the same sicknesses and diseases.[79] Some of these ailments, which can lead to the death of infants, are due to poor nutrition. For example, teeth, often the only intact remains of infants and children, provide evidence of poor nutrition. Almost every field report with a section on physical anthropology will note the teeth with caries (cavities) and describe the teeth as showing signs of malnutrition around age two and a half to three years, corresponding with the time of weaning.

Malnutrition can be seen in the bones as well. A deficiency in vitamin D and calcium is commonly noted in skeletal remains as rickets and osteomalacia. In infants, this causes the bone protein to fail to mineralize,

---

75. Volk, "Kinderkrankheiten," 6. Translation from the German my own.

76. Kenyon suggested that the mass burials of families at Jericho might be due to disease or epidemic. Kathleen Kenyon, *Excavation at Jericho I: Tombs Excavated in 1952–54* (Jerusalem: British Schools of Archaeology in Jerusalem, 1960), 267–68.

77. If this is indeed the case, then a similar storyline is seen in the Achan narrative in Josh 7. Achan's children must all die for his transgression (Josh 7:24).

78. For example, the modern question "why do bad things happen to good people" is a question that brings to the fore the idea that bad things should only happen when someone "deserves" them. Notably, the book of Job struggles with this mindset. For death by divine will, or "acts of God" as we might now call them, see Job 1, the *ketev* in Ps 91:6 and Deut 32:24; and *dever* in Exod 9:3; Hos 13:14; Hab 3:5; 2 Sam 24:13, 15.

79. The scientific study of bones in fields such as osteoarchaeology, bioarchaeology, and paleopathology is a rather recent development. Unfortunately, skeletal remains from those early excavations were not routinely subject to studies looking for pathologies. Moreover, infant and child bones were often overlooked in the early excavations.

resulting in deformed bones, which is a cause of death in premodern societies.[80] Scurvy, usually thought of as a sailor's disease, is due to the lack of vitamin C. Skulls require vitamin C to bind and form connective tissues. These tissues are made at a rapid rate throughout infancy and early childhood. Without these strong connective tissues, a trauma, or even normal movements can cause a skull to hemorrhage and death to ensue.[81] Skeletal reports often reference spongy or porous bone tissue (parietal hyperostosis and cribra orbitalia) in infant and children's bones and skulls. These are again due to malnutrition and are linked to a lack of vitamins and iron.[82] Sometimes the crania of infants or children show signs of pitting, which suggests the bones did not form correctly and indicates a period of sickness before death.[83]

In addition to various kinds of ailments evidenced by the skeletal remains, other forms of sicknesses could be contracted via poor hygienic practices. Without knowledge of the germ theory of disease, ancient Israelites had to rely upon their powers of observation to figure out the cause and effect of sicknesses.[84] Rodents, who carried fleas, who themselves carried the *Bacillus pestis* were known culprits that could cause plagues.[85]

---

80. D. J. Ortner and S. Mays, "Dry-Bone Manifestations of Rickets in Infancy and Childhood," *International Journal of Osteoarchaeology* 8 (1998): 44–55.

81. D. J. Ortner and M. F. Eriksen, "Bone Changes in the Human Skull Probably Resulting from Scurvy in Infancy and Childhood," *International Journal of Osteoarchaeology* 7 (1997): 212–20, especially 213.

82. Examples of malnutrition in infants can be seen at Tel Qashish in Israel, as well as other places in the eastern Mediterranean. Pamela Sabari and Patricia Smith, "The Human Skeletal Remains from Tel Qashish," in *Tel Qashish: A Village in the Jezreel Valley; Final Report of the Archaeological Excavations 1978–1987*, ed. Amnon Ben-Tor (Jerusalem: Institute of Archaeology, 2003), 413–14; J. Lawrence Angel, "Porotic Hyperostosis, Anemias, Malarias, and Marshes in the Prehistoric Eastern Mediterranean," *Science* 153.3737 (1966): 760–63.

83. Patricia Smith, Almut Nebel and Marina Faerman, "The Bio-anthropology of the Inhabitants of Middle and Late Bronze Age Yoqne'am," in *Yoqne'am III: The Middle and Late Bronze Ages, Final Report of the Archaeological Excavations (1977–1988)*, ed. Amnon Ben-Tor, Doron Ben-Ami and Ariella Livneh (Jerusalem: Hebrew University, 2005), 386.

84. The long litany of purity laws found throughout the book of Leviticus may be understood as equating pure things with cleanliness. Mary Douglas, *Purity and Danger* (London: Routledge & Kegan Paul, 1976).

85. Fleas and parasites are found throughout the ancient Near East. For example, in Egypt the Workman's Village of Amarna has produced evidence of squalid condi-

Central to the narrative of the wandering ark in 1 Sam 4–7 is the plague that affects the Philistine cities that host the ark. In the Septuagint, the plagues appear linked with mice that come off ships in the harbor (1 Sam 5:6). The incense stands/braziers found in many Iron Age houses may have been used not only for rituals and heat, but also used as a means of producing smoke that repelled pesky fleas, flies, mosquitoes, and the like (fig. 8.1).[86]

Excavations of upper-class homes in cities from the Bronze through Iron Ages found some attempt at incorporating a drainage system, demonstrating some attempt to keep waste from accumulating in commonly trafficked areas.[87] Houses with actual toilets dating to the Iron Age were found in Jerusalem (four different houses), as well as at Buseirah, and Tell es-Saʿidiyeh.[88] One of the cesspits under the toilet found in Jerusalem's Area G was thoroughly excavated and the remains subject to another relatively new field: archaeoparasitology.[89] The analysis of the cesspit remains

tions with "high levels of parasite infestations, in particular fleas: all in all, an ideal environment to support epidemic disease" (Dodson, *Amarna Sunset*, 17).

86. Mesopotamians and Egyptians also drew a connection between flies, fleas, and other nuisances and disease. Papyrus Ebers includes an entire section on "Medicines for Removing Lice and Fleas." Georg Ebers had great difficulty in correlating the Egyptian prescriptions to known diseases and their causes. Since the discovery of the papyrus in 1867, many have taken up the task. R. Hoeppli, "The Knowledge of Parasite and Parasitic Infections from Ancient Times to the Seventeenth Century," *Experimental Parasitology* 5 (1956): 398–419; Faisal R. Ali and Alexander Finlayson, "Pharaonic Trichology: The Ebers Papyrus," *JAMA Dermatology* 149 (2013): 920; Rami Bou Khalil and Sami Richa, "When Affective Disorders Were Considered to Emanate from the Heart: The Ebers Papyrus," *American Journal of Psychiatry* 171 (2014), 275. In Mesopotamia, a fly symbol was found on a seal depicting Nergal, the God of Death and Disease (Hoeppli, "Knowledge of Parasite and Parasitic Infections," 401).

87. Neufeld suggests some houses in Jericho, Tell Beit Mirsim, Bethel, and maybe the gates of Megiddo and Gezer had drains. Edward Neufeld, "Hygiene Conditions in Ancient Israel (Iron Age)," *BA* 34 (1971): 43–45.

88. Children and infant remains are not the only items misidentified in the archaeological record. Le Père Louis-Hugues Vincent famously called the stone found on his excavation "a magnificent chair of 'royal' stone," i.e., a throne. Louis-Hugues Vincent, *Underground Jerusalem* (London: Cox, 1911), 29. Little did he know it was a throne of a different kind.

89. The remains were also examined for pollen remains to determine the foods ancient Israelites of Area G's house were eating. Jane Cahill et al., "It Had to Happen," *BAR* 17.3 (1991): 64–69.

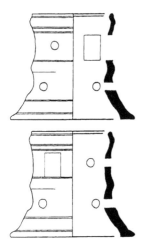

Fig. 8.1. Incense stand, Tell Halif, Iron Age II. Reproduced by permission from James Hardin, *Lahav II: Households and the Use of Domestic Space at Iron II Tell Halif: An Archaeology of Destruction* (Eisenbrauns, 2010), pl. 4.7. © 2010 Eisenbrauns.

identified two parasites: tapeworms and whipworms.[90] Tapeworms are found in poorly cooked meat. Whipworm is a result of poor hygiene; it comes from eating food that has encountered human feces. The scientists suggest that vegetables may have been grown in soil that was fertilized with human excrement. Moreover, if washed, the vegetables were washed poorly or with unsanitary water.[91] Each of these parasites can cause anemia, as well as diarrhea.[92] Diarrhea, either from these parasites, or from unclean drinking water remains a leading cause of child and infant death in developing countries.[93]

Parasitic diseases leading to epidemics are also attested to in the ancient world.[94] Outbreaks, such as malaria caused by the *Plasmodium* parasite, are prone to happen in the wet, rainier months. It affects people five years and younger, those with weaker immune systems, and can

---

90. Other worms have been referenced in the Mesopotamian literature. Kinnier Wilson, "Organic Diseases of Ancient Mesopotamia," in *Diseases in Antiquity: A Survey of the Diseases, Injuries and Surgery of Early Populations*, ed. Don R. Brothwell and A. T. Sandison (Springfield, IL: Thomas, 1967), 194–95.

91. Cahill, "It Had to Happen."

92. Mesopotamians and Egyptians also experienced parasites of this nature (Hoeppli, "Knowledge of Parasite and Parasitic Infections," 400–401; A. Sandison, "Parasitic Diseases," in Brothwell and Sandison, *Diseases in Antiquity*, 178–83).

93. World Health Organization, "Diarrhoeal Diseases," 2 May 2017, https://tinyurl.com/SBL1729q.

94. Zias, "Health and Healing in the Land of Israel," 15

cause death as soon as ten days after contraction.[95] Malarial symptoms can include "excruciating headaches, nausea, paroxysms, chills, tertian fevers, vomiting, severe gastric pain, enlarged spleen, physical weakness, an emaciated and gaunt appearance."[96] Evidence of malarial outbreaks can be found in cemeteries for infants and children, such as the one at the fifth-century CE site of Lugnano in Italy, caused by the most deadly of the *Plasmodium* parasites: *Plasmodium falciparium*.[97] Formal infant and children's cemeteries are not part of the ancient Israelite burial practice and make it difficult to identify outbreaks.[98]

One could add many observations from ethnographic accounts that support the conditions found in the analysis of the archaeological data. Since the aforementioned literature is so vast, a few anecdotal examples will serve as representative. Stomach disorders are quite common in all Near Eastern populations. While the parasitic cause of diarrhea is unknown to most ethnographic populations, they nonetheless have cures for it. In Arab Palestine an ailing child is reportedly given special medicine consisting of mutton, onions, cinnamon, cloves, and other herbs cooked into a loaf of bread. The medicinal loaf is then broken open over the sick child's face. The strong smell frightens away the evil causing the stomach troubles. Another possible cure is to drink the urine of another child or the urine of a postmenopausal woman. Here again, the shock (smell?) is believed to drive away the evil demon.[99] In the category of infection, Granqvist notes that "they [the fellaheen] know nothing of the modern theories concerning bacilli, the fear of germs and germ carriers. They have their own explanations, and attribute illness and accidents to the mysterious

---

95. World Health Organization, "Malaria," 11 June 2018, https://tinyurl.com/SBL1729s.

96. David Soren, "The Children's Cemetery of Lugnano in Teverina, Umbria: Hierarchy, Magic and Malaria," in *The Archaeology of Childhood*, ed. Güner Coşkunsu (Albany, NY: State University of New York, 2015), 246.

97. Soren, "Children's Cemetery," 235–50; Angel, "Porotic Hyperstosis," 761.

98. The presence of the *Plasmodium falciparum* parasite in bones of infants and children from other areas in Anatolia, Greece, and Cyprus (11,000–440 BCE) has been positively identified and linked to marshy or wet areas (Angel, "Porotic Hyperstosis," 160–63). It is unclear if the Egyptian and Mesopotamian medical literature reference malaria, or another disease like it (Hoeppli, "Knowledge of Parasite and Parasitic Infections," 414).

99. Granqvist, *Child Problems among the Arabs*, 97–98 and 98 n. 6.

enmity of supernatural powers."[100] Lacking such knowledge, the fellaheen have no problem with keeping their children filthy and, in fact, see a dirt and filth as protecting the children from harmful spirits.[101] Unfortunately, the ethnographic reports note that the practice seems to do more harm than good.[102]

In sum, the overview here of the various kinds of deaths referenced in the textual and archaeological sources stresses the vulnerability of ancient Israelite infants and children.

8.3. Reactions to Deaths Caused by Human Hands

After examining data concerning the various ways that ancient Israelite children and infants could have died, the next step is to think about how their families reacted to their deaths. Did ancient Israelites mourn the death of their children? Did they care when an infant died soon after birth, or were they callous to the death of these little ones, accepting the fate of their children as beyond their control? One might be tempted to think that those in the ancient world did not feel any remorse or mourn the death of children succumbing to deaths caused by human hands. Sacrifice and infanticide, for example, were acts intentionally carried out. The archaeological and ethnographic data could be interpreted to suggest that causing the death of younglings was considered routine and not met with any shock or horror. Yet, the extant archaeological evidence comes from later periods and foreign nations, so it is necessary to first ask what can be learned about children and deaths caused by human hands from the biblical text.[103]

To begin, the biblical infanticide narratives use generic words for children, and one must rely upon context to infer that the children were indeed infants.[104] By skirting around the age issue, not calling the infant

---

100. Granqvist, *Child Problems among the Arabs*, 99.

101. See §4.4.

102. See especially the section on eyes and blindness, Granqvist, *Child Problems among the Arabs*, 99.

103. Contra to contemporary Jewish, Christian, and Muslim beliefs, the ethnographic literature attests to attitudes which understand the infant as a "nonbeing" and therefore causing the death of the infant is of little concern (Scott, "Killing the Female?," 14–16).

104. Gen 21:12–21 uses ילד and נער interspersed. Exod 1:15 refers to the moment of birth and looking at the birthing stool to determine if it is a son (בן) or daughter

by a word specifically meaning infant, the text abstracts the infanticide.[105] Additionally, every text describing the death of an infant highlights the vulnerability of the infant: they cannot survive on their own. The prevailing attitude of the biblical text is that infants are valued.

The texts state that both Hagar and Moses's mothers do not want to subject their children to such a death. A healthy baby was indeed something to be prized in the ancient world. Hagar subjects her baby to his fate out of sheer desperation and after doing so bursts into tears (Gen 21:15–16). Moses's mother tries to keep her baby as long as she can before "fulfilling" the decree of Pharaoh. Indeed, when she did "throw him into the Nile" (à la Exod 1:22) she does so to save him.[106] The only infant that appears to be tossed out and rejected is the female, Jerusalem.[107] Yet the text does not leave her to die but quickly rescues her from her fate (Ezek 16:6–7). Child sacrifice, whether it be a regular sacrifice, emergency sacrifice, or *mlk* sacrifice, are all spun as negative. The (almost) death of Isaac and the death of Jephthah's daughter caused Abraham and Jephthah great distress.[108] Regular sacrifice of the firstborn child may have been accepted by some YHWHists but was later modified into redemption of the firstborn, and replaced by the Levites.[109] Emergency sacrifices are just that—emergency measures not to be undertaken every day. When war and siege presented themselves, kings could sacrifice their most valuable possession, their children, on the city walls to

---

(בת). Exod 1:22 uses similar language. When Moses is hidden on the Nile he is three months old, and called a ילד (Exod 2:2–3). Ezek 16:4 does not use any word for child or infant but refers to the day of birth (ביום הולדת).

105. Parker, *Valuable and Vulnerable*, 67–72. The words used for infants in these contexts are: גמל, ינוק, עולל, or עול.

106. Stiebert, *Fathers and Daughters in the Hebrew Bible*, 196 n. 111. Moses's birth narrative has been linked to that of Sargon and understood as part of the literary motive of a "rags to riches" narrative of a leader's nation, or the abandoned hero tale (*ANET* 119; Odell, *Ezekiel*, 187; Greenberg, *Ezekiel 1–20*, 275; Propp, *Exodus 1–18*, 155–58).

107. The verb used is געל, indicating extreme abhorrence elsewhere (Jer 14:19; Steibert, *Fathers and Daughters in the Hebrew Bible*, 196).

108. Noting the shock of God's request, Gen 22:2 is careful to specify which son Abraham should take (Rashi on Gen 22:2). Judg 11:35 shows Jephthah's distress.

109. Dewrell, *Child Sacrifice in Ancient Israel*, 72–90; Garroway, *Children in the Ancient Near Eastern Household*, 185–86. For a comparison of the general firstborn sacrifices (Exod 22:28b–29) and that of extraordinary firstborn sacrifices found in the 2 Kgs 3 and Mic 6, see Dewrell, *Child Sacrifice in Ancient Israel*, 107–8.

draw the attention of a deity.[110] Finally, the *mlk* sacrifice, which entered Israel via the Phoenicians, is presented as something not to do.[111] The thread linking all these texts together is a discomfort with causing the death of an infant or child. This discomfort may also have to do with who is being killed. There is no indication that the younglings killed are weak, disfigured, or otherwise deemed unacceptable. We are led to assume that they are all healthy individuals.

Another way the biblical authors demonstrated disapproval of deaths by human hands was to emphasize the foreign nature of killing a child. As referenced above, King Mesha of Moab and the Sepharvim are explicitly foreign. Yet, it is not just these narratives, but all of the categories explored above, infanticide, sacrifice, cannibalism, and bear-eating, have some element of foreignness in them.[112] Hagar is an Egyptian, Jerusalem is born of foreign parents, and Pharaoh issued the decree to kill. Francesca Stavrakopoulou has demonstrated how the Deuteronomist's goal was to craft a text that presented the Northern Kingdom as foreign.[113] In light of this, Jephthah's story might be considered foreign. His narrative takes place in an area (Tob and its surrounds) later associated with the Northern Kingdom, and his parentage is metaphorically foreign as he an illegitimate child.[114] The cannibalistic mothers of 2 Kgs 6 fall into an outsider

---

110. Garroway, "2 Kings 6:24–30," 53–70; Dewrell, *Child Sacrifice in Ancient Israel*, 91–99. Matthews discusses the discomfort and risk inherent in sacrificing a child. Victor H. Matthews, "Taking Calculated Risks: The Story of the Cannibal Mothers (2 Kings 6:24–7:20)," *BTB* 43 (2013): 4–13.

111. The *mlk* sacrifices are part of the Deuteronomic agenda, wherein the sins of the Southern Kingdom (Judah) are retroactively placed on the Northern Kingdom (Israel) in an attempt to denigrate the Northern Kingdom (Dewrell, *Child Sacrifice in Ancient Israel*, 142–43). Polemically speaking, this also serves to call out the South for the sins they were committing.

112. Only the regular child sacrifices exemplified by Exod 22:28–29 (Eng. 29–30), and the near sacrifice of Isaac do not have any overt foreign elements.

113. Stavrakopoulou, *King Manasseh and Child Sacrifice*.

114. The city of Tob is associated with the city of Tubu, which is referenced in the el-Amarna letters (EA 205). Judg 11:2 says בן־אשה אחרת אתה. C. F. Burney suggests that "the *district* is personified as the father of Jephthah," meaning his mother was a prostitute and his father was simply a man of Gilead (*The Book of Judges*, 2nd ed. [London: Rivingtons, 1930], 308). Robert C. Boling suggests that Jephthah "had no patronym, and no Gileadite future" (*Judges*, AB 6A [Garden City, NY: Doubleday, 1975], 197). In the eyes of Jephthah's brothers, and perhaps also the author, Jephthah is seen as an Other and outsider who will not inherit from his father's estate. Cut off

category as they are from Samaria. Samaria, as the capital of the Northern Kingdom, can be understood by the Judean writer to represent the center of this foreign influence. The condemnation of the *mlk* sacrifices, linked again to the Northern Kingdom, also becomes foreign.[115] Finally, even the children mocking Elisha, may be seen as foreign. These children come from the northern town of Bethel, a place associated with Jeroboam's idolatrous cult (1 Kgs 12:28–31).

Expressed in some cases by abstracting a narrative or the reluctance to carry out a sacrifice and in other cases by qualifying an act as foreign, some biblical authors rule that a child's death caused by human hands is to be met with disapproval.

8.4. Reactions to Other Deaths

The data above suggest that infant and child death was not uncommon, and likely every family experienced or knew someone who had experienced the death of an infant or child. This section first explores reactions to deaths not caused by human hands in the biblical and ancient Near Eastern sources and then looks to ethnography as a way of further expanding an assessment of ancient Israelite reactions to the deaths of children.

8.4.1. Reactions in Biblical Sources

The miracles of Elisha have been observed to replicate (and at times surpass) those of his master, Elijah, and thus provide the successor with credibility. The "revival of the woman's son" can be understood as one such miracle. One can also understand these two narratives as independent, employing the same motive.[116] A third way to look at them is to examine them with respect to what they say about children of different socioeconomic situations. The first narrative relates to a boy whose mother is destitute (1 Kgs 17:12, 17–24).[117] The second narrative concerns a boy

---

from the inheritance line of Gilead, Jephthah has no claim in Israel and can be seen metaphorically as a foreigner.

115. Dewrell, *Child Sacrifice in Ancient Israel*, 142.

116. Cogan and Tadmor, *II Kings*, 59–60.

117. I am understanding the narrative in 1 Kgs 17:7–24 to be a single unit. The miracle of the replenishing oil and the revival of the son are separated in 2 Kgs 4.

who comes from a well-to-do family (2 Kgs 4:8–37).[118] Despite their different social standings, the death of both boys elicits the same response from their mothers: both are appalled at their sons' death, and rather than accept their fate, call upon the man of God to provide them with some solace (1 Kgs 17:18; 2 Kgs 4:22, 27–30). Both the rich and the poor have an emotional reaction to the death of a son. For both women, the son is their only child. This is the child who will care for them when they grow old, act as heir, and carry on the family name. For both women, the child is important.

The third death explored is that of a prince. The royal infant who dies in 2 Sam 12:18 is unusual for it is unnamed. In most biblical birth announcements, a child is conceived, born, and then named.[119] The narrative of this child's birth is spread out over two chapters. He is conceived in 2 Sam 11:5 and born in 2 Sam 11:17, but he is never named.[120] The text also leaves out the specific age of the royal infant at his death. Everything is being done here to make the identity of this infant as ambiguous as possible. Despite the ambiguous nature of the infant, David's reaction to his son's illness and death signifies his deep connection to his son. Upon discovering his infant son is deathly ill, "David entreated God for the boy; David fasted, and he went in and spent the night lying on the ground" (2 Sam 12:16). He continues thus for seven days. David's reaction here is one of great emotion, but it is not immediately clear what was driving the emotion. On the one hand, one might read this as David proleptically mourning the death of his son, whom he knows God will take as atonement for his sin.[121] On the other hand, one could read it as David's petition to God to spare his son's

---

118. The term גדולה can be understood as "great in social standing" or "great in wealth" (Cogan and Tadmor, *II Kings*, 56). Either way, the fact that the family is able to build separate quarters for Elisha requires some amount of wealth and denotes and upper-class family.

119. Pardes, *Countertraditions in the Bible*, 39–59.

120. Hélène Nutkowicz, "Propos autor de la mort d'un enfant 2 Samuel XI, 2–XII 24," *VT* 54 (2004): 110.

121. Von Rad, among others, understands 2 Sam 11:27b to be the first of many curses that will be played out in fulfillment of Nathan's prophecy regarding David's actions. Gerhard von Rad, *The Problem of the Hexateuch and Other Essays* (London: Oliver & Boyd, 1966), 198–201; P. Kyle McCarter, *II Samuel*, AB 9 (Garden City, NY: Doubleday, 1984), 304–9.

life. [122] Either way one reads the text, David is deeply invested in whether his son lives.[123]

8.4.2. Reactions in Ancient Near Eastern Sources

The hero Gilgamesh, king of Uruk, is best known for his friendship and adventures with Enkidu. One of the less popular parts of his adventures, the Sumerian account of his descent to the netherworld, finds him visiting a dead Enkidu and inquiring whether Enkidu has seen his stillborn children. Enkidu says: "<Yes, I saw them>: they play at a table of gold and silver with honey and ghee."[124] Of all the questions Gilgamesh could have asked Enkidu, he chose to ask this one, and as true friends do, Enkidu's answer provides comfort to his dear friend who cannot forget his stillborn children.

The palace correspondences of Essarhaddon record another instance in which a king frets over his children. The child in question here is a sickly son. These letters report that his son experienced many fevers and that his father spared no expense when it came to treating his son; the prince met with multiple court doctors. No price was too high to pay to find a cure for his son. This sentiment was not limited to Essarhaddon, indeed the doctor of King Adad-šumu-uṣur notes that if something could be done to solve the illness of his children, the king would give up half of his kingdom.[125] On the one hand, such devotion to these sons could be attributed to the fact they were royalty. High quality expert care came by way of the family's social status, and surely the desire for the king's lineage to carry on also provided some impetus for seeking out expert care.[126] On the other hand,

---

122. G. Gerleman, "Schuld und Sühne: Erwägnungen zu 2 Sam 12," in *Beiträge zur alttestamentlichen Thehologie: Festschrift für Walther Zimmerli*, ed. Herbert Donner, Robert Hanhart, and Rudolf Smend (Göttingen; Vandenhoeck & Ruprecht, 1977), 138. Nutkowicz finds nuance in the petition in so much as 2 Sam 12:22 should read "Who knows? God may spare me [and kill the child] or may let the child live [and kill me]." She argues that the child and David are one entity and that one of them must go, so to speak, as an atonement sacrifice for David's transgression (Nutkowicz, "Propos autour de la mort," 109–10).

123. David's emotional attachment to other sons and grief upon their deaths can be seen in 2 Sam 13:30–31, 37–39; 18:5, 29; 19:1.

124. Rivkah Harris, *Gender and Aging in Mesopotamia: The Gilgamesh Epic and Other Ancient Literature* (Norman Oklahoma: University of Oklahoma, 2000), 16.

125. Volk, "Kinderkrankheiten," 8, CT 53.69.obv.10–12.

126. Those with means could and would seek medical care. Volk notes that par-

just because a parent is royal does not mean one should discount a royal parent's love for his or her child.

Two other examples demonstrate a parent's grief over the loss of a child. The first case is found in a letter from Mari. It implores the bearer "before the king (Zimri-Lim) reaches Mari, tell him that his infant daughter is dead, and may he understand."[127] Perhaps the sender wished that the king should be told of this tragedy ahead of time so that he could mentally prepare and be king-like in the face of bad news once he arrived home. The letter may also be an attempt to spare his wife the agony of telling him the information.[128] The second example comes from the Royal Tomb at Amarna. In a series of three chambers, reliefs depict Akhenaten and Nefertiti mourning the death of a child. One room identifies the female child as Meketaten, their second-born child, who would have been about eleven at the time of death. Many hypothesize that she died from the plague that was sweeping through the Levant during Akhenaten's rule. The fact that two other younger daughters (Neferneferure and Setepenre) disappear from the historical record around this time have led some to conclude that the other two chambers depicting the pharaoh and his queen mourning are the tombs of these two daughters.[129] Figure 8.2 comes from chamber *gamma*.[130] The scenes show the royal family weeping and mourning before the birth canopy, under which Meketaten stands. The scene may mean she died in childbirth, or more likely, show her death and rebirth.[131] In a different frieze, a nurse can be seen breastfeeding a baby with two royal fan bearers nearby. The wet-nurse is

---

ents from as far away as Aleppo sent their children to the "best doctors" (those in OB Mari) for medical treatment (Volk, "Kinderkrankheiten," 29–30, and examples therein).

127. Stephanie Dalley, *Mari and Karana: Two Old Babylonian Cities* (London: Longman, 1984), 98.

128. Harris, *Gender and Aging in Mesopotamia*, 16.

129. Dodson, *Amarna Sunset*, 24, n. 54; Donald Redford, *Akhenaten: The Heretic King* (Princeton, NJ: Princeton University, 1984), 187.

130. The double death scene appears in TA 26 (Dodson, *Amarna Sunset*, 22, fig. 17).

131. Jacobus Van Dijk, "The Death of Meketaten," in *Causing His Name to Live: Studies in Egyptian Epigraphy and History in Memory of William J. Murnane*, ed. Peter J. Brand and Louise Cooper, CHANE 37 (Leiden: Brill, 2009), 84, 87–88; Dodson, *Amarna Sunset*, 19–20.

Fig. 8.2. Royal Tomb of Meketaten, Amarna, Egypt, Eighteenth Dynasty.

just exiting the birthing chamber, adding to the hypothesis that one is to understand Meketaten as reborn.[132]

The latter two sources are interesting because they discuss the death of girls, providing a counter-measure to the argument that a king would only feel grief upon his son's death because the son was the crowned prince.

8.4.3. Reactions in Ethnographic Literature

Ethnographic literature has been quick to point out that those in the Western world find the death of infants and children much more shocking than our counterparts in other areas of the world. For example, in shantytowns of Brazil, where infant mortality is also high, the following interaction between a white, well-educated, woman from California and a local woman from the Shantytown of Bom Jesus was recorded: "Noting my red eyes and tear-stained face, the woman turned to comment to a neighbor woman standing by, 'Hein, hein, coitada! Engraçada, não é; Tsk! Tsk! Poor thing! Funny, isn't she?' What was funny or amusing seemed to be my inappropriate display of grief and my concern over a matter of so little consequence."[133] The matter of little consequence to the villagers was the death of a sickly, malnourished baby. As far back as Cicero, one can find

---

132. Van Dijk, "Death of Meketaten," 83.

133. Nancy Scheper-Hughes, *Death without Weeping: The Violence of Everyday Life in Brazil* (Berkeley: University of California Press, 1993), 270–71. A study of Papel women in Guinea-Bissau in West Africa resulted in a more nuanced view of infant death and mourning. These women do mourn children who die and seek treatment for them when they are ill. Jónína Einarsdóttir, *Tired of Weeping: Mother Love, Child Death, and Poverty in Guinea-Bissau* (Madison: University of Madison, 2004).

the same attitude. Speaking about children under two years of age Cicero states, "If he dies in the cradle, one doesn't even pay attention."[134]

Closer to the land of Israel, Watson investigated the graves of infants and adults in the western Iranian villages of Hasanabad and Shirdasht.[135] She reported that adults were buried in trenches 1–1.5 m deep, with stone slab grave markers distinguishing them as a man or a woman. Babies and younger children were buried in a shallower trench, a 0.5 m deep. Graves of babies and children were marked with a simple fieldstone. Furthermore, babies were buried separately from adults because "such young children die innocent, not having grown old enough to know sin, and are therefore not interred among adults and older children."[136] In these western Iranian villages, babies and young children were in a different category than older children and adults. The attitude towards these youngest members suggests that they were "purer" than their older counterparts. On the other hand, the relatively shallow graves support the notion that their communities were not as invested in the children.[137] Not only was less energy required to dig the shallow graves, but shallow graves meant that the babies and small children would be subject to wolves, jackals, and dogs that dig up the graves looking for food in the winter months.[138] The reaction to young children's death in these societies presents their deaths as different from that of other members in their society; one might say their societies ascribed a lesser value to their deaths.

---

134. Golden, "Did Ancients Care When Their Children Died?," 155. Cicero, *Tusc* 1.39.93.

135. Watson, *Archaeological Ethnography in Western Iran*, 214–15.

136. Watson, *Archaeological Ethnography in Western Iran*, 215. Granqvist notes that newborns and children were buried the same as adults (Granqvist, *Child Problems among the Arabs*, 91).

137. Burials can be examined and interpreted according to the energy expended to make the grave. The energy expenditure for a shallow grave can indicate a lesser status within the community. Garroway, *Children in the Ancient Near Eastern Household*, 220–21; L. Binford, "Mortuary Practices: Their Study and Their Potential," in *Approaches to the Social Dimension of Mortuary Practices*, ed. James Allison Brown, Memoirs of the Society for American Archaeology 25 (Washington: Society for American Archaeology, 1971), 6–29.

138. Adult graves were specifically dug deeper to prevent the bodies from being eaten by wild animals (Watson, *Archaeological Ethnography in Western Iran*, 215). Nothing was said in the report about beliefs in the afterlife, whether infants and small children had a role in the afterlife, or whether their role was different from that of the adults in their community.

Reports of reactions to infant and child death among the Arab Palestinians is described much differently. Peppered throughout her reports, Granqvist notes the double entanglement with which women viewed children. On the one hand, a child was a lot of work, and women took pains to space out their pregnancies. On the other hand, even if a pregnancy came at an undesired time, once the infant was born the mother had a deep connection with the baby.[139] Women cry, weep, and wail at the loss of a child. Recording the death of a small girl, she says:

> Her mother wept inconsolably and the father's mother told me that the child had died in the night quite suddenly and then the mother had begun to wail and weep so loudly that all the neighbours hear it.... She took her dead child on her lap, felt its arms and face and stroked it and wept over her loss.[140]

Special sayings are recited to boost a woman's morale, such as: "The pregnant ones—the women—have conquered the graveyard!" Not only is the child's death difficult for the mother, but the father too feels remorse. Comfort is taken in the fact that as long as both parents are alive, they can have more children.[141] Other comfort is found in the notion that dead children act as guides to the afterlife.[142]

8.5. Death in the Archaeological Record

The burial record from Iron Age Israel offers another perspective on the death of children. When analyzing the burial record, we are limited to what has been found. What has been found is further limited by the socioeconomic status of the individuals, which is to say that the picture of the burial record is skewed towards those with more means. Some insights regarding infant and child burials may be found by looking at the more elite strata of ancient Israel, those who could afford burials.[143]

Those infants who have been found were found because they were preserved in some way, shape, or form. The fact that parents with means took

---

139. Granqvist, *Child Problems among the Arabs*, 92.
140. Granqvist, *Child Problems among the Arabs*, 92.
141. Granqvist, *Child Problems among the Arabs*, 92–94.
142. Granqvist, *Child Problems among the Arabs*, 167.
143. Rachel Hallote, *Death, Burial and Afterlife in the Biblical World* (Chicago: Ivan Dee, 2001), 32.

care to bury their infants shows some amount of emotional attachment may have been present. Examining cross-cultural studies, Sarah Baitzel points out that:

> In many cultures, children's, in particular infants,' funerals are perfunctory, less elaborate, and marginal, as cultural attitudes toward an early death carry connotations of stigma or indifference.... Such funerary conditions may contrast with the immediate, intense, but often immaterial expression of parental grief, such as vocalizations and gestures that are unobservable posthumously. The result is a biased material record that challenges archaeologists to identify and reconstruct emotional experiences.[144]

Baitzel's observation raises an important issue: Does the burial record provide information regarding parental grief, and what is the correlation between the burial rites and parental grief? This question is easier answered in societies that only employ single interment or ones in which children are provided with grave goods. This can be challenging for ancient Israel where many different burial styles were used. While it is often difficult to determine which grave goods belong to which individuals within a tomb or cave, single interments, such as jar burials demonstrate that infants were given grave goods. In the Middle Bronze Age, the grave goods were most often juglets. Sometimes bowls or small jars also accompanied the burials.[145] This suggests that adults took care to provide even the youngest members of their family with the food (or drink) necessary to survive in the afterlife.[146] However, the tendency to bury infants with juglets switched in the Iron Age, when juglets or other ceramic items became less favored. Instead, jewelry became the preferred grave good (tables 1 and 2).[147]

---

144. Sarah Baitzel, "Parental Grief and Mourning in the Ancient Andes," *Journal of Archaeological Method and Theory* (2017): https://doi.org/10.1007/s10816-017-9333-3.

145. Garroway, *Children in the Ancient Near Eastern Household*, 295, table 31.

146. Garroway, *Children in the Ancient Near Eastern Household*, 235. For a discussion of burial kits, see Jill Baker, *The Funeral Kit: Mortuary Practice in the Archaeological Record* (Walnut Creek, CA: Left Coast Press, 2012).

147. Part of this might be attributed to the decline in jar burials, which often include a juglet. The discovery of fewer primary child and infant burials also plays a role. It is difficult to assign grave goods in family tombs. The issue of changing beliefs about the afterlife is also something to consider. It is possible that families no longer believed infants required liquid nourishment in the afterlife.

Table 1. Number of Iron Age I–II Burials with Ceramics

	Juglet	Jar	Jug	Bowl	Lamp	Store Jar	Imports
Infant	0	1	0	0	0	0	1
Child	0	0	0	1	0	0	0

Table 2. Number of Iron Age I–II Burials with Personal Grave Goods

	Ring/Earring	Bracelet/ Anklet	Bead	Scarab
Infant	1	6	3	0
Child	3	2	3	1

The provision of personal grave goods does not necessarily demonstrate a shift in the way infants were treated. It can be seen as a shift in a society's understanding of the afterlife, representative of the increase in a society's wealth or the socioeconomic status of the individual in the specific burial.[148]

Iron Age burial practices in general tend to continue those seen in previous periods, with burial styles including cave or bench tombs, cist, jar, pit (simple burials), anthropoid coffins, and cremations.[149] Table 3 presents the number of burial sites that have been discovered including children and infants. Table 4 presents the total number of infants and children found at these burial sites.

Table 3. Number of Sites with Infants and Children
according to Burial Method and Time Period

	Jar Burial	Cave	Tomb	Cist	Pit	Coffin	Cremation
IA I	4	1	3	0	1	0	2
IA II	6	4	3	0	4	0	0

---

148. A. Maeir, "Tomb 1181," in *Hazor V*, ed. Amnon Ben-Tor et al. (Jerusalem: Israel Exploration Society and the Hebrew University of Jerusalem, 1997), 325; Assaf Yasur-Landau, "Socio-political and Demographic Aspects of the MB Cemetery in Jericho," *TA* 19 (1992): 240.

149. Bloch-Smith, *Judahite Burial Practices and Beliefs about the Dead*, 25–59.

Table 4. Number of Infants and Children
according to Burial Method and Time Period

	Jar Burial	Cave	Tomb	Cist	Pit	Coffin	Cremation
IA I	20	1	14	0	1	0	4
IA II	91[149]	43	16	0	7	0	0

During the Iron Age children are found buried in all but two burial types; however, infants are treated differently.[151] As table 3 demonstrates, jar burials, caves, and tombs make up the bulk of all infant and child burials discovered. Upon closer examination of the cave and tomb burials, one finds a mix in the ages of infants and children. Tables 5 and 6 demonstrate that both infants and children appear alongside adult burials. This goes along with the use of tombs and caves as family burials; families using tombs and caves buried their infants and children with them.[152] The collection of caves at Ketef Hinnom represents this well. It included 10 percent infants (zero to one years old), 23 percent children (one to nine years old), 15 percent juveniles (ten to nineteen years old), and the remainder adults aged twenty to sixty (or more) years old.[153]

Table 5. Cave Burials with Children

Site	Adults Present?	Age of Child	Body Position	Period
Megiddo	N	Infant	P A	IA I
Kh. Abu-Musrrah	Y	4 children, 1.5yr- ~15 yrs	P	IA II
Har Yona	Y	<1 yr and 3–4yr	P A	IA IB/ IIA

---

150. Seventy-seven of these jar burials were found at Zeror.

151. Garroway, *Children in the Ancient Near Eastern Household*, 218–44, 281–98.

152. The use of tombs and caves as family burials is a practice carried over from earlier periods. See, for example, the analysis of the EBI burial caves at Sha'ar Efrayim and 'En Esur. Yossi Nagar, "Human Skeletal Remains from the Burial Caves at Sha'ar Efrayim," *'Atiqot 66* (2011): 75–78; Yossi Nagar, "Human Skeletal Remains from T. 80 in the 'En Esur Cemetery," 121–24.

153. Yossi Nagar, "Skeletal Remains from the Excavation at Ketef Hinnom, Jerusalem" [Hebrew], *'Atiqot 80* (2015): 55–58*.

Ketef Hinnom	Y	5 infants <1yr, 11 children 1–9yr	?	IA II
S. Horbat Tittoria	Y	13 infants 0–4 years, 5 children 5–9 years, 3 older children 10–14 years	?	IA II

Key to body position: S = supine, P = primary, NA = not articulated, A= articulated, FL = flexed.

Table 6. Tomb Burials with Children

Site	Adults Present?	Age of Child	Body Position	Period
Khirbet Nisya	Y	1 child over 5 yrs	? NA	IA I
Beth-Pelet	Y	11 children	P	IA I
Achzib	Y	MNI 2 children	P	IA I
Achzib	Y	MNI 5 children	P	IA II
Tell Dan North	Y	6 mo, 1.5 yrs	P	IA II
Tel 'Ira	Y	< 5 years, 7–8 yrs, 7 juveniles	P	IA II

Key to body position: S = supine, P = primary, NA = not articulated, A= articulated, FL = flexed.

However, not all families used burial caves and tombs, and not all cemeteries in the Iron Age included infants and small children. For example, the Iron Age cemetery at Yavne produced pit graves and cist tombs, in which no individuals under the age of ten were found.[154] Alternatively, jar burials, another burial style seen throughout Israel's history, are the resting place almost exclusively of infants and very young children (tables 7 and 8).[155]

---

154. Kletter and Nagar, "Iron Age Cemetery and Other Remains at Yavne," 1–33.

155. The way in which infants and children are buried in comparison to the rest of the community sheds light on the attitudes that the living society had regarding their deaths and correlates to their perceived membership within their particular society (Garroway, *Children in the Ancient Near Eastern Household*, 218–44).

Table 7. Number of Jar Burials by Period

EB I	EB II	EB III	EB IV	MB II	LBA	IA I	IA II	Total
19/ 18[156]	—	—	—	80/ 77[157]	8	22	92[158]	215/ 209[159]

Table 8. Jar Burials with Children

Site	JB/Site	Adults Present?	Age of Child	Body Position	Period
Azor	17	N	Children	?	IA I
Achzib	1+	N	Infants	P	IA I
Tel es-Safi	1–2	N	Infants/ Children	P	IA I (late)
Megiddo	2	N	Infants	P Supine	IA I
Megiddo	4	Y	Infants	?	IA II
Dothan	6	N	Infants, Child	P	IA II
Tel Dan North	1[160]	N	Juvenile	S	IA II
Achzib[161]	1	N	Child	S	IA II
Zeror	66 Jars 11 Pithos	N	Children and Infants	P	IA II
Gezer	2	Y	Infants	?	IA II

Key to body position: S = supine, P = primary, NA = not articulated, A= articulated, FL = flexed.

156. The first number is the total found, including adults. The second number is the total number of children.

157. The first number is the total found, including adults. The second number is the total number of children.

158. Seventy-seven of these are from Tel Zeror.

159. Total number of jar burials/total number of jar burials specifically of children and infants. The other six jar burials belonged to adults or juveniles.

160. An additional jar burial contained a cremated adult.

161. This jar burial was found inside of a shaft tomb.

Jar burials are usually found apart from the burials of the general population and are almost always placed within the city confines, often within domestic quarters.[162] Most scholars hypothesize that infants were placed within jars and buried inside the domestic quarters to facilitate a physical representation of a metaphysical belief; jar burials are a return to the womb.[163]

8.5.1. Difficulties in Analyzing the Archaeological Record

Infant and child burials, be they in tombs, caves, or jars, present some difficulties. The first issue concerns the number of expected infants buried versus the number of infants discovered. Even in sites that utilize multiple burial methods for infants and children (e.g., Achzib, Azor, Megiddo), the number of infants recovered in the burial record does not match the number of infants expected to be found based on projections from the number of adults found.[164] The numbers are closer for child burials and increase the older a child becomes. The most likely answer to "where are the infants" is that the infants were not buried in formal graves, but were, like the lower classes, buried in unmarked graves.[165] The fact that infants are not regularly found within Iron Age domestic confines supports the conclusions that most infants were buried outside of the site and separately from the rest of the burial population.

The burials of infants and young children that *are* found pose an even more perplexing problem than the lack of infants and young children found in the archaeological record. For example, why were some, but not all, infants buried in jars under house floors? Research has estimated that a woman would need six pregnancies to produce three children who

---

162. Garroway, *Children in the Ancient Near Eastern Household*, 221–26, 239.e

163. Lewis Binford, *An Archaeological Perspective* (New York: Seminar Press, 1972), 219; David Ilan, "Mortuary Practices in the Middle Bronze Age: A Reflection of Canaanite Society and Ideology," in *The Archaeology of Death in the Ancient Near East*, ed. Stuart Campbell and Anthony Green, Oxbow Monographs 51 (Oxford: Oxbow, 1995), 117–37; Garroway, *Children in the Ancient Near Eastern Household*, 240–41. For tomb as womb in general, see Richard Huntington and Peter Metcalf, *Celebrations of Death: The Anthropology of the Death Ritual* (Cambridge: Cambridge University Press, 1991), 115–16; J. Romer, *Romer's Egypt: A New Light on the Civilization of Ancient Egypt* (London: Joseph, 1982), 167; Gabriel Barkay, "Burial Headrests as a Return to the Womb: A Reevaluation," *BAR* 14.2 (1988): 48–50.

164. Smith, "Approach to the Paleodemographic Analysis," 2–13.

165. Hallote, *Death, Burial and Afterlife in the Biblical World*, 31.

survived beyond five years of age.[166] Where were the other infants born by the same woman buried? One suggestion may be that the first infant to succumb to death was buried under the house floor. As ethnographic studies have demonstrated, some cultures have a belief that burial under house floors (or other places frequented by women) will allow the infant's spirit to be reborn in the woman.[167] Consider too, what factors drove some parents to include their infants and children in the family tombs, while other families chose not to include them in their family tombs? Were burial practices regarding infants and young children dependent on geographical, or local burial customs? Questions such as these demonstrate the need for further study of burial practices.

8.6. Summary

What can be said about how the ancient Israelites reacted to infant and child death? Were they, like the women of the shantytowns in Brazil, callous to the death of infants? Or did ancient Israelites truly mourn the death of their infants and children? The answer may be somewhere in between, as it is in the Greco-Roman world. Faced with the realities of a high infant mortality rate, Mark Golden suggests that mourning mothers provided an emotional outlet for society as a whole.[168] The Greco-Roman model allowed for individual mourning to be displaced onto a certain group of people, thus alleviating the need for every single person experiencing trauma related to child death to mourn. Wailing women may also have

---

166. Meyers, *Rediscovering Eve*, 99.

167. Rebirth in this way was found in Borneo, Malaysia, West Africa, and the Huron Native Americans (George N. Appell and Laura W. R. Appell, "Death among the Rungus Momogun of Sabah, Malaysia: The Dissolution of Personhood and Dispersion of the Multiple Souls and Spiritual Counterparts," in *Journeys of the Soul: Anthropological Studies of Death, Burial and Rebirth Practices in Borneo*, ed. William D. Wilder, Borneo Research Council Monograph 7 (Philips, ME: Borneo Research Council, Inc. 2003), 41–121; Matthew Amster, "Gender Complementarity and Death among the Kelabit," in Wilder, *Journeys of the Soul*, 251–308; Antonia Mills and Richard Slobodin, *Amerindian Rebirth: Reincarnation Belief among North American Indians and Inuit* (Toronto: University of Toronto Press, 1994), 46; J. E. King, "Infant Burial," *The Classical Review* (1903): 83.

168. Mark Golden, "Mortality, Mourning and Mothers," in *Naissance et petite enfance dans l'Antiquité*, ed. Véronique Dasen (Firbourg: Academic Press, 2004), 156–67.

played a similar role in ancient Israelite society, as they provided a socially sanctioned way for society to face extreme trauma.[169]

The textual corpus suggests that infant and child death was not something to be taken nonchalantly. When comparing reactions to death, it appears that the biblical text presents stronger reactions to deaths caused by human hands. A discomfort with these deaths is demonstrated by abstract language and an emphasis on the foreign nature of the practices. The Bible presents intentional killing of infants and children as something not condoned by Israelite society. Other deaths, while also unsettling, are perhaps easier to accept because they are understood as inevitable; infants and children get sick and die. This is not to say that they were easily accepted or that parents did nothing to try and prevent the deaths. Indeed, texts and sources from the Bible and the wider ancient Near East attest to the energy put into trying to save sick children; but in the end, death comes to us all. On the other hand, biblical children subject to a death by human hands are not described as sickly but appear quite healthy.[170] To kill (or attempt to kill) these children could be seen as a double death: shortening the life of the youngster and cutting off the life of a potential productive member of Israelite society.

From the anthropological record, it is well documented that societies that experience high rates of infant mortality are slow to form strong bonds with their infants, waiting instead to see whether the child will prove hearty enough to survive.[171] The phenomenon of the "missing" infants within the archaeological record could indicate a calculated indifference to neonates and infants, an indifference born out of a need to emotionally survive the trauma of losing a child. In a related vein, it has been noted that in those societies practicing infanticide:

---

169. Claassens describes the role of the women in Jer 9:17–20 in much the same way as Golden sees mourning mothers. According to Claassens, the keeners in Jeremiah as the "release-valve" for an Israelite society experiencing the trauma of the exile. L. Julianna Claassens, "Calling the Keeners: The Image of the Wailing Woman as a Symbol of Survival in a Traumatized World," *JFSR* 26 (2010): 63–77.

170. This conclusion applies specifically to the attitude of the biblical text. Ethnographical and historical societies practicing infanticide for population control or regular sacrifice to deities do not appear to have this same attitude.

171. Scheper-Hughes, *Death without Weeping*, 402; Lancy, "Accounting for Variability in Mother-Child Play," 273–84; Hewlett et al., "Culture and Early Infancy among Central African Foragers and Farmers," 653–61. See also ch. 6.

The killing is made easier by a cultural belief that a child is not fully human until accepted as a member of the social group. This acceptance may take place when the child is named, or when it appears strong enough to survive, or when it shows "human" characteristics, such as walking and talking. The time varies from a few days to several years after birth. The Peruvian Amahuaca, for instance, do not consider children fully human until they are about three years old.[172]

One can extrapolate the concept of personhood and membership in society as it applies to infanticide and apply it to the perception of ancient Israelite infants and children in general.[173] The fact that some infants were buried outside of the family tombs, either in jar burials or simple burials, may reflect an attitude of differentiated personhood.

The chapter has discussed a world where children succumbed to illness and were subject to death by the hand of others. To those living in a modern, Western society, a world with modern medical advancements where children are highly desired, this world is far removed in both time and culture. For those wanting some happy take-away, I offer one final example from the archaeological record. While this is not the final word on the matter of death and mourning of infants and children, it does serve as a *nechemtah* to a topic that can be difficult to digest.[174] At Tel ʿIra, a site in the Negev, near Beersheba, excavators uncovered a cemetery dating to the ninth to eighth century BCE. Over 130 tombs were uncovered, all of which were bench tombs typical of the Iron Age. The tombs were mass burials of adults and children. Tomb 15 contained twenty-three individuals, placed both on the floor and on benches. On the left bench lay a female in a flexed position; the woman's fingers were cupped over the ribs of a small child, seven to eight years old. The excavators report the following: "The fingers of the woman's right hand were curved across the ribs of the child, with her arm bent and elevated, as if she had been interred holding the child in her arms."[175] This appears to be the burial of a mother and her child.

---

172. Laila Williamson, "Infanticide: An Anthropological Analysis," in *Infanticide and the Value of Life*, ed. Marvin Kohl (Buffalo: Prometheus Books, 1978), 64.

173. For a full treatment of the correlation between an individual's status within the household and his or her social age, see Garroway, *Children in the Ancient Near Eastern Household*, 243–53.

174. In Jewish homilies a *nechemtah*, coming from the root נחם, "to comfort," serves as a closing piece of comfort to a difficult text.

175. Izhaq Beit-Arieh, *Tel ʿIra: A Stronghold in the Biblical Negev* (Tel Aviv: Yass

The study of the archaeology of death has pointed out that the presentation of the dead is arranged by the living. The presentation of the woman and child means that the living members of the Tel 'Ira society chose to bury them not just in the same tomb but to place the child safely in the mother's arms.[176] This, to me, indicates that at least *some* of those living in ancient Israel did not treat the matter of a youngling's death with callous indifference. While there may have been a variety of reactions to infant death, I would assert, as Golden does for the Greco-Roman world, that unless we have compelling evidence to the contrary, we might assume the ancient Israelites cared when the youngest members of their society died.[177]

Publications in Archaeology of the Institute of Archaeology, Tel Aviv University, 1999), 152–53.

176. Based on the positioning of the skeletal remains, it seems possible that the mother and child died at the same time. In her study of Palestinian villages, Granqvist noted that when an adult and child died at the same time, the child was placed on the knees of the adult. The idea was that the innocent and pure child would protect the grown-up on his or her way to the afterlife. "The death angels Nakir and Munkar, come at night to question the dead and they may strike and trouble him terribly in the grave. When, however, they see the child on his knee they have mercy on him for its sake, they do not want to frighten the child" (Granqvist, *Child Problems among the Arabs*, 167–68). It is tempting to consider the possibility that such a belief might also have existed in societies of the distant past as well.

177. Golden, "Did Ancients Care When Their Children Died?," 160.

9
Concluding Remarks

"Children are the future. Teach them well and let them lead the way." These words, sung by Whitney Houston, could well be mistaken for a phrase from Deuteronomy or Proverbs. Just as we understand children as the future, so too did the ancient Israelites. Children were a valued part of society. The well-known stories of Sarah, Rachel, and Hannah exemplify how important children were to the Israelite family. Names such as "YHWH has heard" (Shemaiah), "Happy" (Asher), and "Gift of God" (Nathaniel) personify the ancient Israelite desire for children. Yet, for a portion of society deemed so important, children are given relatively little "page time" in the biblical text. Aside from stories describing the miraculous birth and survival of (male) national heroes like Moses and David, one must hunt for information about children and their world. *Growing Up in Ancient Israel* engages the biblical texts and supplements them by bringing together a wide variety of sources to fill in the gaps. The previous chapters trace the development of a child's biological and social stages, and in doing so, some overarching trends can be seen: the value and vulnerability of a child, the role of enculturation and gendering, and the use of material culture in constructing a child's world. To supplement the discussion of these themes found peppered throughout the individual chapters, the concluding discussion examines them diachronically in an effort to provide a way forward for child-centered biblical studies.

9.1. The Valued Child

With a high infant mortality rate, one might question whether Israelite parents cared about their children. By gathering together sources from other ancient Near Eastern textual traditions, archaeology, and ethnography to supplement the biblical text, it becomes evident that parents invested in their children. The first chapter noted the difficulties in getting pregnant and staying pregnant. While contraceptive measures were known, the default attitude seems to be that these measures were employed only when necessary. For example, the command to "be fruitful and multiply" can be understood as deeming abstinence (within marriage) a bad thing. Consider too how Onan's actions incur a moral judgment; he is wicked. Even the more creative forms of accepted contraception, such as anal sex, were not widespread, but limited to a specific class of women. One might also think about breastfeeding in this milieu. While it causes lactational amenorrhea, a form of contraception, breastfeeding was confined to a specific group of women: mothers and wet-nurses. Moreover, the purpose of breastfeeding was not to stop pregnancy but to nourish the infant. Children were desired.

Despite the many miscarriages or infant deaths women might have experienced, they continued to try to have children. Without hospitals and modern medicine, women relied on the knowledge of midwives and found solace in the rituals of religious practitioners. When the much-desired child was finally born, his or her umbilical cord was cut, and the infant was cleaned, swaddled, and named. These actions in and of themselves indicate the child was valued. Even the act of naming was a vehicle for expressing how much the parent valued the child.

In light of Ezekiel's comments regarding the infant Jerusalem (Ezek 16:4) we can see that some infants were not wanted but thrown to the streets. The discussion in chapter 2 did not discuss in-depth what happens to such a child. While there were some cases of infanticide by exposure, in many cases a child unwanted by one person was desired by another.[1] Since the book's discussion focused mostly on the biological and social stages of a child's life rather than the individual experiences of a child, class distinctions were not often highlighted. However, when discussing the value of a child, it is important to step aside to mention class. In most cases, children who were born in one class stayed in that class. Thus, a freeborn child remained free, and a slave child, a slave.[2] Most children who

---

1. Using the frame of the child-deity relationship, Flynn explores the value such children had within the household (Flynn, *Children in Ancient Israel*, 71–83).

2. Kristine Garroway, "Neither Slave Nor Free: Children Living on the Edge of a Social Status," in *Windows to the Ancient World of the Hebrew Bible: Essays in Honor of Samuel Greengus*, ed. Bill T. Arnold, Nancy Erickson, and John H. Walton (Winona Lake, IN: Eisenbrauns, 2014), 121–38; Jonathan Tenney, *Life at the Bottom of Babylo-*

were slaves were born as slaves, but one could also change status from free to enslaved. Consider, for example, children abandoned by their parents and rescued by someone else who needed a slave.[3] On the one hand, this was an inexpensive way to obtain a slave. On the other hand, rescuing an infant meant an investment in raising that infant. Here we can think about a child having not only inherent value, but also economic value.

Outside of slavery, a child's economic value can be seen by thinking about a child's contribution to the overall household economic system.[4] Young children are able to do simple chores, such as gathering wood for a fire (Jer 7:18). Older children can watch the family flocks (Gen 29:9; 1 Sam 16:11) or fetch water for the family or the herds (Gen 24:16–20; Exod 2:16). Tending small family gardens, helping make the daily bread, and participating in mending clothing, mats, or nets would also be among the many other ways a child could contribute to the household. In some cases, a child might also labor outside of the household on behalf of the family.[5] Helping the family in whatever way they could highlights the economic value of a child.

Despite a parent's best efforts, infants and children did get sick and die. The parents' reactions to a child's death both as explored through the biblical and ancient Near Eastern texts, and through the very act of burial itself, suggest that parents cared when their children died. On the other hand, the subject of intentionally caused deaths might appear to contradict the idea that parents valued children. Voluntarily sacrificing a child or killing him upon birth might seem to argue for a world in which every child was not valued. One might make the counterargument that offering a child as a sacrifice was the highest form of religious expression possible.[6] The biblical text certainly presents passages that support the

----

nian Society: Servile Labor at Nippur in the Fourteenth and Thirteenth Centuries B.C. (Leiden: Brill, 2011). Of course, status is much more nuanced than this. Social status was not quite as simple as "slave and free" but existed on a sliding scale (Garroway, *Children in the Ancient Near Eastern Household*, 141–55).

3. Neo-Babylonian contracts also attest to the possibility of adopting a child that was rescued from the street. See Garroway, *Children in the Ancient Near Eastern Household*, 99–112, and sources within.

4. Koepf-Taylor, *Give Me Children*.

5. Garroway, *Children in the Ancient Near Eastern Household*, 153–58.

6. The summary conclusions drawn here, while made independently, are similar to those of Flynn, who explores in-depth the cultic value of children and child sacrifice (Flynn, *Children in Ancient Israel*, 125–29, 163–69).

presence of child sacrifice in ancient Israel. However, while some rogue groups may have understood child sacrifice as part of the cult of Yahweh, the general impression of child sacrifice in the Hebrew Bible is that it is undesirable and should not be carried out. Child sacrifice, even in times of emergency, is associated with foreign, idolatrous peoples. The same can be said for infanticide; the biblical texts related to humans abandoning or attempting to kill infants all have a foreign element. The overall message concerning children is that they are valuable, and their untimely deaths are not welcomed.

9.2. The Vulnerable Child

The projection that a woman would need to have five to six pregnancies to produce three children who survived beyond five years of age paints a stark picture. Infants faced the most vulnerable time of their life in the first seven days. The single reference to an infant's death in the Bible seems to refer to a death soon after birth. The Lord places a deathly illness on Bathsheba and David's infant, an action that seems from a narrative perspective to take place almost as soon as the infant is born (2 Sam 12:15–19). Where the biblical text is relatively silent on the many dangers of infancy and the means of protecting these most vulnerable family members, the archaeological record provides a richer picture. The burial record in particular provides a means of thinking about just how vulnerable infants and children were. Based on the demographic projections for various sites, it is evident that many infants and children are missing from the burial record. It is possible these "missing" children were given an informal pit burial, and due to the friable nature of their bones, they are now lost to the archaeological record. It might also be that parents did not formally bury some infants or children, but left them out for a sky burial of sorts. In both cases, it would seem the earth itself capitalized on their vulnerability, consuming their remains.

Facing the reality of a high mortality rate, parents turned to talismans and incantations to ward off danger. Amulets, stones, shiny objects, and figurines played an important role in domestic religion and keeping the demonic forces at bay. Texts such as Ps 18:28 equate God with a light who protects one from the darkness. Prayers such as this one acknowledge the scariness of "things that go bump in the night." Even a mundane object such as a lamp could provide protection as the light emanating from it spread a protective glow over the inhabitants of a room. Infants and children especially needed protection from nighttime demons like Lamaštu, who was thought to kill infants in their sleep.

The vulnerability of infants, however, was not limited to the supernatural sphere.[7] As hinted at above, parents or caregivers could pose a threat to children as well. Regardless of the reason, child sacrifice still placed the child in a vulnerable position. Too young to fight back or run away, victims of child sacrifice were truly victims. Unlike Jephthah's daughter, who seemingly went willingly to her death, the prophetic texts imply that parents were the ones behind the killings. The historical narratives and prophetic texts are clear it is the parents who make their children walk through the fire (Deut 18:18; 2 Kgs 16:3; 17:17; 21:6; Jer 7:31; 32:25).

Parents were also the final arbiters on who would be raised in the house. When the family exceeded capacity, it was possible that an infant would be abandoned or a child sold into slavery. Regarding the former, data from the Greco-Roman brothel at Ashkelon showed how infants could be disposed of when they were deemed economically unviable. As mentioned above, slavery was not explored in depth here as it is not a social or biological age, but it should be noted that this was a possible fate. The sale of children born into slavery was not unusual. However, the sale of free-born children into slavery seems to be an exception to the rule.[8] Looking at children through the lens of social and legal status highlights the vulnerability of children; they were not in charge of their lives but were subject to the whims of their legal guardians.

9.3. The Gendered Child

Gendering started as soon as a child was born. The biblical texts suggest that along with their mothers, male and female infants were secluded for different amounts of time before being welcomed into the community. When the mother's seclusion for a male child was over, the biblical text states he was circumcised on the eighth day. Archaeological information

---

7. Warfare is another area that affected children. As the youngest, frailest members of a society, they, along with the elderly, were often the first to succumb to the effects of a siege, resulting famine, or other war brutalities. See Jason Anthony Riley, "Children and Warfare in the Hebrew Bible and the Iron Age II: Rhetoric and Reality in Textual, Iconographic, and Archaeological Sources" (PhD diss., Fuller Theological Seminary, 2018).

8. Garroway, "Neither Slave Nor Free," 121–38.

attests to the fact that ancient Israelite males indeed were circumcised, but as discussed, circumcision originally started as a puberty rite. Other possible acts of gendering at infancy might have happened during an official welcoming ceremony. This might have included holding objects representative of the infant's gender, such as was done in other ancient Near Eastern cultures. Naming too, also acted as a moment where gender could be imposed upon an infant.[9] If the mother named the child at his birth but was then immediately secluded due to impurity, it is possible that a public naming ceremony took place when the mother's seclusion ended. Ruth 4:17 could represent such a public naming ceremony. Following Albertz, one might also envision the possibility that circumcision was moved to the eighth day to correspond with a public naming ceremony.

Parents put time and energy into the children who were expected to thrive. They provided their children not just with food, clothing, and shelter, but also with the skills set to grow into a new generation of Israelites. As children grew, both boys and girls were gendered through the education they received. Rather than a formal, schoolhouse education, children received informal "life" education via socialization. Thus, boys were taught how to become Israelite men, and girls how to become proper Israelite women. The process of gendering is closely related to the process of socialization. Parents repeated and performed gendered acts that were replicated by their children.

The gendering process can also be identified through a visual representation of gender. While circumcision is certainly a visual marker, it was not one put on public display. Clothing, on the other hand, is for public consumption. According to the texts and reliefs, infants wore gender neutral clothing (swaddling clothes) or no clothing at all. As discussed in chapter 6, nakedness in infants and small children was not considered shameful. It does appear that once a child was able to sit on his own, or perhaps even toddle, that he started to wear clothing. What kind of clothes children wore as very young children is unclear. The child riding on the back of a cart, seen in figure 6.1 and the close-up in figure 6.2, wears a little gown. This again suggests a gender-neutral presentation of gender in the young, as the gown is not similar to any of the clothing other individuals,

---

9. It was possible to have a gender-neutral name like Abijah (2 Kgs 18:2 // 2 Chr 29:1; 2 Chr 12:16).

young or old, are wearing. A loose-fitting gown would make sense for very young children, as it could aid in the toilet-training process.[10]

As children got older, they were dressed according to their gender. The Lachish reliefs depict girls all wearing ankle-length dresses with long outer mantles covering their hair. Whereas these girls appear to be cookie-cutter replicas of adult women, the boys in the reliefs have more variation in their clothing. Boys wear the short tunic found on all the males in the relief, but how they adorn the tunic changes as they grow older. Using height as an indication of age, one can see the ornateness and length of the boy's belt increases as he ages. One might also think of male facial hair as adornment and an outward expression of gender. Adult men have a beard, whereas the boys and teenagers in the relief do not. Biblical texts such as 2 Sam 10:4–5 reinforce the idea that beards belong to men, especially manly men who can fight in wars.

Gender can also be seen in death. Since burials are done by the living, the living have the opportunity to shape the way in which the deceased are seen and remembered.[11] "Cultural attitudes dictate where and how infants and children are buried, when they assume their gender identity, whether they are exposed to physical abuse, and at what age they are con-sidered adults."[12] Examining grave goods is one way of learning about the deceased child's gender. In cave or tomb burials, infants and children are often accompanied by adult burials. When multiple burials occur together, it is difficult to tell if a grave good was meant for a particular person or if the grave goods were meant to be shared. In the Bronze Age, infants who received a burial were most often found in jar burials. Jar burials are important because of their uniformity and because it is easy to determine for whom the grave goods were meant. Jar burials continued into the Iron Age. The burials of infants were not marked as "boy infant" or "girl infant"; rather, the jar burials consisted of the same gender-neutral burial kit: a

---

10. On cross-cultural studies referencing children's clothing and potty-training, see Martin W. deVries and M. Rachel deVries, "Cultural Relativity of Toilet Train-ing Readiness: A Perspective from East Africa," *Pediatrics* 60 (1977): 170–77; Laurie Boucke, *Infant Potty Training: A Gentle and Primeval Method Adapted to Modern Living* (Lafayette, CO: White-Boucke Pub, 2008), especially part 4.

11. Kathryn Kamp, "Where Have All the Children Gone? The Archaeology of Childhood," *Journal of Archaeological Method and Theory* 8 (2000): 24; Pearson, *Archaeology of Death and Burial*, 102–4.

12. Mary Lewis, *Bioarchaeology of Children: Perspectives from Biological and forensic Anthropology* (Cambridge: Cambridge University Press, 2007), 1.

store jar, a juglet, and in some cases a bowl. Each individual infant or child that was buried in a jar burial, regardless of gender, was afforded the essential items needed to reach the afterlife.[13]

At times grave goods contain items of personal adornment, such as arrowheads, knives, anklets, bracelets, scarabs, or sets of beads. Depending on the burial custom of the site it can be possible to extrapolate gender based on these personal items.[14] For example, at the Transjordanian site of Tell es-Saʿidiyeh, anklet pairs have been found on women and children but not on men. This suggests that deceased boy children were not presented as "boys," but rather as "non-men" or maybe "non-adult-male." Without a large (adorned) burial population like that of Tel es-Saʿidiyeh, it is difficult to know how adornments in death were related to presentations of gender in ancient Israel.[15]

As this discussion of gender highlights, gender in ancient Israel was both imposed upon the child, modeled for the child, and carried out by the child. Gender was infused into every part of the child's world.

9.4. The Playing Child

Exploring what it means to grow up in ancient Israel and what the child's world was means exploring not just the world inhabited by the child, but also the world created by the child. Children, like adults, interacted with material culture daily. At times the material culture was created for them, but at other times they created it. In thinking about the way in which children interacted with the material culture, one needs to keep in mind the multi-faceted nature of material culture. It is a complex set of symbols.[16] Thus, an object might be used one way, or mean a certain thing to one person, but mean something different to another person. Moreover, the primary use of an object might be much different than the secondary use.

---

13. Items identified as "essential grave goods" are those items needed to ensure a proper transition to the afterlife (Baker, *Funeral Kit*, 27, and sources within).

14. In general, items are assigned as "male" or "female" based on the social perceptions of males and females among the living of a society (Baker, *Funeral Kit*, 52–54).

15. Baker notes, "Imposing gender biases upon burials and their grave goods is more complex than would first appear, and there are not absolutes" (Baker, *Funeral Kit*, 54).

16. Garroway, *Children in the Ancient Near Eastern Household*, 30–34; Hodder, *Present Past*, 139–40, 206–9.

For example, adults might use a JPF for magicoreligious purposes, but a young child might see it as something different. An adult teaches the child proper usage, models the socially accepted way of manipulating a JPF, and thus explains the culturally coded set of symbols. The fact that scholars today cannot always come to a consensus on how an object, such as a JPF, was used highlights the complexity involved in decoding culturally coded symbols.

The chapter on playing briefly explored some of the ways in which a child interacted with objects, and in doing so bestowed new, or different meanings on them. Ceramic figures once used for magicoreligious purposes may have enjoyed a second use as a toy. Ceramic vessels intended for serving food or drink, might, once broken, be transformed by a child or an adult into an object of play, such as a "buzz" or spinning top. Other ceramic objects appear to have been made specifically as toys, such as little animals, game boards, and gaming pieces. Miniature vessels created by children offer an example of times when play served the dual purpose of socialization, as children learned skills needed for later in life. While these are all cases where a child's imprint can be seen on the material record, there are other cases wherein a child's imprint is lost to time. Such instances include, among others, children playing with biodegradable objects, children playing with animals, or children making an object and then destroying it.

9.5. The Next Years

In exploring everything from prebirth and birth to aspects of life and death, it should become clear that there is much more to be done to uncover the lives of ancient Israelite children and what it meant to grow up in ancient Israel. The information gathered in this volume presents a childist method, examining the extant data from a new perspective in order to focus on the child, not the adult. In acknowledging the child as an actor, the child moves out of the realm of passive participant in society and into the realm of agent. At times, such a distinction might be difficult to see; however, if one analyzes the data from a childist perspective, even the seemingly passive child has agency. For example, one might consider the fetus or infant to not have much agency. But through the texts describing the depth with which a child is desired, the value placed on the pregnancy, and the measures taken to protect the infant, one starts to see how the "passive" fetus or infant exerts significant control over the actions of an entire family. Or consider a child who is acquiring skills needed in adulthood; the time and energy invested in successfully rearing children who will become the next generation of Israelites should not be underestimated nor devalued. Ancient Israelite culture will reflect what the child learns in his or her youth. Thus, as contributors to the material culture, a child also has agency.

In collating and framing the data through a childist lens, *Growing Up in Ancient Israel* sets the stage for future research. The broad categories of value, vulnerability, gender, and material culture are all areas that are a part of the child's life and world and areas that can be explored further in a diachronic manner. Issues of children as contributors to the household economic system, children as participants in Israelite household religion, and children in ancient warfare are other examples of areas needing more attention.[17] Finally, from the perspective of childhood archaeology, additional investigation is needed with respect to children's spaces, children as producers, and children as laborers and actors in the household economy.

This study represents a beginning. It has heeded the call of child-centered biblical interpretation to pay attention to children in the biblical text by providing an interdisciplinary approach to the child in ancient Israel. After reading this book, scholars, students, and indeed any reader of the Hebrew Bible should no longer ask where the children are but rather what more we can learn about children. I hope that the methods, sources, and theories found within will inspire some to go on and contribute their own answers.

---

17. Shawn Flynn's book (*Children in Ancient Israel*) was just coming out as this manuscript was being completed. His work is an example of how a child-centered approach can successfully bring together the topics of value and domestic religion as they pertain to children.

Bibliography

Aasgaard, Reidar. *El Evangelio de la Infancia de Tomás*. Salamanca, Spain: Ediciones Sigueme 2009.

Abusch, Tzvi. "Mesopotamian Anti-Witchcraft Literature: Texts and Studies Part I; The Nature of Maqlû; Its Character, Divisions, and Calendrical Setting." *JNES* 33 (1974): 251–62.

Ackerman, Susan. "The Blind, the Lame and the Barren Shall Not Come into the House of the Lord." Pages 29–46 in *Disability Studies and Biblical Literature*. Edited by Candida Moss and Jeremy Schipper. New York: Palgrave MacMillian, 2011.

———. "Household Religion, Family Religion, and Women's Religion in Ancient Israel." Pages 127–58 in *Household and Family Religion in Antiquity*. Edited by John P. Bodel and Saul M. Olyan. Oxford: Wiley-Blackwell, 2012.

Albenda, Pauline. "Western Asiatic Women in the Iron Age: Their Image Revealed." *BA* 46 (1983): 82–88.

Albertz, Rainer. "Family Religion in Ancient Israel and Its Surroundings." Pages 89–112 in *Household and Family Religion in Antiquity*. Edited by John P. Bodel and Saul M. Olyan. Oxford: Wiley-Blackwell, 2012.

———. "Names and Family Religion." Pages 245–386 in *Family and Household Religion in Ancient Israel and the Levant*. Edited by Rainer Albertz and Rüdiger Schmitt. Winona Lake, IN: Eisenbrauns, 2012.

Albright, William Foxwell. *The Archaeology of Palestine*. Harmondsworth: Penguin, 1949.

———. *The Excavation of Tell Beit Mirsim (Joint Expedition of the Pittsburgh-Xenia Theological Seminary and the American School of Oriental Research in Jerusalem)*. 3 vols. AASOR 12–13, 17, 21–22. New Haven: American Schools of Oriental Research, 1932–1943.

———. "The Israelite Conquest of Canaan in the Light of Archaeology." *BASOR* 74 (1939): 11–23.

———. "The Kyle Memorial Excavation at Bethel." *BASOR* 56 (1934): 2–15.

Ali, Faisal R., and Alexander Finlayson. "Pharoanic Trichology: The Ebers Papyrus." *JAMA Dermatology* 149 (2013): 920.

Ali, Nabil. "Ethnographic Study of Clay Ovens in Northern Jordan." Pages 9–18 in *Modesty and Patience, Studies and Memories in Honour of Nabil Qadi, "Abu Salim."* Edited by Hans Georg Gebel, Zeidan Abdel-Kafi Kafafi, and Omar Al-Ghul. Jordan: Yarmuk University, 2009.

Allan, Robert. "Now That Summer's Gone: Understanding *qz* in *KTU* 1.24." *SEL* 16 (1999): 19–25.

Alt, Albrecht. *Die Landnahme der Israeliten in Palästina: Territorialgeschichtliche Studien.* Leipzig: Druckerei der Werkgemeinschaft, 1925.

Alter, Robert. "How Convention Helps Us Read: The Case of the Bible's Annunciation Type-Scene." *Prooftexts* 3 (1983): 115–30.

Amit, Yariah. *Hidden Polemics in Biblical Narrative.* Translated by Jonathan Chipman. Leiden: Brill, 2000.

Amster, Matthew. "Gender Complementarity and Death among the Kelabit." Pages 251–308 in *Journeys of the Soul: Anthropological Studies of Death, Burial and Rebirth Practices in Borneo.* Edited by William D. Wilder. Borneo Research Council Monograph 7. Philips, ME: Borneo Research Council, 2003.

Angel, J. Lawrence. "Porotic Hyperstosis, Anemias, Malarias, and Marshes in the Prehistoric Eastern Mediterranean." *Science* 153.3737 (1966): 760–63.

Appell, George N., and Appell, Laura W. R. "Death among the Rungus Momogun of Sabah, Malaysia: The Dissolution of Personhood and Dispersion of the Multiple Souls and Spiritual Counterparts." Pages 41–121 in *Journeys of the Soul: Anthropological Studies of Death; Burial and Rebirth Practices in Borneo.* Edited by William D. Wilder. Borneo Research Council Monograph 7. Philips, ME: Borneo Research Council, 2003.

Ariès, Philippe. *Centuries of Childhood: A Social History of Family Life.* Translated by Robert Baldick. New York: Vintage, 1962.

Avissar-Lewis, Rona. "Childhood and Children in Material Culture of the Land of Israel from the Middle Bronze Age to the Iron Age" [Hebrew]. PhD diss., Bar-Ilan University, 2010.

———. המקרא בתקופת ישראל בארץ וילדות ארכיאולוגי מבט קדם ילדי. [Children of Antiquity: A View of Archaeology and Childhood in the Land of Israel During the Biblical Period]. Haifa: Haifa University Press, forthcoming.

Baby Center. "Best Baby Carriers for Nursing." https://tinyurl.com/
SBL1729a.

Baden, Joel. "The Nature of Barrenness in the Hebrew Bible." Pages 13–27
in *Disability Studies and Biblical Literature*. Edited by Candida Moss
and Jeremy Schipper. New York: Palgrave Macmillian, 2011.

Baines, John. "Egyptian Twins." *Or* 2/54 (1985): 461–82.

Baitzel, Sarah. "Parental Grief and Mourning in the Ancient Andes."
Journal of Archaeological Method and Theory (2017): https://doi.
org/10.1007/s10816-017-9333-3.

Baker, H. D. "Degrees of Freedom: Slavery in Mid-First Millennium BC
Babylonia." *WA* 33 (2001): 18–26.

Baker, Jill. *The Funeral Kit: Mortuary Practice in the Archaeological Record*.
Walnut Creek, CA: Left Coast Press, 2012.

Barkay, Gabriel. "Burial Headrests as a Return to the Womb: A Reevaluation." *BAR* 14.2 (1988): 48–50.

———. *Ketef Hinnom: A Treasure Facing Jerusalem's Walls*. Israel Museum
Catalogue 274. Jerusalem: Israel Museum, 1986.

Barnett, R. D., et al. *Sculptures from the Southwest Palace of Sennacherib at
Nineveh*. London: British Museum Press, 1998.

Batten, Alicia. "Clothing and Adornment." *Biblical Theology Bulletin* 40
(2010): 148–59.

Bauks, Michaela. "L'enjeu théologique du sacrifice d'enfants dans le milieu
biblique et son dépassement en Genèse 22." *Études théologiques et religieuses* 76 (2001): 529–42.

Baxter, Eva, ed. *Children in Action: Perspectives on the Archaeology of
Childhood*. Archaeological Papers of the American Anthropological
Association 15. Arlington: American Anthropological Association,
2006.

Baxter, Judith. *The Archaeology of Childhood: Children, Gender, and Material Culture*. Walnut Creek, CA: AltaMira, 2005.

Beaumont, Lesley. "The Social Status and Artistic Presentation of 'Adolescence' in Fifth Century Athens." Pages 29–50 in *Children and Material
Culture*. Edited by Joanna R. Sofaer Derevenski. London: Routledge,
2000.

Bechtel, Lyn. "What If Dinah Is Not Raped? (Genesis 34)." *JSOT* 62 (1994):
19–26.

Beek, Gus van. "The Buzz: A Simple Toy from Antiquity." *BASOR* 275
(1989): 53–58.

Beck, P. "A New Type of Female Figurine." Pages 29–34 in *Insights through Images: Studies in Honor of Edith Porada*. Edited by M. Kelly-Buccellati. Malibu, CA: Udena, 1986.

Beckman, Gary. "Hittite Birth Rituals." PhD diss., Yale University, 1977.

———. *Hittite Birth Rituals: An Introduction*. Malibu, CA: Undena, 1978.

Beit-Arieh, Izhaq. "A Phallus-Shaped Clay Object." Page 580 in *Tel Malḥata: A Central City in the Biblical Negev*. Edited by Itzhaq Beit-Arieh and Liora Freud. Winona Lake, IN: Eisenbrauns, 2015.

———. *Tel 'Ira: A Stronghold in the Biblical Negev*. Tel Aviv: Yass Publications in Archaeology of the Institute of Archaeology, Tel Aviv University, 1999.

Ben-Arieh, Sara. *Bronze and Iron Age Tombs at Tell Beit Mirsim*. Jerusalem: Israel Antiquities Authority, 2004.

Ben-Dov, Jonathan. "The Poor's Curse: Exodus XXII 20–26 and Curse Literature in the Ancient World." *VT* 56 (2006): 431–51.

Bender, Shunya. *The Social Structure of Ancient Israel: The Institution of the Family (beit ʾav) from the Settlement to the End of the Monarchy*. Jerusalem: Simor, 1996.

Bennett, W. J., Michael David Coogan, and Jeffrey A. Blakely, eds. *Tell el-Hesi: The Persian Period (Stratum V)*. ASOR 3. Winona Lake, IN: Eisenbrauns, 1989.

Bergant, Dianne. "An Anthropological Approach to Biblical Interpretation: The Passover Supper in Exodus 12:1–20 as a Case Study." *Semeia* 67 (1994): 43–62.

Betsworth, Sharon. *Children in Early Christian Narratives*. LNTS 521. London: Bloomsbury, 2015.

Biddle, Mark. *Deuteronomy*. Smyth and Helwys Bible Commentary. Macon, GA: Smyth & Helwys, 2003.

Biggs, Robert. *ŠÀ.ZI.GA Ancient Mesopotamian Potency Incantations*. Texts from Cuneiform Sources 2. Locust Valley, NY: Augustin, 1967.

Binford, Lewis. *An Archaeological Perspective*. New York: Seminar Press, 1972.

———. "Mortuary Practices: Their Study and Their Potential." Pages 6–29 in *Approaches to the Social Dimension of Mortuary Practices*. Edited by James Allison Brown. Memoirs of the Society for American Archaeology 25. Washington: Society for American Archaeology, 1971.

Blair, Peter, Peter Sidebotham, Carol Evanson-Coombe, Margaret Edmons, Ellen Heckstall-Smith, and Peter Fleming. "Hazardous Co-sleeping Environments and Risk Factors Amenable to Change: Case-Control

Study of SIDS in South West England." *The BMJ*. 13 October 2009. http://dx.doi.org/10.1136/bmj.b3666.

Blenkinsopp, Joseph. "The Family in First Temple Israel." Pages 48–103 in *Families in Ancient Israel*. Edited by Leo Perdue, Joseph Blenkinsopp, John J. Collins, and Carol Meyers. Louisville: Westminster John Knox, 1997.

———. *Isaiah 56–66: A New Translation with Introduction and Commentary*. AB 19B. New York: Doubleday, 2003.

Bliss, Fredrick. *A Mound of Many Cities, or Tel el-Hesy Excavated*. London: Palestinian Exploration Society, 1898.

Bloch-Smith, Elizabeth. "The Cult of the Dead in Judah: Interpreting the Material Remains." *JBL* 111 (1992): 213–24.

———. *Judahite Burial Practices and Beliefs about the Dead*. JSOT Sup. 123. Sheffield: JSOT, 1992.

Bogin, Barry, and Holly Smith. "Evolution of the Human Life Cycle." Pages 515–86 in *Human Biology: An Evolutionary and Biocultural Perspective*. Edited by Sara Stinson, Barry Bogin, and Dennis O'Rourke. Hoboken: Wiley & Sons, 2012.

Bohak, Gideon. *Ancient Jewish Magic*. Cambridge: Cambridge University Press, 2008.

Bohmbach, Karla. "Names and Naming in the Biblical World." Pages 33–39 in *Women in Scripture*. Edited by Carol Meyers. Grand Rapids Eerdmans, 2000.

Boling, Robert C. *Judges*. AB 6A. Garden City, NY: Doubleday, 1975.

Booth, Charlotte. *Lost Voices of the Nile: Everyday Life in Ancient Egypt*. Glouchestershire: Amberley, 2015.

Borghouts, Joris. *Ancient Egyptian Magical Texts*. Leiden: Brill, 1978.

Borowski, Oded. *Lahav III: The Iron Age II Cemetery at Tell Halif (Site 72)*. Winona Lake, IN: Eisenbrauns, 2013.

Boswell, John. *The Kindness of Strangers: The Abandonment of Children in Western Europe from Late Antiquity to the Renaissance*. New York: Pantheon, 1988.

Bosworth, David. *Infant Weeping in Akkadian, Hebrew, and Greek Literature*. Winona Lake, IN: Eisenbrauns, 2016.

Boucke, Laurie. *Infant Potty Training: A Gentle and Primeval Method Adapted to Modern Living*. Lafayette, CO: White-Boucke, 2008.

Bowie, Fiona. *The Anthropology of Religion*. Oxford: Blackwell, 2000.

Braun, Joachim. *Music in Ancient Israel/Palestine*. Translated by Douglas W. Stott. Grand Rapids Eerdmans, 2002.

Brody, Aaron J. "Late Bronze Age Intramural Tombs." Pages 515–30 in *Askhelon I: Introduction and Overview 1985–2000*. Edited by Lawrence E. Stager, J. David Schloen, and Daniel M. Master. Winona Lake, IN: Eisenbrauns, 2008.

Brown, Judith K. "A Note on the Division of Labor by Sex." *AA* 72 (1970): 1073–78.

Brueggemann, Walter. *1 and 2 Kings*. Smyth and Helwys Bible Commentary. Macon, GA: Smyth & Helwys, 2000.

Brunner, Hellmut. "Das Besänftigungslied im Sinuhe (B 269–279)." *ZÄS* 80 (1955): 5–11.

Bunimovitz, Shlomo, and Zvi Lederman. "Iron Age Artifacts." Pages 560–602 in vol. 2 of *Tel Beth-Shemesh A Border Community in Judah: Renewed Excavations 1990–2000; The Iron Age*. Edited by Shlomo Bunimovitz and Zvi Lederman. Tel Aviv: Yass Publications in Archaeology; Winona Lake, IN: Eisenbrauns, 2016.

———, eds. *Tel Beth-Shemesh A Border Community in Judah: Renewed Excavations 1990–2000; The Iron Age*. 2 vols. Tel Aviv: Yass Publications in Archaeology; Winona Lake, IN: Eisenbrauns, 2016.

Burney, C. F. *The Book of Judges*. 2nd ed. London: Rivingtons, 1930.

Butler, Judith. *Gender Trouble: Feminism and the Subversion of Identity*. London: Routledge, 1990.

Bullogh, Vern. "Deviant Sex in Mesopotamia." *The Journal of Sex Research* 7 (1971): 184–203.

Bunge, Marsha, ed. *The Child in the Bible*. Grand Rapids Eerdmans, 2008.

Byrne, Ryan. "Lie Back and Think of Judah: The Reproductive Politics of Pillar Figurines." *NEA* 67 (2004): 137–51.

Cadelli, D. "Lorsque l'enfant paraît ... malade." Pages 11–34 in *Ktèma: Civilisations de l'Orient, de la Grèce et de Rome antiques, 1997*. Ktèma 22. Centre de recherche sur le Proche-Orient et la Grèce antiques. Strasbourg: Université Marc Bloch, 1998.

Cahill, Jane M., Karl Reinhard, David Tarler, and Peter Warnock. "It Had to Happen." *BAR* 17.3 (1991): 64–69.

Campbell, Edward. *Ruth: A New Translation with Introduction, Notes and Commentary*. AB 7. Garden City, NY: Doubleday, 1975.

Center for Disease Control. "Infant Health." https://tinyurl.com/SBL1729b.

Chamberlain, Andrew. *Demography in Archaeology*. Cambridge: Cambridge University Press, 2006.

———. "Minor Perspectives on Children in Past Societies." Pages 206–12 in *Children and Material Culture.* Edited by Joanna R. Sofaer Derevenski. London: Routledge, 2000.

Chapman, Cynthia. *The House of the Mother: The Social Role of Maternal Kin in Biblical Hebrew Narrative and Poetry.* New Haven, CT: Yale University Press, 2016.

Childs, Brevard. *Exodus.* Philadelphia: Westminster, 1974.

Chodorow, Nancy. "Family Structure and Feminine Personality." Pages 43–66 in *Woman, Culture, and Society.* Edited by Michelle Zimbalist Rosaldo and Louise Lamphere. Stanford: Stanford University Press, 1974.

Claassens, L. Julianna. "Calling the Keeners: The Image of the Wailing Woman as a Symbol of Survival in a Traumatized World." *JFSR* 26 (2010): 63–77.

Clem, Carl. *Die Phönikische Religion.* Leipzig: Hinrichs, 1939.

Cogan, Mordechai, and Hayim Tadmor. *II Kings: A New Translation with Introduction and Commentary.* AB 11. New York: Doubleday, 1988.

Cohen, Mark E. "Literary Texts from the Andres University Archaeological Museum." *RA* 70 (1976): 129–44.

Cohen, Yoram. "Feet of Clay at Emar: A Happy Ending?" *Or* 74 (2005): 165–70.

Collon, Dominique. "Clothing and Grooms in Ancient Western Asia." Pages 503–16 in vol. 1 of *Civilizations of the Ancient Near East.* Edited by Jack Sasson. New York: Scribner, 1995.

Cornelius, Izak. "A Terracotta Horse in Stellenbosch and the Iconography and Function of Palestinian Horse Figurines." *ZDPV* 123 (2007): 28–36.

Cosgrove, Charles. "A Woman's Unbound Hair in the Greco-Roman World, with Special Reference to the Story of the 'Sinful Woman' in Luke 7:36–50." *JBL* 124 (2005): 675–92.

Coşkunsu, Güner, ed. *The Archaeology of Childhood: Interdisciplinary Perspectives on an Archaeological Enigma.* Albany: State University of New York Press, 2015.

Costin, Cathy Lynne. "Use of Ethnoarchaeology for the Archaeological Study of Ceramic Production." *Journal of Archaeological Method and Theory* 7 (2000): 377–403.

Crawley, Sara, Lara Foley, and Constance Shehan, eds. *Gendering Bodies.* Lanham: Rowman & Littlefield, 2008.

Crenshaw, James. "Education in Ancient Israel." *JBL* 104 (1985): 601–15.

Dalley, Stephanie. *Mari and Karana: Two Old Babylonian Cities.* London: Longman, 1984.

Darby, Erin. *Interpreting Judean Pillar Figurines: Gender and Empire in Judean Apotropaic Ritual.* FAT 2/69. Tübingen: Mohr Siebeck, 2014.

Daviau, P. M. Michèle. "Family Religion: Evidence for the Paraphernalia of the Domestic Cult." Pages 199–229 in *The World of the Arameans II: Studies in History and Archaeology in Honor of Paul-Eugène Dion.* Edited by Paul-Eugène Dion. JSOT Supp 325. Sheffield: Sheffield Academic, 2001.

Day, John. *Molech: A God of Human Sacrifice in the Old Testament.* University of Cambridge Oriental Publications 41. Cambridge: Cambridge University Press, 1989.

Day, Peggy. "From the Child Is Born the Woman: The Story of Jephthah's Daughter." Pages 58–74 in *Gender and Different in Ancient Israel.* Edited by Peggy Day. Minneapolis: Fortress, 1989.

Decker, Wolfgang, and Michael Herb. *Bildatlas zum Sport im alten Ägypten Corpus der bildlichen Quellen zu Leibesülangen, Spiel, Tanz, und verwandten Themen.* 2 vols. Leiden: Brill, 1994.

Delaney, Carol. "Untangling the Meanings of Hair in Turkish Society." *Anthropological Quarterly* 67.4 (1994): 159–72.

Derevenski, Joanna R. Sofaer, ed. *Children and Material Culture.* London: Routledge, 2000.

———. "Engendering Children, Engendering Archaeology." Pages 192–202 in *Invisible People and Processes: Writing Gender and Childhood into European Archaeology.* Edited by Jennie Moore and Eleanor Scott. London: Leicester University Press, 1997.

———. "Where Are the Children? Accessing Children in the Past." *ARC* 13.2 (1994): 7–20.

deVries, Martin W., and M. Rachel deVries. "Cultural Relativity of Toilet Training Readiness: A Perspective from East Africa." *Pediatrics* 60 (1977): 170–77.

Dever, William G. *Did God Have a Wife? Archaeology and Folk Religion in Ancient Israel.* Grand Rapids: Eerdmans, 2005.

———. *The Lives of Ordinary People in Ancient Israel: Where Archaeology and the Bible Intersect.* Grand Rapids: Eerdmans, 2012.

———. *Who Were the Early Israelites and Where Did They Come From?* Grand Rapids: Eerdmans, 2006.

Dever, William G., H. Darrell Lance, and Reuben G. Bullard. *Gezer IV: The 1969–71 Seasons in Field VI, the "Acropolis."* 4 vols. Jerusalem: Keter Press; Jerusalem: Nelson Gleuck School of Biblical Archaeology, 1986.

Dewrell, Heath. *Child Sacrifice in Ancient Israel.* Winona Lake, IN: Eisenbrauns, 2017.

Dodson, Aidan. *Amarna Sunset: Nefertiti, Tutankhamun, Ay, Horemheb, and the Egyptian Counter-Reformation.* Cairo: The American University in Cairo Press, 2009.

Doman, A. D., P. C. Zuttermeister, and R. Friedman. "The Psychological Impact of Infertility: A Comparison with Patients with Other Medical Conditions." *Journal of Psychosomatic Obstretics and Gynecology* 14 (1993): 45–52.

Dommasnes, Liv Helga. "Introduction: The Past-Worlds of Children and for Children?" Pages xi–xxx in *Children, Identity and the Past.* Edited by Liv Helga Dommasnes and Melanie Wrigglesworth. New Castle: Cambridge Scholars, 2008.

Dommasnes, Liv Helga, and Melanie Wrigglesworth, eds. *Children, Identity and the Past.* New Castle: Cambridge Scholars, 2008.

Dornan, Jennifer. "Agency and Archaeology: Past, Present, and Future Directions." *Journal of Archaeology and Theory* 9 (2002): 303–29.

Dothan, Trude, and Baruch Brandl. *Deir El-Balaḥ: Excavations in 1977–82 in the Cemetery and Settlement.* Qedem 50. Jerusalem: Institute of Archaeology, Hebrew University, 2010.

Dothan, Trude, and Dalit Regev. "Iron Age I Limestone Phallus." Pages 469–70 in *Tel Miqne-Ekron Excavations 1985–1988, 1990, 1992–1995: Field IV Lower, The Elite Zone.* Edited by Seymour Gitin, Trude Dothan, and Yosef Garfinkel. Harvard Semitic Museum. Winona Lake, IN: Eisenbrauns, 1996.

Douglas, Mary. *Purity and Danger.* London: Routledge & Kegan Paul, 1976.

Drewal, Henry John. "Pageantry and Power in Yorba Costuming." Pages 189–230 in *The Fabrics of Culture: The Anthropology of Clothing and Adornment.* Edited by Justine Cordwell and Ronald A. Schwarz. Berlin: de Gruyter, 1979.

Drower, Ethel S. "Women and Taboo in Iraq." *Iraq* 5 (1938): 105–17.

Edwards, I. E. S. *Oracular Amuletic Decrees of the Late New Kingdom.* Hieratic Papyri in the British Museum 4th series. London: British Museum, 1960.

Eilberg-Schwartz, Howard. *The Savage in Judaism: An Anthropology of Israelite Religion and Ancient Judaism*. Bloomington, IN: Indiana University Press, 1990.

Einarsdóttir, Jónína. *Tired of Weeping: Mother Love, Child Death, and Poverty in Guinea-Bissau*. Madison: University of Madison Press, 2004.

Einsler, Lydia. *Mosaik aus dem heiligen Lande: Schilderung einiger Gebräuche und Anschauungen der arabischen Bevölkerung Palästinas*. Jerusalem: Druck des Syrischen Waisenhauses, 1898.

el Guindi, Fadwa. *Veil: Modesty, Privacy, and Resistance*. Oxford: Berg, 1999.

Elkins, Kathleen G., and Julie Parker. "Children in the Biblical Narrative and Childist Interpretation." Pages 422–34 in *The Oxford Handbook to Biblical Narrative*. Edited by Danna Fewell. New York: Oxford University Press, 2014.

Erman, Adolf. *Zaubersprüche für Mutter und Kind: Aus dem Papyrus 3027 des Berliner Museums*. Berlin: Akademie der Wissenschaften, 1901.

Ewbank, Douglas, and James N. Gribble. *Effects of Health Programs on Child Mortality in Sub-Saharan Africa*. Washington DC: National Academy Press, 1993.

Faerman, Marina, Gila Kahila Bar-Gal, Dvora Filon, Charles L. Greenblatt, Lawrence Stager, Ariella Oppenheim, and Patricia Smith. "Determining the Sex of Infanticide Victims from the Late Roman Era through Ancient DNA Analysis." *Journal of Archaeological Sciences* 25 (1998): 861–65.

Faerman, Marina, A. Nebel, N. Angel-Zohar, and P. Smith. "The Bioarchaeology of the Human Remains." Pages 283–94 in *Tel Kabri: The 1986–1993 Excavation Seasons*. Edited by Aharon Kempenski. Tel Aviv: Yass Publications in Archaeology, 2002.

Farber, Walter. *Lamaštu: An Edition of the Canonical Series of Lamaštu Incantations and Rituals and Related Texts from the Second and First Millennia B.C.* Mesopotamian Civilizations 17. Winona Lake, IN: Eisenbrauns, 2014.

———. "Magic at the Cradle: Babylonian and Assyrian Lullabies." *Anthropos* 85 (1990): 13–148.

———. *Schlaf, Kindchen Schlaf! Mesopotamische Baby-Beschworungen und-Rituale*. Mesopotamian Civillizations 2. Winona Lake, IN: Eisenbrauns, 1989.

Farmer, Henry G. "The Music of Ancient Egypt." Pages 255–82 in vol. 1 of *The New Oxford History of Music*. Edited by Egon Wellesz. 10 vols. London: Oxford, 1957–1974.

———. "The Music of Ancient Mesopotamia." Pages 228–54 in vol. 1 of *The New Oxford History of Music*. Edited by Egon Wellesz. 10 vols. London: Oxford, 1957–1974.

Faust, Avraham. "The Archaeology of the Israelite Cult: Questioning the Consensus." *BASOR* 360 (2010): 23–35.

———. "The Bible, Archaeology, and the Practice of Circumcision in Israelite and Philistine Societies." *JBL* 134 (2015): 273–90.

Fensham, F. Charles. "Salt as a Curse in the Old Testament and the Ancient Near East." *BA* 25 (1962): 48–50.

———. "Widow, Orphan, and Poor in Ancient Near Eastern Legal and Wisdom Literature." *JNES* 21 (1962): 129–39.

Feucht, Erika. *Das Kind im Alten Ägypten*. Frankfurt: Campus, 1995.

———. "Childhood." *OEAE* 1:261–64.

Fewell, Danna Noel. *The Children of Israel: Reading the Bible for the Sake of Our Children*. Nashville: Abingdon, 2003.

Fewell, Danna Nolan, and David Gunn. "Tipping the Balance: Sternberg's Reader and the Rape of Dinah." *JBL* 110 (1991): 193–211.

Finkelstein, Israel. *The Archaeology of the Israelite Settlement*. Jerusalem: Israel Exploration Society, 1988.

———. "The Emergence of Israel in Canaan: Consensus, Mainstream and Dispute." *SJOT* 5 (1991): 47–59.

———. "Environmental Archaeology and Social History: Demographic and Economic Aspects of the Monarchic Period." Pages 56–66, 70 in *Biblical Archaeology Today, 1990: Proceedings of the Second International Congress on Biblical Archaeology*. Edited by Avraham Biran and Joseph Aviram. Jerusalem: Israel Exploration Society; Israel Academy of Sciences and Humanities, 1993.

———. "Ethnographic Origins of Iron I Settlers in the Highlands of Canaan: Can the Real Israel Stand Up?" *BA* 59 (1996): 198–212.

Finkelstein, Israel, and Nadav Na'aman. *From Nomadism to Monarchy: Archaeological and Historical Aspects of Early Israel*. Jerusalem: Yad Izhak Ben-Zvi: Israel Exploration Society, 1994.

Finlay, Nyree. "Kid Knapping: The Missing Children in Lithic Analysis." Pages 203–12 in *Invisible People and Processes: Writing Gender and Childhood into European Archaeology*. Edited by Jennie Moore and Eleanor Scott. London: Leicester University Press, 1997.

Findlay, Timothy D. *The Birth Report Genre in the Hebrew Bible*. FAT 12. Tübingen: Mohr Siebeck, 2005.

Finsterbusch, Karin. "The Firstborn between Sacrifice and Redemption in the Hebrew Bible." Pages 87–108 in *Human Sacrifice in the Jewish and Christian Tradition*. Edited by Karin Finsterbusch, Armin Lange, and Diethard Römheld. Leiden: Brill, 2007.

Fishbane, Michael. *Biblical Interpretation in Ancient Israel*. Oxford: Oxford University Press, 1985.

Fleishman, Joseph. "Legal Innovation in Deuteronomy XXI 18–20." *VT* 3 (2003): 311–27.

Fleming, Daniel. "The Integration of Household and Community Religion in Ancient Syria." Pages 37–59 in *Household and Family Religion in Antiquity*. Edited by John P. Bodel and Saul M. Olyan. Oxford: Wiley-Blackwell, 2012.

Flynn, Shawn. *Children in Ancient Israel: The Hebrew Bible and Mesopotamia in Comparative Perspective*. Oxford: Oxford University Press, 2018.

———. "The Teraphim in Light of Mesopotamian and Egyptian Evidence." *CBQ* 74 (2012): 694–711.

Fontinoy, Charles. "La naissance de l'enfant chez les Israélites de l'Ancien Testament." Pages 103–18 in *L'enfant dans les Civilisations Orientales*. Edited by Aristide Théodoridès, Paul Naster, and Julien Ries. Leuven: Peeters, 1980.

Foster, Catherine P., and Bradley J. Parker. "Introduction: Household Archaeology in the Near East and Beyond." Pages 1–14 in *New Perspectives on Household Archaeology*. Edited by Bradley J. Parker and Catherine P. Foster. Winona Lake, IN: Eisenbrauns, 2012.

Fowler, Mervyn. "Excavated Figurines: A Case for Identifying a Site as Sacred?" *ZAW* 97 (1985): 333–44.

Fox, Nili, and Angela Roskop. "Of Rattles and Rituals: The Anthropomorphic Rattle from the Nelson Glueck Collection at the Cincinnati Art Museum." *HUCA* 70–71 (1999–2000): 15–26.

Freidman, Richard Elliot. *Commentary on the Torah*. San Francisco: HarperSanFrancisco, 2001.

Friedl, Erika. *Children of Deh Koh: Young Life in an Iranian Village*. Syracuse, NY: Syracuse University Press, 1997.

———. "Islam and Tribal Women in a Village in Iran." Pages 159–73 in *Unspoken Worlds: Women's Religious Lives in Non-Western Cultures*. Edited by Nancy Falk and Rita Gross. San Francisco: Harper & Row, 1980.

Friedrich, Johannes. "Der Hethitische Soldateneid." *ZA* 35 (1924): 161–92.

Frymer-Kensky, Tivka. *In the Wake of the Goddesses*. New York: Free Press, 1992.

———. *Studies in Bible and Feminist Criticism*. JPS Scholars of Distinction Series. Philadelphia: Jewish Publication Society, 2006.

Furman, Nelly. "History Versus Her Story: Male Genealogy and Female Strategy in the Jacob Cycle." Pages 107–16 in *Feminist Perspectives on Biblical Scholarship*. Edited by Adele Collins. Atlanta: Scholars Press, 1985.

Gabbay, Uri. "A Collection of Pazuzu Objects in Jerusalem." *RA* 95 (2001): 149–54.

Gadot, Yuval, and Assaf Yasur-Landau. "Beyond Finds: Reconstructing Life in the Courtyard Building of Level K-4." Pages 526–43 in *Megiddo IV: The 1998–2002 Seasons*. Edited by Israel Finkelstein, David Ussishkin, and Baruch Halpern. Tel Aviv: Yass Publications in Archaeology, 2006.

Galil, Gershon. "Israelite Exiles in Media: A New Look at ND 2443+." *VT* 59 (2009): 71–79.

Gammie, S. C., A. Negron, S. M. Newman, and J. S. Rhodes. "Corticotrophin-Releasing Factor Inhibits Maternal Aggression in Mice." *Behavioral Neuroscience* 118 (2004): 805–14.

Garroway, Kristine. "2 Kings 6:24–30: A Case of Unintentional Elimination Killing." *JBL* 137 (2018): 53–70.

———. "Childist Archaeology: Children, Toys, and Skill Transmission in Ancient Israel." Paper presented at the Annual Meeting of American Schools of Oriental Research. Boston, MA, 18 November 2017.

———. "Children and Religion in the Archaeological Record of Ancient Israel." *JANER* 17 (2017): 116–39.

———. *Children in the Ancient Near Eastern Household*. Winona Lake, IN: Eisenbrauns, 2014.

———. "Neither Slave Nor Free: Children Living on the Edge of a Social Status." Pages 121–38 in *Windows to the Ancient World of the Hebrew Bible: Essays in Honor of Samuel Greengus*. Edited by Bill T. Arnold, Nancy Erickson, and John H. Walton. Winona Lake, IN: Eisenbrauns, 2014.

Gennep, Arnold van. *The Rites of Passage*. Chicago: University of Chicago Press, 1960.

Gerleman, G. "Schuld und Sühne: Erwägungen zu 2 Sam 12." Pages 132–39 in *Beiträge zur alttestamentlichen Thehologie: Festschrift für*

Walther Zimmerli. Edited by Herbert Donner, Robert Hanhart, and Rudolf Smend. Göttingen: Vandenhoeck & Ruprecht, 1977.

Gilmore, David. *Manhood in the Making: Cultural Concepts of Masculinity*. New Haven: Yale University Press, 1990.

Gilmour, Garth. "The Nature and Function of Astragalus Bones from Archaeological Contexts in the Levant and Eastern Mediterranean." *Oxford Journal of Archaeology* 16 (1997): 167–75.

Givon, Shmuel. *The Fifth Season of Excavation at Tel Harasim (Nahal Barkai) 1994: Preliminary Report 5* [Hebrew]. Tel Aviv: Tel Aviv, 1995.

Golden, Mark. *Children and Childhood in Classical Athens*. Baltimore: Johns Hopkins University Press, 1990.

———. "Did the Ancients Care When Their Children Died?" *Greece and Rome* 35 (1988): 152–63.

———. "Mortality, Mourning and Mothers." Pages 156–67 in *Naissance et petite enfance dans l'Antiquité*. Edited by Véronique Dasen. Firbourg: Academic Press, 2004.

Gottwald, Norman. *The Tribes of Yahweh: A Sociology of the Religion of Liberated Israel 1250–1050 BCE*. Sheffield: Sheffield Academic, 1999.

Graham, Sarah. "Hormone Found Linked to Mother's Protective Instincts." 2 August 2004. Scientific American. https://tinyurl.com/SBL1729d.

Granqvist, Hilma. *Birth and Childhood among the Arabs: Studies in a Muhammadan Village in Palestine*. Helingsfors: Söderström, 1947.

———. *Child Problems among the Arabs: Studies in a Muhammadan Village in Palestine*. Helingsfors: Söderström, 1950.

———. *Marriage Conditions in a Palestinian Village*. Helsingfors: Societas Scientiarum Fennica, 1931.

Gray, John. *1 and 2 Kings*. OTL. Philadelphia: Westminster Press. 1963.

Green, John. "Anklets and the Social Construction of Gender and Age in the Late Bronze and Early Iron Age Southern Levant." Pages 283–311 in *Archaeology and Women: Ancient and Modern Issues*. Edited by Sue Hamilton, Ruth D. Whitehouse, and Katherine I. Wright. Walnut Creek, CA: Left Coast Press, 2007.

———. "Social Identity in the Jordan Valley During the Late Bronze and Early Iron Ages: Evidence from the Tall as-Sa'idiyya Cemetery." Pages 419–29 in *Studies in the History and Archaeology of Jordan XI*. Amman: Department of Antiquities, 2013.

Greenberg, Moshe. *Ezekiel 1–20*. AB 22. Garden City, NY: Doubleday, 1983.

Grimm, Linda. "Apprentice Flintknapping: Relating Material Culture and Social Practice in the Upper Paleolithic." Pages 53–71 in *Children and Material Culture.* Edited by Joanna R. Sofaer Derevenski. London: Routledge, 2000.

Gruber, Mayer. "Breast-Feeding Practices in the Bible and Old Babylonian Mesopotamia." *JANES* 19 (1989): 61–83.

———. "Private Life in Ancient Israel." Pages 633–48 in vol. 1 of *Civilizations of the Ancient Near East.* Edited by Jack Sasson. New York: Scribner, 1995.

Halcrow, Siân, and Nancy Tayles. "The Bioarchaeological Investigation of Childhood and Social Ages: Problems and Perspectives." *Journal of Archaeological Theory and Method* 15 (2008): 190–215.

Hallo, William. "Games in the Biblical World" [Hebrew]. *EI* 24 (1993): 83–84.

Hallote, Rachel. *Death, Burial and Afterlife in the Biblical World.* Chicago: Ivan Dee, 2001.

Hanuš, L. O., T. Řezanka, J. Spížek, and V. M. Dembitsky. "Substances Isolated from Mandragora Species." *Phytochemistry* 66 (2005): 2415–16.

Hardin, James. *Lahav II: Households and the Use of Domestic Space at Iron II Tell Halif; An Archaeology of Destruction.* Reports of the Lahav Research Project. Winona Lake, IN: Eisenbrauns, 2010.

Harrington, Rebecca. "Twins Are Remarkably Common in One Area of the World." *Business Insider.* 17 September 2015. https://tinyurl.com/SBL1729e.

Harris, Rivkah. *Ancient Sippar.* Belgium: Nederlands Instituut voor het Nabije Oosten, 1975.

———. *Gender and Aging in Mesopotamia: The Gilgamesh Epic and Other Ancient Literature.* Norman: University of Oklahoma Press, 2000.

Harris, W. V. "Child Exposure in the Roman Empire." *Journal of Roman Studies* 84 (1994): 1–22.

Hasan, I., M. Zuhlkifle, A. H. Ansari, A. M. K. Sherwani, and M. Shakir. "History of Ancient Egyptian Obstetrics and Gynecology: A Review." *Journal of Microbiology and Biotechnology Research* 1 (2011): 35–39.

Hays, Christopher B. *Hidden Riches: A Sourcebook for the Comparative Study of the Hebrew Bible and Ancient Near East.* Louisville: Westminster John Knox. 2014.

Henniger, Josef. *Die Familie bei den heutigen Beduinen Arabiens: Und seiner Randgebiete; Ein Beitrag zur Frage der ursprünglichen Familienform der Semiten.* Leiden: Brill, 1943.

Hewlett, Barry, M. E. Lamb, D. Shannon, B. Leyendecker, and A. Schölm-
    erich. "Culture and Early Infancy among Central African Foragers
    and Farmers." *Developmental Psychology* 344 (1998): 653–61.
Hockings, Paul. "Badaga Apparel: Protection and Symbol." Pages 143–74
    in *The Fabrics of Culture: The Anthropology of Clothing and Adorn-
    ment.* Edited by Justine Cordwell and Ronald A. Schwarz. Berlin: de
    Gruyter, 1979.
Hodder, Ian. "Agency and Individuals in Long Term Processes." Pages
    21–33 in *Agency in Archaeology.* Edited by Marcia-Anne Dobres and
    John Robb. London: Routledge, 2000.
──────. *The Present Past: An Introduction to Anthropology for Archaeolo-
    gists.* London: Batsford, 1982.
──────. *Symbols in Action: Ethnoarchaeological Studies of Material Culture.*
    New Studies in Archaeology. Cambridge: Cambridge University Press,
    1982.
Hoeppli, R. "The Knowledge of Parasite and Parasitic Infections from
    Ancient Times to the Seventeenth Century." *Experimental Parasitol-
    ogy* 5 (1956): 398–419.
Holladay, John. "Religion in Israel and Judah under the Monarchy: An
    Explicitly Archaeological Approach." Pages 249–99 in *Ancient Israelite
    Religion: Essays in Honor of Frank Moore Cross.* Edited by Patrick D.
    Miller, Paul D. Hanson, and S. Dean McBride. Philadelphia: Fortress,
    1987.
Holladay, William. *Jeremiah 1: A Commentary on the Book of the Prophet
    Jeremiah, Chapters 1–25.* Hermeneia. Edited by Paul Hanson. Phila-
    delphia: Fortress, 1986.
Holland, Thomas. "A Typological and Archaeological Study of Human and
    Animal Representations in the Plastic Art of Palestine during the Iron
    Age." PhD diss., Proefschrift Oxford, All Souls College, 1975.
Horn, Cornelia, and John Martens. *Let the Little Ones Come to Me: Chil-
    dren and Childhood in Early Christianity.* Baltimore: John Hopkins,
    2007.
Horne, Rosemary, Fern Hauck, and Rachel Moon. "Sudden Infant Death
    Syndrome and Advice for Safe Sleeping." *The BMJ.* 28 April 2015.
    https://doi.org/10.1136/bmj.h1989.
Hornsby, Teresa J. *Sex Texts from the Bible.* Woodstock, VT: Skylight Paths,
    2007.
Hot Sling. "Homepage." https://www.hotslings.com/

Hui-Chin, Hsu. "Play during Infancy and Early Childhood: Cultural Similarities and Variations." Pages 218–25 in *International Encyclopedia of the Social and Behavioral Sciences*. Edited by James D. Wright. 2nd ed. Amsterdam: Elsevier, 2015.

Hübner, Ulrich. *Spiele und Spielzeug in antiken Palästina*. Universitätsverlag Freiburg Schweiz: Vandenhoeck & Ruprecht Göttingen, 1992.

Huffmon, Herbert B. "Shalem שׁלם." *DDD*, 755–57.

Hughes, A. L. "Female Infanticide: Sex Ration Manipulation in Humans." *Ethology and Sociobiology* 2 (1981): 109–11.

Huizinga, Joshua. *Homo Ludens: A Study of the Play Element in Culture*. London: Routledge & Paul, 1980.

Huntington, Richard, and Peter Metcalf. *Celebrations of Death: The Anthropology of the Death Ritual*. Cambridge: Cambridge University Press, 1991.

Ilan, David. "Mortuary Practices in the Middle Bronze Age: A Reflection of Canaanite Society and Ideology." Pages 117–37 in *The Archaeology of Death in the Ancient Near East*. Edited by Stuart Campbell and Anthony Green. Oxbow Monographs 51. Oxford: Oxbow, 1995.

Janssen, Rosalind M., and Jac J. Janssen. *Growing Up in Ancient Egypt*. London: Rubicon, 1990.

Jeon, Jaeyoung. "Two Laws in the Sotah Passage (Num V 11–31)." *VT* 57 (2007): 181–207.

Jobling, David. *I Samuel*. Edited by David Cotter. Berit Olam. Collegeville, MN: Liturgical Press, 1998.

Johnson, M. "Concepts of Agency in Archaeological Interpretation." Pages 211–27 in *Interpretation of Archaeology: A Reader*. Edited by Julian Thomas. London: Leicester University Press, 2000.

Johnston, Philip. "Figuring out Figurines." *TynBul* 54 (2003): 81–104.

Josephus, Flavius. *The Works of Flavius Josephus: Antiquities of the Jews; A History of the Jewish Wars; and the Life of Flavius Josephus*. English translation by William Whiston. Philadelphia: Smith, 1860.

Justel, Daniel. *Infancia y legalidad en el Próximo Oriente antiguo durante el Bronce Reciente (ca. 1500–1100 a. C.)*. Atlanta: SBL Press, 2018.

Kamp, Kathryn. "Dominant Discourses; Lived Experiences: Studying the Archaeology of Children and Childhood." Pages 115–22 in *Children in Action: Perspectives on the Archaeology of Childhood*. Edited by Eva Baxter. Archaeological Papers of the American Anthropological Association 15. Arlington: American Anthropological Association, 2006.

———. "Where Have All the Children Gone? The Archaeology of Childhood." *Journal of Archaeological Method and Theory* 8 (2000): 1–34.

Karp, Harvey. "The 5 S's for Soothing Babies." Happiestbaby.com. https://tinyurl.com/SBL1729f.

Keel, Othmar. "Kanaanäische Sühneriten auf ägyptischen Tempelreliefs." *VT* 25 (1975): 413–66.

Keel, Othmar, and Christopher Uehlinger. *Gods, Goddesses, and Images of God in Ancient Israel.* Edinburgh: T&T Clark, 1998.

Kenyon, Kathleen. *Digging Up Jericho.* London: Benn, 1957.

———. *Excavation at Jericho I: Tombs Excavated in 1952–54.* Jerusalem: British Schools of Archaeology in Jerusalem, 1960.

———. *Excavations at Jericho II: The Tombs Excavated in 1955–58.* Jerusalem: British School of Archaeology, 1965.

Khalil, Rami Bou, and Sami Richa. "When Affective Disorders Were Considered to Emanate from the Heart: The Ebers Papyrus." *American Journal of Psychiatry* 171 (2014): 275.

Kilmer, Anne. "An Oration on Babylon." *AoF* 18 (1991): 9–22.

King, J. E. "Infant Burial." *The Classical Review* (1903): 83–84.

King, Philip. "Gezer and Circumcision." Pages 333–39 in *Confronting the Past: Archaeological and Historical Essays on Ancient Israel in Honor of William G. Dever.* Edited by Seymour Gitin, J. Edward Wright, J. P. Dessel. Winona Lake, IN: Eisenbrauns, 2006.

King, Philip, and Lawrence Stager. *Life in Biblical Israel.* Louisville: Westminster John Knox, 2001.

Kinney, Hannah, and Bradley Thach. "The Sudden Infant Death Syndrome." *New England Journal of Medicine* 361 (2009): 795–805.

Kletter, Raz. "Anthropomorphic and Zoomorphic Figurines and Hollow Vessels." Pages 546–57 in *Tel Beth-Shemesh A Border Community in Judah: Renewed Excavations 1990–2000; The Iron Age.* Vol 2. Yass Publications in Archaeology. Winona Lake, IN: Eisenbrauns, 2016.

———. "Between Archaeology and Theology: The Pillar Figurines from Judah and the Asherah." Pages 179–216 in *Studies in the Archeology of the Iron Age in Israel and Jordan.* Edited by Amihai Mazar. JSOTSup 331. Sheffield: Sheffield Academic, 2001.

———. "Clay Figurines." Pages 1075–1136 in *Beersheba III: The Early Iron Age IIA Enclosed Settlement and the Late Iron IIA–Iron IIB Cities.* Edited by Zev Herzog and Lily Singer-Avitz. Winona Lake, IN: Eisenbrauns, 2016.

———. *Judean Pillar Figurines and the Archaeology of Ashera*. BARIS 636. Oxford: Tempus Reparatum, 1996.

———. "A Monkey Figurine from Tel Beth Shemesh." *Oxford Journal of Archaeology* 21 (2002): 147–52.

Kletter, Raz, and Yossi Nagar. "Iron Age Cemetery and Other Remains at Yavne." *'Atiqot* 81 (2015): 1–33.

Knight, Douglas. *Law, Power and Justice in Ancient Israel*. Library of Ancient Israel. Louisville: Westminster John Knox, 2011.

Koepf-Taylor, Laurel. *Give Me Children or I Shall Die*. Minneapolis: Fortress, 2013.

Kraft, Paul. "Worked Bone." Pages 2434–440 in *Lachish V*. Edited by D. Ussishkin. Tel Aviv: Yass Publications in Archaeology, 2004.

Králik, Miroslav, Petra Urbanová, and Marin Hložek. "Finger, Hand and Foot Imprints: The Evidence of Children on Archaeological Artefacts." Pages 1–15 in *Children, Identity and the Past*. Edited by Liv H. Dommasnes and Melanie Wrigglesworth. Newcastle: Cambridge Scholars, 2008.

Kuntzmann, Raymond. *Le symbolism des jumeaux au Proche-Orient ancient: Naissance, function et evolution d'un symbole*. Beauchesne: Paris, 1983.

Kunz-Lübke, Andreas. *"Schaffe mire Kinder …" Beiträge zur Kindheit im alten Israel und in seinen Nachbarkulturen*. ABG 21. Leipzig: Evangelische Verlagsanstalt, 2006.

Labat, René. *Traité akkadien de diagnostics et prognostics médicaux (TDP)*. Paris: International Academy for the History of Science, 1951.

Laderman, Carol. "Symbolic and Empirical Reality: A New Approach to the Analysis of Food Avoidances." *American Ethnologist* 8 (1981): 46.

Laes, Christian. *Children in the Roman Empire: Outsiders Within*. Cambridge, UK: Cambridge University Press, 2011.

Lambert, Wilfred, and Allan Millard. *Atra-hasīs: The Babylonian Story of the Flood*. Oxford: Oxford University Press, 1969.

Lancy, David. "Accounting for Variability in Mother-Child Play." *AA* 1092 (2007): 273–84.

Landsberger, Benno. "Einige unerkannt gebliebene oder verkannte Nomina des Akkadiaschen." *Wiener Zeitschrift für die Kunde des Morgenlandes* 56 (1960): 109–29.

Leavitt, Judith W. *Brought to Bed: Childbearing in America 1750–1950*. New York: Oxford University Press, 1986.

Lehmann, Gunnar. "The United Monarchy in the Countryside: Jerusalem, Judah and the Shephelah during the Tenth Century B.C.E." Pages 117–62 in *Jerusalem in Bible and Archaeology: The First Temple Period*. Edited by Andrew G. Vaughn and Ann E. Killebrew. Atlanta: Society of Biblical Literature, 2003.

Leichty, Erle. "Demons and Population Control." *Expedition* 13 (1971): 22–26.

———. *The Omen Series Šumma Izbu*. Locust Valley, NY: Augustin, 1970.

Lewis, Mary. *Bioarchaeology of Children: Perspectives from Biological and Forensic Anthropology*. Cambridge: Cambridge University Press, 2007.

Lewis, Naphtali. *Life in Egypt under Roman Rule*. Oxford: Clarendon, 1985.

Lewis, Theodore. "Family, Household, and Local Religion at Late Bronze Age Ugarit." Pages 60–88 in *Household and Family Religion in Antiquity*. Edited by John P. Bodel and Saul M. Olyan. Oxford: Wiley-Blackwell, 2012.

Lichtheim, Miriam. *The New Kingdom*. Vol. 2 of *Ancient Egyptian Literature*. Berkeley: University of California Press, 2006.

Lichty, Erle. "Demons and Population Control." *Expedition* (1971): 22–26.

Lillehammer, Grete. "A Child Is Born: The Child's World in an Archaeological Perspective." *Norwegian Archaeological Review* 22 (1999): 89–105.

Linde, Kirsten. "Swaddling." Pages 802–3 in vol. 3 of *The Encyclopedia of Children and Childhood in History and Society*. Edited by Paula S. Fass. 3 vols. New York: Macmillian, 2004.

Livingstone, Alasdair. "The Pitter Patter of Tiny Feet in Clay." Pages 15–27 in *Children, Childhood and Society*. Edited by Sally Crawford and Gillian Shepherd. BARIS 1696; IAA Interdisciplinary Series 1. Oxford: Archaeopress, 2007.

Louis-Hugues, Vincent. *Underground Jerusalem*. London: Cox, 1911.

Low, Katherine. "Implications Surrounding Girding the Loins in Light of Gender, Body, and Power." *JSOT* 36 (2011): 3–30.

Lundbom, Jack. *Jeremiah 1–20*. AB 21A. New York: Double Day, 1999.

Lurker, Manfred. *The Gods and Symbols of Ancient Egypt*. London: Thames & Hudson, 1974.

Lyman, R. Lee, and Michael J. O'Brien. "The Direct Historical Approach, Analogical Reasoning, and Theory in Americanist Archaeology." *Journal of Archaeological Method and Theory* 8 (2001): 303–42.

Macalister, R. A. S. *The Excavation of Gezer 1902–1905 and 1907–1909*. 3 vols. London: Palestine Exploration Fund, 1912.

Maeir, Aren. "A New Interpretation of the Term ʿopalim (עפלים) in the Light of Recent Archaeological Finds from Philistia." *JSOT* 32 (2007): 23–40.

———. "Tomb 1181." Pages 295–327 in *Hazor V.* Edited by Amnon Ben-Tor, Ruhama Bonfil, Baruch Arensburg, and Alan Paris. Jerusalem: Israel Exploration Society and the Hebrew University of Jerusalem, 1997.

Maeir, Aren, and Nava Panitz-Cohen. *Bronze and Iron Age Tombs at Tel Gezer, Israel: Finds from Raymond-Charles Weill's Excavation in 1914 and 1932.* Oxford: Archaeopress, 2004.

Malinowski, Bronislaw. *A Scientific Theory of Culture.* New York: Oxford University Press, 1944.

Malaise, Michel. "Bes." *OEAE* 2:179–81.

Makujina, John. "Male Obstetric Competence in Ancient Israel: A Response to Two Proposals." *VT* 66 (2016): 78–94.

Malul, Maier. "Adoptions of Foundlings in the Bible and Mesopotamian Documents: A Study of Some Legal Metaphors in Ezekiel 16:1–7." *JSOT* 46 (1990): 97–126.

Manor, Dale. "Toys 'R' Us at Tel Beth-Shemesh." Paper presented at the Annual Meeting of American School of Oriental Research, Boston, MA, 16 November 2017.

Margalith, Othniel. "A New Type of Ashera-Figurine?" *VT* 44 (1994): 109–15.

Mark, Elizabeth Wyner. "Wounds, Vows, Emanations: A Phallic Trope in the Patriarchal Narrative." Pages 3–17 in *The Covenant of Circumcision.* Edited by Elizabeth Wyner Mark. Lebanon, NH: Brandeis University Press, 2003.

Master, Daniel, et al. *Dothan I: Remains from the Tell (1953–1964).* Winona Lake, IN: Eisenbrauns, 2005.

Matthews, Victor H. "Taking Calculated Risks: The Story of the Cannibal Mothers (2 Kings 6:24–7:20)." *BTB* 43 (2013): 4–13.

Mays, Simon. "Infanticide in Roman Britain." *Antiquity* 67 (1993): 883–88.

Mazar, Amihai, and Nava Panitz-Cohen. *Timnah (Tel Batash) II: The Finds from the First Millennium BCE.* Jerusalem: The Institute of Archaeology, Hebrew University, 2001.

Mazar, Benjamin. *Jerusalem through the Ages* [Hebrew]. Jerusalem: Israel Exploration Society, 1968.

McCarter, P. Kyle. *II Samuel.* AB 9. Garden City, NY: Doubleday, 1984.

McClellan, Theresa. "Man Charged with Trying to Hurt Fetus: He Is Accused of Attacking His Pregnant Girlfriend with the Intention of Causing a Miscarriage." 3 Edition. *The Grand Rapids Press*. 11 September 2003: A.18.

McGeough, Kevin. "Birth Bricks, Potter's Wheels and Exodus 1:16." *Biblica* 87 (2006): 305–18.

McKay, Heather. "Gendering the Discourse of Display." Pages 169–200 in *On Reading Prophetic Texts: Gender Specific and Related Studies in Memory of Fokkelien van Dijk-Hemmes*. Edited by Bob Becking and Meindert Dijkstra. Brill: Leiden, 1996.

Meeks, Dimitri. "Dance." *OEAE* 1:356–60.

Meier, Samuel A. "Destroyer משחית." *DDD*, 240–44.

Mendenhall, George. "The Hebrew Conquest of Palestine." *BA* 25 (1962): 65–87.

Meskell, Lynn. *Archaeologies of Social Life*. Oxford: Blackwell, 1999.

Metropolitan Museum of Art, "Atropaic Wand," http://www.metmuseum.org/art/collection/search/545740.

Meyers, Carol. "Engendering Syro-Palestinian Archaeology: Reasons and Resources." *NEA* 66 (2003): 185–97.

———. *Exodus*. NCBC. Cambridge: Cambridge University Press, 2005.

———. "The Family in Early Israel." Pages 1–47 in *Families in Ancient Israel*. Edited by Leo Perdue, Joseph Blenkinsopp, John J. Collins, and Carol Meyers. Louisville: Westminster John Knox, 1997.

———. "From Household to House of Yahweh: Women's Religious Culture in Ancient Israel." Pages 277–303 in *Congress Volume Basel 2001*. Edited by André Lemaire. VTSup 92. Leiden: Brill, 2002.

———. *Household and Holiness: The Religious Culture of Israelite Women*. Minneapolis: Fortress, 2005.

———. "Household Religion." Pages 118–35 in *Religious Diversity in Ancient Israel and Judah*. Edited by Francesca Stavrakopolou and John Barton. T&T Clark, 2010.

———. "Material Remains and Social Relations: Women's Culture in Agrarian Households of the Iron Age." Pages 425–44 in *Symbiosis, Symbolism, and the Power of the Past: Canaan, Ancient Israel, and Their Neighbors, form the Late Bronze Age through Roman Palaestina*. Edited by William G. Dever and Seymour Gitin. Winona Lake, IN: Eisenbrauns, 2003.

———. *Rediscovering Eve: Ancient Israelite Women in Context* Oxford: Oxford University Press, 2013.

———. "Terracottas without a Text: Judean Pillar Figurines in Anthropological Perspective." Pages 115–30 in *To Break Every Yoke, Essays in Honor of Marvin L. Chaney.* Edited by Robert B. Coote and Norman Gottwald. Sheffield: Sheffield Phoenix, 2007.

Michel, Andres. *Gott und Gewalt gegen Kinder im Alten Testament.* FAT 37. Tübingen: Mohr Siebeck, 2003.

Milgrom, Jacob. *The JPS Torah Commentary: Numbers.* Philadelphia: Jewish Publication Society, 1990.

———. *Leviticus 1–16.* AB 3. New York: Doubleday, 1991.

Mills, Antonia, and Richard Slobodin. *Amerindian Rebirth: Reincarnation Belief among North American Indians and Inuit.* Toronto: University of Toronto Press, 1994.

Moby Wrap. "Home Page." http://mobywrap.com/

———. "Instructions." http://mobywrap.com/pages/instructions-the-moby-wrap.

Moltz, Howard. "God and Abraham in the Binding of Isaac." *JSOT* 96 (2001): 59–69.

Moore, Jennie, and Eleanor Scott, eds. *Invisible People and Processes: Writing Gender and Childhood into European Archaeology.* London: Leicester University Press, 1997.

Moorey, P. R. S. "Bronze Age Catalogue—Akkadian to Old Babylonian Periods in Babylon." *Catalogue of Terracotta Figurines in the Ashmolean.* http://www.ashmolean.museum/ash/amocats/anet/pdf-files/ANET-23Bronze1MesII-Catalogue-1.pdf.

———. *Cemeteries of the First Millennium BC at Deve Hüyuk, Near Carchemish, Salvaged by T. E. Lawrence and C. L. Woolley in 1913 (with a Catalogue Raisonné of the Objects in Berlin, Cambridge, Liverpool, London and Oxford.* BARIS 87. Oxford: British Archaeological Reports, 1980.

———. *Idols of the People: Miniature Images of Clay in the Ancient Near East.* The Schweich Lectures of the British Academy 2001. Oxford: British Academy, 2003.

———. "Terracotta Plaques from Kish and Hursagkalama." *Iraq* 37 (1975): 79–99.

Mosca, P. G. "Child Sacrifice in Canaanite and Israelite Religion: A Study in *Mulk* and מלך." PhD diss., Harvard University, 1975.

Murphy, A. James. *Kids and Kingdom: The Precarious Presence of Children in the Synoptic Gospels.* Eugene, OR: Pickwick, 2013.

Musil, Alois. *Arabia Petraea*. Ethnologischer Reisebericht 3. Wein: Kaiserliche Akademie der Wissenschaften, 1908.

Mustakallio, Katarina, Christian Laes, and Ville Voulanto. *Children and Family in Late Antiquity: Life, Death and Interaction*. Leuven: Peeters 2015.

Nagar, Yossi. "Human Skeletal Remains." Pages 471–72 in *Megiddo IV: The 1998–2002 Seasons*. Edited by Israel Finkelstein, David Ussishkin, and Baruch Halpern. Tel Aviv: Yass Publications in Archaeology, 2006.

———. "Human Skeletal Remains from T. 80 in the 'En Esur Cemetery." *Atiqot* 64 (2010): 121–24.

———. "Human Skeletal Remains from the Burial Caves at Sha'ar Efrayim." *'Atiqot* 66 (2011): 75–78.

———. "Skeletal Remains from the Excavation at Ketef Hinnom, Jerusalem" [Hebrew]. *'Atiqot* 80 (2015): 55–58.

Nagar, Yossi, and Vered Eshed. "Where Are the Children? Age-Dependent Burial Practices in Peqi'in." *IEJ* 51 (2001): 27–35.

Nakhai, Beth Alpert. "Female Infanticide in Iron II Israel and Judah." Pages 257–72 in *Sacred History, Sacred Literature: Essays on Ancient Israel, the Bible, and Religion in Honor of Richard Elliott Friedman*. Edited by Shawna Dolansky. Winona Lake, IN: Eisenbrauns, 2008.

———. "Mother-and-Child Figurines in the Levant from the Late Bronze Age through the Persian Period." Pages 165–98 in *Material Culture Matters: Essays on the Archaeology of the Southern Levant in Honor of Seymour Gitin*. Edited by John R. Spencer, Robert A. Mullins, and Aaron Jed Brody. Winona Lake, IN: Eisenbrauns, 2014.

Nelson, Antonia. "Risks and Benefits of Swaddling Healthy Infants: An Integral Review." *MCN American Journal of Maternal Child Nursing* 42 (2017): 216–25.

Nelson, E. A., et al. "International Child Care Practices Study: Infant Sleeping Environment." *Early Human Development* 62 (2001): 43–55.

Nelson, Sarah, ed. *Handbook of Gender in Archaeology*. Lanham: Alta Mira, 2006.

Neufeld, Edward. "Hygiene Conditions in Ancient Israel (Iron Age)." *BA* 34 (1971): 43–45.

Niditch, Susan. *My Brother Esau Is a Hairy Man: Hair and Identity in Ancient Israel*. New York: Oxford University Press, 2008.

Nielsen, Mark. "Pretend Play and Cognitive Development." Pages 870–87 in *International Encyclopedia of the Social and Behavioral Sciences*. Edited James D. Wright. 2nd ed. Amsterdam: Elsevier, 2015.

Noth, Martin. *Exodus*. OTL. Philadelphia: Westminster, 1962.

———. *The History of Israel*. 2nd ed. New York: Harper & Row, 1958.

Novak, Tzvi. "Mother and Child Postpartum Defilement and Circumcision." thetorah.com. https://tinyurl.com/SBL1729g.

Nunn, John F. *Ancient Egyptian Medicine*. Norman: University of Oklahoma Press, 1996.

Nutkowicz, Hélène. "Propos autor de la mort d'un enfant 2 Samuel XI, 2–XII 24." *VT* 54 (2004): 104–18.

Odell, Margaret. *Ezekiel*. Macon, GA: Smyth & Helwys, 2005.

Olyan, Saul. "Family Religion in Israel and the Wider Levant of the First Millennium BCE." Pages 113–26 in *Household and Family Religion in Antiquity*. Edited by John P. Bodel and Saul M. Olyan. Oxford: Wiley-Blackwell, 2012.

Oppenheim, A. Leo. *Letters from Mesopotamia*. Chicago: University of Chicago Press, 1967.

Oruene, Taiwo. "Magical Powers of Twins in the Socio-religious Beliefs of the Yoruba." *Folklore* 96 (1985): 208–16.

Oren, Sarah. "A Small Plant Gives Birth to Great Drama—The Mandrake." Neot Kedumim Park website. https://tinyurl.com/SBL1729h.

Oren, Tal. "An Amulet of the Demon Pazuzu." Pages 517–22 in *From the Late Bronze Age IIB to the Medieval Period*. Vol. 1 of *Excavations at Tel Beth-Shean 1989–1996*. Edited by Amihai Mazar. Jerusalem: Israel Exploration Society, 2006.

Ortner, D. J., and S. Mays. "Dry-Bone Manifestations of Rickets in Infancy and Childhood." *International Journal of Osteoarchaeology* 8 (1998): 44–55.

Ortner, D. J., and M. F. Eriksen. "Bone Changes in the Human Skull Probably Resulting from Scurvy in Infancy and Childhood." *International Journal of Osteoarchaeology* 7 (1997): 212–20.

Out, D., S. Pieper, M. J. Bakermans-Kranenburg, and M. H. van Ijzendoorn. "Physiological Reactivity to Infant Crying: A Behavioral Genetic Study." *Genes, Brains and Behavior* 9 (2010): 868–76.

Özgüc, Tahsin, and Mahmut Alok. *Horoztepe: Eski Tunç Devri Mezarlig ve Iskân Yeri; An Early Bronze Age Settlement and Cemetery*. Turk Tarih Kurumu, Yayinlarindan 5/18. Ankara: Turk Tarih Kurumu Basimevi, 1958.

Pardes, Ilana. *Countertraditions in the Bible: A Feminist Approach*. Cambridge: Harvard University Press, 1992.

Parker, Bradley, and Catherine Foster. *New Perspectives on Household Archaeology.* Winona Lake, IN: Eisenbrauns, 2012.

Parker, Julie. "I Bless You by YHWH of Samaria and His Barbie: A Case for Viewing Judean Pillar Figurines as Children's Toys." Paper presented at the Annual Meeting of Society of Biblical Literature, Boston, MA, 18 November 2017.

———. *Valuable and Vulnerable: Children in the Hebrew Bible, Especially the Elisha Cycle.* BJS 355. Providence, RI: Brown University, 2013.

Payne, Blanche. *History of Costume: From the Ancient Egyptians to the Twentieth Century.* New York: Harper & Row, 1965.

Pearson, Michael Parker. *The Archaeology of Death and Burial.* College Station: Texas A&M Press, 2000.

Petrie, W. M. Flinders. *Gerar.* Jerusalem: British School of Archaeology, 1928.

———. *Objects of Daily Use.* London: British School of Archaeology in Egypt, 1927.

Pezzulla, Nadia. "Neonati, Infanti e Bambini nel Vicino Oriente Antico." Master's Thesis, Università ca' Foscari Venezia, 2012.

Philip, Tarja S. *Menstruation and Childbirth in the Bible: Fertility and Infertility.* StBiblit 88. New York: Lang, 2006.

Pinch, Geraldine. *Magic in Ancient Egypt.* London: British Museum, 1994.

Polak, Jakob E. *Persien: Das Land und seine Bewohener.* Ethnographische Schilderungen 1. Leipzig: Brockhaus, 1865.

Pomeroy, Sarah. "Infanticide in Hellenistic Greece." Pages 207–22 in *Images of Women in Antiquity.* Edited by Averil Cameron and Amélie Kuhrt. Detroit, MI: Wayne State University Press, 1985.

Porada, Edith. "An Emaciated Male Figure of Bronze in the Cincinnati Art Museum." Pages 159–66 in *Studies Presented to A. Leo Oppenheim.* Edited by Robert D. Biggs and John A. Brinkman. Chicago: University of Chicago Press, 1964.

Pritchard, James B., ed. *Ancient Near Eastern Texts relating to the Old Testament with Supplement.* 3rd ed. Princeton, NJ: Princeton University Press, 1969.

Propp, William. *Exodus 1–18.* AB 2. New York: Doubleday, 1998.

———. *Exodus 19–40.* AB 2A. New York: Doubleday, 2006.

———. "Origins of Infant Circumcision in Israel." *HAR* 11 (1987): 355–70.

Rad, Gerhard von. *Genesis: A Commentary.* OTL. Philadelphia: Westminster, 1972.

———. *The Problem of the Hexateuch and Other Essays.* London: Oliver & Boyd, 1966.

Rathbun, Andy. "Prescott, Wis.: Man Accused of Punching Pregnant Woman in Stomach." *Saint Paul Pioneer Press.* 10 July 2013.

Redford, Donald. *Akhenaten: The Heretic King.* Princeton, NJ: Princeton University Press, 1984.

Reeder, Greg. "Same-Sex Desire, Conjugal Constructs, and the Tomb of Nianhkhnum and Khnumhopte." *WA* 32 (2000): 193–208.

Reiner, Erica. "Babylonian Birth Prognoses." *ZA* 72 (1982): 124–38.

Riddle, John. *Goddesses, Elixirs, and Witches.* New York: Palgrave MacMillan, 2010.

Riley, Jason Anthony. "Children and Warfare in the Hebrew Bible and the Iron Age II: Rhetoric and Reality in Textual, Iconographic, and Archaeological Sources." PhD diss., Fuller Theological Seminary, 2018.

———. "The Motif of Children as Victims of War." Paper presented at the Annual Meeting of the Southwestern Region of the Society of Biblical Literature. Irving, TX. March 11, 2017.

Ritner, Robert. "Magic: An Overview." *OEAE* 2:321–26.

———. "Magic: Magic in Daily Life." *OEAE* 2:329–33.

Röder, Brigitte. "Archaeological Childhood Research as Interdisciplinary Analysis." Pages 68–82 in *Children, Identity and the Past.* Edited by Liv Helga Dommasnes and Melanie Wrigglesworth. New Castle: Cambridge Scholars, 2008.

Romer, John. *Romer's Egypt: A New Light on the Civilization of Ancient Egypt.* London: Joseph, 1982.

Rost, Leonhard. "Weidewechsel und altisraelischer Festkalender." *ZDPV* 66 (1943): 205–15.

Roth, Ann Macy. *Egyptian Phyles in the Old Kindgom: The Evolution of a System of Social Organization.* Studies in Ancient Oriental Civilization 48. Chicago: University of Chicago Press, 1991.

Roubach, Sharon. "Two Who Donned the Veil: The Image of Twins in the Bible" [Hebrew]. *Beit Mikra* 183 (2005): 366–90.

Roveland, Blythe. "Footprints in the Clay: Upper Palaeolithic Children in Ritual and Secular Context." Pages 26–38 in *Children and Material Culture.* Edited by Joanna R. Sofaer Derevenski. London: Routledge, 2000.

Rowe, Ignacio Márquez. "Ceramic Stamp-Seal Amulets in the Shape of the Head of Pazuzu." *Iraq* 71 (2009): 151–59.

Rystedt, Eva. "Notes on the Rattle Scenes on Attic Geometric Pottery." *Opuscul a Atheniensia* 19 (1992): 125–33.

Sabari, Pamela, and Patricia Smith. "The Human Skeletal Remains from Tel Qashish." Pages 413–14 in *Tel Qashish: A Village in the Jezreel Valley; Final Report of the Archaeological Excavations 1978–1987*. Edited by Amnon Ben-Tor. Jerusalem: Institute of Archaeology, 2003.

Salem, Hamed. "Implications of Cultural Tradition: The Case of Palestinian Traditional Pottery." Pages 66–82 in *Archaeology, History, and Culture in Palestine and the Near East: Essays in Memory of Albert E. Glock*. Edited by Tomis Kapitan. ASOR Books 3. Atlanta: Scholars Press, 1999.

Sandison, A. T. "Parasitic Diseases." Pages 178–83 in *Diseases in Antiquity: A Survey of the Diseases, Injuries and Surgery of Early Populations*. Edited by Don R. Brothwell and A. T. Sandison. Springfield, IL: Thomas, 1967.

Sandnes, K. O., O. Skarsaune, and R. Aasgaard, eds. *Når jeg så skal ut i verden: Barn og tro i tidlig kristendom*. Trondheim: Tapir, 2009.

Sarna, Nahum. *The JPS Torah Commentary: Genesis*. Philadelphia: Jewish Publication Society, 1989.

Schenkel, W. *Memphis—Herakleopolis—Theben: Die epigraphischen Zeugnisse der 7.–11. Dynastie Ägyptens*. ÄAT 12. Weisbaden: Harrassowitz, 1965.

Scheper-Hughes, Nancy. *Death without Weeping: The Violence of Everyday Life in Brazil*. Berkeley: University of California Press, 1993.

Schloen, J. David. *The House of the Father as Fact and Symbol: Patrimonialism in Ugarit and the Ancient Near East*. Studies in the Archaeology and History of the Levant 2. Winona Lake, IN: Eisenbrauns, 2001.

Schmidt, Brian B. *Israel's Beneficent Dead: Ancestor Cult and Necromancy in Ancient Israelite Religion and Tradition*. Tübingen: Mohr Siebeck, 1994.

———. *The Materiality of Power: Explorations in the Social History of Early Israelite Magic*. FAT 105. Tübingen: Mohr Siebeck, 2016.

Schmidt, H., and P. Kahle. *Volkserzählungen aus Pälästina I–II*. Göttingen: Vandenhoeck & Ruprecht, 1918–1930.

Schmitt, Rudiger. "Typology of Iron Age Cult Places." Pages 265–86 in *Family and Household Religion in Ancient Israel and the Levant*. Edited by Rainer Albertz and Rüdiger Schmitt. Winona Lake, IN: Eisenbrauns, 2012.

Schmitz, Philip. "Queen of Heaven." *ABD* 5:586–88.

Schneider, Thomas. "God's Infanticide in the Night of Passover: Exodus 12 in the Light of Egyptian Rituals." Pages 52–76 in *Not Sparing the Child: Human Sacrifice in the Ancient World and Beyond*. Edited by Vita Daphna Arbel, Paul C. Burns, J. R. C. Cousland, Richard Menkis, and Dietmar Neufeld. London: T&T Clark, 2016.

Schwartz, Joshua. "Ball Play in Jewish Society in the Second Temple and Mishnah Periods." *Zion* 60 (1995): 247–76.

———. "Play and Games." Pages 641–53 in *The Oxford Handbook of Jewish Daily Life*. Oxford: Oxford University Press, 2012.

Schwartz, J. H. "Bones, Teeth and Estimating Age of Perinates: Carthaginian Infant Sacrifice Revisited." *Antiquity* 86 (2012): 738–45.

———. *What the Bones Tell Us*. New York: Holt, 1993.

Schwartz, Jeffrey H., Frank Houghton, Roberto Macchiarelli, and Luca Bondioli. "Skeletal Remains from Punic Carthage Do Not Support Systematic Sacrifice of Infants." *PLOS ONE* 5 (2010): e9177. https://doi.org/10.1371/journal.pone.0009177.

Schwarz, Ronald A. "Uncovering the Secret Vice: Towards an Anthropology of Clothing and Adornment." Pages 23–46 in *The Fabrics of Culture: The Anthropology of Clothing and Adornment*. Edited by Justine M. Cordwell and Ronald A. Schwarz. The Hague: Mouton, 1979.

Schwyn, Irène. "Kinderbetreuung im 9.–7. Jahrhundert: Eine Untersuchung anhand der Darstellungen auf neuassyrischen Reliefs." *Lectio Dificilor* 1 (2000): 1–14.

Scott, Eleanor. "Killing the Female? Archaeological Narratives of Infanticide." Pages 1–22 in *Gender and the Archaeology of Death*. Edited by Bettina Arnold and Nancy L. Wicker. New York: AltaMira, 2001.

Scott, Susan, and Christopher J. Duncan. *Demography and Nutrition: Evidence from Historical and Contemporary Populations*. Oxford: Blackwell Science, 2002.

Scurlock, JoAnn. "Baby Snatching Demons, Restless Souls and the Dangers of Childbirth: Medio-Magical Means of Dealing with Some of the Perils of Motherhood in Ancient Mesopotamia." *Incognita* 2 (1991): 137–85.

Scurlock, JoAnn, and Burton R. Andersen. *Diagnoses in Assyrian and Babylonian Medicine: Ancient Sources, Translations, and Modern Medical Analyses*. Chicago: University of Illinois Press, 2005.

Sebbane, Michael. "ḥnn Gaming Board Section A: Two-Sided Gaming Board Fragment Bearing and Ownership Inscription." Pages 639–46 in *Tel Beth-Shemesh A Border Community in Judah: Renewed Excava-*

tions 1990–2000: The Iron Age. Edited by Shlomo Bunimovitz and Zvi Lederman. Vol. 2. Yass Publications in Archaeology. Winona Lake, IN: Eisenbrauns, 2016.

Sellers, Ovid R., et al. *The 1957 Excavation at Beth-Zur.* AASOR 38. Cambridge, MA: ASOR, 1968.

Shanks, Herschel. "Buzz or Button?" *BAR* 17.3 (1991): 62–63.

Sharp, Casey, Chris McKinny, and Itzahq Shai. "The Late Bronze Age Figurines from Tel Burna." *Strata* 33 (2015): 61–76.

Short, R. V. "Breast Feeding." *Scientific American* 250.4 (1984): 35–41.

Simoes, Eric A. F., Thomas Cherian, Jeffrey Chow, Sonbol A. Shahid-Salles, Ramanan Laxminarayan, and T. Jacob John. "Acute Respiratory Infections in Children." Pages 483–98 in *Disease Control Priorities in Developing Countries.* Edited by Dean T. Jamison et al. New York: Oxford University Press, 2006.

Smith, Jonathan Z. *Imagining Religion.* Chicago: University of Chicago Press, 1982.

Smith, Patricia. "An Approach to the Paleodemographic Analysis of Human Skeletal Remains from Archaeological Sites." Pages 2–13 in *Biblical Archaeology Today, 1990: Proceedings of the Second International Congress on Biblical Archaeology.* Edited by Avraham Biran and Joseph Aviram. Jerusalem: Israel Exploration Society; Israel Academy of Sciences and Humanities, 1993.

———. "Skeletal Remains from Level VI." Pages 2504–7 in *The Renewed Archaeological Excavations at Lachish (1973–1994).* Edited by David Ussishkin. Tel Aviv: Yass Publications in Archaeology, 2004.

Smith, Patricia, and Gal Avishai. "The Use of Dental Criteria for Estimating Postnatal Survival in Skeletal Remains of Infants." *Journal of Archaeological Science* 32 (2005): 83–89.

Smith, Patricia, Gal Avishai, Joseph A. Greene, and Lawrence E. Stager. "Aging Cremated Infants: The Problem of Sacrifice at the Tophet at Carthage." *Antiquity* 85 (2011): 859–74.

Smith, Patricia, Lawrence E. Stager, Joseph A. Greene, and Gal Avishai. "Age Estimations Attest to the Practice of Infant Sacrifice at the Carthage Tophet." *Antiquity* 87 (2013): 1991–99.

Smith, Patricia, and Marina Faerman. "Has Society Changed Its Attitude to Infants and Children? Evidence from Archaeological Sites in the Southern Levant." *Servei D'investigacions Arqueològiques Prehistòriques* (2008): 211–29.

Smith, Patricia, Almut Nebel, and Marina Faerman. "The Bio-anthropology of the Inhabitants of Middle and Late Bronze Age Yoqne'am." Pages 383–94 in *Yoqne'am III: The Middle and Late Bronze Ages, Final Report of the Archaeological Excavations (1977–1988)*. Edited by Amnon Ben-Tor, Ben-Ami Doron, and Ariella Livneh. Jerusalem: Hebrew University, 2005.

Smits, Jeroen, and Christiaan Monden. "Twinning across the Developing World." *PLOS ONE* (2011): http://doi.org/10.1371/journal.pone.0025239.

Smoak, Jeremy. "Amuletic Inscriptions and the Background of YWHW as Guardian and Protector in Psalm 12." *VT* 60 (2010): 421–32.

Soltis, Joseph. "The Signal Function of Early Infant Crying." *Behavioral and Brain Sciences* 27 (2004): 443–90.

Soren, David. "The Children's Cemetery of Lugnano in Teverina, Umbria: Hierarchy, Magic and Malaria." Pages 235–50 in *The Archaeology of Childhood*. Edited by Güner Coşkunsu. Albany: State University of New York Press, 2015.

Specht, Edith. "Girls' Education in Ancient Greece." Pages 125–36 in *Children, Identity and the Past*. Edited by Liv Helga Dommasnes and Melanie Wrigglesworth. New Castle: Cambridge Scholars, 2008.

Speiser, E. A. *Genesis*. AB 1. Garden City, NY: Doubleday, 1964.

Stager, Lawrence. "Ashkelon and the Archaeology of Destruction: Kislev 604 BCE" [Hebrew]. *ErIsr* 25 (1996): 61–74.

———. "The Fury of Babylon: Ashkelon and the Archaeology of Destruction." *BAR* 22.1 (1996): 56–69, 76–77.

Stager, Lawrence, and Sam Wolf. "Child Sacrifice at Carthage—Religious Rite or Population Control?" *BAR* 10.1 (1984): 31–51.

Stanford University. "Low Birthweight." Standford Children's Health. https://tinyurl.com/SBL1729i.

Stavrakopoulou, Francesca. *King Manasseh and Child Sacrifice: Biblical Distortions of Historical Realities*. Berlin: de Gruyter, 2004.

Steinberg, Naomi. "Exodus 12 in Light of Ancestral Cult Practices." Pages 89–103 in *The Family in Life and in Death*. Edited by Patricia Dutcher-Walls. New York: T&T Clark, 2009.

———. *Kinship and Marriage in Genesis: A Household Economic Perspective*. Minneapolis: Augsburg Fortress, 1993.

———. *The World of the Child in the Hebrew Bible*. HBM 51. Sheffield: Sheffield Phoenix, 2013.

Steinkeller, Piotr. "The Organization of Crafts in Third Millennium Babylonia: The Case of Potters." *AoF* 23 (1996): 232–53.

Stern, Ephraim. "The Beginnings of Greek Settlement in Palestine in Light of the Excavations at Tel Dor." Pages 107–24 in *Recent Excavations in Israel: Studies in Iron Age Archaeology.* Edited by Seymour Gitin and William G. Dever. AASOR 49. Winona Lake, IN: Eisenbrauns, 1989.

Stiebert, Johanna. *Fathers and Daughters in the Hebrew Bible.* Oxford: Oxford University Press, 2013.

Stol, Martin. *Birth in Babylonia and the Bible: Its Mediterranean Setting.* Groningen: Styx, 2000.

———. "Private Life in Ancient Mesopotamia." Pages 485–501 in vol. 1 of *Civilizations of the Ancient Near East.* Edited by Jack Sasson. New York: Scribner, 1995.

Storrs, C., and D. Goldenschmidt. "U.S. Twin Birth Rate Hits Record High." 23 December 2015. CNN. https://tinyurl.com/SBL1729j.

Stowers, Stan. "Theorizing Ancient Household Religion." Pages 5–19 in *Household and Family Religion in Antiquity.* Edited by John P. Bodel and Saul M. Olyan. Oxford: Wiley-Blackwell, 2012.

Sullivan, Frank, and Susan Barlow. "Review of Risk Factors for Sudden Infant Death Syndrome." *Paediatric and Perinatal Epidemiology* 15 (2001): 144–200.

Sutton-Smith, Brian. *The Ambiguity of Play.* Cambridge: Harvard University Press, 2001.

Sweeney, Deborah. "Egyptian Objects." Pages 1062–74 in *Beer-Sheba III: The Early Iron IIA Enclosed Settlement and the Late Iron IIA–Iron IIB Cities.* Edited by Zeʾev Herzog and Lily Singer-Avitz. Winona Lake, IN: Eisenbrauns, 2016.

Talis, Svetlana. "An Early Bronze Age IB–II Settlement at Abu Qurinat" [Hebrew]. *ʿAtiqot* 85 (2016): 45–55.

Tambiah, Stanly J. "The Magical Power of Words." *Man* 2/3.2 (1968): 175–208.

Tenney, Jonathan. *Life at the Bottom of Babylonian Society: Servile Labor at Nippur in the Fourteenth and Thirteenth Centuries B.C.* Leiden: Brill, 2011.

Thareani, Yifat. "Ancient Caravanserais: An Archaeological View from ʿAroer." *Levant* 39 (2007): 123–41.

———. "The Judean Desert Frontier in the Seventh Century BCE: A View from ʿAroer." Pages 227–66 in *Unearthing the Wilderness: Studies on the History and Archaeology of the Negev and Edom in the Iron Age.* Edited by Juan Tebes. Leuven: Peeters, 2014.

Thenius, Otto. *Bücher der Könige.* Leipzig: Weidermann, 1849.

Thiessen, Matthew. "The Legislation of Leviticus 12 in Light of Ancient Embryology." *VT* 68 (2018): 1–23.

Thureau-Dangin, F. "Rituel et Amulettes Contre Labartu." *RA* 18 (1921): 161–98.

Tooley, Michael. *Abortion and Infanticide.* Oxford: Clarendon, 1983.

Toorn, Karel van der. *Family Religion in Babylonia, Syria, and Israel: Continuity and Change in the Forms of Religious Life.* Leiden: Brill, 1995.

———. "Family Religion in Second Millennium West Asia (Mesopotamia, Emar, Nuzi)." Pages 20–36 in *Household and Family Religion in Antiquity.* Edited by John P. Bodel and Saul M. Olyan. Oxford: Wiley-Blackwell, 2012.

———. *From Her Cradle to Her Grave.* Translated by Sara Denning-Bolle. Sheffield: JSOT 1994.

———. "Israelite Figurines: A View from the Text." Pages 45–62 in *Sacred Time, Sacred Place: Archaeology and the Religion of Israel.* Edited by Barry M. Gittlen. Winona Lake, IN: Eisenbrauns, 2000.

———. "Parallels in Biblical Research: Purpose of Comparison." Pages 1–8 in *Proceedings of the Eleventh World Congress of Jewish Studies, Division A: The Bible and Its World.* Jerusalem: World Union of Jewish Studies, 1993.

Toorn, Karel van der, Bob Becking, and Pieter Willem van der Horst, eds. *Dictionary of Deities and Demons in the Bible.* Leiden: Brill, 1995.

Torres, Sara, J. Campbell, D. W. Campbell, J. Ryan, C. King, P. Price, R. Y. Stallings, S. C. Fuchs, and M. Laude. "Abuse during and before Pregnancy: Prevalence and Cultural Correlates." *Violence and Victims* 15 (2000): 303–21.

Trible, Phyllis. *Texts of Terror: Literary-Feminist Readings of Biblical Narratives.* Philadelphia: Fortress, 1984.

Tufnell, Olga. "Burials in Cemeteries 100 and 200." Pages 11–13 in *Beth-Pelet I.* Edited by W. F. Petrie. London: British School of Archaeology in Egypt, 1930.

———. *Lachish III (Tell ed. Duwier) The Iron Age.* London: Oxford University Press, 1953.

———. *Lachish IV: The Bronze Age.* 2 vols. London: Oxford University Press, 1958.

Turner, Bryan. *The Body and Society: Explorations in Social Theory.* Los Angeles: SAGE, 2008.

Turner, Victor. *The Forest of Symbols: Aspects of Ndembu Ritual.* Ithaca: Cornell University Press, 1967.

———. *The Ritual Process: Structure and Anti-Structure.* Chicago: Aldine, 1969.

Ucko, Peter. "The Interpretation of Prehistoric Anthropomorphic Figurines." *The Journal of Royal Anthropological Institute of Great Britain and Ireland* 92 (1962): 38–54.

United Kingdom, Government. "Conditions of Heat Exhaustion and Heatstroke." NHS.uk. https://tinyurl.com/SBL1729k.

University of Southern California West Semitic Research Project. "Training Program." https://tinyurl.com/SBL1729m.

University of Pennsylvania. "Essarhaddon's Succession Treaty." ORACC. https://tinyurl.com/SBL1729n.

Ussishkin, David. "Tombs from the Israelite Period at Tel 'Eton." *TA* 1 (1974): 109–27.

Uziel, Joel, and Rona Avissar Lewis. "The Tel Nagila Middle Bronze Age Homes—Studying Household Activities and Identifying Children in the Archaeological Record." *PEQ* 145 (2013): 284–92.

Van Buren, E. Douglas. "Clay Relief in the Iraq Museum." *AfO* 9 (1933–1934): 165–71.

Valler, Shulamit. "King David and 'His' Women." Pages 129–42 in *A Feminist Companion to Samuel and Kings.* Edited by Athalya Brenner. Sheffield: Sheffield Academic, 1994.

Van Dijk, Jacobus. "The Death of Meketaten." Pages 83–88 in *Causing His Name to Live: Studies in Egyptian Epigraphy and History in Memory of William J. Murnane.* Edited by Peter J. Brand and Louise Cooper. CHANE 37. Leiden: Brill, 2009.

Vasiljević, Vera. "Embracing His Double: Niankhkhnum and Khnumhotep." *Studien zur Altägyptischen Kultur* 37 (2008): 363–72.

Vaux, Roland de. *Ancient Israel.* Translated by John McHugh. London: Darton, Longman & Todd, 1961.

Velde, Herman Te. "Theology, Priests, and Worships in Ancient Egypt." Page 1733 in vol. 3 of *Civilizations of the Ancient Near East.* Edited by Jack Sasson. New York: Scribner, 1995.

Vermaak, P. S. "A New Interpretation of the Playing Objects in the Gilgamesh Epic." *Journal for Semitics* 20 (2011): 109–38.

Viezel, Eran. "The Influence of Realia on Biblical Depictions of Childbirth." *VT* 61 (2011): 685–89.

Vogelzang, M. E., and W. J. van Bekkum. "Meaning and Symbolism of Clothing in Ancient Near Eastern Texts." Pages 265–84 in *Scripta Signa Vocis: Studies about Scripts, Scriptures, Scribes and Languages in the Near East Presented to J. H. Hospers.* Edited by J. H. Hospers and H. L. J. Vanstiphout. Groningen: Forsten, 1986.

Voigt, Mary. "Çatal Höyük in Context: Ritual at Early Neolithic Sites in Central and Eastern Turkey." Pages 253–94 in *Life in Neolithic Farming Communities: Social Organization, Identity and Differentiation.* Edited by Ian Kuijt. New York: Kluwer Academic/Plenum, 2000.

Volk, Konrad. "Kinderkrankheiten nach der Darstellung babylonisch-assyrischer Keilschrifttexte." *Or* 2/68 (1999): 1–30.

Voulanto, Ville. *Children and Asceticism in Late Antiquity. Continuity, Family Dynamics and the Rise of Christianity.* Farnham: Ashgate, 2015.

Voulanto, Ville, with Reider Aasgaard, Oana Maria Cojocaru, Camilla Christensen, Cecilie Krohn, and Camilla Roll. "Children in the Ancient World and the Early Middle Ages: A Bibliography." https://tinyurl.com/SBL1729o.

Watson, Patty Jo. *Archaeological Ethnography in Western Iran.* Tuscan: University of Arizona Press, 1979.

Wegner, Josef. "A Decorated Birth-Brick from South Abydos: New Evidence on Childbirth and Birth Magic in the Middle Kingdom." Pages 447–96 in *Archaism and Innovation: Studies in the Culture of Middle Kingdom Egypt.* Edited by David P. Silverman, William Kelley Simpson, and Josef William Wegner. New Haven: Yale University Press, 2009.

Wenig, Steffen. *The Women in Egyptian Art.* Leipzig: Leipzig Edition, 1969.

Westbrook, Raymond. *Property and the Family in Biblical Law.* Sheffield: JSOT Press, 2009.

White, Gwen. *Antique Toys and Their Background.* New York: Arco, 1971.

White, Robert. "Motivation Reconsidered: The Concept of Competence." *Psychological Review* 66 (1959): 197–333.

Wiggerman, F. A. M. "Lamaštu, Daughter of Anu, a Profile." Pages 217–52 in *Birth in Babylonia and the Bible, Its Mediterranean Setting.* Edited by Martin Stol. Groningen: Styx, 2000.

Wilcke, Claus. "Noch einmal: Šilip rēmim und die Adoption *ina mêšu*; Neue und alte einschlägige Texte." *ZA* 71 (1981): 87–94.

Wileman, Julie. *Hide and Seek: The Archaeology of Childhood.* Stroud: Tempus, 2005.

Wilk, Richard, and William Rathje. "Household Archaeology." *American Behavioral Scientist* 25 (1982): 617–39.

Wilson, Ian D. "Judean Pillar Figurines and the Ethnic Identity in the Shadow of Assyria." *JSOT* 36 (2012): 259–78.

Wilson, Stephen. *Making Men: The Male Coming of Age Theme in the Hebrew Bible.* New York: Oxford University Press, 2015.

Williams, B. G., E. Gouws, C. Boschi-Pinto, J. Bryce, and C. Dye. "Estimates of Worldwide Distribution of Child Deaths from Acute Respiratory Infections." *Lancet Infectious Diseases* 2 (2002): 25–32.

Williamson, Laila. "Infanticide: An Anthropological Analysis." Pages 61–75 in *Infanticide and the Value of Life.* Edited by Marvin Kohl. Buffalo: Prometheus Books, 1978.

Wilson, Ian. "Judean Pillar Figurines and the Ethnic Identity in the Shadow of Assyria." *JSOT* 36 (2012): 259–78.

Wilson, Kinnier. "Organic Diseases of Ancient Mesopotamia." Pages 191–208 in *Diseases in Antiquity: A Survey of the Diseases, Injuries and Surgery of Early Populations.* Edited by Don R. Brothwell and A. T. Sandison. Springfield, IL: Thomas, 1967.

Winkler, Hans Alexander. *Ghost Riders of Upper Egypt.* Translated by Nicholas S. Hopkins. Cairo: American University of Cairo Press, 2009.

Wolkenstein, Diane, and Samuel Noah Kramer. *Inanna Queen of Heaven and Earth: Her Stories and Hymns from Sumer.* New York: Harper & Row, 1983.

World Health Organization. "Diarrhoeal Diseases." 2 May 2017. https://tinyurl.com/SBL1729q.

———. "Low Birthweight: Country, Regional and Global Estimates." 2004. https://tinyurl.com/SBL1729r.

———. "Malaria." 11 June 2018. https://tinyurl.com/SBL1729s.

Wright, Ernest. *Biblical Archaeology.* New and rev. ed. Philadelphia: Westminster, 1962.

Wyatt, Nick. "Circumcision and Circumstance: Male Genital Mutilation in Ancient Israel and Ugarit." *JSOT* 33 (2009): 405–31.

Xella, P., et al. "Phoenician Bones of Contention." *Antiquity* 87 (2013): 1199–1207.

Yadin, Yigal, et al. *Hazor II: An Account of the Second Season of Excavations, 1956.* Jerusalem: Magnes, 1960.

Yahalom-Mack, Naama, and Amihai Mazar. "Various Finds from the Iron Age II Strata in Areas P and S." Pages 468–504 in *From the Late Bronze Age IIB to the Medieval Period*. Vol. 1 of *Excavations at Tel Beth-Shean 1989–1996*. Edited by Amihay Mazar. Jerusalem: Israel Exploration Society, 2006.

Yasur-Landau, Assaf. "Socio-political and Demographic Aspects of the MB Cemetery in Jericho." *TA* 19 (1992): 235–46.

Yasur-Landau, Assaf, Jennie Ebeling, and Laura Mazow. *Household Archaeology in Ancient Israel and Beyond*. Leiden: Brill, 2011.

Zaccagnini, Carlo. "Feet of Clay at Emar and Elsewhere." *Or* 63 (1994): 1–4.

———. "War and Famine at Emar." *Or* 64 (1995): 92–109.

Zevit, Ziony. *The Religions of Ancient Israel: A Synthesis of Parallactic Approaches*. London: Continuum, 2001.

Zias, Joe. "Health and Healing in the Land of Israel—A Paleopathological Perspective" [Hebrew]. Pages 13–23 in *Illness and Healing in Ancient Times*. Haifa: University of Haifa, 1996.

Zimmerli, Walther. *Ezekiel 1: A Commentary on the Book of the Prophet Ezekiel, Chapters 1–24*. Hermeneia. Translated by Ronald Ernest Clements. Philadelphia: Fortress, 1969.

Ancient Sources Index

Modern Authors Index

CPSIA information can be obtained
at www.ICGtesting.com
Printed in the USA
BVHW07s0752251018
531047BV00001B/1/P

9 781628 372113